CW00798063

MEDIEVAL LANDSCAPES

Medieval Landscapes

Edited by Mark Gardiner and Stephen Rippon

Landscape History after Hoskins

Volume 2

Series Editor: Christopher Dyer

WIND*gather*
PRESS

Medieval Landscapes: Landscape History after Hoskins, Volume 2

Copyright © Windgather Press 2007

All rights reserved. No part of this publication may be reproduced, stored in a retrieval system, or transmitted in any form or by any means (whether electronic, mechanical, photocopying or recording) or otherwise without the written permission of both the publisher and the copyright holder.

Published by: Windgather Press Ltd, 29 Bishop Road, Bollington, Macclesfield, Cheshire SK10 5NX

Distributed by: Oxbow Books, 10 Hythe Bridge Street, Oxford, OX1 2 EW

British Library Cataloguing-in-Publication Data

A catalogue record for this book is available from the British Library

ISBN 978-1-905119-18-9

Designed, typeset and originated by Carnegie Book Production, Lancaster
Printed and bound by Cambridge Printing, Cambridge

Contents

List of Figures

Abbreviations

BaRAS	Bristol and Region Archaeological Services
BRO	Buckinghamshire Record Office
CAT	Cotswold Archaeological Trust
CIPM	*Calendar of Inquisitions Post Mortem and other analogous documents preserved in the Public Record Office*
CPR	*Calendar of the Patent Rolls preserved in the Public Record Office. Prepared under the superintendence of the Deputy Keeper of the Records*
CVMA	Corpus Vitrearum Medii Aevi
DoE	Department of the Environment
ERYARS	East Riding of Yorkshire Archive and Record Service
HS	Historic Scotland
HUL	Hull University Library
NAS	National Archives of Scotland
NLS	National Library of Scotland
NMR	National Monument Record
NRO	Northamptonshire Record Office
NTS	National Trust for Scotland
OS	Ordnance Survey
PRO:TNA	Public Record Office: The National Archives
RCHME	Royal Commission on the Historical Monuments of England
RCAHMS	Royal Commission on the Ancient and Historical Monuments of Scotland
RHP	Register House Plans
Stat. Acct.	*The Statistical Account of Scotland*

Acknowledgements

The conference on which this book is based was organised by a committee drawn from the School of Archaeology and Ancient History and the Centre for English Local History in the University of Leicester, with David Palliser as a representative of the Royal Historical Society, and Tony Brown for the Society for Landscape Studies. It attracted support and sponsorship from English Heritage, the British Academy, the Friends of the Centre for English Local History, the Historical Geography Research Group, the Medieval Settlement Research Group, Oadby and Wigston Borough Council, Oxbow Books, the Royal Historical Society, the Society for Landscape Studies and Windgather Press. The excursions were led by the late Harold Fox, Graham Jones and Charles Phythian-Adams. Impeccable organisation was provided by Barbara Johnson, with help from David Johnson and Mike Thompson. Publication of the papers in a series of three volumes has depended on the services of the editors: P. S. Barnwell, Andrew Fleming, Mark Gardiner, Richard Hingley, Marilyn Palmer and Stephen Rippon. An anonymous referee gave valuable service. All of the editors and contributors are indebted to Richard Purslow of Windgather Press for his help and support in producing this series, and to Sarah Harrison, who prepared the index for each volume. Financial help for the costs of publication from the Aurelius Trust is gratefully acknowledged.

Christopher Dyer

Landscape History after Hoskins,
Series Editor, Christopher Dyer

Landscape History after Hoskins

··

Christopher Dyer

This book celebrates a great scholar; it emerged from an inspiring occasion; and it reflects the vigour of an enthralling subject, the history of the landscape. It contains a selection of the papers presented to a conference called *W. G. Hoskins and the Making of the British Landscape*, held at the University of Leicester on 7–10 July 2005 to mark the fiftieth anniversary of the publication of *The Making of the English Landscape* by W. G. Hoskins. A Devon man, Hoskins spent the early part of his life as a student in that county, and returned to it in retirement. He held the post of Reader in Economic History at Oxford in 1951–65, and he lived in London when he held a wartime post in the civil service. Leicester was the appropriate place for a conference to honour his work in landscape history, as he had developed his approach to local history and topography in his time on the staff of the University College in the 1930s and late 1940s (he briefly returned as Professor in 1965–8). He was active in the Leicestershire Archaeological Society, and contributed some notable articles to that Society's *Transactions*. He attracted an enthusiastic following to his adult education lectures at Vaughan College. His books on Leicestershire included *The Midland Peasant* and, for a wider readership, the Shell Guide. While at Leicester he founded the University's Department (later Centre) of English Local History.

The Making of the English Landscape appeared in 1955 and had a major impact on the reading public, as it was well written, accessible, and revealed a new way of looking at the past. Hoskins showed that our everyday surroundings – roads, hedges, trees, buildings – had an historical significance, and he was tapping a new source of evidence. The Ordnance Survey map became in his hands a vital document, and he asserted that the landscape was 'the richest historical record we possess'. *The Making* was admired by academics as well as a wider readership, and went through a number of versions, including a Penguin paperback and a Folio Society edition. It was followed by a series of studies of individual counties, which made good progress but was not completed. The book produced a rather delayed response in academia, in the sense that the discipline of Landscape History did not grow rapidly until the 1970s and 1980s, when it was widely practised by archaeologists and geographers, rather than historians. It gained a society and journal with the foundation of the Society for Landscape Studies in 1979, which has published *Landscape*

History ever since. So much research and writing was being done on the subject, and it attracted so much interest from the public as well as professional scholars, that a second journal, *Landscapes*, was launched in 2000.

At the 2005 Leicester conference sixty papers were given in two parallel sessions under ten themes: prehistoric/Roman landscapes; rural settlement; towns; industry; buildings; designed landscapes; environments; ritual; perceptions; and techniques of mapping. The conference was attended by 250 people, and indeed the need to limit the numbers in each lecture room meant that latecomers had to be turned away. Plenary talks were given at the beginning by Christopher Taylor (a landscape archaeologist who knew Hoskins well), Elisabeth Zadora Rio (who provided a continental European perspective), and Fiona Reynolds of the National Trust, who had been influenced by *The Making* when she read it as a student. Three receptions were held, and excursions on three alternative routes occupied one afternoon. The beginning of the conference on 7 July was overshadowed by the London bombings but, in spite of this setback, a cheerful and positive atmosphere prevailed, helped by the sunny weather, good hospitality and attractive surroundings.

Those who gave papers at the conference were encouraged from the beginning not to think of the event as a memorial or a retrospective. W. G. Hoskins was the starting point, and almost every speaker made some reference to the pioneer, but they were focused on recent research and future developments. A number of themes covered subjects which Hoskins himself did not consider in much detail and used techniques that have emerged since 1955. The organisers had hoped that the conference would attract representatives of different disciplines, and would promote interdisciplinary contacts, and this was achieved. Younger scholars were encouraged to attend and to contribute, and a good number responded. The papers in this book, only a selection of those presented at the conference, reflect the progress in landscape history after Hoskins, and readers will gain an impression of the liveliness of the discipline, the new thinking, and the wide range of subject matter.

Christopher Dyer
Professor of Regional and Local History and Director of the
Centre for English Local History
Chair of the Conference Organising Committee

CHAPTER ONE

Introduction:
The Medieval Landscapes
of Britain

Mark Gardiner and Stephen Rippon

Hoskins, in a memorable and often-repeated metaphor, described the English landscape as a palimpsest (Hoskins 1955, 271). It was an idea which he had toyed with for many years before he began to write *The Making of the English Landscape*, and had borrowed from Maitland (Maitland 1897, 15; Hoskins 1943, 81). Though it is a vivid conceit, it is in many ways an imprecise and misleading description. A palimpsest is a piece of parchment from which the earlier text has been expunged so that it can be used a second time. At very few points in the past has the landscape been even partially wiped clear and rarely, if ever, has it been recreated with little regard for its earlier usage, as a palimpsest was. More often, elements of the existing landscape have been taken and reworked into new forms. Some elements have been retained, particularly those with symbolic importance (Bradley 1987; Semple 1998; Williams 1998), and others have been recast into entirely different patterns to meet changing demands and perceptions.

Landscape historians have long recognised the early medieval period as one of the crucial moments in the formation of the countryside of Britain which we have inherited. During that period, though the palimpsest was not scrubbed clean, it was very thoroughly over-written. For Hoskins's generation the great events which changed the landscape were the period of the English settlements in the fifth and sixth centuries when villages were, they thought, established and open fields were laid out. More recently, the period of parliamentary enclosure between 1750 and 1850, when those early fields were swept away and the countryside remade, was also seen as being crucial in shaping the character of the modern countryside. Recent thinking has shifted the chronology of the origins of villages and open fields forward to the ninth and tenth centuries when, under pressure from a rising population, many of the features which characterise the landscape – towns, churches, villages, manors and, until relatively recently, open fields – first began to take enduring forms which have survived, in most cases, until the present.

The idea that the English landscape gradually took shape as boundaries were defined and areas demarked has emerged strongly from a recent study of settlement forms. Reynolds (2003, 130) has identified three phases of change. In the first, during the fifth to mid sixth century, settlements were often sprawling and morphologically unstable. They have been compared to the *Wandersiedlungen*, or 'wandering' settlements, of continental Europe, the centres of which gradually drifted as farmsteads were rebuilt on adjoining land (Hamerow 1991). From the late sixth century a stronger sense of a managed and bounded landscape began to emerge. High-status settlements show more certain evidence of planning, and enclosures around farmsteads became more common. The third phase began in the crucial period of the ninth century, when manorial sites began to emerge; many settlements established in this period have a clear rectilinear arrangement suggesting that they were laid out with care, perhaps even using methods of survey and measurement.

The changes in the morphology of settlements were reflected more generally in that of the English landscape, which might be said to 'crystallise' during the course of the early medieval period as a framework of boundary features was first established and then was infilled. By the ninth and tenth centuries the outlines of the present-day landscape were rapidly emerging. This change did not take place across England at the same time for, as Rippon argues in his paper (this volume), the crucial period of change in the South West appears to have been the seventh and eighth centuries, a time which also seems to be important in the formation of the landscapes of Norfolk, Suffolk and perhaps Cambridgeshire (Newman 1992; Moreland 2000; Oosthuizen 2005). As has been argued above, these new landscapes were not established on a *tabula rasa*, for they inherited a number of 'antecedent features'. This is the term that Roberts (1987, 22) has used for those elements which survived from earlier generations. It has been suggested, for example, that in some areas of East Anglia and the East Midlands the furlong boundaries of the open fields were established over Roman or other ditches, and recent work has reinforced this suggestion (Rodwell 1978; Taylor and Fowler 1978; Upex 2003). Elsewhere, the features of the Iron Age and Roman landscape had apparently been lost or were removed and the medieval fields ignored the earlier pattern (Unwin 1983).

This great change in landscape form marks a point beyond which it is very difficult to proceed. We can say a great deal about the landscape from the tenth century onwards, but we can only dimly discern fragments of evidence relating to the eighth-century countryside. It is therefore hardly surprising that most papers in this volume concentrate on the landscape of the central and later Middle Ages, passing only briefly over the earlier period. However, one of the issues which underlie a number of the papers in this volume is the question of origins. Where did the pattern of fields, manors and towns spring from? And on the tail of that question comes a further issue: how rapidly did the landscape crystallise into the form which then persisted until the period of parliamentary enclosure?

The pursuit of origins can have a distorting effect on our interpretation of the landscape. If we consider that by the end of the first millennium the structure of the landscape was largely in place, the period from 1000 to 1500 – the end point of this volume – is reduced to a study of the way in which the countryside first filled up with people and was then partially emptied, rather like water poured into a jug and then decanted. There is a danger that the study of the later medieval period may simply become a repetitious demonstration of the grand picture which Duby (1968) and Postan (1975) outlined many decades ago. Marshes were drained, woodlands were cleared and uplands were colonised as people sought ever more land to feed the rising population, activity which was brought to a halt by the Malthusian crisis of the early fourteenth century. This has been described by Beresford, in a memorable phrase, as 'the journey to the margin' (Beresford and St Joseph 1979, 94). Stricken by famine and disease, the population shrank, retreating from these marginal lands, which were then left uncultivated or only partially used. Details of this bald picture, which places economic forces as the sole determinant of landscape change, have been rightly criticised (Bailey 1989; Dyer 1989), but there is still much to do to produce a more sophisticated view of this period. One way to re-examine the older interpretation, as a number of papers, particularly in the last section of this volume, indicate, is to give greater emphasis to social and ideological considerations. What types of organisation lay behind the very considerable works required to clear trees and drain wetlands? Were lands left uncultivated for reasons of social prestige? Finally, was the treatment of uncultivated countryside conditioned by the ways in which this type of landscape was perceived?

The study of the landscape is not, of course, only about the study of the countryside. The urban landscape is a complementary field, even though it was treated rather briefly by Hoskins, as Slater notes in his paper below. There are fundamental differences in the way in which rural and urban landscapes have been studied. This partly results from the fact that the degree of survival of evidence is much greater in the countryside than the town; it is possible to find some rural areas of Britain today where the landscape is broadly similar in form to that of six or seven hundred years ago. The hedged fields, farms and woods, though changed in detail, resemble those of the late medieval period. By contrast, there are few, if any, towns where the same is true. It is hard even to find a street in which it is possible to walk down the road and see a significant number of houses much as they would have appeared in, say, the fourteenth century. Perhaps, however, we should not wonder why old buildings survive, but why they have not been demolished. For as one buildings historian has noted, a house survives from the 'last period at which its owner or occupier had the means and motive to rebuild it' (Currie 1988, 6). The paucity of surviving medieval buildings in London is a reflection of the sustained prosperity of the capital city which has allowed the frequent replacement of houses and shops (Schofield 1994). In contrast, Lincoln's substantial stock of medieval buildings is testimony to its relative decline from the thirteenth century and the subsequent paucity of investment in new property (Stocker

2003). On the whole, Britain's continuing prosperity has meant that there are fewer places like Lincoln and more, with a dearth of medieval buildings, like London.

As a consequence, the study of the landscape of towns has not generally been an examination of the physical fabric, but of the maps of towns, for one of the features which may have remained little altered is the pattern of roads and building plots. Conzen, one of the founding fathers of the study of the urban historical landscape, established the methodology for dissecting the plans of towns and relating them to their growth. Beresford, another of the pioneers of urban landscape study, was also interested in urban patterns and chose planned towns for his initial studies. Even in the unpromising situation of the streets of Leeds, where he was appointed professor, Beresford (1984, 12–13) was able to identify evidence for a new town founded in the early thirteenth century. The problem of picking out the ancient elements and recording them precisely is considered in the paper below by Lilley and his colleagues. They show that it is not sufficient to select elements from historic maps; in order to understand how towns may have been laid out in the field, it is necessary to measure them precisely. They demonstrate how this may be done using a Global Positioning System and how the results can be analysed with a Geographical Information System.

Slater, like Lilley *et al.*, argues that the plan of streets and plot boundaries is only one element of the urban landscape and it is necessary for the understanding of the similarities and differences of towns to examine also the patterns of defences and the building types. The subject of defences is considered further by Creighton, who questions not only their military function, but also whether they defined the extent of the town. It is arguable that town walls had various functions: their purpose in Wales, or even on the coast of south-east England, where towns were subject to French raids in the mid and later fourteenth century, were rather different to the walls around towns in the Midlands, where defence was not a consideration. The regional nature of towns is further emphasised in the final paper in this section, which discusses urban development in the North West. Towns in this area were late to appear and, with the exception of Chester, did not achieve the wider importance gained by places in southern and Midland England. In the North West, towns reflect the nature of the marketing systems in their region, and the lack of access to continental markets. The farming system in this region, which operated at little more than subsistence level, meant that the volume of trade was much smaller here than to the south and east. This study provides an important corrective to much of the work on urban growth, which has hitherto focused on the Midlands and southern England.

Higham's study also draws attention to the second theme of this volume, the regional character of landscape. The renewed interest in regional variation is in part a response to two volumes by Roberts and Wrathmell (2000; 2002), cited by a number of papers. These two scholars brought together a number of maps showing both existing information and newly gathered data. As Roberts indicates in his paper below, maps pose questions and demand answers. In some cases their maps suggest their own answers. By plotting the distribution of various pre-Conquest place-name elements indicative of woodland and setting these against the boundaries of the 'village belt' of England's 'central province', they demonstrate that nucleated settlement grew up where there was little available uncleared land (Roberts and Wrathmell 2002, fig. 1.10). On the other hand, their subsequent map shows that there was no relationship between the availability of timber and the use of cruck construction for houses (Roberts and Wrathmell 2002, fig. 1.11). Their maps raise important questions about the relative importance of environmental and cultural factors. The first of these factors has been rather downplayed in recent years and Williamson, in his paper, wishes to reassert its importance. His is certainly not a crude environmentally deterministic argument, but he seeks to emphasise the fundamental business of the countryside – farming. He is able to speak with some authority on this subject since he has experience of the problems of cultivating claylands.

Rippon takes a very different view in his study of the emergence of the village-dominated countryside of the 'central province', emphasising the importance of individual agency in the creation of landscapes. In particular, in Somerset, he identifies the influence of the abbots of Glastonbury in the creation of nucleated villages and open fields, and contrasts it with the behaviour of their less interventionist colleagues the bishops of Bath and of Wells, who left individual sub-tenants to structure the landscape of newly reclaimed wetlands in a variety of ways. Other factors appear to have played a significant part in explaining why the management of the landscape through villages and open fields did not spread any further into the South West: this region had developed its own successful system of rotational husbandry which meant that open-field agriculture offered little evident benefit for the farmer. In East Anglia, Martin adopts a multi-causal explanation to understand the distribution of field systems. While the 'Gipping divide' seems to be the result of different topographies to the north and south, he suggests that Viking settlement may explain the development of common fields in northern and western Suffolk. It is notable that both Williamson and Martin revive explanations for regional difference which had fallen into disfavour in recent years – soils and the settlement of incomers – but both employ a more sophisticated interpretation of these mechanisms. It is apparent that there is still much to understand about the ways in which regional differences in landscape may have developed during the course of the Middle Ages.

The third group of papers examines the processes of landscape change at a different scale – that of the settlement. The paper by Page and Jones is directly relevant to the preceding section, because it discusses the stability of settlement forms and questions whether the nineteenth-century maps employed by Roberts and Wrathmell for one of their key studies (Roberts and Wrathmell 2000, 9–17, 27) can be utilised as a guide to earlier settlement forms. They take a series of villages in the Whittlewood area of Buckinghamshire and

Northamptonshire and show that half of these have radically altered in plan since the Middle Ages. It remains to be demonstrated whether this area is typical of England, but there is no reason to believe that it is exceptional. Many settlements will have experienced considerable changes to their form. We might treat village desertion as an extreme case of settlement change. Many other villages were reduced in size, either by the abandonment of houses within the settlement leaving empty plots, or by the contraction of the area of occupation through shrinkage. The issue of stability or change is a particularly English issue, because in other areas there is hardly a question over whether the settlements retained their medieval form. In Scotland, for example, where the Clearances allowed whole landscapes to be radically reordered, the problem is how to ascertain the form of settlements before these radical changes of the eighteenth and nineteenth centuries. Dixon suggests that the landscape has been in a period of flux since at least the twelfth century when planned settlements were introduced, perhaps as the result of the influx of Flemish and Anglo-Norman landholders. Comparison is made with row settlements in England and elsewhere in Europe, but it might be particularly relevant to compare the Scottish examples with similar planned villages in Pembrokeshire (Kissock 1997). A second phase of change occurred from the fifteenth century onwards, when settlement in Scotland expanded into marginal land, but the most radical changes happened when the landscape was improved by reforming lairds who amalgamated holdings to create larger farms. Permanency of settlement patterns is also examined in the third paper in this section, by Gardiner. He considers the extent to which the manor house was an unchanging feature of the landscape and concludes that it, too, was often impermanent: manor houses did not tend to occupy the same position for century after century.

The final group of studies charts a developing interest in the phenomenology, symbolism and design of landscapes. This approach has been developed particularly in prehistoric studies (Tilley 1994; Bradley 2000; Tilley 2004), but the opportunities for understanding the landscapes of the Middle Ages are even greater. Written evidence allows the context of the creation of 'made landscapes' to be understood more clearly and lets us approach more closely the perceptions and ideas of those who occupied them. This type of study is not without its difficulties, and one of the most ambitious attempts to date to interpret the medieval landscape, by Altenberg (2003), is not entirely satisfactory. It employs a range of evidence, including folklore, and utilises a classification of landscape developed in the rather different cultural context of Japan. The papers presented here are altogether more cautious. McDonagh continues the examination of the movement or persistence of manor houses also considered in the preceding paper. She discusses the way in which the spatial relationship between the church, settlement and manor house might have been perceived, and how this may have been manipulated to imply that the church was the possession of the lord. This may have been achieved by echoing the architectural features of the church in the manor house, or by surrounding the two buildings with a single enclosure. Liddiard, in his examination of seigniorial landscapes, also considers the ways in which the setting of houses was managed. However, his paper concerns the landscapes of great houses rather than the manorial dwellings of the gentry. He suggests that we might consider the concept of a 'design threshold' separating the more elaborate designed landscapes from those which were less ambitious in scope. Future research will show whether there really was such a sharp distinction between the landscapes of the nobility and the gentry.

These two papers are largely concerned with secular landscapes, but it is very likely that the surroundings around monastic houses were organised in a similar manner to enhance the buildings' setting. Liddiard suggests that the monks of Clairvaux in France saw their labours as bringing order to the landscape in both practical and metaphoric terms. It is remarkable that the symbolism of the landscape of monasteries has not been investigated in greater detail, which is no doubt a reflection of the greater interest in the claustral buildings at the expense of the outer court and the wider setting more generally. Work at Bordesley Abbey has demonstrated how archaeology might be undertaken using a broader perspective (Astill *et al.* 2004), but the significance of some of the buildings of the monastery still remains poorly understood, as Everson and Stocker demonstrate. They identify a class of chapel which escaped antiquarian notice, the monastic chantry chapel, but more importantly they show that this allows us to look again at the way the monastic precinct was regarded. This, with their earlier work on the setting of ecclesiastical sites in the Witham valley (Stocker and Everson 2003), indicates a way in which the study of the landscapes of monasteries might develop.

The papers within this volume are, we would suggest, broadly representative of the directions of current research on the *English* landscape. The themes which we have picked out in organising this volume – towns, regions, settlement and conceptual landscapes – are those in which there is the greatest scholarly activity. A number of papers here report on work in progress or recent methodological developments, and indicate the likely direction of future studies. However, it is hardly possible within the scope of a single book to cover all the areas of research, let alone all aspects of the British landscape. Readers will note that areas beyond England are poorly served in the papers here. It is hoped that the gaps in this book will be made up by the publication of recent work, supported by Cadw, on rural settlement in Wales and, beyond Britain, by the Medieval Rural Settlement module of the Discovery Programme in Ireland.

The papers here demonstrate how far the heirs of Hoskins have taken forward the study of landscape in the fifty years since the publication of *The Making of the English Landscape*. The primary message of his highly influential study was to show that the landscape had been recast in different ways over a period of centuries and to suggest how the various traces of the past might be distinguished. He was concerned with how one might be able to learn to 'read' the evidence of the landscape (Hoskins 1955, 14–15). The present papers suggest that the emphasis of study has now very largely shifted from description of the landscape towards explanation. The authors below grapple with such difficult problems as why were there regional differences, what remained permanent in the changing landscape of the Middle Ages and how we might study the ritual and symbolic landscapes of the past. Fifty years after the publication of *The Making of the English Landscape*, the discipline which Hoskins helped to initiate has moved forward to examine new questions and problems. It is hoped that some of the excitement of the discovery of landscape which was generated by Hoskins's volume will also be conveyed by the papers published here.

PART ONE

Urban Landscapes

CHAPTER TWO

The Landscape
of Medieval Towns:
Anglo-European Comparisons

Terry R. Slater

The Making of the English Landscape gives towns short shrift. Hoskins (1955, 230) recognised this and suggested that 'the Landscape of Towns requires a whole book to itself'. A number of such books have, of course, been published in English over the past half-century, some with an emphasis on the chronologies of history (Reynolds 1977), some the artefacts of archaeology (Carver 1987; Ottoway 1992; Schofield and Vince 1994), and some the development of plan forms (Lilley 2001a). Very few of these volumes, however, have ventured far into providing readers with comparative material across the cultures and societies of Europe. Even experts in particular urban specialities are hard-pressed to present a Europe-wide comparative survey on a particular theme, so it is certainly not the intention to attempt such a feat in this brief chapter. But I do want to make the initial point that I think it is important that we begin to widen our horizons if we are to understand better what is distinctive about our own regional or national townscapes. Even *within* most European countries there is a clear geography of difference, deriving from the medieval period, in the character of historic towns: in the character of the towns of north, south and east Germany, for example (Meckseper 2004).

That geography of difference is greater still if the scale of comparison is raised to the European level. If we have an interest in understanding historic towns, enhancing their character and preserving their uniqueness, then we need to understand precisely what it is that makes towns of medieval origin in Ireland, Gascony, Bavaria, Poland and Tuscany (to take just a few examples) so different from one another. Some of the answers are to be found in differences of medieval economy (the merchant cities of north Italy and the mining towns of Lower Saxony, for example); in differences of local environment engendering different building responses (rain-swept Bergen and sun-soaked Lucca, for instance); in differences of law and administration (the city states of Tuscany and the nation state of England, for example); and in the different post-medieval histories of different regions and states (the traumatic effects of the Thirty Years War in north-central Europe, of early industrialisation in Britain, or of Second-World-War bombing across northern Germany, for instance (Slater 1999a)).

My own interest in the geographies and histories of difference in the character of towns of medieval origin focuses upon their plan forms. The sheer complexity of most European medieval urban plans has deterred many investigators and led others to simplistic analyses. It is still all too common to see medieval towns represented only by their street plans, whereas it is the combination of street plan, plot pattern, and building plans that is minimally necessary for even the most basic understanding of medieval towns from this perspective. Only then can we begin to appreciate why the very long narrow plots of the Bryggen harbour frontage in Bergen (Øye 1994) produce a fundamentally different townscape to the broad, shallow plot pattern found in Aigues Mortes, and understand that these two places stand as examples of two regional plan types: the Hanseatic port towns of the North and Baltic Sea littorals, and the high medieval bastides of south-west France (Lauret *et al.* 1988). And only then can we begin to conserve these places successfully, because we can understand the things that make them special. These perspectives on plan characteristics will be explored in more detail in what follows.

The map of European nations today is, of course, not a map of culture areas, still less a map of medieval culture areas, though for England that is perhaps rather less true than for almost any other European nation. Since the eleventh century, England has been a single unified state and, though there are undoubtedly differences between the cultures of northern England, East Anglia and the South West, for instance, as well as between the landscape and medieval agrarian economies of these regions, the differences in regional townscapes and plan forms are small-scale, though still comparatively poorly identified, let alone explained and understood, compared with those of towns in many other parts of Europe.

The landscape of towns is an important theme because towns carry an enormous weight of social and cultural value in all European societies. Their meaning is part of our social and cultural identity and therefore of our well-being. Hoskins recognised this half a century ago in answering his own question regarding the value of the study of towns. The answer was that 'one gets a greater depth of pleasure out of knowing the anatomy of a town and why it takes that particular form' (Hoskins 1955, 211). For Conzen, too, the complexity of urban landscapes represented an 'objectification of the spirit' of local culture, society and economy translated into built and plan forms that have been transformed and selectively replaced through time (Conzen 1972).

It is the Conzenian world of urban morphology which has formed the grounding of my own work, and that of others, in seeking to understand more of the plan forms and development processes taking place in medieval towns. So it will be the Conzenian framework of town-plan analytical studies which will be used here to point up what I would see as some of the critically distinctive features of English medieval towns compared with their counterparts in other culture areas. There is sufficient space to consider briefly five themes: first, defences; secondly, the composite character of town plans; thirdly, the nature of medieval town planning; fourthly, the metrology of plots; and, finally, building types.

Defences

For much of medieval mainland Europe, a pattern of stable nation states with unchanging boundaries and firm, centralised government was rarely achieved, in considerable contrast to the pattern in England. Apart from in England, medieval towns in most other parts of Europe were therefore the defensible spaces of political elites, as well as trading places; the military capture of a town meant that both the town and its territory were transferred from one '(es)state' to another (see Lilley 2000b for the example of Norman Wales). 'National' boundaries and a sense of nationhood were far more fluid for the majority of European peoples than we perceive today. The consequence was that the majority of European towns were heavily defended, not just in the medieval period, but through into the nineteenth century (Pollack 1992), and those defences had dramatic morphological effects that define one of the major differences between English and other European towns. Only the largest English cities, such as Norwich, York and Bristol, together with the 'gateway' towns on the Scottish border (Carlisle and Berwick) and the dockyard towns of the south coast (Plymouth, Portsmouth and Chatham), maintained their town walls and gates into the sixteenth and seventeenth centuries (Creighton and Higham 2005), and for the larger cities it was mostly for prestige and toll-collection purposes. Similarly, only Bristol shows the successive enlargement of medieval defensive circuits to enclose new suburbs, which is such a feature of most European towns of any size. No English city had elaborate water-filled ditches supplementing its medieval walls, such as those around cities in the Low Countries and north Germany, whilst Renaissance-style bastion defences are unknown, again excepting the border and dockyard towns (Duffy 1979).

This has important morphological consequences. The most dramatic is that very few English towns have the spatio-temporal discontinuity between their medieval and early modern phases of development, and their industrial-era development, that is such a distinctive feature of other European realms. In very many central-European towns, this spatio-temporal discontinuity is marked by relict defensive structures which could be wholly or partially demolished in the nineteenth century and utilised for the construction of '*Ringstrassen*' (ring roads). Demolition also gave space for parks and green open spaces, high-status institutional buildings such as universities, art galleries and hospitals, and high-income housing consisting of detached mansions in extensive grounds. Examples include the university city of Göttingen (Denecke 1979), the market centre of Braunschweig (Kalanke and Kuchen 1982 has maps and illustrations), and the much-studied *Ringstrasse* zone of Vienna (Oppl 1982). These *Ringstrassen* zones constitute the classical inner fringe belt of European cities. In English cities, inner fringe belts usually consist of irregularly developed zones of back-land industrial use, warehouses and narrow access lanes. Alnwick is the type site (Conzen 1960). Ring roads are the exception rather than the rule (the eastern side of early modern Exeter is one of those exceptions because the medieval walls were retained there), so there is no temporal discontinuity between medieval, early modern and industrial era development. Consequently, when the motor vehicle demanded ring roads in the twentieth century, they could only be created through the processes of post-1945 'slum clearance' and centralised urban planning. This often effectively eliminated early industrial-era housing developments and created a spatio-temporal discontinuity in English cities as dramatic as those in European cities, but for a later morphological period, as in 1960s Birmingham (Cherry 1994) or 1970s Leeds and Newcastle-upon-Tyne.

Composite town plans and plan units

Research investigating the plan units of composite-plan towns has been dominated by the work of the Conzenian school, myself included (Slater 1987; 1990b; 1998; 2005a), which has tried to discover more about the empirical characteristics of the planning processes within medieval towns. Conzen's work itself was important here in demonstrating that even planned towns are usually 'composite' in their plan development; that is, they are made up of distinctively different 'plan units', each representing different temporal phases of the development process (Conzen 1960). Ludlow is the type site, though it is interesting to reflect that, forty years on, arguments continue as to the definition and chronology of its plan units (Conzen 1968; 1988; Hindle 1990; Slater 1990b; Lilley 1999). The vast majority of English medieval new towns are less complex; they are simple one-street plans with burgage series ranged along both sides of a highway, which is sometimes broadened in the middle to provide a market place. Yet even the simplest of these towns often have composite plans (Slater 2004). Such one-street planned towns are found all over Europe, but less frequently than in England, and there are still distinctive regional differences. First, even small one-street European towns are usually characterised by wall defences and fortified gates, and in Italy and the Iberian peninsula such defences are combined with defensible ridge-top locations, whereas few English towns have so much as a ditch marking their outer boundary. Secondly, the circular churchyard precinct at one end of the street town, or at the core of more complex plans, such as Kempen, north Germany, is extremely common in central European regions and in northern Italy, giving what we might characterise as a 'tadpole' form to the single-street plans, and a spider-like radial-concentric form to the others. These circular churchyards often give form to the market space which surrounds them, or takes their place, in later medieval times (see the German historic towns' atlases for examples: Stoob 1973–93). Thirdly, many of these small European towns are much more geometrically planned than their English counterparts.

It is perhaps appropriate to take a number of well-studied exemplar towns to illustrate the importance of plan-unit definition in telling the story of the medieval urban development process and its differences and similarities across Europe. Considered first is the small north German town of Duderstadt

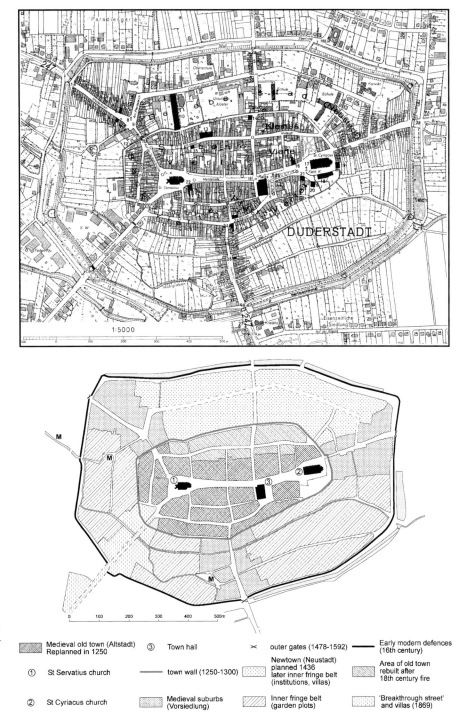

FIGURE I.
A town-plan analysis of Duderstadt, Lower Saxony, Germany (source: 1:5,000 Stadtplan von Duderstadt 1964).

Medieval old town (Altstadt) Replanned in 1250

① St Servatius church

② St Cyriacus church

③ Town hall

town wall (1250-1300)

Medieval suburbs (Vorsiedlung)

× outer gates (1478-1592)

Newtown (Neustadt) planned 1436 later inner fringe belt (institutions, villas)

Inner fringe belt (garden plots)

Early modern defences (16th century)

Area of old town rebuilt after 18th century fire

'Breakthrough street' and villas (1869)

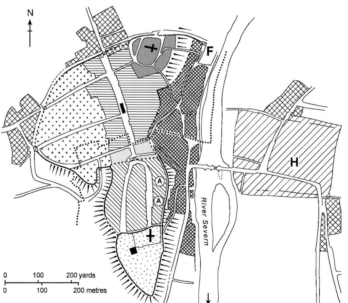

N↑

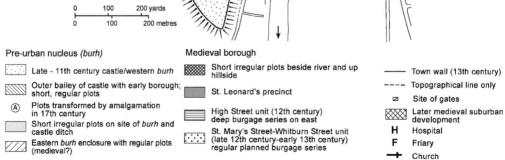

| 0 | 100 | 200 yards |
| 0 | 100 | 200 metres |

Pre-urban nucleus (*burh*)

:::: Late - 11th century castle/western *burh*

▨ Outer bailey of castle with early borough; short, regular plots

Ⓐ Plots transformed by amalgamation in 17th century

▨ Short irregular plots on site of *burh* and castle ditch

▨ Eastern *burh* enclosure with regular plots (medieval?)

Medieval borough

▨ Short irregular plots beside river and up hillside

■ St. Leonard's precinct

☰ High Street unit (12th century) deep burgage series on east

:::: St. Mary's Street-Whitburn Street unit (late 12th century-early 13th century) regular planned burgage series

—— Town wall (13th century)

- - - Topographical line only

▨ Site of gates

▨ Later medieval suburban development

H Hospital

F Friary

✝ Church

(Figure 1). To those practised in reading town plans the differentiation are immediately obvious of (i) the medieval old town within the stone walls with its balance of townscape dominants (two churches and the town hall); (ii) the three medieval suburbs beyond the wall circuit; (iii) the inner fringe belt of institutional land uses inside and outside the medieval walls, especially to the north where a 'new town' was planned in 1436, but failed to develop; (iv) the earthwork and moated sixteenth-century defences with their allotment gardens between the two wall circuits (another part of the fringe belt); and (v) the nineteenth-century breakthrough street of villa houses leading to the railway station. Further investigation, particularly in the field, reveals the distinctive built forms along the northern intramural street caused by a major fire in the eighteenth century, which thereby created an important sub-unit of the old-town plan unit. Though small, Duderstadt has a complex plan which has been splendidly conserved in the modern period.

The second example is Bridgnorth in the Severn valley of midland England (Figure 2). Here a distinctive topography must be added to the complexity of its plan development. High Town, to the west of the river, has a very different plan form to Low Town, on the east. The latter may derive from a rectangular tenth-century defensible *burh* defending this important river crossing and linked to another enclosure on the hill-top to the west (Slater 1990b). The latter became a Norman castle town in the late eleventh century. A 'high street' of long narrow plots developed in front of the castle town gate with a church enclosure marking its northern end, that enclosure being, very unusually for England, sub-circular in form. An irregular, zig-zag road down a steep hill and associated plots linked the High Town to the medieval bridge. A carefully planned parallel-street system with regular plots, surrounded by a wall, was added to the western side of the high street and marks the final medieval development phase (Slater 1990b).

A third example from southern Europe will extend the range of case studies to a completely different culture area. Trani, in southern Italy, has been the subject of a detailed study in the Italian morphological tradition (Strappa *et al.* 2003), but I have translated this into town-plan analytic mode (Figure 3). So, again, there is a defended 'old town' core which is either (as the Italians suggest) derived from an underlying Roman set of buildings, plots and streets, or (as I believe) was planned anew by the Normans in the eleventh century with new townscape dominants in the form of castle and cathedral church on the waterfront. There are small Romanesque churches in the centre of the town (St Martin's) and – probably – outside the western gate (St James's), and a synagogue within the walls. The street plan is a classic example of a single spine road (later lined with the grand palaces of the elite) with a series of parallel access roads at right angles to the spine and slightly offset from one another on each side of the spine. They are linked by a continuous intramural lane. There was probably already development on the western frontage of the harbour, which may have preceded the walled town and which therefore had to be incorporated into the plan, hence the

FIGURE 2.
A town-plan analysis
of Bridgnorth,
Shropshire, England
(source: 1:2,500
Ordnance Survey
County Series, sheets
58/8 and 58/12, second
edition 1914).

17

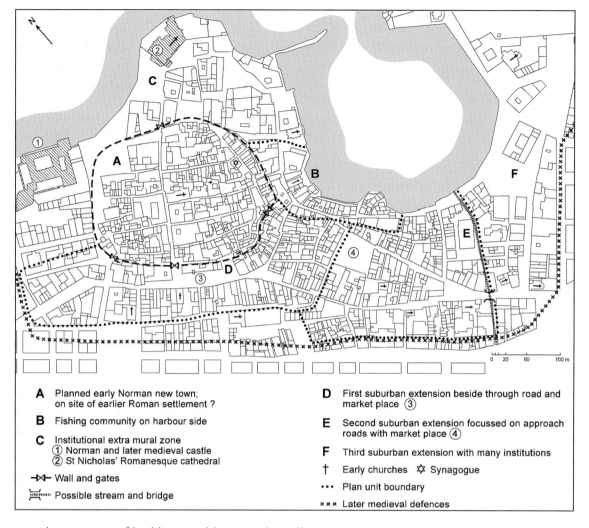

A Planned early Norman new town;
on site of earlier Roman settlement ?

B Fishing community on harbour side

C Institutional extra mural zone
  ① Norman and later medieval castle
  ② St Nicholas' Romanesque cathedral

⊢⋈⊣ Wall and gates

⊓⋯ Possible stream and bridge

D First suburban extension beside through road and
market place ③

E Second suburban extension focussed on approach
roads with market place ④

F Third suburban extension with many institutions

† Early churches ✡ Synagogue

••• Plan unit boundary

××× Later medieval defences

FIGURE 3.
A town-plan analysis
of Trani, Puglia, Italy
(source: base map
redrawn from Strappa
et al. 2003, fig. 14).

complex junction of buildings and lanes at the still surviving Antiqua Porta. Later, but not very much later, there was further development on the major approach road to the town and harbour, and along the coast road towards the provincial capital at Bari, again possibly with Roman antecedents. This gave two further distinctive plan units (D and E), while ecclesiastical institutions and churches formed initial markers for these developing areas. All was enclosed within a later medieval wall which formed a fixation line for the construction of the railway and the large-scale nineteenth-century planned housing developments that form another distinctive plan unit with a grid street plan, which can be subdivided further as its development took place in phases (Slater 2005b).

So, here we have three examples of relatively small towns from central, northern and southern Europe respectively that can be understood by using plan analysis and which demonstrate a complexity of forms, but a commonality of the processes leading to those forms, whilst recognising the distinctive regional and national histories that have given rise to these features. Notable characteristics of these towns include the dispersed character of Bridgnorth compared with Duderstadt and Trani, though all are defensible towns; the dominance of the early modern defences in Duderstadt (thanks to the Thirty Years War) compared with the others; and the distinctive differences of plot pattern and building plans between all three towns, of which more below. Furthermore, even at this level of analysing plan complexity it should be obvious that modern managerial planning and conservation policies that deal with such towns as single, undifferentiated entities are bound to fail because they do not recognise the distinctive features of 'old town', 'high-street' layout, inner fringe belt, townscape dominant (major buildings such as churches and town halls) and 'break-through' street, to name but the most common of plan-unit categories. All of these require different managerial policies if their distinguishing characteristics are to be conserved and enhanced and thereby give meaning to today's historical townscapes. Once the third dimension of the built forms are added to the plan, then the managerial complexities are multiplied manifold since they are much more subject to national, regional and local cultural variations, styles and building materials.

Medieval town planning

The third theme, medieval planned towns, provides a very much larger literature, beginning with that developed by town planners and planning historians to legitimise their new subject at the beginning of the twentieth century (Scrase 2002). Much of the more recent material has developed from a second book, almost as iconic as Hoskins: namely, Beresford's magisterial *New Towns of the Middle Ages in England, Wales and Gascony*, in which is contained a very clear recognition that processes of English new town creation in the twelfth to fourteenth centuries was part of a Europe-wide urbanisation process (Beresford 1967). Unfortunately, it has had the partial consequence of fixating our English-speaking comparative lens concerning town planning on Gascony, particularly since that region is a favoured location for English summer holidays! We therefore have far less comparative material easily available from Spain and Portugal, Italy, other parts of France, and the whole of Slavic and German-speaking eastern and central Europe, where new town planning was equally common (Friedman 1988 provides some comparative material from these regions).

A number of research themes can be discerned in the post-Beresford investigation of medieval town planning. The first is the search for regional plan types, which is almost untouched in Britain (though see Lilley 2001b). The most notable example from the wider European realm is the categorisation of the Gascon bastide towns into four basic plan 'families' by Lauret and his co-researchers at the University of Toulouse (Lauret *et al.* 1988); Figure 4 illustrates only the most important 'Aquitaine' and 'Gascon' types. Meckseper has recently attempted something similar for central European regular plan types in the thirteenth century, where he suggests that there is distinct regional variation in German medieval urban planning (Meckseper 2004).

The second theme of research on medieval planning processes has been geometry. Architectural historians, in particular, have long sought to discover the imagined geometrical complexity of both medieval cathedral buildings and that underlying seemingly simple grid town plans. Lavadan's studies of Monpazier are amongst the earliest and are comparatively straightforward (Lavadan and Hugueny 1974). Much more complex (and controversial) has been Francois Bucher's original interpretation of the geometry of Grenade-sur-Garonne's odd-length street blocks (Bucher 1972) which generated an intense debate in the pages of the journal *Urban Morphology* a few years ago, leading, I think, to the comprehensive demolition of Bucher's hypotheses (Lilley 1998; Slater 1999b; 2001; Scrase 1999; Boerefijn 2000). This sort of critical analysis of complex plan interpretations is all too rare in this field. Equally well-known is Friedman's interpretation of the new towns planned by the merchant commune of Florence in its newly expanded territory in the early fourteenth century, especially at San Giovanni Valdarno (Friedman 1988). Its complex sine geometry is unique and, since it was discovered and published by an American, to many Italian scholars is as controversial as Bucher's interpretation of Grenade, though the uniquely detailed documentation, and his careful field measurements, places Friedman's research on a very firm footing (Friedman and Pirillo 2004). As context, Lilley has recently written much on the importance of geometry in the neo-Platonic academic world of the thirteenth-century monastic European Church (Lilley 2004). This is incontrovertible, but whether this ideal world of geometry burst forth into the realities of town planning in any context other than the time-space context of early fourteenth-century Florence, where Renaissance knowledge was already fermenting, is difficult to prove.

Equally controversial have been Nitz's attempts to suggest that Austrian new towns of the thirteenth century were based on both a model and a street-block metrology derived from the *borgo novo* of the city states of northern Italy (Nitz 2001). Most of his work is based on cartographic evidence, rather than field metrology, and there is need of both further critical analyses of maps and their supporting documentation, and for field measurement of plot dimensions. Rather less work has been done on the plan principles of east European grid-planned towns, and earlier research tended to concentrate on the geometric 'ideal' plan, rather than the reality of the evidence on the ground (Kalinowski 1972; see also Koter and Kulesza 1999). A third set of researches that provokes intense argument derives from a group of Italian academic architects and planners. They have undertaken much work on the continuities from Roman to medieval dwellings in particular Italian towns, such as at Trani (referred to above). But there is little by way of documentary or archaeological support for these theoretical transformations of building structures (Cataldi *et al*. 2003 provides a brief example of this type of study, using Pienza).

The third planning theme has not so much dominated the agenda as

FIGURE 4. Gascon bastide town plans. The 'Gascon model', with central street blocks equal in size to the market square and no back lanes: A. Pavie; B. Geaune. The 'Aquitaine model', with rectangular street blocks divided by narrow back lanes for rear access to properties: C. Monflanquin; D. Miramont-de-Guyenne (source: redrawn from Lauret *et al*. 1988, 66, 72).

0   100m

crept up slowly on the English-speaking world. This is what Baker has called 'ground-works' planning and which we might subsume in a wider categorisation of environmental planning in medieval towns. The recent publication of Baker and Holt's study of Worcester and Gloucester (2004) has brought to wider notice the enormous earth-moving task of infilling a huge Roman ditch that was undertaken as a preliminary to planning Anglo-Saxon Worcester. The diversion of major rivers to provide mill reaches at places such as Tewkesbury and Salisbury has received little comment, even in the copious literature devoted to the latter place, whilst the creation of very large impounded lakes which marked the plans of places such as Stafford, Kenilworth, Lichfield and Newcastle-under-Lyme, to take only a selection of examples from the English Midlands, excites even less interest in the literature. By contrast, the spectacularly engineered timber waterfronts of medieval London are now well known (Milne 2003), and Harrison's recent study of medieval bridges has rightly drawn attention to the lengthy causeways which often needed to be constructed across floodplain approaches to major bridges, as well as the bridges themselves where they spanned significant rivers, such as Rochester

Bridge across the Medway, and London Bridge across the Thames (Harrison 2004).

European interest in the environmental planning realm is more long-standing. One obvious difference with England is in the Mediterranean world, where questions of urban water supply loom large, especially in those towns perched high on ridge tops. Both the huge stone-lined cisterns (there are well-displayed examples at Assisi and Bergamo (Italy), for example) and the aqueducts which brought water from upland catchments elsewhere were often derived from Roman times and had only to be repaired and maintained. The other major difference is the huge effort expended on fortifications, especially when accompanied with moats and, in the sixteenth and seventeenth centuries, by brick-built or stone-lined bastions, such as those at Estremoz and Badajoz on the Portuguese–Spanish border.

Plot forms

The fourth research strand that is summarised here is the attempts to understand the dimensional character of the initial plots in newly developing towns and the ways in which these were then subdivided in the subsequent stages of the development process. This is something which has occupied me for the past quarter-century (Slater 1981), but there were earlier studies of this kind in Germany, Switzerland and Poland (Strahm 1948; Pudełko 1959; 1960). Interdisciplinary studies integrating documents, plans and archaeology have been important here in providing a convincing body of evidence for some of these early development processes and the continuity of plot boundaries, especially in Britain and Germany (Fehring 1991; Baker and Holt 2004). However, we are still far from any Europe-wide comparative survey of urban plot characteristics and development processes.

Much of the early work of this kind was concerned with recognising the plot dimensions of planned towns of the twelfth and thirteenth centuries. Strahm's analysis of medieval Bern, one of the well-known group of Zahringian planned new towns, is perhaps the best-known of these early metrological analyses (Strahm 1948). It is interesting to note that recent archaeological work has overturned Strahm's chronology for the development of Bern's distinctive plan, pointing to the importance of interdisciplinary investigation in this sort of work. The long-term research by groups of historians, archaeologists and geographers in places such as Lübeck, Winchester and London have had considerable success in mapping processes of plot and building change over the long term (Keene 1985; Fehring 1991). Such processes of change have also been fundamental to the methodologies of the Italian school of architectural urban morphologists, though with a concentration on buildings rather than plots, and on theorising developmental processes rather than using the evidence of documents and archaeology. My own work, begun with Stratford-upon-Avon, has been important in pointing up the particular measuring systems used in medieval English towns (the statute perch and acre) and included the ways in which the ideals of plot form were easily sacrificed to the realities of the site and initial large plot sizes were immediately subdivided by their owners to begin a capitalist land market (Slater 1987; 1997). However, we have only the broadest idea of both the chronology of medieval urban plot dimensions (in northern Europe they seem to get shorter and narrower between the tenth and the fourteenth centuries) and the geography of urban plot dimensions (though they seem to be distinctively squarer across most of southern Europe). This last is clearly related to the similar geography of the courtyard-house type.

Domestic buildings

There is little space to provide examples of this fifth thematic strand – the geographies of the urban domestic building types which occupied the medieval ground plan and which give our medieval old towns their third dimension. Urban buildings have received rather more attention from academic studies, especially by architectural historians, and we are more familiar with a Europe-wide perspective in terms of architectural style, though this is mostly couched in terms of what in English is often called 'polite' or elite styles, rather than the vernacular (Büttner and Meissner 1981; Griep 1985).

The first theme of interest must be the relationship between plot dimensions and building orientation in towns. Generally speaking, low-density occupation sees buildings constructed with their long axis parallel to the street. Since the majority of English towns were not constrained by fortifications, they were more spacious and built at a lower density than in most other culture realms; most English urban medieval buildings therefore have their long axis to the street (Smith 1992). Where plots are narrow and building densities high, then there is a greater propensity for buildings to be constructed gable-end to the street, as at Celle and Rothenburg-an-der-Tauber in Germany (Griep 1985), and plots can be narrower still if access to the rear of plots is provided by back lanes rather than through, or beside, the frontage building. This became the particular building tradition in the towns of north-central Europe, from the Low Countries across to the Vistula and southwards to the Danube.

Again, there are time-space constraints to these building traditions, particularly when we insert building materials and their technologies into the equation (Dolgner and Roch 1987). Archaeologists have demonstrated clearly that in the timber-building realm across the whole of northern Europe, including Britain, the development of timber-frame construction sometime in the later twelfth century made the urban building as valuable as the plot because it no longer had to be rebuilt every twenty years or so, as was the case with earth-fast timber buildings. It also allowed for a dramatic increase in the density of urban buildings (and populations) because they could now be constructed several storeys, rather than a single storey, high (Palliser *et al.* 2000). The fairly recent archaeological discovery of previously unknown earth-fast, single-storey buildings underlying large areas of such well-known new towns as Freiburg-im-Breisgau in southern Germany, with its double-depth cellars, has meant a dramatic reconsideration of their urban developmental history. On the outer fringes of Europe, in Scandinavia, Scotland, Ireland and east of the Vistula, single-story timber buildings continued to be built in towns well into the early modern period.

Before the development of timber-framing, stone buildings marked out the wealthy elite. There are few surviving examples in England: the so-called Jews' houses in Lincoln are probably the best-known (Harris 1993). In the larger merchant towns of northern Europe, in contrast, there are far more, often several storeys high, with capacious cellars for storing commodities below, and often with clear signs that they were defensible. An example is the retractable timber ladder which originally gave access to the first-floor entrance of 19 Simeonstrasse, a beautifully-restored Romanesque house in Trier (Wiedenau 1983, 272–3). In many German merchant towns the stone houses were to the rear of the plot, as in the preserved house in Hagenbrücke, Braunschweig (illustrated in Stadt Braunschweig 1985; see also Wiedenau 1983, 50–1). The fine Romanesque stone houses in the principal streets of Cluny are also well known (Büttner and Meissner 1981). Another important early stone house type was the tall tower house, found in many towns in northern Italy, and occasionally north of the Alps, most notably in Regensburg. The best-known surviving examples are those in the small Tuscan town of San Gimignano and in Bologna, but the relics of others can be seen in places such as Siena and Florence.

The greatest contrast in medieval house types from the thirteenth century onwards is between northern and southern Europe, rather than between England and the rest of Europe. In southern Europe the courtyard house is the standard type. It usually presented a rather forbidding front to the street, with few windows; those that did exist were often barred and shuttered, whilst a similarly fortified door gave access to a passageway into the courtyard. The living rooms were distributed around the courtyard and a substantial staircase gave access to the upper floors, where the principal living quarters were often accessed by open galleries. Outward-looking upper windows often gave access to wooden galleries with awnings built out from the walls on the street frontage; it was not unknown for such structures to collapse into the street. From the fourteenth century, developing Renaissance ideals emanating from Florence led to an increasing regularity in the design of both courtyard houses overall and, more particularly, in their façade, with the 'invention' of the street (Friedman 1992).

Another significant contrast with English urban building traditions in the later medieval period derives from the fact that in some central European regions, towns were occupied by large numbers of farmers as well as by traders and people engaged in craft production. In these so-called 'Ackerbürger' towns of Germany, farmsteads dominated the urban landscapes. They were huge buildings, gable-end to the street (such as those in Lippstadt, north Germany), which contained the living quarters for family, oxen and cows on the ground floor, and capacious storage for hay and grain on the upper floors (Klockow

1964). There are few villages in these regions, only towns, but they are very different towns to those with which we are familiar in England.

Another urban tradition in a number of European regions, including the bastide towns of Gascony and the new towns of the Portuguese–Spanish border, is the pattern of ground-floor storage and first-floor living in small two-storey houses. In these houses, the ground floor is dominated by a large arched entrance and a single unheated room. This could be used as a shop, a workshop, or for storage, whilst today it often provides the space for a garage. A separate entrance gives on to a staircase up to the first floor where the principal living room, with fireplace, looks out on to the street. The grand Romanesque houses of Cluny are planned in the same way. Finally, there are particular traditions in single towns: the double-depth cellars in Freiburg-im-Breisgau, for example (Diel 1981), or the arcaded buildings that have been a tradition in Bologna from medieval times through to the present (Bocchi 1997).

Conclusions

Enough has been said to suggest that even for the selected five themes Europe-wide comparisons would considerably enhance our knowledge and understanding of the physical characteristics of medieval towns. English towns (and it requires to be noted that even comparisons within the British Isles provide contrasting material on these themes) are mostly not encircled by constricting medieval walls beyond the fifteenth century, whereas in many parts of Europe walls were extended, improved, moated, and sometimes completely replaced by new circuits. With a very small number of exceptions, English towns were not further constrained by extensive Renaissance-style defences as were so many towns in all parts of Europe, most particularly those in political border regions.

The majority of medieval towns in both England and elsewhere in Europe are composite in plan, reflecting periods of development, standstill and decline over more than 500 years. Generally speaking, the larger the town the greater the degree of compositeness in the town plan, but even small towns, such as the three examples used in this chapter, have as many as seven or eight major plan divisions in their layout. The recognition of these plan units is an important preliminary both to further more detailed analysis of medieval urban topographies and for successful urban conservation policies in these historic towns.

An enormous number of the smaller towns in England and elsewhere in Europe which were established between the twelfth and the fourteenth centuries were carefully and deliberately planned by their founders. From today's perspective, that planning can often seem to have as much irregularity as regularity, especially in the early part of this period, but medieval town designers were adaptable to topographical constraints and problems. Though they certainly carried 'ideal' designs in their minds, practicalities almost always took precedence over ideals. In a few regions, such as Gascony, it is already clear that the number of new towns being founded was sufficiently large for particular 'ideal' plans to gain wider regional adoption. Sufficient research has also been completed to suggest that over time new planned towns were becoming more regular and geometric in their layout, thanks to advances in mathematics and surveying.

Planning was not just a matter of street layouts, the plan element that gets most attention in early work on medieval urban topography. Plots, too, were carefully laid out with regulated dimensions. Since urban taxes and the voting rights of plot owners were often determined by the occupation of particular plots, or plots of a particular size, their initial layout and their continued recording in borough courts, or by stones or pins hammered into the ground, was also important, providing us with a rich record of documentary sources in many places. Plot dimensions and orientation also provide distinctive rhythms to the street facades of towns, which are enhanced by the orientation of buildings. The gable-end-to-the-street building tradition of central-European towns, and the very large storage capacities of their two- or three-storey attics, create a very different townscape to the two- or three-storey, long-axis-to-the-street buildings (rarely with any attic storage) of the typical English high street.

Finally, the almost ubiquitous medieval English timber-framed house found in towns large and small, though it has small-scale regional variants, has little to match the distinctive regional timber-framing traditions to be found just within Germany, for example. Domestic or commercial stone buildings were comparatively rare in most English towns, whilst defensible tower houses are exceptional, in considerable contrast to Ireland, for example, where almost every town had one or more stone-built tower houses. Despite the spread of the new styles of the Renaissance outwards from Florence and the other merchant cities of northern Italy, they did not affect the domestic building tradition of English towns until the later seventeenth century, whilst the courtyard dwelling never became fashionable.

This has been a very summary survey of selected comparative material on the plans and built forms of continental European and English towns. I hope enough has been said to suggest some of the principal themes that might form the structure of a wider study. The landscape of medieval European towns deserves a very large book indeed and, echoing Hoskins, that book has still to be written.

CHAPTER THREE

Mapping Medieval Townscapes: GIS Applications in Landscape History and Settlement Study

Keith Lilley, Chris Lloyd and Steve Trick

Mapping traditions and approaches

> There are, of course, many scholarly books on boroughs in their institutional aspects, their political history and their administrations. But one looks in vain for any discussion of their physical growth, where their original core lay, of the directions in which they grew, and when and why, and of what accounts for their street plan and shape today. (Hoskins 1955, 210)

At around the time Hoskins wrote these words two scholars – one an historian and one a geographer – were beginning to give the urban landscape the scholarly attention that he felt it deserved. Hoskins himself, though, while he saw the need to study the landscapes of towns and cities, had his gaze more on rural settings – the countryside, with its farms, fields and villages – rather than on townscapes (Meinig 1979; Taylor 1988). Certainly he saw potential in using the same approach he was applying to rural landscapes 'to get behind the superficial appearances, to uncover the layers of the palimpsest' that was the urban landscape (Hoskins 1955, 211). But rather than Hoskins taking the lead in 'studying towns in this way' (Hoskins 1955, 211), it was through the work of Beresford, an economic historian, and Conzen, an urban geographer, that his wishes were fulfilled.

With their differing scholarly backgrounds, but their shared belief that the landscape, whether urban or rural, is a palimpsest, Beresford and Conzen were to move the study of urban landscapes forward during the 1950s and 1960s in ways that, when Hoskins wrote *The Making of the English Landscape*, had barely been tried before. To them both, and indeed also to Hoskins, the key lay in the use of maps and mapping. It was through maps that the landscape palimpsest could be read; and it was through mapping that palimpsest landscapes could be represented. By drawing upon work from a recent research project, 'Mapping the Medieval Urban Landscape', this paper is an attempt to build on these foundations laid down by Conzen, Beresford and Hoskins.

It follows in their tradition of trying to use maps to unravel how urban land-scapes had formed during the Middle Ages, but uses new computer-based mapping technologies, in particular a Geographical Information System (GIS), as a methodological basis for mapping medieval townscapes.

Hoskins, Beresford and Conzen were only too aware that in Britain many of today's towns and cities – and their landscapes – trace their early origins and evolution back to the Middle Ages, particularly the period between the ninth and fourteenth centuries. The principle they worked on is that a landscape is a palimpsest – a record of its own evolution (although *cf.* Introduction, this volume). Townscapes are palimpsests too. Hoskins (1955, 211) recognised that it was possible 'to see, for example, a piece of the tenth century in the way a street makes an abrupt turn or does something else unexpected'. His approach was to read the shape of the urban landscape as an indicator of the past forces that had been at work in doing the shaping. What Beresford and Conzen did, more than Hoskins, was develop ways of interpreting the shapes of urban landscapes to reach back to their early histories, using large-scale Ordnance Survey plans of towns and cities as documents of urban history.

Conzen's approach was to develop a systematic and scientific (in his view) approach. He set out his method of 'town-plan analysis' in a characteristi-cally detailed study of Alnwick, a medieval market town in Northumberland (Conzen 1960). He used the shapes of the town's 'plan elements' – particu-larly its street and plot patterns – to identify areas – 'plan units' – which he interpreted to be stages of urban growth. These plan units are simply areas characterised by morphological homogeneity: unique areas evident in the town plan that have a distinct pattern of streets and plots (Lilley 2000a). Conzen later wrote 'the recognition of distinct plan-units is of great importance and can often illuminate the growth stages of a medieval town, especially earlier ones, when available written records fail to give any information' (Conzen 1968, 17). Through plan analysis, Conzen was using Ordnance Survey plans as an unwritten record of settlement history, not only to identify differently shaped areas that make up a town's plan but also as a means of reconstructing a town's historical evolution.

Beresford too saw the importance of studying what he called 'urban topography' from town plans. This is clear both in his 'Journey to New Towns' chapter of *History on the Ground* (Beresford 1957), as well as his better-known *New Towns of the Middle Ages*, in which he remarked how town plans were 'dumb witness' to their own making (Beresford 1967, 147). Like Conzen, Beresford was using modern maps to create maps of medieval urban landscapes but, unlike Conzen, his approach used urban topography and town plans in a less systematic way. In his sojourn to Hedon in east Yorkshire, for example, Beresford uses 'an examination of the map', commenting on the town's layout, 'the grid pattern of parallel streets' (Beresford 1957, 141, 143), and mapping out its plan. But this was no plan analysis in the Conzenian tradition: while they communicated on the subject, for example in the case of Alnwick's town plan (Beresford 1967, 470), there was a fundamental difference between them.

For Conzen it made sense not to talk of 'planned' and 'unplanned' medieval towns at all but rather to see towns – even some of Beresford's so-called 'new towns', such as Conwy in north Wales – as having evolved through successive stages of planned development (Conzen 1968). The reason for this difference between them possibly lies in their differing scholarly traditions, and the place of maps and mapping in history and geography.

Conzen placed an emphasis on looking not just at street patterns but plot patterns too. Indeed, it was this approach that was crucial to identifying the units that made up a town's plan and which made it a 'composite' of differently shaped areas. Conzen was critical of those who failed to recognise the 'period-compositeness' of town plans and those who tried simply to classify town-plans according to their overall street pattern (Conzen 1968; 1988). This, he argued, overlooked the complexity of urban form, for it was the details of the shapes of streets and plots that were the vital clues that made it possible to read the urban landscape as a record of its own evolution. Interestingly, Hoskins himself later picked this up in the second of his two books on local history, *Fieldwork in Local History* (Hoskins 1967). Like Beresford, though, Hoskins continued to refer to the 'topography' of towns, rather than Conzen's urban 'morphology', a pointer to the two differing disciplinary traditions from which they were approaching mapping and the urban landscape.

While, from the Conzenian point of view, Beresford's and Hoskins's unsystematic approach to mapping urban landscapes may have left something to be desired, there is no doubt that Conzen's town-plan approach could have benefited from greater use of historical sources. Here we see, perhaps, the two historians having the upper hand, with their concern over who was doing what in the shaping of past urban landscapes. Indeed, Hoskins (1967, 66, 73) points out that in the study of Alnwick, 'a minute geographical analysis', Conzen 'is chiefly concerned with geographical influences on a town plan and very little with the personalities behind the development'. It was not that Conzen's work was ahistorical, or that he was unwilling to engage with historians. For example, in 1965 he participated in a conference on urban history organised by H. J. Dyos, a meeting at which Hoskins was also present (Conzen 1968). It was just that in his 'disembodied' mapping of medieval urban landscapes, Conzen (more so than Beresford) tended to overlook, at least in his earlier work, the importance of agency, although he later tried to correct this in a paper on 'secular' agency in the creation and transformation of Ludlow (Salop) (Conzen 1988).

Beresford and Conzen – whether consciously or not – had answered Hoskins's call of 1955. Soon after *The Making of the English Landscape*, Beresford gave medieval town foundation the attention it deserved, recognising the importance of using urban topography to understand urban history, while simultaneously Conzen had shown that medieval urban histories were to be written from the forms left behind in modern urban landscapes. In their work there was an acceptance of the palimpsest principle and the use of maps and mapping. However, although they were contemporaries with each other and shared an interest in mapping medieval townscapes, there were distinct differences separating Hoskins and Beresford from Conzen. While the two historians tended to deal with 'urban topography' and saw this as a useful adjunct to studying past landscapes through more conventional historical sources, the latter was concerned with the detailed 'morphology' of the medieval town, and worked first from large-scale plans and maps. Despite the differences, though, it was through the contribution made by these three scholars that the situation Hoskins had described back in 1955 had itself become history.

New approaches to mapping medieval townscapes

During the 1970s and into the 1980s and 1990s, the groundwork laid down by Hoskins, Beresford and Conzen in the 1950s and 1960s developed into two distinct sub-disciplines. One was landscape history, a field of study with a more rural focus, developed from Hoskins's English local history (Hooke 2001) and tucked into which was Beresford's contribution on medieval rural settlement. Alongside landscape history, Conzen's urban morphology was continued, particularly by historical geographers (Whitehand and Larkham 1992), again with some influence coming from Beresford's work on new towns of the Middle Ages (Slater 1990a). The study of medieval urban landscapes developed more through the latter than the former, but increasingly as an interdisciplinary endeavour. Those following in Conzen's footsteps included medieval historians and archaeologists as well as historical geographers (Brooks and Whittington 1977; Spearman 1988; Baker and Slater 1992). Two issues received particular attention: first, the gradual improvement of Conzen's technique of plan-analysis for, despite his writing on the subject, he had not himself set out a specific methodology; and secondly, the application of Conzen's work to reappraise the processes that had shaped urban landscapes in the Middle Ages, in particular Beresford's 'new towns'. Through this work, new approaches to mapping medieval townscapes emerged.

Although Conzen set out the principles of town-plan analysis in his study of Alnwick, and remarked upon it in later papers, he was not clear on how to undertake a plan analysis (Conzen 1960; 1968; 1988). While this did not prevent plan analysis being used by those interested in the landscapes of towns (Aston and Bond 1976), it was not until the 1990s that attempts were made to explain, step-by-step, how to conduct a plan analysis on nineteenth-century large-scale maps, and how to use them to reconstruct how a town or city had evolved nearly a thousand years earlier. Baker and Slater (1992) examined Conzen's idea of 'morphological regions', while Lilley (2000a) set out the plan-analysis technique as a 'transferable methodology'. The principles Conzen had defined in the 1960s remained the same, but now there was an explicit account of how to extract 'plan elements' from Ordnance Survey 1:2,500 scale plans, how to use these to define 'plan units', and how to then integrate these with archaeological and historical sources to reconstruct the stages of urban landscape evolution, mapping out for different time-periods the formation of a town's layout. This approach involved mapping techniques that Conzen himself had used, using tracing paper to extract the patterns of streets and plots from historic mapping of the eighteenth and nineteenth centuries, and pencils, crayons and pens to do the line work. By the late 1990s the potential for using computer-based mapping to do this instead was clear (Koster 1998), but not just to create attractive-looking maps: computers also offered a means of integrating those data sources for analysing town plans.

In addition to the improvement of plan-analysis techniques, Conzen's approach was being applied to particular towns to examine their medieval development. Some earlier studies focused on one individual place, mapping out its stages of spatial evolution through plan units (e.g. Brooks and Whittington 1977; Spearman 1988). Slater, in particular, reappraised some of the 'classic' new towns that Beresford (1957; 1967) had been interested in, including Hedon (Yorks.), Stratford-upon-Avon (Warks.) and Bridgnorth and Ludlow (Salop) (Slater 1985; 1987; 1990b). He showed that these places had themselves grown through successive phases of development, and were not laid out all in one go, *de novo*. Here, the idea Conzen (1968, 119) had put forward about the 'widespread compositeness of medieval town plans' was being reinforced, and a new perspective afforded on Beresford's 'new towns'. Moreover, the plan-analysis technique offered a means of revealing the often otherwise undocumented stages of development that these towns had undergone in their formative periods – usually the twelfth and thirteenth centuries.

With more plan analyses of medieval new towns being undertaken in the 1980s and 1990s (as well as studies of larger urban centres such as Coventry: Lilley 2000a), there was scope for comparative work on groups of towns. Such comparative study was something Conzen (1968) had envisaged too, and in the 1990s a plan analysis of a group of Norman towns in England, Wales and Ireland revealed some interesting common design traits (Lilley 1999; 2000b). Here again, though, the potential of using computer-based mapping software was beginning to become clear, for a Geographical Information System (GIS) – sometimes defined as a 'spatial database' – could be used not only to create and store the reconstructed towns' plans, but also to compare them.

Through the development of Conzen's mapping approaches, and the reappraisal of Beresford's study of medieval new towns, the last two decades in particular have begun to address what Hoskins had identified in 1955 as lacking in studies of urban landscapes: 'discussion of their physical growth, where their original core lay, of the directions in which they grew, and when and why, and of what accounts for their street plan and shape today' (Hoskins 1955, 210). Even so, questions remain, especially over the processes that shaped urban landscapes in the Middle Ages.

With these two issues in mind – analysing town plans and comparing them – a research project was set up in 2003 to apply GIS techniques to undertake a comparative study of one group of medieval new towns. The 'Mapping the Medieval Urban Landscape' project sought to develop existing techniques of morphological study by using computer-based spatial technologies, while at the same time focusing on the new towns founded in England and Wales in the reign of King Edward I to establish whether their urban landscapes had common design features (Figure 5; Lilley et al. 2005a). It was, then, a comparative plan analysis but, unlike earlier such studies, it was to be entirely GIS-based. The thinking behind the project was to concentrate on a well-studied and comparatively well-documented group of 'new towns', which in the context of medieval Britain really means those of thirteenth-century date (Lilley 2001b). This was 'near the end of the story' of medieval town plantation (Beresford 1967, 3); a period when aspects of town planning get documented in detail for the first time, thanks to the work of Edward's administrators (Tout 1934). Over the past century Edward's 'new towns' have

FIGURE 5. Location of Edward I's new towns, with dates of foundations (source: Lilley et al. 2005a).

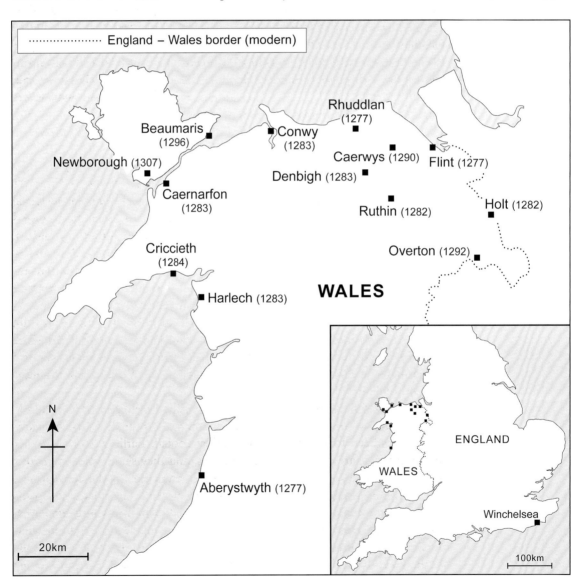

been copiously cited by historians as examples of medieval town planning (for example, Unwin 1909; Tout 1934; Beresford 1967), but in contrast to the detailed comparative architectural histories of the king's castles (e.g. Taylor 1986), no comparative detailed morphological study has been carried out on his towns. Instead, frequently they are wrongly described as bastides, their layouts over-simplified and generalised as being 'grid plans', and sometimes looked upon as British imports of continental town-plantation practices, coming over from Gascony, for example, through trading and territorial links with Edward's lands in south-west France (Morris 1979).

Edward's new towns are thus long overdue closer scrutiny, and GIS computer-based mapping offers a way of analysing and comparing their plans to help address unanswered questions about how they were originally designed and planned. The remainder of this paper draws upon the work undertaken by this project, and examines the advantages to be gained by using GIS for mapping medieval townscapes. It does so in two ways: first, by looking at how GIS helps to integrate spatial data sources, in particular different kinds of mapping, to visualise in map-form the layouts of medieval towns; and, secondly, by using GIS to compare the plans of Edward's new towns, to see what this can reveal about their design and planning.

Computer-based mapping of medieval townscapes

There are, of course, no contemporary maps for the new towns of Edward's time to show what their townscapes looked like. This is the case for medieval Europe in general and it means that their town plans have to be recreated using a combination of cartographic, archaeological and documentary sources. One of the problems of undertaking plan analyses is integrating these different sources with each other. Here GIS proves to be a helpful solution, for not only does it comprise a spatial database capable of analysing large (spatial) data sets but it also makes possible mapping of settlement and landscapes in two and three dimensions (e.g. Heywood *et al.* 1998). This process of creating maps of medieval townscapes by integrating data sources in GIS is described here, the specific aim in the project being to create maps showing Edward's new towns as they looked soon after their foundation, *c*.1300, for use as a basis for comparative study.

Conzen (1960; 1968) advocated using Ordnance Survey 1:2,500 scale first edition mapping of towns and cities as a basis for plan analysis and this convention has been followed ever since (Lilley 2000a). Earlier historic maps of medieval towns are drawn to different scales, and they show different degrees of detail of the layout and form of an urban landscape. In the conventional Conzenian approach plan elements are traced off from these maps and plans on to paper overlays. Conducting a GIS-based plan analysis begins with scanned maps (rasters), from which a town's street and plot patterns are digitised on-screen (so-called 'heads-up' digitisation), so creating a series of layers in the GIS. The primary source layer is the first edition Ordnance Survey

1:2,500 plan, and the digitised plan elements (vector data) derived from this are an interpretative layer. Further source layers are then added, including pre-Ordnance Survey town maps and plans. All the source layers (rasters) are geo-rectified to spatial co-ordinates derived from field survey undertaken in each town using a Global Positioning System (GPS) (Lilley *et al.* 2005b). Selected Ground Control Points (GCPs), reference points to link the source mapping with a position given by the GPS, are used for this (for example, a corner of a building). Combining source layers in this way provides a means of identifying 'lost' plan features, particularly patterns of former streets and plots destroyed in redevelopment. These features, as well as buildings and structures such as churches and town defences, are also digitised to add another inter-pretative layer. This process of linking field-survey data and map-derived data provides a measure of the relative distortion between different historical map sources (quantified as an Root Mean Square Error), and reveals that the Ord-nance Survey first edition plans so favoured by Conzen and his followers in plan analysis are indeed the most accurately surveyed historic maps available on a national scale.

Using this approach, a 'composite map' derived from different map sources is built up (Lilley *et al.* 2005a), and to signify which historic maps are used to digitise the different elements a 'symbology' is applied in the GIS identifying the origins of each vector line feature. Therefore, each digitised plan element (such as plot boundaries and streets) can be traced back to its original map-source. This makes for a greater degree of transparency in the mapping process. The integration of map-layers and plan-analysis in this way was conducted for thirteen 'new towns' founded in England and Wales, each attributed to Edward I rather than his chief overlords (Figure 5). Only those places that survive today as settlements were included (not the 'lost' towns of Newton (Dorset) and Bere (Merionydd), for example: Beresford 1967; Beresford and St Joseph 1958). None of the historic maps used to extract plan elements dates from much before the early eighteenth century.

To work towards creating a map of the towns, to show how they looked at around the time they were founded *c.*1300, archaeological and historical data are added as further 'source layers' in the GIS. This has two main advan-tages: first, it helps check that the townscape features shown on historic maps and digitised in the GIS have a medieval provenance; and secondly, it adds 'lost' medieval townscape features not shown on the maps. Archaeological site-maps of excavations and evaluations (from 'grey literature' and published sources), along with published architectural plans and surveys, were scanned and then geo-rectified in the GIS (as the historic maps were). From these, fur-ther interpretative layers are added – for example, the alignment of a town's medieval defences, or the position of its original quayside. Plot and street patterns are also confirmed where possible. Urban excavation sites typically provide only a relatively small 'window' on to the medieval townscape as a whole (see Ottaway 1992, 16–24), though in a GIS archaeologically proven features can sometimes be extrapolated by linking them with digitised plan elements taken from the historic maps. For example, even if only a small section of a town's defences has been excavated it becomes possible to suggest their course by seeing how the excavated section relates to nearby street and plot patterns. In this way a fuller picture of the medieval townscape emerges, populated with its main features, lost and extant, conjectured and certain, as shown here (Figure 6) in the case of Rhuddlan (see also Lilley *et al*. 2005c).

In essence the process used here is the same as that of a conventional paper-based plan analysis; however, the GIS also provides a means of storing and retrieving the different data layers, geo-rectifying the various sources and adding (through digitising) new interpretative layers to create a map of the town as close as possible to how it appeared in *c*.1300. There are also other advantages when it comes to trying to link historical sources with the GIS-based maps of medieval townscapes. In some cases, as at Winchelsea (E. Sussex) and Beaumaris (Anglesey), Edward's new towns were surveyed soon after their foundation and rentals drawn up at that time list their properties in terms of the number of burgages and the names of burgesses (Anon. 1877; Homan 1949). In some cases, too, the area of the town's original burgages was stated (Lewis 1912). Using these written sources it is possible to relate documented morphological elements to features on the ground. This can help to establish the former size and extent of medieval plot-patterns, street-blocks and built-up areas of a town, and so build up a picture of the town's layout as it was *c*.1300. Since the degree of distortion in source maps can be estimated (using the Root Mean Square Error or other statistics), this sort of exercise in reconstructive mapping can be done with quantifiable confidence (Lilley *et al*. 2005b). In some cases, though, surviving documentation is not detailed enough to do this. Not all of Edward's towns have rentals, and burgage sizes varied and were not always recorded. Nevertheless, what can emerge from integrating written and morphological evidence for towns such as Caernarfon, Rhuddlan and Winchelsea, is a map that is perhaps as close as we can be to how a town looked soon after its foundation at the end of the thirteenth century (Figure 7).

Thanks to the visualisation tools within GIS software these townscape maps can be projected either in two or three dimensions, the latter drawing upon elevation data incorporated into the GIS as a source layer (Figure 8; Lilley *et al*. 2005a). These various output maps are also easily overlaid with each other, as well as other imagery layers, such as modern aerial photography or historic maps. Above all, the integration of data sources within the GIS helps in the plan analysis process to create new maps of medieval townscapes which are suitable for further, comparative, analysis.

GIS offers not only the means of integrating digitised cartographies to create new maps of medieval townscapes, but also a way of comparing the layouts of groups of medieval towns. Comparing the forms of medieval towns, as Conzen recognised, has the potential to reveal similarities and differences between urban landscapes that may point to otherwise hidden details about the processes of their formation: 'what is of generic significance originating in general historical causes or in the activity of important planning agencies' (Conzen 1968, 119). Since contemporaries left little in the way of details in conventional records about the processes that shaped urban landscapes in the Middle Ages, the landscape itself becomes the key source, Beresford's (1967, 147) 'dumb witness', though 'silent witness' may be a better turn of phrase. Comparison of medieval town plans is easily undertaken within a GIS. They can be scaled and orientated the same, a simple but nevertheless revealing way of identifying similarities and differences between towns. Particular aspects of their forms can be compared in more detail. Shared locations of features such as castles, churches and market places can emerge, while other aspects of 'design grammar' are identifiable, such as similarities in the configuration of street patterns. GIS makes it possible to lay different town plans over each other or manipulate them to reveal other ways in which their features can be

FIGURE 6. Rhuddlan: the town and its Edwardian castle and defences (source: Lilley *et al.* 2005a).

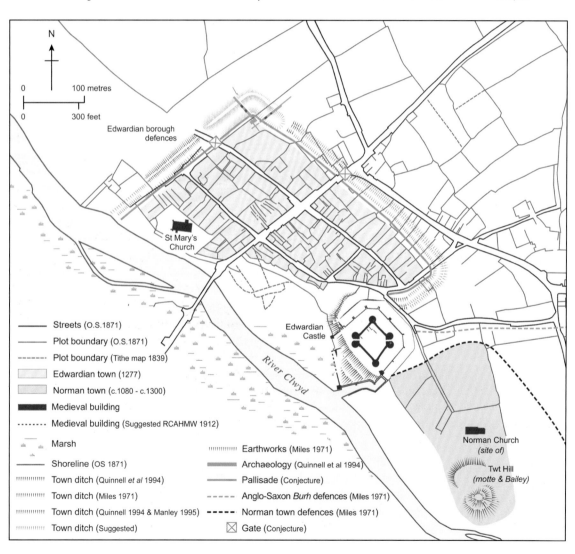

seen to correspond. All this provides insight on the hidden urban design and planning processes that were at work in the Middle Ages, and the largely silent decision-makers whose ideas and practices are fossilised in the traces of streets and plots they left behind.

Since the thirteen towns covered by the project were all founded within a relatively short time period (between 1277 and 1303), under the same authority (King Edward I), for the same commercial and strategic purposes, and within close geographical proximity (especially in north Wales, for example), it might be expected that Edward's new towns would share some common features in their layouts. This is not the case, however. Where similarities do occur, they are specific and limited to a few examples.

Two particular 'castle towns' where comparative analysis has suggested a shared design, and designer, are Conwy and Beaumaris, both located on coastal sites in north Wales and founded in 1283 and 1296 respectively (Lilley

FIGURE 7. Rhuddlan: reconstruction of town plan, *c.*1300 (source: Lilley *et al.* 2005a).

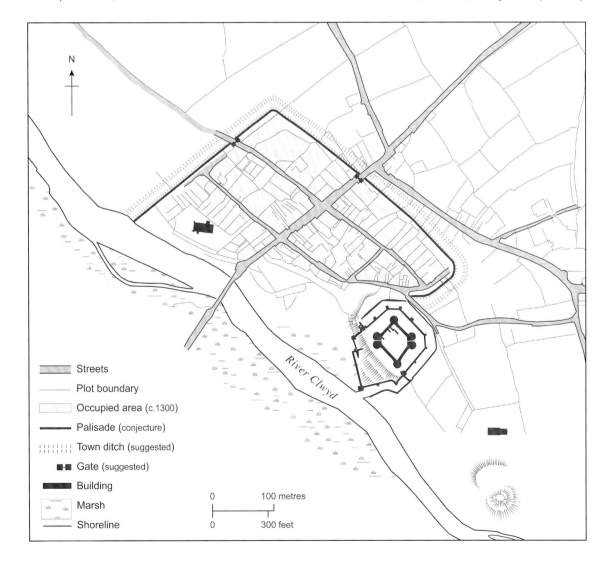

Streets
Plot boundary
Occupied area (c.1300)
Palisade (conjecture)
Town ditch (suggested)
Gate (suggested)
Building
Marsh
Shoreline

0   100 metres

0   300 feet

River Clwyd

N

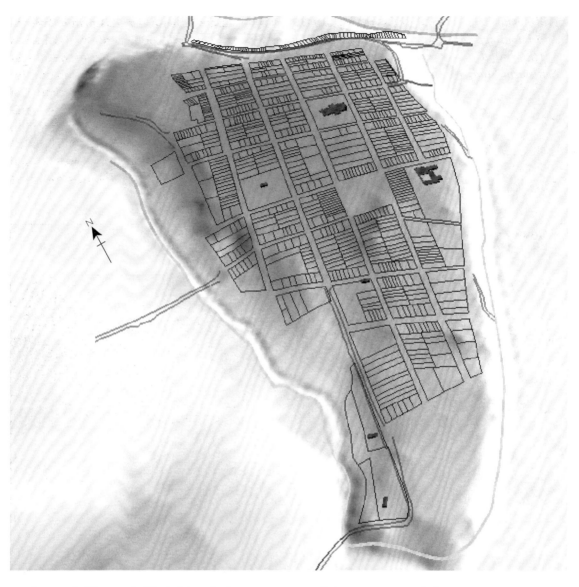

FIGURE 8.
Winchelsea, *c.*1300,
projected in 3D
(with 1.5x vertical
exaggeration) (source:
Lilley *et al.* 2005a).

et al. 2005a) (Figure 9). Their historical contexts are well known, as are their celebrated Edwardian castles (Lewis 1912; Beresford 1967; Taylor 1986). Their morphological similarities lie in the configuration of principal streets, notably in the use of a T-shape where one street (Berry Street at Conwy and Castle Street at Beaumaris) runs parallel to the shoreline (and quayside in the thirteenth century) and another extends perpendicular to it (High Street and Church Street respectively). The two streets intersect at a ninety-degree angle and where they meet a further, shorter street runs down to the shore, giving the street-layout a cruciform-shape overall. The relative positions of the towns' castles and churches also show similarities: in both cases the street along the shoreline is also the one that extends up to the castles' gates, and the church is situated in the same south-western corner of the two main streets. These

FIGURE 9.
The layouts of
Beaumaris and Conwy
compared (source:
Lilley *et al.* 2005a).

similarities are even more striking if, in the GIS, Beaumaris's plan is inverted and matched against Conwy. Then it looks as if both were derived from a common blueprint. Interestingly, the castles in both places were overseen right from the start by Master James of St George, the king's master mason for the castle-building programme in north Wales, while the borough charter of Beaumaris was also modelled on that of Conwy (Taylor 1986). As an architect with geometrical training, Master James would have been well suited to designing urban landscapes. Since his work on castles in north Wales, such as Harlech, has been identified through stylistic comparison of architectural form and design (Taylor 1963), why not also the plans of the new towns set out alongside his castles?

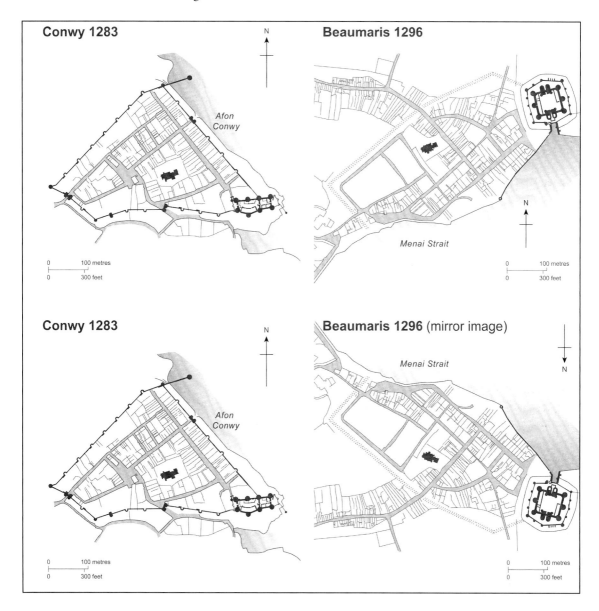

39

Using a GIS it is thus possible to undertake comparative analyses of the medieval layouts of Conwy and Beaumaris, revealing not just their shared forms but identifying common design rules used in their making – their 'design grammar'. These rules were not written down in a literal sense but emerge through reading the form of the urban landscape by breaking down a town's plan into its constituent plan elements, using these to look at the angles at which streets intersect, for example, and the degree to which streets were laid out straight. Such comparisons can be done in the GIS by overlaying the towns' plans and seeing how well they match up, but also they can be quantified using tools to measure aspects of a town's geometry, for example comparing the relative size of street blocks or searching for common units of town planning (Lilley *et al.* 2005b). Given the historical connections between Conwy and Beaumaris, some shared aspects in their design might have been expected.

Connections between urban designs are suggested by similarity in form for other places too. This is the case for Flint and Holt, both in north-east Wales, founded within a few years of each other (1277 and 1282 respectively). Flint's regular pattern of longitudinal streets contained within a playing-card-shaped defensive circuit has long been recognised (Tout 1934; Beresford and St Joseph 1958), although the similarity it bears with nearby Holt has not been commented upon before. Here, too, longitudinal streets are present; the castle is situated at one end of the town and a market place is situated across the streets about midway along their length. There is also a hint that Holt was originally intended to have been a defended town (Pratt 1965). A defensive circuit encompassing its streets would have made Holt rectangular in form, and thus similar to Flint. Being in adjoining counties, with shared town-plans, both places may have been designed by the same individual, possibly a local official such as Nicholas Bonel, who in the autumn of 1277 was appointed by the king as 'surveyor of his works … both at Le Cheynou [Flint] and at Rothelan [Rhuddlan]' (Taylor 1986, 19). To complicate matters, though, Rhuddlan differs in layout from both Holt and Flint. If each had been Bonel's work some reason is needed to explain why this is: unless there was another agent involved? Either way, Holt and Flint's similarity in form seems too close to be without significance.

These morphological comparisons between Edward's new towns of north Wales suggest that, rather than some exotic, continental influence coming either from Gascony or Savoy (cf. Tout 1934; Beresford 1967), there were more local or regional influences at work. Aberystwyth's layout (of 1277) has strong similarities with Bristol's, for example. In a recent reappraisal of Taylor's (1963) work, an English influence on the design of Edward's castles of north Wales has been put forward by Coldstream (2003). The same seems to have been the case with the shapes chosen for Edward's new towns. As Conzen (1968) pointed out, comparisons between medieval town-plans – based upon their reconstructed layouts – are revealing of the unwritten processes that shaped them during their initial stages of formation. When these plans are examined by comparing them with the earliest available documentary sources some interesting conclusions may be drawn about the decision-making process involved in laying out Edward's new towns, and in some cases the individuals who may have been responsible for carrying out the work on the ground: it was certainly not Edward himself. The GIS-based study of Edwardian new towns has begun to reveal the potential of this approach and underlines the importance of first having detailed and evidence-based maps of medieval townscapes, and then being able to draw upon the analytical capability of the GIS itself to begin to interpret unwritten histories contained within the forms of urban landscapes.

Conclusion – towards a remapping of medieval townscape

The aim of this paper was to set out how GIS has advantages for landscape history and settlement study. The focus has been on medieval townscapes, drawing upon recent research on the towns founded in England and Wales in the reign of Edward I. The ways in which GIS was used in this project as a means to analyse and compare the layout of these new towns has been addressed here, which may be of benefit to those who wish to conduct similar work on other historic settlements or landscapes. The approach taken builds upon a tradition of scholarship that emerged during the 1950s and 1960s in the UK through the work of Hoskins, Beresford and Conzen. These scholars, though slightly different in their interests and methods, all shared a common concern to understand past landscapes through the use of maps and mapping. Conzen's work on town-plan analysis as a means of mapping medieval townscapes, and its subsequent development, has been commented upon, and from this a case is made to use GIS as a tool to advance plan analysis by helping to integrate different data sources and create new maps of medieval towns. These can then themselves provide a sound basis for undertaking comparative study, again using GIS.

In the context of medieval urban design and planning – the formative processes that shaped towns and cities in the Middle Ages – this approach has particular advantages, for conventional sources are generally silent on such matters. Hoskins himself recognised this when he made use of the idea that landscape is a palimpsest – a record of its own evolution. The agenda he set in 1955, on 'studying towns in this way', has since been expanded upon by both urban morphologists and landscape historians mapping medieval townscapes. So far, though, there has in this regard been little application of spatial technologies, and yet, as this paper has suggested, their potential is great for presenting new visual perspectives on medieval townscapes, increasing the appeal of those townscapes to a widened audience and helping our understanding of the processes at work in the making of medieval urban landscapes in Britain.

Acknowledgements

The research on which this paper is based was funded by the Arts and Humanities Research Council (RG/AN3206/APN14501) ('Mapping the Medieval Urban Landscape: Edward I's new towns of England and Wales', 2003–2005). Detailed discussion of the project's findings are accessible via the Archaeology Data Service (www.ads.ahds.ac.uk), including an online interactive atlas of the thirteen towns studied in the project (Lilley *et al.* 2005a). For their assistance the authors wish to thank David Martin of Archaeology South East, as well as staff of Cadw, Clwyd-Powys Archaeological Trust, Gwynedd Archaeological Trust, the National Library of Wales, the National Trust, the Royal Commission on the Ancient and Historical Monuments of Wales, and archivists at Anglesey, Caernarfon, Conwy, Denbighshire, East Sussex, Flintshire, and Merionydd record offices. Conor Graham, Mike Fradley and Cormac McConaghy provided assistance in the field.

CHAPTER FOUR

Town Defences and the Making of Urban Landscapes

Oliver Creighton

While this paper is concerned with medieval town defences, it will not focus, as many archaeological studies have done, on the physical fabric of walls, gates and related structures. Rather than examining these fortifications as discrete features in abstraction from their historic urban contexts, it seeks to explore some of the ways in which town defences were not only intimately bound up with the form of townscapes, but also closely linked to the creation of urban identities. This last point is important: town walls fundamentally served to exclude as well as to embrace sectors of populations and could be socially divisive features within townscapes – a fact still glaringly apparent in modern-day cities as far removed as (London)Derry and Jerusalem. More specifically, this paper seeks to address several aspects of a common assumption about the relationship between towns and their defences: namely, that walls and gates were *defining features* of urban settlements (see, for example, Astill 2000, 478). This assumption works at two levels. First, it is commonly presumed that possession of defences was an important – indeed even a defining – characteristic of what constituted a settlement of 'urban' status in the medieval period. Secondly, it might reasonably be supposed that defences acted to demarcate townscapes physically – the walls constituting an unambiguous boundary that marked where the countryside stopped and the townscape started. In both cases it is argued that these assumptions deserve greater critical treatment than is, perhaps, normally afforded. The first of these two points – the connection between the possession of defences and definition of urban status – is dealt with fairly briefly, prior to more detailed analysis of the physical relationships between walls and townscapes and the implications of this for our understanding of medieval urban identities.

Town walls and urban status

In the period between the eleventh and sixteenth centuries, England and Wales had something in the region of 230 towns that possessed defences, whether earthwork or masonry circuits or gates alone; Scotland had perhaps twenty-five more (Bond 1987; Creighton and Higham 2005, 253–75). These fortifications had an extremely diverse range of origins, including circuits of Roman date surviving in both unchanged and expanded forms into the Middle Ages, the defences of new *burh*-type settlements laid out in the ninth and tenth centuries and which continued in use after the Norman Conquest, and a wide variety of planted towns and boroughs that acquired circuits in the later medieval period. Yet, while from one point of view the possession of surrounding defences might be thought of as a characteristic quality of medieval towns, given the overall level of urbanisation in later medieval Britain and the distribution of these settlements across the landscape, it is clear that those towns possessing defences were actually in the minority (Palliser 1995, 106). Historians and archaeologists have always found it hard to agree on a workable definition of a medieval town, yet no matter where the urban threshold is drawn, it is clear that no more than one third of towns in Wales and one quarter of those in England were defended, and the proportion is lower still in Scotland.

On the wider European stage the defences of British towns seem particularly limited in scale, ambition and in their overall imprint on urban form. For example, the larger British medieval towns generally lacked the successive concentric defensive rings that shaped the growth of great medieval cities such as Bruges, Cologne and Paris; in sharp contrast, medieval London remained encircled within its ancient Roman *enceinte* (see below). In Germany the proportion of walled medieval towns is estimated at 53 per cent (of a total of 1,083), a figure that excludes those with earthworks or palisades (Tracy 2000, 82). In comparison to Germany, a regional study of the generally open medieval urban settlements of East Anglia has characterised these places as 'towns without walls' (Brodt 1997). While the reasons for these contrasts are complex and deep-rooted, strong royal government and relative internal peace in later medieval Britain, combined, crucially, with the generally smaller scale of urbanism and the lower levels of independence attained by these communities would seem to be the principal factors (Palliser 1995, 117).

Significantly, the number of defended towns as a proportion of the whole was far higher before the Norman Conquest than at the peak of urbanisation around *c*.1300. The proportion of post-Conquest planted towns possessing primary defences is particularly low: provision for enclosing defences is remarkably rare in foundation charters, for instance, and in many cases defensive circuits were clearly secondary additions to composite town plans rather than features present from a settlement's plantation and deemed essential for its functioning. For instance, in a recent study of the townscapes of three Norman plantations, Alnwick (Northumb.), Bridgnorth (Salop) and Ludlow (Salop), in no case was the town wall an 'original' feature of urban planning, with the circuit forming an original morphological frame for an arrangement of streets and burgage plots (Lilley 1999). Instead, walls were frequently later additions, and it was exceptionally rare for *enceinte* and town plan to be conceived in unison. Even in the case of Edward I's so-called 'bastides' in north Wales – representing, perhaps, the 'apogee' of new town foundation in Britain – a planted town was not necessarily a defended town (Beresford 1967, 35–51). Of this famous group of ten towns, whose plantation represented part and parcel of a campaign of military conquest and consolidation, only four possessed primary defences: Flint and Rhuddlan (Flint) were embraced by unusual double earthworks that seemed to have served to demarcate rather than to defend, while Conwy (Caernarvon) and Caernarfon had masonry circuits (although a new survey of the latter has raised the intriguing possibility that the walls and town plan were conceived separately: Lilley *et al.* 2005c). This argument can usefully be extended to embrace the numerous English bastides founded in Aquitaine in the thirteenth and fourteenth centuries, only a small minority of which possessed primary defences (Creighton forthcoming).

Furthermore, in those cases where medieval towns were defended, walls were not always the monumental structures we might assume. Previous studies of urban defences have, perhaps understandably, focused predominantly on masonry fortifications, and murage grants (representing a royal grant of permission enabling a town to levy a tax for the explicit purpose of wall-building) have been used as the key documentary source for their study (Turner 1970). While such sources provide us with a relatively full record of the intent to build walls after the middle of the thirteenth century, in numerous cases this investment did not result in the construction of full circuits. An instructive example is that of Bridgwater (Somerset), which was granted the right to levy murage for a period of five years in 1269. Here, John Leland observed in the sixteenth century that, while the town possessed four gates, its 'wall' was made up of joined-together sections of stone houses (Toulmin Smith 1907, 162). Moreover, we remain remarkably ignorant about those towns encircled not by stone but with earth and timber perimeters, or which were defended in more piecemeal and partial fashion. On currently available evidence, the number of towns provided with defences of these sorts exceeded those with masonry walls. The enormous range of settlements defended in the post-Conquest period with earth and timber ranged in status from shire towns such as Bedford and Ipswich (Suffolk) and major ecclesiastical boroughs such as Lichfield (Staffs.) and Salisbury (Wilts.) to more modest seigniorial plantations such as Bolsover (Derbys.), Devizes (Wilts.) and New Buckenham (Norfolk). Numerous medieval market towns such as Banbury (Oxon), Halesowen (Worcs.) and Oakham (Rutland), meanwhile, had stone gates over their main thoroughfares, rather than full circuits. This tendency towards the partial defence of towns was more marked still in Scotland, where the piecemeal 'back-dyking' of plots to produce irregular and often partial circuits and the provision of freestanding masonry 'ports' over major roads was far more commonplace than the provision of formal walls (Wallace *et al.* 2004). Here, urban wall-building schemes were exceptional and mostly the result of royal initiative (Edinburgh, Midloth.) and/or English influence (Berwick (Northumb.), Stirling and perhaps Perth); far more characteristic of the Scottish burgh, however, are places such as Aberdeen, Glasgow (Lanarks.) and St Andrews (Fife), where freestanding gates were used to control commerce and did not represent vestiges of more ambitious defensive schemes.

It is also interesting to consider the broader positioning of defended towns within the full spectrum of medieval urban settlements. The way in which walled towns are distributed unevenly within this overall urban hierarchy is particularly striking. At the upper end of the spectrum, it is instructive to assess the defences of Britain's twenty-five most important and populous towns at the end of the fourteenth century, as defined by the *Cambridge Urban History of Britain* (Kermode 2000a, 442–3). Within this elite group of towns, places of the status of Beverley (Yorks.) and Boston (Lincs.) were embraced not within walls but by ditches or earthworks of little or no defensive value, while at others, such as Bury St Edmunds (Suffolk), Cambridge, (King's) Lynn (Norfolk) and Salisbury (Wilts.), wall-building projects were left half-complete or never got off the ground. At the opposite end of the urban hierarchy, meanwhile, it is clear that there was no 'cut-off' point of population level, wealth or size beneath which towns were not provided with defences. Indeed, it is striking how far down the hierarchy we find fortified towns, to the extent that a great many fall into the notoriously 'grey area' between urban and rural settlement, a large number of these being castle-dependent and seigniorially dominated nucleations of the type common on the Anglo-Welsh border – places such as Caus (Shropshire), Kilpeck (Herefordshire) and Richard's Castle (Herefordshire) (Creighton 2005, 167–72).

Nonetheless, even if enclosed towns are not spread evenly within the overall urban hierarchy, there is little question that walls featured heavily in medieval society's own image of the city. Walls and gates were powerful and evocative landmarks in urban cosmologies. To some extent walls were always symbolic of towns: one of their first representations is the Egyptian hieroglyph depicting a cross within a circle, representing the unity of street plan and circuit, and the tradition is perpetuated in Roman and early medieval coinage and ultimately in later medieval art, picture-maps and seals. The point is illustrated particularly well by the image of Oxford's first seal (Figure 10; Davis 1968). In use in 1191 and apparently the earliest municipal seal in Britain, this flaunts the powerful image of a crenellated wall that both defines the city physically and represents its independence (other symbols represent the 'Ox' of Oxford and cylindrical towered structures signifying the castle and/or churches). Rather less obviously, it is far from certain that Oxford actually possessed a freestanding masonry wall at this date. The masonry *enceinte* was built in the period *c.*1226–40, to replace an earthen circuit supplemented in places with a partial revetment wall, as revealed by excavation (Dodd 2003, 21–5, 135–200). The Oxford seal thus represents an imagined townscape showing the place of the city wall in the community's self image and, arguably, in medieval urban ideology.

A number of other seals similarly depict town walls as civic symbols that proclaimed status and independence and were clearly integral to the construction of collective identities: those of Barnstaple (Devon), London and York are instructive examples (Steane 2001, 226–32). Whatever its origins, this link between the medieval urban image and the town wall was enduring, and was

FIGURE 10.
The late twelfth-century municipal seal of Oxford, showing an idealised image of a city wall, along with an ox and a symbol probably representing the royal castle and/or churches (after Davis 1968, plate VI).

propagated in other ways. In local memory walls might be strongly associated with figures in foundation myths. The late fourteenth-century civic annals of Colchester (Essex), for example, credited the foundation of the city's ancient *enceinte* to King Cole (Rosser 2000, 339, 345). The 'show fronts' of town gates, meanwhile, sometimes displayed representations of the heroes of foundation myths alongside more conventional symbols such as the royal arms, the city arms and those of ecclesiastical authorities. Above Bristol's St John's Gate, for example, were displayed statuettes of the city's mythical founders, Brennus and Belinus; the portal of Southampton's (Hants.) north gate was flanked by Sir Bevis and the giant, Ascupart; and London's legendary king is remembered in the name 'Lud'gate, over which the mythical king sat with his two sons, following a sixteenth-century refurbishment (Rosser 1996, 14; Creighton and Higham 2005, 166–73).

Walls and the townscape

Besides being strongly linked to the urban image as perceived by contemporaries, walls clearly played important roles in the delineation of urban space. In simple terms, walls made physical the definition of the 'non feudal islands in the feudal sea' famously described by Postan (1975, 212). A growing body of archaeological and historical work is, however, now beginning to challenge over-simplistic urban/rural dichotomies to examine lines of contact and zones of interface between town and country (see, for instance, Epstein 2001; Perring 2002; Giles and Dyer 2005). It is now more clearly understood that in a physical sense the 'outer face' of the medieval city was not always as rigidly defined as we might imagine; for instance, immediately beyond the urban limits commonly lay a belt of essentially rural resources to which urban populations had access (Dyer 2005, 314). Here we might ask how urban defences fitted into this pattern? Did walls really mark such a sharp dividing line between towns and their hinterlands?

Defences certainly exerted an enduring influence on urban form, yet they did not bound townscapes in simple linear fashion. Rather, they were rather part and parcel of a far more complex layering of features, defensive and otherwise, that created a 'zone of transition' on the urban fringe. The zoning of activities, ranging from industrial processing to prostitution, displays a consistent relationship with the immediately extra-mural area. In addition, the location of market places outside gates is well known in larger earlier centres such as Canterbury (Kent) and Hereford, while other townscapes display a 'funnelling' of intra-mural development in towards the gates, as at Winchester (Hants.). Intra-mural routes were other characteristic features of urban planning closely related to defensive topographies, while less widely acknowledged is the maintenance of thin girdles of land immediately within defences as open spaces: this was a characteristic of burghal-period foundations, such as Wallingford (Oxon), and was maintained well into the post-Conquest centuries in Exeter (Devon) and London.

It is, however, crucial to note that the area under the jurisdiction of a town and the zone physically embraced within defences were very often not the same thing. Frequently, the medieval traveller would know he or she had reached the urban limits not because of formal walls and gates, but because of movable bars, chains or turnstiles that marked toll-collection points, often well in advance of the walls. While archaeologically invisible, their construction and maintenance is recorded in civic records and they are sometimes remembered in street-names: Whirligig Lane in Taunton (Somerset) is a little-known example. Alternatively, at Gloucester, Chester and elsewhere, freestanding stone gates marked the limits well in advance of formal town walls.

The example of Beverley (Figure 11) brings many of these issues into focus. Growing up around an important minster church, this large and wealthy borough – by the late fourteenth century the eleventh most populous in England – was embraced not within a masonry circuit but a humble earthwork, known as the Bar Dyke. Despite agitations in the 1320s from the burgesses to build a wall, a combination of restrictive ecclesiastical lordship and royal favour towards Kingston-upon-Hull (Yorks.), which received murage grants, resulting in the construction of new brick circuit, ensured that a more piecemeal approach to enclosure and defence continued. Sections excavated across the Bar Dyke in 1985 and 2003 demonstrate that it was not primarily defensive: comprising a broad low bank and a shallow flat-bottomed ditch built in the twelfth century, it was, at best, sporadically maintained and virtually derelict before the four main bars or gates (including the famous surviving North Bar) were rebuilt at great cost in brick in the late fourteenth and early fifteenth

FIGURE 11.
The medieval topography of Beverley, showing the line of the Bar Dyke, or town ditch, and the town 'bars' (after Miller *et al.* 1982, folding map 1, with additions).

centuries (Miller 1984b; Youngs *et al.* 1986; Tibbles 2003). Also notable is that to the east, where the town outgrew its confines, rather than a formal extension to what was essentially a jurisdictional earthwork being constructed, more temporary barriers were erected: the Town Keepers' accounts record expenditure on features such as chains, timber bars, turnstiles and lengths of earthwork in outlying positions on the approach roads in the fourteenth and fifteenth centuries (Miller *et al.* 1982, 39–45; Miller 1984a).

Town defences therefore comprised far more than linear obstacles; rather, they consisted of complex and a multi-layered 'belts' of features that might stretch from outer ditches through walls and/or ramparts and ditches to intra-mural banks, roads and open strips, and were used as resources by urban populations in a multitude of ways. The earthwork berms between walls and

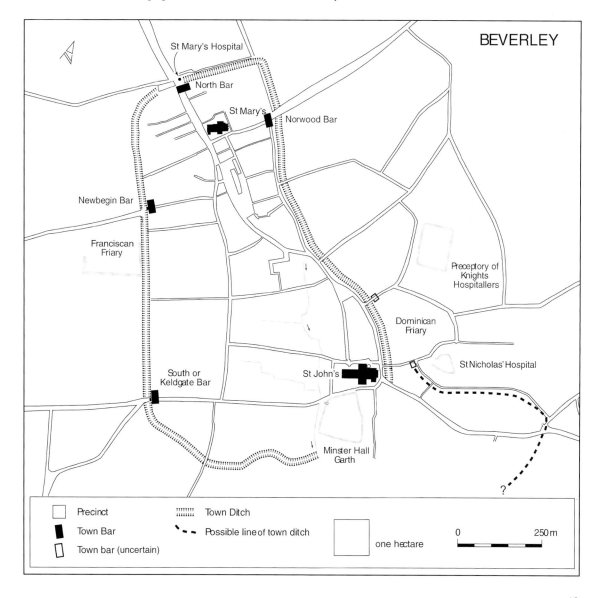

BEVERLEY

St Mary's Hospital
North Bar
St Mary's
Norwood Bar
Newbegin Bar
Franciscan Friary
Preceptory of Knights Hospitallers
Dominican Friary
St Nicholas' Hospital
South or Keldgate Bar
St John's
Minster Hall Garth
?

	Precinct		Town Ditch
	Town Bar		Possible line of town ditch
	Town bar (uncertain)		

one hectare

0   250 m

ditches (and sometimes the ditches themselves) were valued grazing areas, for instance: the city wall of Oxford contained a postern recorded from the mid sixteenth century as the 'Turl', after the wooden turnstile that kept cattle out of the town (Elrington 1979, 303). At Exeter, Stafford and elsewhere these spaces were used for stretching out manufactured cloth. City ditches were also fishponds, mill-races and (unofficially) municipal dumps; walls were perambulations, playgrounds and sources for stone, while their gates might house guildhalls or gaols, or were let out both as prestige dwellings and as tenements for the poor. It comes as no surprise that medieval civic records (especially in the form of bye-laws) show that urban authorities could be in more or less constant conflict over the regulation of activities such as building, grazing, gardening and dumping in the vicinity of defensive zones – a typical example being the ordinance of 1366 in London that prohibited the construction of gardens, houses and other structures against the wall (Barron 2004, 244).

Religious buildings were another important element in the structuring of the urban fringe and have important relationships with defences – gate chapels and churches especially so. Canterbury had at least five, Bristol and Winchester had four and Warwick two; other lesser-known examples include the 'Hanging Chapel' at Langport (Somerset) and St Peter's, Wallingford (Berks.) (Morris 1989, 201–2, 214–17). This characteristic pattern may have arisen, in part, for pragmatic reasons: prominent churches by gates naturally attracted donations from travellers. Some church-gates at London were of minster status and served to 'anchor' the wards, while at Oxford and perhaps elsewhere late Saxon church towers by gates may have originally stood next to, or formed parts of, the residences of noblemen (Haslam 1988; Renn 2003, 85–9). Yet the phenomenon of gate-churches and chapels also, inescapably, lent something of a spiritual dimension to a town's defence. Charitable institutions in general, and *leprosaria* in particular, were further markers of the fringe, forming rings around larger towns and clustering at gates – at Yarmouth (Norfolk), for instance, the buildings of the leper hospital of St Mary Magdalen flanked both sides of the town's east gate (Rawcliffe 2005, 261). These institutions were landmark features in the mental geography of a town's fringe, as were those hermitages located in gates, mural towers and in the corners of town walls, and the many nunneries and friaries built immediately against circuits (as at Beverley: Figure 11). As well as frequently resulting in uncertainty and occasionally disputes over ownership and access rights, such activities contributed further to the creation of distinctive 'city fringe' zones that were liminal socially as well as physically (Gilchrist 1995, 116, 173–5).

Town walls by no means always provided protection for urban populations at large. As the only British urban centre in any way reaching the status of a front-rank medieval city by European standards, London (Figure 12) is remarkable in that the line of its Roman defences was never extended to embrace any of its massive suburbs (and nor did it by any means represent the largest defended area in Britain). The only extension to London's ancient circuit, circumscribing some 132 ha, was out to the Fleet on the west side of the

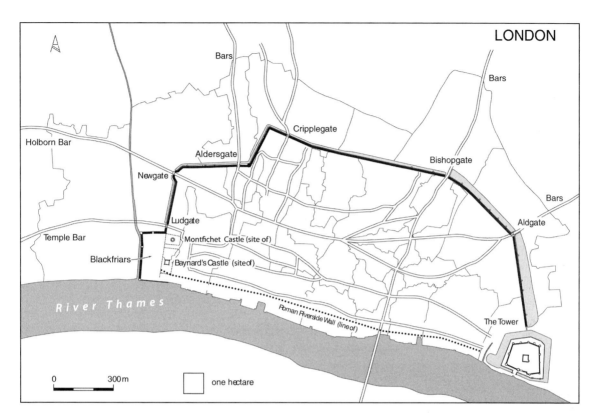

Bars

Bars

Holborn Bar

Cripplegate

Aldersgate

Bishopgate

Newgate

Bars

Ludgate

Aldgate

Temple Bar

Montfichet Castle (site of)

Blackfriars

Baynard's Castle (site of)

River Thames

Roman Riverside Wall (line of)

The Tower

0   300 m

one hectare

FIGURE 12.
The medieval defences
and wards of London.
Note the disappearance
of the Roman
riverside wall (dotted
line), as well as the
westward expansion
of the *enceinte* around
Blackfriars (after
Sheppard 1998, fig. 15,
with additions).

city in the 1270s, to include a monastic precinct, although in the same period the Tower's expansion on the opposite (south-east) side of the city took in a large area (Barron 2004, 242–3). Piecemeal reclamation on the north bank of the Thames, following systematic demolition of the riverside wall, meanwhile, saw a small net increase in the enclosed zone, but at the expense of making the city arguably less defensible than before the Conquest. Thus, despite the high levels of independence attained by the growing city, its growth in status and size was never reflected in an extension to the defences, the true urban limits being marked in the later medieval period by outlying bars and barriers. It is also notable that here, as in most other major British towns, the wards (or units around which the manning and watch of walls was organised, presumably from the burghal period) extended to embrace large areas of extra-mural space. That London's wards were referred to in later medieval documents as the *patriae* (or 'homelands') of their inhabitants provides a tantalising glimpse of a deep-rooted network of local loyalties both inside and outside the walls, quite at odds with the superficial unity of the walled *enceinte* (Rosser 2000, 344). Winchester, where the ancient walls embraced a minority of its inhabitants at the city's peak around *c.*1100, provides another clear example. Its sprawling suburbs took up at least two and perhaps as much as three times as much space as the 58-ha walled zone; as at Canterbury and Lincoln, partial earthworks well beyond the circuit enclosed portions of these suburbs, though in no case were defences formally extended (Barlow *et al.* 1976, 484).

We should therefore recognise that as well as embracing certain sectors of urban populations, town walls excluded others and were not necessarily symbols of universal commercial advantage. At London, for instance, restrictions on access through designated gates ensured that some streets within the city that terminated at the wall were 'commercial backwaters' (Schofield 2000, 227). In settlements which gained defences late in the day, the construction of fresh defensive lines might cut across built-up areas or infringe on property rights. At Southampton, for instance, the fourteenth-century wall was built across a series of merchant's houses on the south-west side of the town (Figure 13), helping to reverse permanently the fortunes of a once prosperous area (Platt 1973, 123–7, 269). A combination of royal initiative and civic endeavour, this wall-building scheme played a major role in the recasting of the town's economic geography: by cutting across the network of lanes around the town's mercantile waterfront zone, the new wall ensured a concentration of trade away from the complex of private wharfs towards the two public quays (Hughes 1994, 126–36). At Coventry (Warks.), which became a walled community only in the late fourteenth century, the wall similarly 'amputated' certain zones of development and embraced the assets of the privileged. On the north side of the city, for instance, a prominent 'dog-leg' in the circuit marked where the wall line deviated to include the prior's fish stews and the pond known as St Osburg's Pool, while elsewhere it cut across gardens and through houses (Gooder *et al.* 1966, 94–5; Pugh 1969, 21–3). Other clear

FIGURE 13.
Southampton town wall in the south-west part of the medieval city, showing an earlier merchant's house cut across by the new fourteenth-century curtain wall.
O. CREIGHTON

examples of the severing of settlements from redefined urban cores by new town walls are provided by the late-thirteenth-century circuit of Norwich (Norfolk) and Edinburgh's fifteenth-century King's Wall.

It follows that the enclosure of a town might not have necessarily enhanced economic opportunities for all. Indeed, while a wall might outwardly appear to encourage security, with its gates acting as a filter system facilitating the ready collection of tolls, there seems to have been a long-standing tension between the needs for defence and commerce. This was particularly acute in port towns. For instance, it was the temporary nature of Southampton's waterfront defences in the first half of the fourteenth century that led to the town's devastation in a French raid in 1338: the defensive 'wall' flanked only the town's northern and eastern sides, the quaysides being provided only with gated streets (Platt and Coleman-Smith 1975, 37–8). Similarly, at Kingston-upon-Hull the magnificent new brick wall of the fourteenth century left the waterfront from the mouth of the Hull to the haven undefended. In contrast, London's Roman riverside wall was toppled into the mud within a couple of generations of the Norman Conquest, presumably in the face of commercial pressure, and never replaced; in the later medieval period only water gates and impermanent timber bretaching defended the waterfront (Turner 1970, 157). On occasion, burgesses might even directly oppose wall-building enterprises: quite exceptionally, the murage grant to Portsmouth (Hants.) in 1342 was reversed two years later following vociferous complaints from the townsmen that the levying of tax was adversely affecting trade (Page 1908, 187).

A surprising number of wall-building projects, meanwhile, were only partially realised. Civic aspirations might be thwarted by the restricting influence of lordship (especially in ecclesiastically dominated towns) or fizzle out due to economic downturn or inefficiencies in the murage system. For instance, it has been calculated that only one sixth of the money raised through murage to finance the maintenance of London's wall in the 1330s was used for this purpose (Barron 2004, 243). At Ipswich (Suffolk), (King's) Lynn (Norfolk), Scarborough (Yorks.) and Stafford, wall-building projects were left half-completed or never got off the ground, with stretches of earth and timber plugging the missing gaps. The planted town of New Winchelsea (E. Sussex) is a famous and extreme example of grand ambition left unrealised: development never filled the circuit as envisaged in the late thirteenth century, leaving the gates as isolated outlying features, and when attempts were made to rebuild the defences on a contracted line in the early fifteenth century, this, too, was left incomplete (Martin and Martin 2004).

A related point of broader significance here is that walls might not always mark 'urban' densities of development, and this holds true not only of those towns that in some way or other failed to live up to their potential or that fell into decline, such as the numerous seigniorial boroughs in Wales where open zones within defences were never filled. For example, Norwich's town wall (built from the 1290s) embraced the largest defended area in Britain – a massive 388 ha – but always enclosed gardens, fields and other unoccupied spaces. Even in those towns where development spilled beyond the confines of a walled area, vast areas of intra-mural space might be taken up by open areas: even the walled city of medieval London at its peak was still 'a city of gardens and open spaces' (Barron 2004, 252). Monastic and other ecclesiastical precincts similarly ate up huge chunks of intra-mural space. At Chester, for instance, friary and nunnery precincts took up almost all of the additional area embraced by the twelfth-century expansion to the Roman *enceinte* (Thacker 2000, 22–6).

Indeed, the image of the city wall as a unifying emblem of communal defence was frequently at odds with the reality of walled topographies, which were often confused and whose ownership was actively contested between interest groups. The three brief concluding examples of Lincoln, Durham and Bristol illuminate further how town defences, rather than necessarily unifying communities, could accentuate the development of separate identities.

In later medieval Lincoln (Figure 14), the city limits were marked by an irregular and visually unimpressive arrangement of ditches, banks and 'enhanced' property boundaries, with only short discontinuous stretches of walling and inconspicuous gates (Stocker 2005; see also Jones *et al.* 2003). Here, the 'walls' defined a more privileged zone dominated by the Roman Upper City, elevated above its surroundings and embracing the castle and cathedral within its ancient masonry defences. In sharp contrast, the city's convoluted outer perimeter was constructed piecemeal in the post-Conquest period to mark the limits of what was a loose amalgamation of suburbs rather than a unified urban entity (Stocker 2005). At Durham (Figure 14) the 'city' wall was clearly nothing of the sort. It was established by Bishop Flambard in the late eleventh century and again encircled a complex of high-status build-ings and precincts rather than a densely settled urban area; it was also built at the same time that the peninsula was reorganised through the clearance of Palace Green in front of the new cathedral (Leyland 1994, 416–17). Indeed, the walled zone was less densely settled after construction of the defences than before, and archaeological evidence suggests that this scheme of urban development may have also included the replanning of displaced tenements beyond the wall, on the northern edge of the peninsula (Lowther *et al.* 1993, 108). Not until the fourteenth century was Durham's commercial heart, rep-resented by the market place of the Bishop's Borough, enclosed, and most of the population was always extra-mural. Despite the superficial appearance of the iconic walled city, the physical reality of medieval Durham was of a 'polyfocal' community of fragmented identities based around a collection of quasi–independent boroughs that were mostly undefended and at least two of which had separate charters (Bonney 1990, 41–9).

Finally, Bristol's thirteenth-century 'Portwall' was a walled extension to the south of the city's early medieval core. Built in a huge arc across a loop of the Avon and fronted with a wide ditch, the wall's construction was a massive engineering operation that entailed the damming and diversion of waterways and went hand in hand with an ambitious scheme of reclamation. A series of

FIGURE 14. The walled topographies of Lincoln and Durham (after Jones *et al.* 2003, fig. 9.72, with additions, and Lowther *et al.* 1993, figs 39 and 42, with additions).

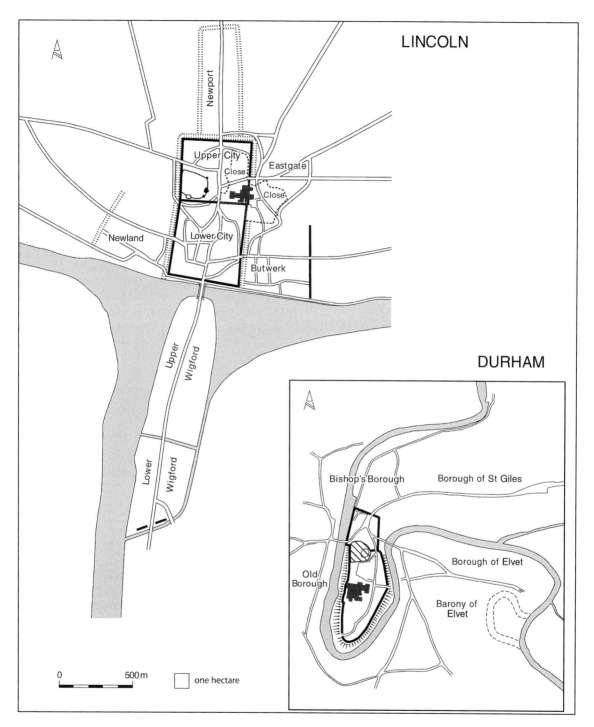

LINCOLN

DURHAM

0   500 m

☐ one hectare

developer-funded excavations between 1994 and 2000 have revealed for the first time the remarkable form of the eastern stretch of this lost wall: in this section only, it was pierced by internal 'casemates', twenty-two in all, providing access to loops regularly placed at intervals of 5.75 m and amounting to a multi-tier 'battery' (BaRAS 1995; 2000). This appearance of immense defensive strength and sophistication – quite unlike most town walls – was enhanced further by loops in the 'spines' of the imposing Tower Harratz that marked the wall's terminus against the river. Crucially, the wall in this part of the city marked the boundary of the Temple Fee of the Knights Templar. While ostensibly a 'city wall', this stretch of the circuit was, it seems, explicitly designed as the symbol and substance of the Templars' authority and was seemingly influenced by their Middle Eastern castles, while the very deliberate blocking of the casemates may relate to the Templars' suppression in the early fourteenth century.

Conclusions

Many of the examples explored in this paper have presented an image of town defences sharply at odds with the familiar view of walled heritage proudly displayed by medieval 'gem' towns such as Conwy and York. To a contemporary medieval visitor, a town's defences – if indeed it possessed any – may not have been visually impressive symbols of communal pride at all but scrappily built features obscured by other activities and encumbered by development. Moreover, the point at which a traveller entered the urban area might not be clear-cut but marked by a broader zone of transition comprising different component parts of defensive systems as well as a range of other characteristic features and activities.

Overall, we can find compelling evidence that, far from being 'communal' defences in the true sense, many town walls embodied the ambitions of elite sectors and other minority stakeholders in urban society. Many circuits not mentioned in this paper started life as enclosures attached to castles – vast outer baileys, even – and were always seigniorial in character. Several instances have been cited of larger cities where vast stretches of circuits marked the boundaries of high-status precincts and were managed and maintained essentially as 'privatised' resources, while huge tracts of populations lived outside the walls. As such, defences served to divide as well as to unite, potentially creating or exacerbating fragmented identities in a manner quite at odds with the enduring image of the walled city as a cohesive entity. These matters, in addition to the 'secret history' of walls and gates as the focus for discontent and as arenas for conflict between competing interest groups, require careful consideration in the future.

Acknowledgements

Thanks to Mike Rouillard for preparing the illustrations.

CHAPTER FIVE

Changing Spaces:
Towns and their Hinterlands
in the North West, AD 900–1500

N. J. Higham

In AD 900, north-west England – by which I mean pre-1974 Cheshire and Lancashire – was a virtually town-free space. The recent processes of town formation in Wessex and parts of Mercia had not impacted here and the region could boast only one identifiable market – the extraordinarily long-lived beach trading and manufacturing site at Meols, on the northern end of the Wirral peninsula (Hume 1863), which has now been lost to the sea. Rather, this seems to have been a thinly populated landscape without settlement nucleation. The little organisation that is detectable consists mostly of very large parishes (Thacker 1987, 264–73; Higham 1993) which may have originated as units of secular lordship. Settlements were dispersed and are difficult to identify, being virtually aceramic and non-coin-using. This paper will explore the landscape contexts of two successive episodes of urban foundation in the region: the first in the tenth and eleventh centuries (generally, see Haslam 1984; Blair 2000); and the second across the period *c.*1250–1360 (see Dyer 2000; Kermode 2000b).

The first episode began with the refoundation of Chester in AD 907 (Mason 1975; 1976; 1985; Thacker 1987; Ward 1994; 2001), followed by the construction of at least five further walled centres by AD 924, stretching from Rhuddlan in the west to Manchester in the east (Figure 15). These sites were part of successive governmental attempts to control Mercia's northern frontiers at a time when these were threatened by Norse forces in the Irish Sea area and southern Northumbria.

Chester, earlier the premier Roman fortress in the region, seems *ab initio* to have been the key to the whole, although whether or not it was already an urban site in the ninth century remains unclear. It was the crux of the Roman road system, by far the largest of these new fortifications, the only site in the region where a mint and more than a single church was established, the only one which looked like a significant town in 1066 – when it had some 487 houses – and the only one which developed as a sea-port. Once the immediate military crisis had dissipated and the kingdom of Northumbria brought

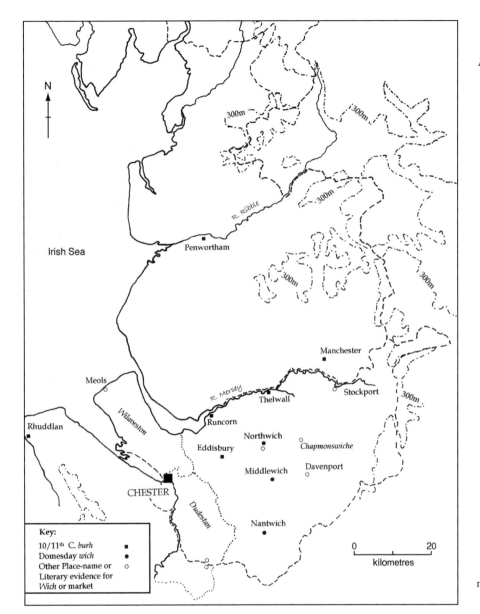

N

Irish Sea

R. Ribble

300m

300m

300m

300m

300m

300m

Penwortham

Manchester

Meols

R. Mersey

Thelwall

Stockport

Wilaveston

Runcorn

Northwich

Rhuddlan

Eddisbury

Chapmonswiche

Middlewich

Davenport

CHESTER

Dudestan

Nantwich

Key:
10/11th C. *burh*   ■
Domesday *wich*   ●
Other Place-name or   ○
Literary evidence for
Wich or market

0   20
kilometres

FIGURE 15.
Walled centres and
markets in the North
West, 900–1086.

into the English state, the Crown only needed a single centre in the region
through which to influence the fast-changing politics of the northern Irish
Sea, to oversee trade, to garrison against raids, to muster ships, to mint coin
and to collect tribute, and Chester fulfilled all these functions during the
remainder of the tenth and eleventh centuries. The fortifications were maintained and manned by means of the shire system, which placed responsibility
for Chester on twelve hundreds stretching from Wat's Dyke to the Pennines.
The collegiate minster of St Werburgh's was strengthened by royal charter
(in AD 958) and Chester ultimately became the focus of power of one of the
most powerful earldoms of the eleventh-century state. That said, numismatic

Towns and their
Hinterlands
in the North West,
AD 900–1500

evidence suggests that its primacy in the Irish-Sea zone was short-lived, being eclipsed by Bristol by the late tenth century (Downham 2003).

The other newly fortified sites of the early tenth century around Chester decayed. Those initially founded in AD 914–15 by Æthelflæd, King Alfred's daughter and widow of Earldorman Æthelfrith of the Mercians, were the hill-top site of Eddisbury, and Runcorn on the Mersey. Eddisbury seems to have been deserted by 1066 and the area was afforested soon after the Conquest, if not before. Runcorn's foundation involved relocation of the local minster outside the walls, arguably from either Daresbury (Greene 1989, 30) or Preston-on-the-Hill (Higham 1993, 157). The new church, which had two priests in 1086, shared its dedication to St Bertelin with Æthelflæd's burh-church at Stafford. However, despite this investment in the permanence of the site, lordship had by 1066 migrated to Halton, nearby, where a baronial stronghold was eventually constructed, leaving the small burh, built on a rocky outcrop jutting out into the Mersey, to fall into ruin.

Further defences were commissioned by Alfred's son and Æthelflæd's brother, Edward the Elder (AD 899–924), around AD 919 at Thelwall and Manchester, and an additional work at Rhuddlan (Cledemutha) around AD 921. Thelwall seems to have been valueless when Domesday Book was commissioned and the site of the burh is now lost. At Manchester, Edward probably refurbished the Roman fort, as Griffiths (2001, 178) has argued, and a few small finds imply some activity in the vicinity (Holdsworth 1983). However, it was the pre-Conquest church which became the focus for the post-Conquest lordship and borough most of a mile to the north-east, so the burh can safely be assumed to have been abandoned.

Rhuddlan's defences have been excavated but there has been some controversy concerning the line and extent of the pre-Conquest fortifications, with later commentators favouring a minimal interpretation (Manley 1987; Quinnell *et al.* 1994; Griffiths 2001). The site retained some importance as a local centre, becoming a stronghold of King Gruffydd of Wales until his death in 1063, and then, after 1071, receiving a new motte which served as the focus of an extensive Norman lordship. However, Rhuddlan was a 'new borough' in 1086 (Morgan 1978, FT2), which implies that it was not thought of as a town previously (see Griffiths 2001, 171). It then failed once more, only to be refounded by Edward I in 1277, slightly downstream.

Further south, royal burh construction accompanied by the development of markets, mints and intra-mural settlement proved a critically important stimulus to the reinvention of urban life (Astill 2000, 41). In the North West, however, only Chester developed into a meaningful urban settlement in the tenth and eleventh centuries, becoming a significant Domesday civitas. The remaining fortified sites of the early tenth century were all comparatively small, of the type more normally thought of as forts than towns, so it may be that urban development was never in prospect. Additionally, King Edward's foundations around AD 919 may have been intended to replace his sister's of AD 914–15 (Higham 1988). That said, signs of continuing occupation at Rhuddlan and removal of a local minster church to Runcorn may imply some intention to refocus local communities on the new fortifications in the longer term, leaving open the possibility that either could have been expected to develop some urban characteristics.

The only other site in the region to have urban pretensions in 1086 was Penwortham, on the south side of the Ribble estuary and beside the new motte, with a mere six burgesses (Morgan 1978, R6). Penwortham was one of King Edward's estates in the region and royal interest in the site may date back to the tenth century, when southern Lancashire was arguably annexed by southern kings keen to disrupt links between Dublin and York (Higham 1988). It need not have been a new town in 1086, therefore, but its compliment of three radmen, eight villeins and four ploughmen clearly outnumbered the burgesses, so Penwortham's claims on urban status were marginal.

Otherwise, three salt-production sites in Cheshire – Northwich, Middlewich and Nantwich – perhaps had some of the characteristics of towns by 1066 (Oxley 1982), but at all three archaeological remains before AD 400 and after 1200 still predominate at the expense of eleventh-century activity. Only Middlewich was a significant parochial centre and the focus of a hundred. There are some further signs of incipient proto-urbanisation, but these are slight indeed. There is a scatter of additional -wich place-names but none is associated with workings that are otherwise attested. The eastern Cheshire site of Davenport – literally, 'market-town by the [river] Dane' – was destroyed by the Norse in the AD 920s. The name survived as that of a minor Domesday manor in 1066, but the later township evidenced no signs of settlement nucleation. Domesday *Cepmundewiche* suggests a market associated with salt works at Ollerton near Knutsford, and another concentration of 'port' names at and around Stockport implies some sort of trading site on the south side of the Mersey, on the very edge of Mercia. Chester apart, however, this does not look like the successful launch-pad from which urbanisation eventually sprang. Penwortham had given way to Preston by 1200. Although the three salt wiches and Stockport emerged as thirteenth-century urban settlements, neither Davenport nor *Cepmundewiche* did, giving way to new foundations at Congleton and Knutsford respectively. Before 1100, urbanisation was tentative indeed.

The landscape contexts of these tenth-century developments were mixed. In the hinterland of Chester, the west Cheshire hundreds of Wilaveston and Dudestan appear virtually devoid of woodland at Domesday and have a distinct concentration of the shire's plough teams and ploughlands (Terrett 1962; Phillips and Phillips 2002; Higham 2004), suggesting a comparatively well-developed agrarian economy capable of providing a surplus. It is possible, but by no means proven, that a degree of village creation had already occurred here (White 1995), but most manors seem still to have been characterised by dispersal (Lewis 1991; Higham 2004, 52–5), and Chester's success perhaps obviated further urban foundations. Further east and south, the wiches required fuel and local woodlands were probably managed to meet this demand, but there

Towns and their
Hinterlands
in the North West,
AD 900–1500

is little sign of a marketable arable surplus. The key manors were Halton and Acton, with twenty and thirty ploughlands respectively, but both were major seigniorial centres surrounded by townships which are unnamed in Domesday Book, suggesting a more dispersed pattern of both rural settlement and ploughlands than one might initially suppose. The degree of market penetration into the countryside seems to have been very limited. While considerable quantities of 'Chester Ware' have been recovered from Chester itself, little has been discovered elsewhere in the region, with just one sherd, for example, coming from the *c.*3,600 square metres of excavation on the eleventh- to fourteenth-century 'village' site at Tatton (Higham 2000). While urbanisation in the tenth and eleventh centuries clearly had some impact on the wider landscape, therefore, its principal influences seem to have been localised comparatively close to Chester itself, leaving much of the hinterland still virtually coin-less and near aceramic. There seem to have been few opportunities for sales of farm produce in regulated markets and settlement was primarily characterised by thinly scattered farms which were tied into a system of political and social patronage but otherwise operated close to subsistence.

This picture seems to have changed little until the later twelfth century, when charters were granted to Preston (1179) and Lancaster (1193). Chester apart, regional society was organised around baronies, many of which were centred on castles, and around a comparatively small number of major church sites. The few specialised sites were predominantly the wiches, and there were in addition several small fishing and/or maritime communities. The urgency with which Norman lords established fortified boroughs at the heart of their lordships in Marcher Wales (Soulsby 1983, 6–12; Courtney 2005) seems lacking in much of the North West, where only Chester had walls, implying a very different context to this next episode of urbanisation and a comparatively secure environment.

Urban settlements tended to develop where advantageous factors coalesced (Figure 16): both Lancaster and Preston were ancient church sites under high-status patronage, overlooking major river crossings and with access to the sea: the priory church and the castle at Lancaster were both clearly pivotal to the development of the town. Frodsham was the earliest settlement in Cheshire to be chartered, a status it achieved by 1215. The site offered a combination of comital lordship, links with hundredal administration, a Roman road and river-crossing, a major church and harbourage, albeit these were dispersed across the parish, rather than focused on the new roadside settlement. Macclesfield was second, with a comital castle, a hundredal role and major routes stretching out of the shire, along and across the Pennines; but the local minster lay over two miles to the north, at Prestbury. The hundredal centre of Salford was chartered in 1231. Again, this was a location where groups must frequently have congregated under high-status patronage, both to attend the court but also to cross the river to the church at Manchester.

All these were likely to have been proto-urban sites where market activity pre-dated the provision of a charter, and where lordship was to an extent

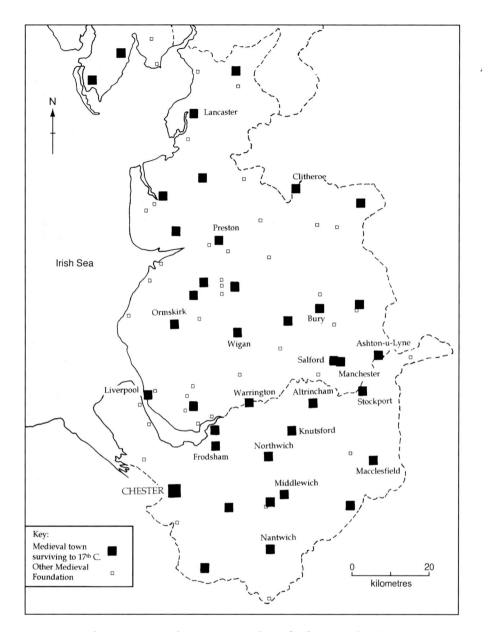

FIGURE 16.
Medieval urban settlements in Lancashire and Cheshire.

Key:
Medieval town surviving to 17th C. ■
Other Medieval Foundation □

Irish Sea

Lancaster
Clitheroe
Preston
Ormskirk
Bury
Wigan
Ashton-u-Lyne
Salford
Manchester
Liverpool
Warrington
Altrincham
Stockport
Knutsford
Northwich
Frodsham
Macclesfield
CHESTER
Middlewich
Nantwich

0   20
kilometres

reactive, seeking to control, promote and profit from trade. In contrast, at Liverpool a new castle-town was founded by King John in 1207 to act as a port for traffic to his interests in Ireland. It was laid out on a 'green-field' site with no previous history of settlement or commerce.

By comparison with other regions, the formalisation of urban communities came late to the North West (compare Cambridgeshire, for example: Galloway 2005; or the North East: Kermode 2000b). On both sides of the Mersey, but more dramatically in Cheshire, the Edwardian conquest and consolidation of North Wales between 1277 and *c.*1320 witnessed a surge in borough foundation, which involved lower strata of the social hierarchy than hitherto.

Towns and their
Hinterlands
in the North West,
AD 900–1500

When it began, Cheshire may have had as few as seven chartered boroughs and Lancashire twelve – that is, assuming all known foundations had succeeded, which seems improbable. By 1320 there were a further dozen in each, after which the whole process ran out of steam. Before 1500, Cheshire's total only advanced by the establishment of Tintwistle (1358–59), in Longdendale, while a further seven urban communities were founded in Lancashire below the Sands (so excluding foundations in Furness, which are best dealt with as part of the north: Kermode 2000b). Edward I's policies may well have encouraged landholders in the North West to attempt borough foundation, taking advantage of a surge in activity on local roads as men and resources flowed towards Chester for redeployment into Wales, or northwards, towards Scotland. This also coincided with the high point of population in Cheshire and Lancashire, which grew dramatically from a mere 10,000 at Domesday to more than 100,000 in 1300 (Higham 2004, 70–4). A rash of new urban communities was integral to this steep demographic rise, as commercialisation of the regional economy increasingly lubricated the market and sustained specialisation (Britnell 1993).

Some of these foundations, like Manchester, Warrington and Malpas, look much like an earlier generation of Welsh baronial boroughs, albeit without the walls, each developing alongside closely juxtaposed seigniorial castle and minster church at sites where traders were probably already active. Other new towns were, however, very different, being inserted into a dispersed settlement pattern in which lordship and parish were already centred on different sites. Some were sited beside a castle, as at Halton (Ches.) or Castleton (Rochdale, Lancs.), with the church at some distance. Others were located beside a church or chapel, as at Bromborough and Burton (Ches.) and Burnley (Lancs.), but distant from the focus of lordship. Often, however, the new town simply added a further element to a determinedly dispersed system of settlement. Take, for example, the development of Altrincham, located on the Roman road between Northwich and Manchester at the centre of the Barony of Dunham Massey, itself a lordship with clear pre-Conquest origins (Higham 1997).

This barony dominated the eastern half of the Domesday Hundred of Bucklow (Figure 17), north-east of the River Bollin, and was approximately coterminous with the ancient parish of Bowdon (Thacker 1987), with its stone church on the heights of the sandstone ridge. This was a colonising landscape of lowland wetlands, mosses and heaths, around patches of comparatively well-drained land characterised by settlement place-names. The foundation of a borough *c.*1290 on the principal route-way close to the centre of the lordship may imply some previous proto-urban development there. The charter itself reveals the baron as interested in matters to do with enclosure of common pasture around and about, at least as much as in commercial matters (Ormerod 1882, I, 536).

On the opposite side of the river Bollin, in the western half of the Domesday hundred, Knutsford was similarly founded in a dispersed landscape, but not on the Roman road, exploiting instead cross-country routes towards

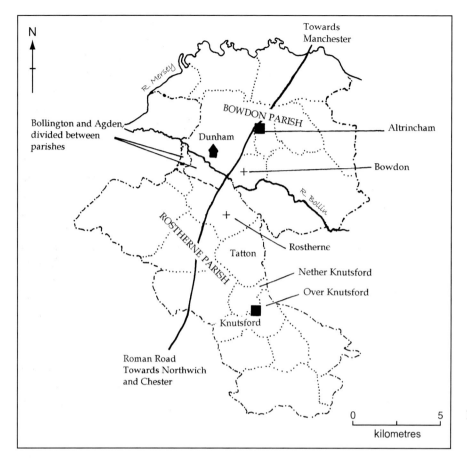

Map labels:
N
Towards Manchester
R. Mersey
BOWDON PARISH
Bollington and Agden, divided between parishes
Dunham
Altrincham
Bowdon
R. Bollin
ROSTHERNE PARISH
Tatton
Rostherne
Nether Knutsford
Over Knutsford
Knutsford
Roman Road
Towards Northwich
and Chester
0   5
kilometres

FIGURE 17.
Bucklow Hundred, the
minster parishes and
Dunham Barony.

Macclesfield and the wiches of the Weaver valley. It lay in the old, multi-
township parish of Rostherne, but around three miles from the church, with
burgesses initially in both Over and Nether Knutsford. The charter, *c.*1292
(Ormerod 1882, I, 488–9), concentrates primarily on the burgesses' access to
arable, common pasture, pannage, right to building and hedging timber, tur-
bary and moorland, beside references to a weekly market and annual fair,
suggesting that this was viewed as much as a nucleated farming community
as one dependant on commerce or manufacturing. This was a part of the
region devoid of major lordships, where local initiative lay with lesser manorial
figures, and it may be significant that the charter was witnessed by the lords
of several neighbouring manors, suggesting an agreed initiative to provide a
market at a location convenient to themselves and their dependants.

Knutsford's market does, however, seem to have stimulated some change
to its immediate hinterland. The nearest settlements to the north lay in Tatton, where recent large-scale research revealed that sherds from cooking and
storage vessels and jugs of the period *c.*1200–1400 mark the end of the near
aceramic phases of its archaeology. The initial appearance of this pottery pre-
dates Knutsford's charter by at least two generations, so presumably reflects
earlier access to trade, perhaps on the same site but prior to the charter. The

range of pottery was dominated by West Midland manufactures and Pennine gritty wares, both of which necessarily reached the site overland. The absence of ceramics from further afield is noticeable, and there was very little other artefactual evidence. A single piece of window glass dates from around 1300 but the earliest coin (from the Old Hall) was from the second half of the fifteenth century, and the excavated settlement of the thirteenth and fourteenth centuries produced very little metalwork of any sort (Higham 2000). The range and number of finds were particularly limited by comparison with village excavations of the same period in eastern and southern England, suggesting that Knutsford attracted few of the long-distance traders apparent at coastal Meols in the same period (for example, Galloway 2005, 204–5). Nor do architectural habits seem to have changed, for local farmers were still using post-hole construction, rather than adopting the new preference for half-walls in stone which was otherwise sweeping across England. The impact of Knutsford's new status as a borough on the behaviour of local farmers was, therefore, at best somewhat limited. Like many other small towns of the period, most traded goods were arguably of comparatively local provenance and of kinds invisible to archaeology (Dyer 2003). That Knutsford was a minor leather-working centre in the sixteenth century may imply earlier activity of a similar kind.

Routeways held the key to viability when it came to new town foundation in the region. Such new boroughs as Halton (Ches.), established at a castle but distant from main roads, failed to develop. Conversely, sites controlling significant river crossings emerged as particularly successful, even with pairs of such towns surviving in some locations. For example, Salford and Manchester were sited on opposite sides of the Irwell, joined with a stone bridge from the 1320s (Morris 1983), and both developed some urban characteristics before 1300. River-crossing settlements provided opportunities to control the passage of goods and people into and out of lordships, to levy tolls and to profit from overnight accommodation. The replacement of fords by bridges enabled towns to improve their competitive position by ensuring that goods passed through their own streets. Chester's bridge over the Dee was already constructed before 1066 and others were built later across the major rivers. A medieval bridge over the Dee survives largely intact at Farndon, although the adjacent settlement around a major minster is not known to have acquired a charter.

The Mersey was particularly difficult to bridge. The place-name Thelwall, first recorded in the tenth century, refers to a 'plank bridge at a pool' (Dodgson 1970, 2, 138), but this need not have actually spanned the river. Ferries plied between Birkenhead and Liverpool and a tidal ford was passable at Runcorn, but medieval bridges were few. At Warrington, a voluminous early fourteenth-century list of tolls suggests that a wide variety of goods was crossing this important bridge (Beaumont 1872), into and out of the baronial borough.

Further east, Stockport was chartered around 1260, on a site overlooking the point at which the old road from Buxton to Manchester crosses the Mersey. A castle had been built by the reign of Henry II, and a church by around

1200. A stone bridge was added across the Mersey by the 1280s, where it ran in a narrow gorge between sandstone cliffs, providing a safe river crossing, and both the castle and church were rebuilt in stone around 1320 (Arrowsmith 1997). The market area even today reflects the layout of the medieval trading centre, the oldest building now surviving, Staircase House, having been built around 1460. But, as already noted, the place-name implies an earlier trading site and the layout does suggest that the market was the primary feature, occupying a north-facing terrace, with the church perched on its upward (southern) edge and the castle on the lower. It remains a distinct possibility that this was a proto-urban settlement by the eleventh century.

Landscapes around such petty towns varied enormously. South of Manchester *c.*1300 lay a scatter of small bond settlements such as Gorton, Bradford and Ardwick, each with a single townfield but dispersed among common pastures, moors, mosses and woods. Some of the latter were improved and enclosed by local free tenants and gentry families during the late thirteenth and fourteenth centuries and exploited on a long-ley system as pasture, meadow and arable (Harland 1856–62). Around Warrington, colonisation of mossland was widespread, with much of Burtonwood converted to farmland by the early fourteenth century. The Beaumont barons of Warrington relocated there following a disastrous fire at their town residence, building themselves the moated complex of Bewsey Old Hall within an extensive deer park (Lewis 2000, 200–6). Stockport lay amid a veritable sea of dispersed settlement. Beyond the townfield lay a landscape characterised by comparatively isolated and often moated halls, such as the surviving fifteenth-century Arden Hall, and small greens, isolated farms and hamlets associated with a mix of hedged assarts, all interspersed with large areas of unreclaimed mosses and moors, woods and heaths.

Not far distant from Stockport were the great expanses of the Forest of the Peak and Macclesfield Forest, which were largely waste uplands used for mining and summer pasture, although both had attracted permanent populations by the fifteenth century. Small quantities of oats were grown for local consumption, but the main focus along the Pennine edge lay in livestock farming, and cattle reared in Macclesfield Hundred were being driven as far as London by the fourteenth century (Hewitt 1967, 33–4). However, export of goods to other regions only really became significant from the 1470s, with a rise in the output of local linen and woollens (Phillips and Smith 1994). Urban settlements around Manchester developed as local centres for the trade, at the western end of cross-Pennine packhorse tracks carrying cloth to Kingston-upon-Hull and other east coast ports (Cunliffe-Shaw 1958; Willan 1980). Successful merchants from the region established themselves at Leicester and London. Sir Edmund Shaw, for example, from a family of mercers in and around Saddleworth and Stockport, became mayor of the metropolis in 1483 and helped Richard III to power. Manchester was the highest taxed part of Lancashire by the reign of Henry VIII, and the hub of an expanding trading network dealing primarily in poor-quality woollen cloth, with new satellite markets and fairs around it

FIGURE 18.
Annotated detail from Thornton's Survey of Stockport, 1824.

Towns and their
Hinterlands
in the North West,
AD 900–1500

at, for example, Bury and Ashton-under-Lyne (Morris 1983; Nevell 1991, 60–1), with rising exports also passing through Liverpool.

A landscape of increasingly dense, but still largely dispersed, settlements lay around these developing markets. The landscape was characterised by fresh colonisation and the foundation of numerous new smallholdings as forests,

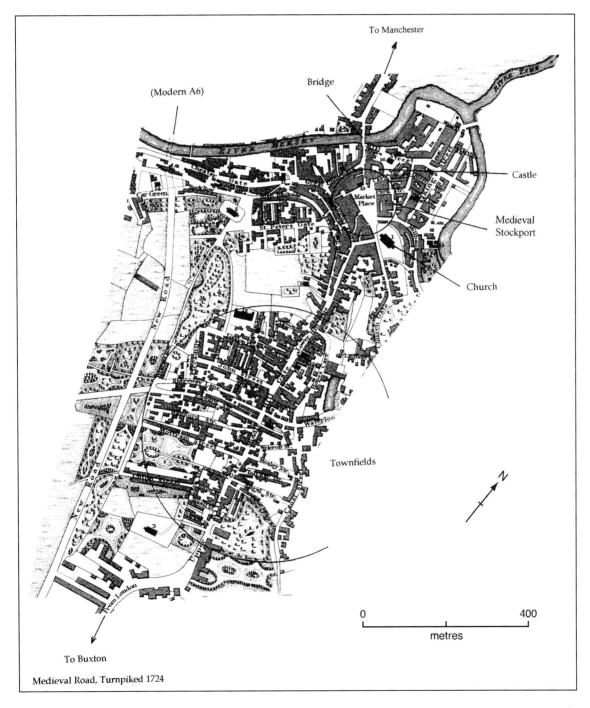

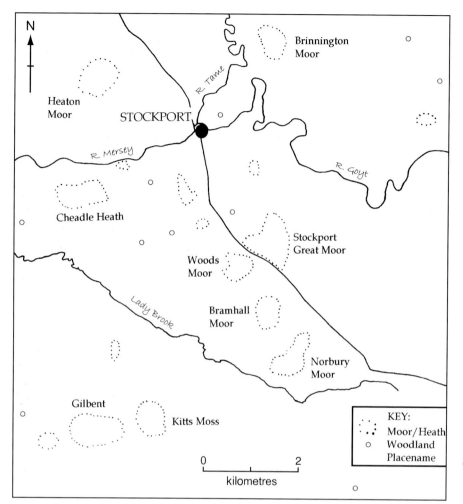

FIGURE 19.
The hinterland of later medieval and early modern Stockport.

uplands and old lowland wetlands were broken up, leased out, drained and improved. Large numbers of tenants combined small-scale farming with weaving, alongside larger, better-capitalised land-holdings which were increasingly dignified by large stone farmhouses. The great expansion of woollen manufacture in the seventeenth and eighteenth centuries developed from the small boroughs, the manorial and parochial systems and the patterns of settlement characterising the fifteenth and early sixteenth centuries, and this general system of settlement and land use was only seriously altered, and even then only in particular localities, by the development of the factory system in the decades around 1800, and subsequently by the processes of mass urbanisation and suburbanisation. And even here, if we stay with Stockport, there remain traces of the earlier landscape. Thornton's survey of 1824 (Figure 18) reveals a road layout in the newly built upper town which appears to have been based on the old open-field strips, while modern street names include Longshut Lane and Hempshaw Lane, and suburbs such as Stockport Great Moor, Cale Green and Woods Moor invoke an earlier landscape (Figure 19). Kitts Moss was built over for housing as recently as 1958–9, having been dug out and improved over previous centuries (Hall *et al.* 1995, 14). All bear witness to the mosaic of mosses, assarts, woods and hamlets which underlies so much of the modern metropolitan borough.

Conclusion

There were two episodes of urban development in the North West between AD 900 and 1500, of which the first was less successful than the second. Royal *burh* foundation in the region during the early tenth century only succeeded in launching Chester on to its unique trajectory as a major urban settlement. Otherwise, the new defensive sites seem to have made little headway as towns and regulated markets are implicit only at the several Cheshire salt wiches and perhaps a few places designated by the suffix 'port'. Low levels of population, poor agricultural yields, the insecurity of a frontier location, a western outlook which excluded profitable trading with the Continent, near subsistence-level farming practices, minimal coin-use and the absence of direct royal influence were arguably all factors holding back the spread of towns in this region.

The period between 1100 and 1349 saw a dramatic demographic increase, coupled with very considerable colonisation of previously under-utilised lands, a degree of economic specialisation and growing commercialisation of the agricultural economy. Urban development came late in comparison with most of England, although small-scale, unchartered and virtually undocumented market sites, which we might term 'proto-towns', may well have been common around 1250. Thereafter, the Edwardian interest in Chester, and to an extent also in Scotland, brought new traffic to the region's roads and waterways and encouraged local lords to found boroughs. While the particular circumstances in which these began did not last, numerous very small market towns did survive the demographic downturn of the period 1350–1500 and more were established. Of the sixty plus boroughs or other urban sites identifiable in the region at some point during the period 1066–1500 (Higham 2004, 187–8), over half exhibited urban characteristics in the seventeenth century (Phillips and Smith 1994, 31), and of those very few had ceased to function as towns within the Middle Ages but then revived (Ormskirk is a candidate). Most of the remainder had already failed soon after foundation, with several new foundations effectively still-born on account of poor situations, as at Murifield and Halton (Ches.) or losing out to more successful neighbours, as did Penwortham and Walton-le-Dale to Preston and West Derby to Liverpool (Lancs.). Other petty seigniorial foundations survived, however, as at Knutsford, Clitheroe and Altrincham, by servicing longer-distance travellers, acting as small-scale manufacturing sites and providing markets for local, dispersed settlements. The more successful were generally ports, such as Liverpool, and/or major river crossings – for instance, Lancaster, Preston, Manchester, Stockport and Warrington. Only Chester, however, really prospered before the late fifteenth century as an urban settlement of greater than local significance, and that was at the expense of seigniorial foundations nearby, such as Aldford and Burton. As at Shrewsbury, there was a distinct scarcity of towns within a half day's ride of Chester, in comparison with other parts of the region's lowlands.

There has been much recent discussion regarding the distribution and roles of small towns across medieval England, with very real differences noted in the incidence of urbanisation from west to east. The adoption of standardised criteria has tended to minimise the numbers reported in the North West: Dyer's (2000, 507) survey, covering the period 1270–1540, included only eleven in Cheshire and fourteen in Lancashire, totalling twenty-five for a region of some 1,650,000 acres (to which one might add the single major town, Chester), in contrast to forty-eight in Devon, which was virtually the same size, and forty-five in Kent (970,000 acres). Of course, a series of environmental factors rendered the North West less productive than either comparator and it was further disadvantaged by its exclusion from continental trade. However, it should be emphasised that this contrast rests heavily on issues of definition and inclusion, and threatens to discriminate against any region with numerous small and under-developed towns. Additionally, it may fail to take account of the frequency with which even failed urban settlements were replaced by new candidates. There is a case for including as towns communities with lesser claims to urban status in a region where nucleated settlements were otherwise either absent or very uncommon across entire localities. Phillips and Smith (1994, 31) identified some forty-five urban settlements of one kind or another in Lancashire and Cheshire in the period 1542–1660, and although this is clearly an optimal figure for the close of the Middle Ages it may well be closer to the reality as then experienced by a regional community which lacked access to towns only along the high Pennines and within the extensive lowland wetlands of northern Amounderness. Very small-scale, petty, seigniorial towns were, therefore, a persistent and comparatively widespread feature of the region from *c.*1280 to 1500, and played a significant role as commercial and social foci within a settlement pattern which was among the most dispersed in England.

PART TWO

Regional Perspectives

CHAPTER SIX

The Village: Contexts, Chronology and Causes

Brian K. Roberts

'Geography and chronology are the two eyes of history.'

(Giambattista Vico 1744, 17)

Hoskins defined some of the research questions touching villages with simplicity and elegance:

> The variety of plan among the villages of England, besides affording one of the most delightful characteristics of the countryside, is profoundly inter-esting – and tantalising – to the historian of landscape. It is interesting because he realises that this variety of forms almost certainly reflects very early cultural or historical differences, and it is tantalising for two reasons. First, because we cannot be sure that the present village plan is not the result of successive changes that had been completed before the earliest maps are available: we cannot be sure we know what the original shape was in many instances. And secondly, even if we are sure of the original shape of a village, we are not in a position to say – for the subject has been so little studied in this country – what the various shapes and plans mean in terms of social history. (Hoskins 1955, 49)

Hoskins would be delighted with the volume of work that has emerged since 1955, and in spite of many difficulties landscape studies, documents and archaeology have produced large amounts of new material to feed our imagi-nation and provide a few answers and, inevitably, a host of further questions (Beresford and St Joseph 1958; Beresford and Hurst 1971; Howell 1983, 114–46; Taylor 1983; Roberts 1987; 1996, fig. 3.2; Lewis *et al.* 1997). What follows is less an attempt to answer any of these new questions in detail than to establish way-markers on possible routes for the journey. While it must be admitted that methodological discussion does underlie this essay, the simple objective is to show how maps can enhance our understanding of the past.

Contexts for study

Individual local studies are, and will remain, the foundation of historical landscape enquiry. Essentially anecdotal in character amid more general historical conversations, they excite, feed and nourish our understanding. They may be quite short – an elegant paper in a local journal – or have the thick description, vast time-depth and weight of publication found at Wharram Percy. In fact, understanding any specific case necessitates, as the quotation from Giambattista Vico at the head of this essay implies, placing it with the twin contexts of space and time. Each example, be this a deserted village or the plan of living settlement, must be positioned within these two frames. In this way what is known and what can be discovered from landscape study and/or documentation, or recovered through excavation, acquires enhanced meaning within broader reconstructions of the world of the past.

While villages and hamlets have traditionally been examined amid the contexts of terrains and soils (Thorpe 1949) the author now bases his own thinking on two national maps: a first map simply places a small dot where there was a town, village or small hamlet in the decades of the nineteenth century when the Ordnance Survey first edition one-inch maps were being created, while a second draws together into one image symbolic representations of the woodland recorded in Domesday Book in 1086, Anglo-Saxon and Anglo-Scandinavian place-names, and the woodlands and open grazing lands recorded in the Land Utilisation Survey of the period 1937–46. These two maps are now widely available and will not be reproduced here (Atkins *et al.* 1998, figs 8.3, 11.9; Roberts and Wrathmell 2000; 2002; Williamson 2003, fig. 18; Britnell 2004, fig. 1.4). Together they provide cultural contexts, and while both maps could be greatly improved – not false modesty – they nevertheless carry information that remains meaningful to the level of the 10 x 10 km^2. Emphatically, they must be seen as tools, overviews, flattened time-matrices and Aunt Sallies, designed to inform national, regional and local studies: those done in the past, those now being done and those to be done in the future. Of course, the regional boundaries suggested by these distributions are not fixed and impermeable, for such boundaries rarely are, but use and careful evaluation are necessary. Even the application of simple terms begs questions; for example, 'commons': are these common wastes, manorial wastes, stinted commons, common pastures, common appendant, common appurtenant, commons in gross, commons by reason of vicinage, common by grant, common by prescription, rough pastures or even temperate savannas? All of this terminological complexity is concealed amid the catch-all general term (HMSO 1958; Harris and Ryan 1967, xxxi, 11–33). It will, eventually, be possible to amplify, improve and perhaps replace the Land Utilisation Survey data from the 1930s. Thus an innocent, yet wholly unwise, decision made over a decade ago to run the mapping of woodland and open common grazing lands into one layer in a computer system because of technical problems arising from copying the data is still used in Figure 21. An approximation of the distribution of national commons and wastes in the second half of the eighteenth century, using the varied county maps, is currently in progress, and this should form a more secure base from which to reassess the 'point' locations provided by the interrelated evidence of Domesday woodlands and place-name elements.

Such synoptic views of the principal elements of cultural landscapes are informative because they establish a basis for asking questions. Polities, early states, kingdoms, counties, shires, small shires and eventually parishes and townships, and their assembly into honours, baronies and fees, always possess spatial contents. The varied distributions of landscape elements of mountain and hill, plain and marsh, seacoast and woodland, terrain and soils, all provide ready summaries of the contents of countrysides and settings for the varied and particular dramas of social and economic life. In cultural terms the divergences between the substantively cleared landscapes of the 'planned' or 'champion' countrysides of the Central Province, and those landscapes with mosaics of wooded and enclosed countrysides, yet with some areas of townfield, all intermixed with open commons and sometimes great tracts of open pastures, that are found to the north and west and south and east of the midland Central Province, remain fundamental to understanding the past. In this brief summary of England and Wales there must be deep apologies to Scotland, where fertile strath and mountain land provide similar important and stark contrasts (Lebon 1952, 21, 28; Rackham 1986, 1–5; Roberts and Wrathmell 2002, *passim*).

Furthermore, there is a dynamic dimension, for landscapes rarely remain static: that which came before always influenced that which followed. To select only three cases: we can note that the place-names indicative of Scandinavian settlement largely concentrate in the champion lands of the east and north-eastern Midlands. Why? To note the fact, and see this familiar distribution in a new light, is not to explain why the Vikings settled amid the cleared lands, even if they utilised the more marginal elements. Roman villas appear in both champion and woodland landscapes, implying perhaps a route for reassessing variations in local 'villa' economies. We suspect that some at least of the medieval woodland in the Central Province was descended from Roman industrial coppices. 'Greens', relatively small tracts of common waste set peripheral to core areas of settlement of ancient foundation, and not true village greens, undoubtedly concentrate in the two outer provinces, signalling a geographically dispersed terminology for the same type of cultural landscape feature (Roberts and Wrathmell 2000, figs 26 and 30; 2002, fig. 5.6). When, why and how did this onomastic terminology develop? All this requires further investigation and thought, and will, one sincerely hopes, be both deconstructed and reconstructed by younger scholars with even more powerful tools at their disposal. Indeed, 'tools' are the name of the game. In the construction of national maps the author used the software program Freehand and an Ordnance Survey base map from 1922 on which a National Grid framework had been projected. While some of his maps are built from scratch, many sources have been borrowed and stolen – but always redrawn and always acknowledged – from work already published. There is both strength and weakness here: strength, because the convergence of data from many and varied sources is itself a powerful investigational tool, and weakness because when bringing distributions from several maps, constructed by several scholars working often several or even many decades apart, to a standard scale, the differences caused by small human errors in plotting, paper shrinkage, distortions caused by photography and projection and the like, often mean that individual boundaries and symbols which should coincide do not do so. None of this really affects the broad pattern seen on the page, but such maps cannot be used for rigorous point-by-point comparison, although experiment suggests that my own national maps are reasonably accurate to the level of a 10 x 10 km². Further, one is indeed well aware that many economic indicators vary on a north to south basis, latitudinal, as well as east to west or longitudinal, so that no single simple deterministic explanation needs to be, or indeed should be, sought. As any farmer knows, rural life and economy are never simple!

Figure 20 presents two maps of Yorkshire, using the software program Freehand to draw together a mass of data into one distribution. The problem of correlating two distributions is seen in the map of plan-regularity and the Domesday vills in the hands of Edward the Confessor and William the Conqueror. Given the small inaccuracies, it is impossible to be certain of the precise significance of the superimposition or near superimposition of symbols. Nevertheless, the map serves to raise important questions about the links between village plan forms and royal rural estates in 1086, with the most regular plans apparently being less prevalent on the royal estates. However, by superimposing the same village plan data over a map of medieval baronies, honours and liberties, more questions arise, questions that necessitate further focused inquiry (Middlebrook 1968, fig. facing 35; Sheppard 1974; 1976; Hallam 1986, 78–94). Thus the concentrations of regular plans in the Ainsty of York, the Honour of Knaresborough, the Honour of Richmond and the extreme west of the Honour of Langburgh demand investigation. The simple point is that maps are not an end-product of enquiry: they are tools, to be used to stimulate questions and steer the direction of future research.

Figure 21 uses a portion of a published map to fly another kite; it is taken directly from a national map of woodlands based on the work of Sir Clifford Darby and his co-workers and studies by many place-name scholars (Roberts and Wrathmell 2002, fig. 1.13). It shows, *inter alia*, two points of interest to the present argument: first, in County Durham (outlined), in a zone not covered by Domesday Book, place-names indicative of woodland suggest a wedge of such land, no doubt intermixed with open commons, extending across the eastern flank of the Pennines as far as the North Sea coast. This coastal termination is precisely where the twin monasteries of Jarrow and Monkwearmouth were located. In contrast, the superimposed darkly shaded zones suggest lowland areas where woodland was largely absent because they had already been

FIGURE 20.
Aspects of settlement in Yorkshire.

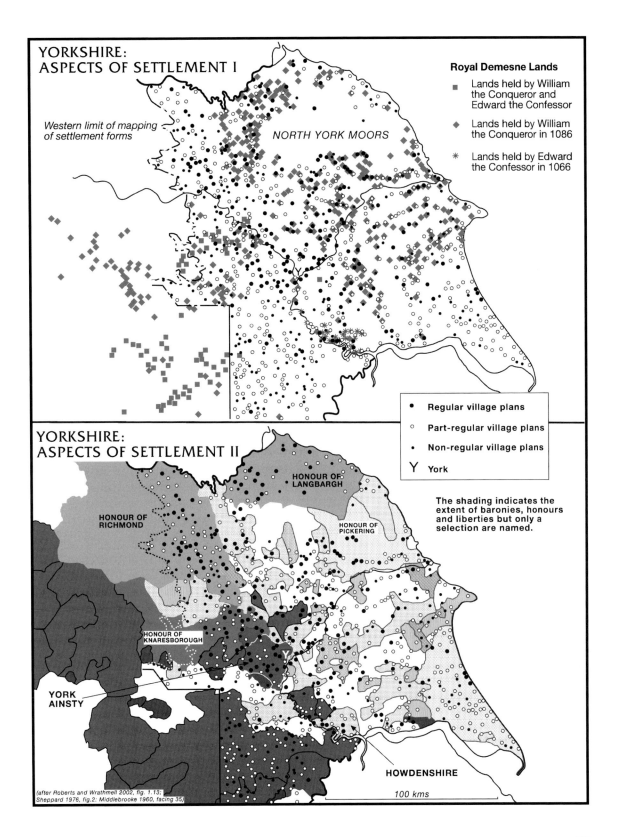

YORKSHIRE:
ASPECTS OF SETTLEMENT I

Western limit of mapping
of settlement forms

NORTH YORK MOORS

Royal Demesne Lands

■ Lands held by William
the Conqueror and
Edward the Confessor

◆ Lands held by William
the Conqueror in 1086

✳ Lands held by Edward
the Confessor in 1066

● Regular village plans

○ Part-regular village plans

• Non-regular village plans

Y York

YORKSHIRE:
ASPECTS OF SETTLEMENT II

HONOUR OF
LANGBARGH

HONOUR OF
RICHMOND

HONOUR OF
PICKERING

The shading indicates the
extent of baronies, honours
and liberties but only a
selection are named.

HONOUR OF
KNARESBOROUGH

YORK
AINSTY

HOWDENSHIRE

(after Roberts and Wrathmell 2002, fig. 1.13;
Sheppard 1976, fig.2: Middlebrooke 1960, facing 35)

100 kms

77

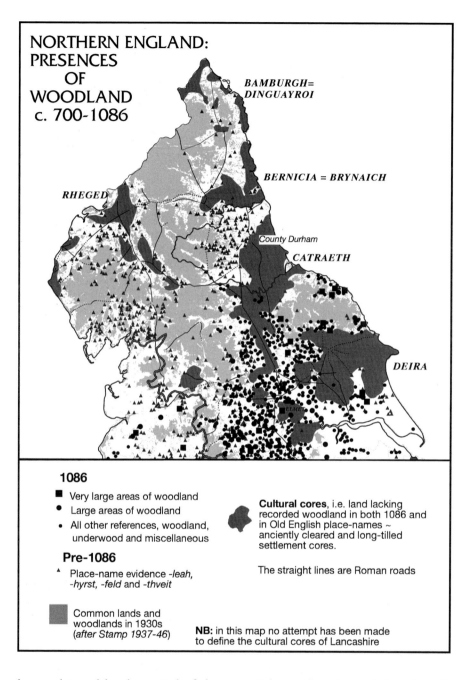

NORTHERN ENGLAND: PRESENCES OF WOODLAND c. 700-1086

BAMBURGH= DINGUAYROI

BERNICIA = BRYNAICH

RHEGED

County Durham

CATRAETH

DEIRA

1086

■ Very large areas of woodland

● Large areas of woodland

• All other references, woodland, underwood and miscellaneous

Pre-1086

▲ Place-name evidence -*leah*, -*hyrst*, -*feld* and -*thveit*

Common lands and woodlands in 1930s (*after Stamp 1937-46*)

Cultural cores, i.e. land lacking recorded woodland in both 1086 and in Old English place-names ~ anciently cleared and long-tilled settlement cores.

The straight lines are Roman roads

NB: in this map no attempt has been made to define the cultural cores of Lancashire

FIGURE 21.
Presences of woodland in pre-Conquest northern England, and core areas of countryside cleared before AD 700.

long-cultivated by the period of the map. It has to be admitted that there is subjectivity, speculation and even a degree of 'doodling' involved, but these territories do suggest the core zones of early polities, each separated by tracts of wood pasture and open pasture. There can be debate over the precise boundaries, but the visual, tangible qualities of this map, even in the face of variable data quality, encourages questions and hypotheses leading to further thought, enquiry and dispute (Higham 1986, fig. 6.3). In this matter, a comparison of

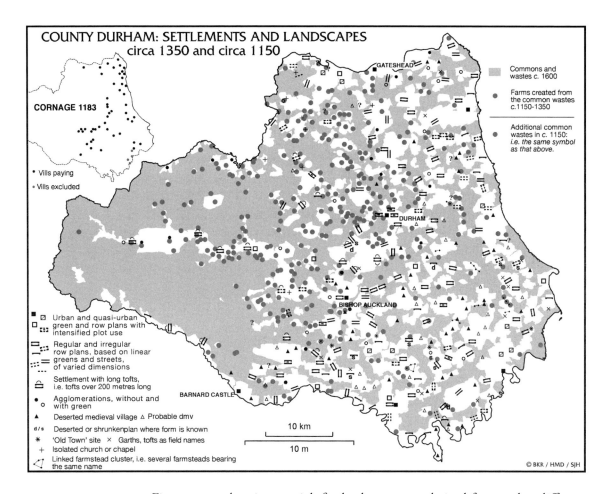

COUNTY DURHAM: SETTLEMENTS AND LANDSCAPES
circa 1350 and circa 1150

CORNAGE 1183

• Vills paying
• Vills excluded

Commons and wastes c. 1600

● Farms created from the common wastes c.1150-1350

● Additional common wastes in c. 1150: *i.e. the same symbol as that above.*

■ ☑ Urban and quasi-urban green and row plans with intensified plot use

⬓ ═ Regular and irregular row plans, based on linear greens and streets, of varied dimensions

⏣ Settlement with long tofts, i.e. tofts over 200 metres long

● Agglomerations, without and ○ with green

▲ Deserted medieval village △ Probable dmv

d / s Deserted or shrunkenplan where form is known

✳ 'Old Town' site ✕ Garths, tofts as field names

+ Isolated church or chapel

◁ Linked farmstead cluster, i.e. several farmsteads bearing the same name

10 km

10 m

© BKR / HMD / SJH

GATESHEAD

DURHAM

BISHOP AUCKLAND

BARNARD CASTLE

FIGURE 22.
County Durham:
settlements and
landscapes *c.*1150
and *c.*1350.

Figures 21 and 22 is essential, for both maps are derived from rather different sources and are presented at different scales.

Scale manipulation

The idea of scale manipulation defines a fundamental *leitmotiv* underlying this paper: not only are maps powerful tools of synoptic landscape analysis, they can also be used by bringing together varied scales of mapping to illuminate questions and formulate hypotheses. Thus, Figure 22 encapsulates in one map three fundamental layers.

First, precious evidence from coal-rich Durham in the form of mid-nineteenth-century regional landownership maps allows a relatively easy step towards the reconstruction of the common wastes in the earlier decades of the seventeenth century (Dunsford and Harris 2003). Thus, beginning by using nineteenth-century maps that record the former common wastes, Dunsford indirectly mapped the improved lands at that stage, no doubt with some errors, but we believe we have here at least 80 per cent accuracy. This stark map of commons, seen as the grey background shading in Figure 22, raises methodological issues. Whatsoever the difficulties of detail, by mapping and shading all commons, white areas then appeared which are the 'non-commons', namely the settled improved lands, with villages, hamlets, farmsteads, arable fields and meadows, involving both enclosed and unenclosed lands. This technique, which we can term positive and negative mapping, effectively involves a process of *tegulation*: thinking of the whole landscape as a complete and perfectly interlocking set of tiles. In this manner the spatial content of the whole land surface can be mapped, for gaps assume significance, and must be explored and explained. Of course, there will be errors; there will be voids that are at first inexplicable, but time and work can remove the most gross of these. As in science, experimental errors can be taken into account at the next level of investigation. Thus in Durham, the irregular bulge visible in the string of enclosures, or inby lands, running through the western centre of the county, in fact up Weardale, appears only because a decision was taken not to approximate the far earlier enclosures within the boundary of the bishops' great park. Earthworks are indeed known, but a continuous picture cannot be easily reconstructed. Similarly, further to the east in the dale, arable enclosures of later thirteenth-century date do exist and can, at least in part, be mapped and documented. Not present in this map, these would be included in a purely local study. Advances and retreats of the commons there may be, but rarely can such a synoptic picture as this have emerged from the 'bottom-up' record, although local studies and local detail will always qualify our understanding of the limits of accuracy of the synoptic map and encourage adjustments.

In order to create a second layer for this analysis, Simon Harris, working with Richard Britnell, laboured through 10,000 land charters and other documents to give us 'all possible' reclamations from the waste between 1150 and 1350 (Dunsford and Harris 2003). The round dots, deliberately shown only slightly darker than the background of commons, can be seen in two ways: either as single farmsteads present in 1350, and of these we know the precise area of one third and the assessed area of another third, while the remainder are merely names; or as former waste, that must be added to that seen on the underlay map (of about 1600) to provide a glimpse of the vast extent of the open commons of 1150.

The third and final layer in this case study involves placing on the map of commons the distribution of nucleated settlements, villages, hamlets and deserted settlements published many years ago by the author and based upon his own analysis of mid-nineteenth-century six-inch-to-the-mile Ordnance Survey maps. Effectively, these three layers blend together to encapsulate in a single distribution. First is a map of County Durham in about 1350, with villages and townfields, single farmsteads and wastes, and to see this we must picture each of the deep grey dots as a reclaimed farmstead. Second is a map of County Durham in about 1150, with villages, hamlets and a glimpse of the extremely extensive wastes of that period, and to see this, each dark grey dot must be pictured as the raw material from which the farms were carved, former common wastes.

If, over the county map, we superimpose a map of parishes and townships, then the county scale synoptic view becomes a distribution that can be related more closely to local detail, revealing such elements as the presence of communal townfields as well as the individual blocks that represent farms reclaimed from the waste between 1150 and 1350. This is a powerful tool for further enquiry. Furthermore, a comparison of the data on Figures 21 and 22 shows the way in which the detailed Durham mapping was foreshadowed by the map of place-name data used in the national and regional mapping. Once again, the data recorded in Figure 22 cannot be perfect, but we defy anyone to prove that it is wholly misleading. Using this detailed evidence, within Durham, a broad but important contrast is to be seen between the south and east and north and west, a contrast found in the Old English 'habitation' names of the former and the 'woodland' names of the latter, giving confidence in the more generalised national picture in Figure 21 (Watts 2002, xiv, xvi). The distribution of cornage (the inset map in Figure 22), an ancient form of cattle tribute, points towards even older layers of antecedent settlement and perhaps to renders made within a post-Roman north lacking coinage as a medium of exchange (Jolliffe 1926, *passim*; Higham 1986, fig. 6.3).

However, the Durham mapping is of a very different character to the Free-hand-based national work. Using the software ArcGIS, it builds upon the Ordnance Survey Old Series six-inch maps of the mid nineteenth century, and the screen image so created can be zoomed from a single field to the entire county and back again. Helen Dunsford's lovingly inserted lines, embracing parish and township boundaries, farm boundaries, landownership boundaries and head dykes, are so accurately placed that even at the closest level of resolution on a 1:10,560 map they can be trusted as a framework upon which to build further work. In fact we have barely begun to use this powerful tool which, in historical geographical terms, resembles an electron microscope! It is also an archival tool, for each and every item of data included is keyed into a spreadsheet so that a record of the evidence is directly attached to what appears on the map, and the material can thus be used, corrected and adapted within future research projects. As noted above, a key framework map, the backdrop to which all other work was eventually related, was a countywide and detailed map of parishes and townships, so that each parish, and more significantly each township, can be viewed within in its appropriate cultural geographical context.

To illustrate this important point, let us turn to one small local study: the small shire and ancient administrative territory of Heighington. The detail of Figure 23 was extracted from the county map and the analysis is based upon landscape evidence from the Boldon Book of 1183 and the Hatfield Survey of about 1381. Cutting an intricate story very short, at the junction of four small shires – Aucklandshire, Staindropshire, Gainford[shire] and Heighingtonshire – there lies a previously unnoticed cluster of very regular village plans. New-biggin, the 'new town near Thickley' in 1183 rendered one mark (13s 4d) and found 'twelve men one day or one man twelve days, to mow in autumn, and

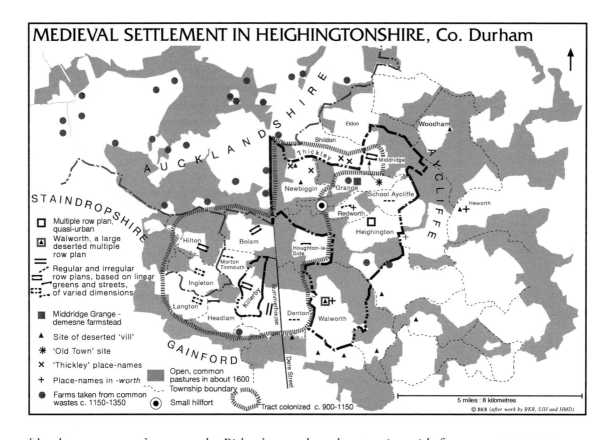

MEDIEVAL SETTLEMENT IN HEIGHINGTONSHIRE, Co. Durham

Legend:
- ▢ Multiple row plan, quasi-urban
- ▣ Walworth, a large deserted multiple row plan
- ═ ╍ Regular and irregular row plans, based on linear greens and streets, of varied dimensions
- ■ Middridge Grange - demesne farmstead
- ▲ Site of deserted 'vill'
- ✳ 'Old Town' site
- ✕ 'Thickley' place-names
- + Place-names in -*worth*
- ● Farms taken from common wastes c. 1150-1350
- ◉ Small hillfort
- ▨ Open, common pastures in about 1600
- ╌╌ Township boundary
- ⣿⣿ Tract colonized c. 900-1150

5 miles : 8 kilometres

© BKR (*after work by BKR, SJH and HMD*)

Map labels: AUCKLANDSHIRE, AYCLIFFE, STAINDROPSHIRE, GAINFORD, Eldon, Woodham, Shildon, Thickley, Middridge, Newbiggin, Grange, School Aycliffe, Heworth, Redworth, Heighington, Hilton, Bolam, Houghton-le-Side, Morton Tinmouth, Ingleton, Summerhouse, Langton, Killerby, Headlam, Denton, Walworth, Dere Street

FIGURE 23.
Medieval settlement
in Heighingtonshire,
County Durham.

[the drengage tenant] goes on the Bishop's errands and carts wine with four oxen'. The dreng – a ministerial tenant – holding this land, Guy de Redworth, had already mentored a new plantation at Redworth itself. This involved 'sixteen *firmars*' – rent-paying tenants – each holding sixteen oxgangs, a tenemental regularity that may have been paralleled in plan regularity, although this cannot be proved in this case because of the later remodelling of the village to empark the great house. These two villages appear to derive from the colonisation of an area of waste and surviving woodland, peripheral to the shire core, a process ending in the later twelfth century but beginning as early as the tenth century. The rent demanded from Newbiggin allowed for either success or failure; indeed, the venture was not a success, for no village appeared. While Thickley itself speaks of a thick wood containing the new buildings to be established at Newbiggin, further to the south-west the place-names Headlam and Morton tell of heath and moor, Bolam of tree stumps, Summerhouse of summer pastures, and Langton, Houghton and Hilton of settlement on hillslopes, spurs and ridges. There is little Scandinavian influence here, although Ingleton and Killerby may contain Scandinavian personal names (Watts 2002, 66, 68). The territory of Heighington 'small shire' was, in the later decades of the twelfth century, still rendering food rents in the form of malt, meal, oats and hens, together with carting, mowing, harrowing and ploughing duties, and the cutting of loads of wood. In addition there was the payment of a milch cow and the render of cornage, indicating that the roots of the 'shire' must lie in a past already distant by 1183. Indeed, a small hill-fort, of uncertain date but of 'Iron Age' form, hints at the long usage of this countryside as cattle pasturage, while the survival of those 'foreign' to Old English settlers is attested by 'Walworth', the 'enclosure of the Welsh' (Watts 2002, 131–2; NZ 229233; NZ 233192). This depopulated village is one of the most enigmatic settlements in the county, the site bearing remarkably clear traces of a large multiple-row plan, almost of urban proportions, although it is not documented.

The maps of County Durham are replete with such micro-potential, but Heighingtonshire exemplifies an important methodology. To undertake this level of analysis a portion of the countywide positive mapping of the commons has been merely cut from the whole. The content of the remaining negative spaces was then realised by pulling in the villages, deserted villages and the few pre-1350 single farms documented in this zone (in contrast to the large number in Aucklandshire, to the north-west), and adding further local detail. The pattern can then be interpreted by recourse to more detailed documentary evidence. Much more analysis is, of course, possible; thus the transplantation of an older settlement from the ridge at Middridge to a new site on the former common lands of the plateau to the north, a regular two-row green plan, probably took place in the twelfth century to create a consolidated demesne at Middridge Grange. Both Redworth and Newbiggin represent new plantations made at about the same time – in the middle decades of the twelfth century – although Redworth is an Old English place-name and there may have been earlier settlement in the locality. In this analysis of the tegulation of the land surface, even the area of the planted single farmstead on former waste to the south of Heighington village becomes visible and noteworthy.

These maps, national, regional, local and parochial, taken together, where national maps inform local maps and *vice versa*, provide a glimpse of what is now possible using existing technologies. They are, in effect, the same maps seen in different ways. Positive and negative mapping, and the mode of thought it generates by adopting a countywide synoptic or 'top-down' approach, represents an important foundation technique. The experimental work done by Stuart Wrathmell and myself indicates what is now feasible at a national scale. To progress further in understanding the historic landscape we must now create a soundly based national and county-scale system of standardised recording, based upon simple and nationally agreed criteria. The maps presented here do show what is possible and work by Steven Warnock, Geoffrey Griffiths, Jane Corbett, Steve Potter and Jonathan Porter within the *Living Landscapes Project* at the University of Reading gives substance to this potential (Warnock 2002). By adopting standardised foundation criteria, landscape characterisation for Kent can be comparable with Yorkshire and that for Cornwall with Cumbria, in spite of significant detailed differences. Then the many complexities, the wonderful detail, and the increasingly inventive techniques of much local work can be informed by an agreed synoptic framework that places new demands upon new local studies. While many counties and local projects are working in this direction, there remains an unacceptable lack of a sound but flexible computer-based national system. Not to formulate and develop this is nonsense: now that the Ordnance Survey first edition six-inch maps are available via *Edina*, a University-based access procedure, there is a serious challenge here to all national bodies monitoring and nurturing the historic and prehistoric past and the management of historic landscapes. It is, and I stress this point, axiomatic that local detail serves to test, to modify, to criticise and to support the panorama derived from top-down nationally based synoptic images. The scale-manipulation of historical, and for that matter prehistoric, datasets within soundly based geographical information systems provides powerful tools for new research. In the few illustrative maps used in this discussion, deliberately pared to a bare minimum, what we see are old maps added to new materials and new maps developed from the content of older maps archived for future use in computers. None is wholly definitive: all ask questions.

Above all, national and regional synoptic views offer to landscape studies the possibility of a scientific approach and appropriate national action in this direction would build for younger, oncoming, scholars – now our most precious resource – the possibility of moving quickly to greater depths of investigation, depths we cannot yet envisage. This would be a magnificent monument to Hoskins, and the greatest compliment to Thirsk, a successor at Leicester, who has herself done so much to give a spatial understanding to agrarian history.

Village chronology and causes

In spite of its title this paper has not presented new arguments for the chronology and causes of villages and indeed no short contribution could readily do this. Figure 24 is what the economic historian Snooks terms an 'existential model'; that is to say, an empirical model of reality, to be contrasted with the logical or deductive models of physics and economics, which are merely constructs of the mind. Snooks suggests that existential models 'based upon dynamic timescapes … set free the imagination to range over the actual patterns of existence … and … in these patterns we can see the dynamic processes of reality' (Snooks 1996, 433–4, 440). It does no injustice to Snooks' views to see all of the present author's many settlement models, and indeed all the maps seen in the figures of this paper, as expressing 'dynamic timescapes', 'actual patterns of existence' and 'the dynamic processes of reality'. All are designed to feed the imagination; they ask questions and allow simple but testable hypotheses to be formulated and evaluated. The content of Figure 24 needs a book-length analysis, but is an attempt to 'visualise' what the author thinks he sees and knows of northern planned villages in a time-space matrix. 'Thinks he sees and knows' is a deliberate qualification because, as was once remarked, 'facts are like cows, they go away if you stare at them'.

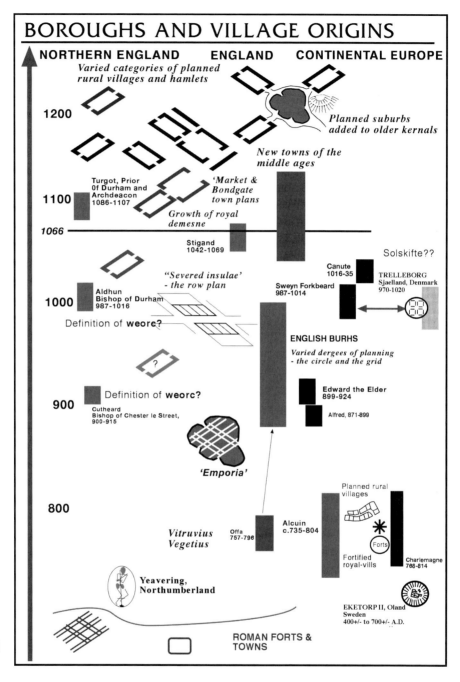

FIGURE 24.
A schematic model exploring the origins of planned villages and hamlets.

The existence of planned villages and planned towns by the later eleventh and twelfth century is now well attested (Taylor 1983, 125–50; Roberts 1987, 33–62, 196–205; Beresford 1967) and there are increasing indications of pre-Conquest origins for planned villages, although this is not yet 'proven' beyond all doubt. Overall, planned villages and hamlets must derive from a milieu in which boroughs and forts were already being planned, and we

can postulate that both planned and unplanned entities developed concur-
rently in the centuries before the Norman Conquest. There was no uniform
or simple pattern of activity. The map of Yorkshire seen in Figure 20 is a
pointer towards the difficulties involved in the next stage of analysis. It seems
likely, indeed probable, that the classic regular two-row plans, comprising
two compartments, each subdivided into a series of tofts and separated by
a street, street-green or broad green, represent two half-*insulae*; that is, the
blocks or checkers of an urban plan-form. Figure 24, a challenging but fragmented model, has to be thought of as a matrix, a textured warp and woof,
in which only limited parts of the overall pattern are picked out. More can
be added. To introduce a social dimension, in the period between the sixth
and the eleventh century we are, *inter alia*, seeing a transition from kin-based
communities, often served by household slaves, to communities containing
varied categories of tenant. In Durham it appears to the author that the
definition of *weorc*, as exemplified in the phrase 'and they work as they of
Boldon' suggests tenth- or even ninth-century roots for the appearance of
regular rural tenements and formalised services. The countywide patterns
of tenurial and fiscal regularity so established were probably focused within
planned rural settlements from the time they were defined. Further, in the
north of England generally important questions must be raised by the careful
measurement of the great seventh-century hall at Yeavering, with the grave of
its possible gate-ward and putative surveyor set in the entrance (Hope-Taylor
1977, fig. 25, 200–3).

As Lang and many others have shown, the Northumbria of the Lindisfarne
Gospels and Alcuin was intellectually linked to the wider worlds of continental Europe and the Mediterranean (Lang 2000, 109–19). It can hardly
be accidental that planned villages are known in the Carolingian empire,
used as a means of extending royal control over territories from which tribute was to be levied (Nitz 1988a, 249–73). The sculpture of Giselbertus and
his contemporaries and successors in Burgundy, that great corridor between
north and south, appeared in a world in which surviving examples of Roman
constructions, literature and travelling churchmen and missionaries helped
build crucial bridges: links between Roman antecedents, the Carolingian
world, and the North Sea lands (Armi 1983, 109–14; Fletcher 1997). In effect,
planned villages may be as Romanesque as the rounded arch and groined
or ribbed vaults, and in their spread we can postulate strong parallels with
the diffusion of architectural and artistic concepts. Charlemagne, writing to
Paul the Deacon at Monte Cassino, creates a marvellous image of transit
and transmission:

> Across the hills and through the valley's shade,
> Alone the small script goes,
> Seeking for Benedict's beloved roof,
> Where waits its sure repose. (Waddell 1982, 141)

Envoi

To conclude, any spatial and environmental understanding of the past must juggle four sets of interwoven conditions:

first, *conditions of antecedence*, for what came before always frames what comes later, and there are few if any new beginnings;

second, *conditions of change*, such as the advent of new skills, new people, new plagues, new weather, all affecting the use of space;

third, *conditions of stability*, for it should never be forgotten that there was a fundamental need for continuity in farming life involving the sustaining of agricultural production and soil fertility. Failure to do this resulted in serious social and economic dislocation. Further, sustaining rural stability is, paradoxically, a wholly dynamic process.

Finally, *conditions of contingency*, linkages, sometimes deliberate, sometimes fortuitous, between natural environments and human activities and events and between cultural developments within both adjacent and more distant areas.

All settlement evolved within a vast and intricate time-space matrix in which physical factors, latitude and terrain, climate, soils, flora and fauna and all medieval settlements, towns, villages, hamlets, single farmsteads and upland shielings, responded to these variables, but also to antecedent cultural land-scape patterns that had already been established. Thus all northern English developments must be set not only amid the varied constraints of the environment, but also amid the prior extent of clearance and cultivation, the political indeterminacies of Viking activities, the substantial southern contacts and political duplicities of the Cuthbertine community of Durham, the local power of the pre-Conquest archbishops of York and the appearance of repeated, indeed sustained local devastations. Perhaps most important of all, there was an extension of pre-Conquest and post-Conquest royal power and control over a fought-over region whose landed wealth comprised long-cultivated arable cores and extensive wood pastures, all set within vast cattle-productive savanna-like open pastures and wolf-haunted inhospitable uplands. From this agricultural base came the wealth to feed and support the lifestyles of those who prayed and those who fought, for goldwork and other metalwork, for brooches, weapons, relics and liturgical vestments, and for fine books and great buildings. Of course, the eventual establishment of post-Conquest feudalism drew anciently productive territorial frameworks, concerned with food, work renders and tribute, into a new dynamism of baronies, honours, liberties, estates, fees and rural production systems that were described in Walter of Henley's textbook on estate management. Hamlets and villages appeared as one means of organising and exploiting communities of tenant farmers who were essentially, if not absolutely, bound to grain-producing soils. In spite of culturally imposed timescales of centuries and developmental phases, reality was always a seamless robe of dynamic timescapes and landscapes. In this matter, cartographic and regional analyses are powerful research tools.

Acknowledgements

Here it is fitting that great debts should be acknowledged: to English Heritage for its funding support and the input of David Stocker; to Stuart Wrathmell, my archaeological counterpoise; to Helen Dunsford, Simon Harris and Richard Britnell, partners in an AHRC-funded project, the results of which have been so prolific that they still defy short-term digestion. I am grateful to them all.

CHAPTER SEVEN

The Distribution of 'Woodland' and 'Champion' Landscapes in Medieval England

Tom Williamson

Introduction: 'woodland' and 'champion'

Landscape historians have long debated about why it was that medieval farmers in a broad band of central England, running from Yorkshire in the north to the chalklands of southern England, organised their agriculture on more cooperative lines than their fellows to the south-east or south-west, and generally lived in nucleated villages, rather than in scattered farms and hamlets. This was the region which Gray (1915), at the start of the twentieth century, recognised as the heartland of his 'Midland System' (Figure 25(a)). In most vills, the holdings of cultivators were distributed fairly evenly across two or three great fields, one of which lay fallow each year. Even the demesne usually lay in strips, intermingled with the lands of the tenants, and farming was, in general, organised on highly communal lines (Gray 1915). The same broad region appears in the maps of nineteenth-century rural settlement produced by Roberts and Wrathmell (2000; 2002). There are, it is true, some differences in detail, especially towards the west, but once again the Midlands and the North East stand out as areas of predominantly nucleated settlement, as do the chalklands of southern England – including in this case the North as well as the South Downs (Roberts and Wrathmell 2000). The distribution of Rackham's 'planned', as opposed to 'ancient', countryside is closely comparable (Figure 25(b)), which is hardly surprising as it represents the landscapes created by the late enclosure of the former champion lands (Rackham 1976, 17).

Settlement outside this belt of 'champion' countryside was more dispersed in character during the Middle Ages, sometimes lacking large nucleated villages altogether, and both woods and common pastures were generally more extensive (Figure 25(c)). But while some of these districts seem to have been characterised by enclosed fields from an early date, and in many of them the demesne land took the form of discrete blocks, open-field systems of a kind usually existed and often covered the majority of the cultivated area. Such

a)

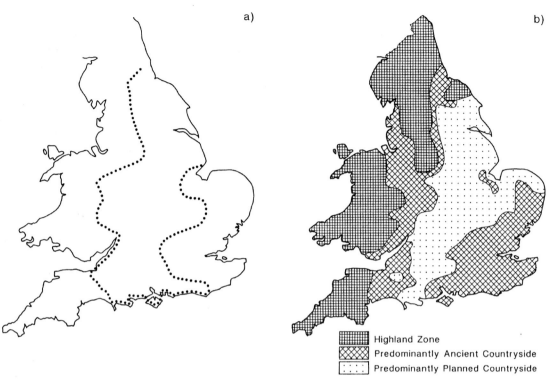

b)

Highland Zone
Predominantly Ancient Countryside
Predominantly Planned Countryside

c)

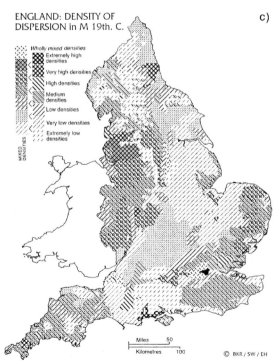

ENGLAND: DENSITY OF
DISPERSION in M 19th. C.

Wholly mixed densities
Extremely high densities
Very high densities
High densities
Medium densities
Low densities
Very low densities
Extremely low densities

MIXED DENSITIES

Miles   50
Kilometres   100

© BKR / SW / EH

open fields were, however, of 'irregular' form: holdings were clustered close to the farmstead, the fields themselves were often multiple and complex in character and – in some areas – communal controls over the organisation of cropping, and other aspect of farming, were less pervasive than in champion districts (Baker 1973, 396–7; Roden 1973; Williamson 2003, 91–122). Such field systems were particularly susceptible to piecemeal enclosure, which proceeded apace from the later fourteenth century. By the start of the seventeenth century the distinction between the open, champion lands and the enclosed and bosky 'woodland' countryside was probably sharper than it had ever been.

Explaining regional variation

In the first half of the twentieth century historians like Gray (1915) and Homans (1953) attributed these important variations in the medieval landscape to patterns of early medieval ethnic settlement, but since the 1960s most scholars have explained them in social and economic terms. The arguments advanced by Thirsk in the 1960s have been particularly influential (Thirsk 1964). She suggested that in districts which came to be characterised by champion landscapes, demographic growth led first to the progressive disintegration of holdings into strips, principally through partible inheritance, and then to a serious shortage of grazing. As pastures dwindled, farmers were obliged to make more intensive use of the marginal grazing afforded by the aftermath of the harvest, and by the fallows: but where arable lands lay intermingled, in unhedged strips, it was difficult or impossible to utilise these resources efficiently unless neighbouring cultivators timed their operations in concert. Cultivators were thus drawn inexorably into increased levels of cooperation, culminating in the institution of a continuous fallowing sector which occupied a half, or a third, of the land of the village. Numerous subsequent commentators have developed this model further, most notably Dyer and his associates. As population rose, as holdings became subdivided and intermixed, and as common pastures contracted, recurrent disputes arose among peasant cultivators:

> A peaceful option for a long-term resolution of their difficulties involved the inhabitants reorganising their numerous farms and hamlets into common fields where the problems of competition would be minimised. The animals of the whole community were pastured together on the land which lay fallow or awaited spring cultivation. (Lewis *et al.* 1997, 199)

These new forms of agrarian organisation 'probably spread by emulation' to all areas, other than those in which population levels were low and reserves of pasture still extensive. Here the older pattern of dispersed farms and hamlets, enclosures, and irregular field systems survived. Champion landscapes had developed in many areas by the time of the Norman Conquest, although in some places their appearance was delayed until the twelfth or even the thirteenth century (Lewis *et al.* 1997, 199–200; and see Rippon, this volume).

FIGURE 25.
Regional variations in the medieval landscape were first mapped in 1915 by Gray (a); the central areas of England were characterised by nucleated villages farming two or three extensive open fields. Because a high proportion of the latter survived into the post-medieval period, the same broad pattern is picked out by Rackham's 'Planned Countryside' of late, rectilinear, planned enclosure (b). In the nineteenth century, and even today, this broad zone is characterised by a more nucleated pattern of settlement than the districts to either side, as shown in this map by Roberts and Wrathmell (c) (sources: (a) Gray 1915, fig. 1; (b) Rackham 1976, fig. 1; (c) Roberts and Wrathmell 2002, fig. 1.3).

To Roberts and Wrathmell the champion landscape of the Midlands – the 'Central Province' – was similarly the core area of Saxon settlement, and woodland districts in contrast were ones of relatively 'late' clearance (Roberts and Wrathmell 2000). Roberts has, perhaps more clearly than other writers, explained the link between late colonisation and individual colonisation. Before the twelfth century the expansion of cultivation had normally added new furlongs to the village fields, but legal and tenurial changes of the twelfth and early thirteenth centuries, culminating in 1236 with the Statute of Merton, meant that the manorial waste was increasingly seen as the property of its lord, who could grant it in the form of ring-fence farms for rents assessed outside the traditional fiscal framework of the vill. In Roberts's words, 'the rise of the doctrine of the lord's ownership of the waste during the twelfth and thirteenth centuries, and the provision of defence against *Novel Disseisin* by the Statute of Merton ... are key factors in explaining the swing to individual colonisation and emphasis on personal rather than communal rights' (Roberts 1973, 229).

But some historians have queried whether regional variations in the medieval landscape can be attributed quite so directly to differences in demographic pressure and the chronology of clearance and settlement. Taylor (2002, 53–4), for example, has recently argued that nucleated villages and cooperative farming systems were simply a 'fashion' which began perhaps in the East Midlands and spread outwards, before fading out at essentially arbitrary boundaries. Others have emphasised the importance of social and, in particular, tenurial factors in the adoption of the new modes of farming and settlement. Campbell (1981, 119), for example, questioned whether 'the co-ordination and systematisation of common fields progressed quite as smoothly, and were quite so directly related to population growth, as the Thirsk model postulates'. The changes in landholding necessary to transform 'irregular' to 'regular' field systems could only have been carried out by manorial lords: 'strong and undivided lordship would have been most favourable to the functional development of the common field system' (Campbell 1981, 127). The emergence of the Midland system would thus be associated with the development, in the course of the Saxon period, of local territorial lordship, as described by historians like Faith (1997).

Problems with current models

These current approaches share a number of problems. The first is a failure to examine medieval field systems in terms of agricultural practice – something which may strike readers who are new to these debates as rather odd, given what fields were for and what most inhabitants of the medieval countryside actually did in them. Not that an agricultural perspective has been entirely absent – in the early part of the twentieth century the Orwins emphasised the importance of joint ploughing, or 'co-aration', in the development of the open fields and, indeed, the more general necessity for close cooperation amongst farmers living in an insecure environment (Orwin and Orwin 1938, 37–44; Seebohm (1890) had earlier made similar suggestions). Nucleated villages simply made it easier for farmers to share implements and cooperate more generally. More recently, Eric Kerridge has described the agricultural logic of open-field systems, albeit concentrating on those found within a relatively limited range of soil types (Kerridge 1992). Agrarian approaches to the medieval landscape have thus always existed, but in recent years especially they have generally been marginalised from the main arenas of academic debate.

The second problem is a failure to deal with – or even engage with – the issue of the actual configuration of the champion belt: to ascertain what features of the social or natural environment it corresponds or fails to correspond with. The suggestion that 'champion' landscapes were areas of highest population density is thus endlessly repeated. Yet it is completely unsupported by the only demographic data for the later Saxon period which we possess – Domesday Book – which suggests, if anything, that 'woodland' districts in general carried the densest populations (Figure 26). It might be argued that the essential distinction between woodland and champion first arose earlier, perhaps in the eighth or ninth centuries, when the distribution of population was different: but given that the Domesday pattern is perfectly explicable in terms of climatic and other environmental factors, such a suggestion is hard to sustain (Williamson 2003, 32–5). At times the argument verges on the circular: champion districts must have been the most densely populated, because high population densities lead to the development of champion landscapes. The evidence from archaeological surveys reveals no consistent pattern in this respect. Some 'woodland' districts do indeed seem to have been sparsely settled in middle and late Saxon times (Dyer 1991), but by no means all. In purely archaeological terms, the development of settlement in 'woodland' East

FIGURE 26.
The distribution of
Domesday population
(left) and free tenures
(right), as mapped
by Darby (1977, figs
19 and 35). Neither
map displays much
similarity with the
distributions shown in
Figure 25.

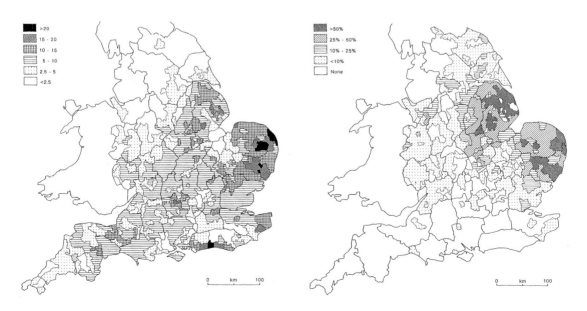

93

Anglia, and in the champion Midlands, for example, seems virtually indistinguishable. In both, the scattered and shifting settlement pattern of the fifth, sixth and seventh centuries began to stabilise in the eighth, usually beside sites now occupied by parish churches, and nucleated villages developed, a process which continued into the ninth and tenth centuries. Thereafter the two regions diverged. In the Midlands an essentially nucleated settlement pattern was perpetuated into post-medieval times: but in East Anglia, from the later tenth or the eleventh century, farms migrated away from older sites, mainly to form garlands of settlement around greens and commons (Brown and Foard 1998; Davison 1990; Hall 1982; Rogerson 1995; Wade-Martins 1980b; Warner 1987).

Tenurial factors, likewise, correspond poorly with the woodland/champion divide. *Domesday* and other sources suggest that both types of landscape could be found in areas of tenurial complexity, with a high density of free tenures and multi-manorial vills (Figure 26). And if nucleation and regular open fields were really a 'fashion' which gradually diffused from some unknown point

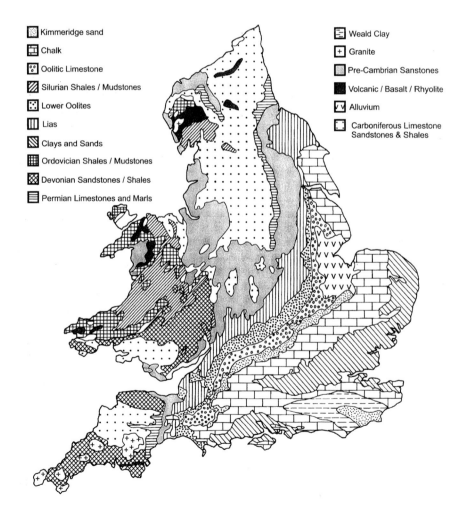

Kimmeridge sand
Chalk
Oolitic Limestone
Silurian Shales / Mudstones
Lower Oolites
Lias
Clays and Sands
Ordovician Shales / Mudstones
Devonian Sandstones / Shales
Permian Limestones and Marls

Weald Clay
Granite
Pre-Cambrian Sanstones
Volcanic / Basalt / Rhyolite
Alluvium
Carboniferous Limestone Sandstones & Shales

FIGURE 27.
The solid geology of England and Wales. Note the general similarity between the broad configuration of formations and the distributions mapped in Figure 25 (source: British Geological Survey).

of origin, like ripples in a pond, why did their resultant distribution take the shape that it did, rather than something more compact and perhaps more circular in form?

This brings us to the most obvious, yet most blatantly ignored, feature of the various distributions mapped in Figure 25. The champion belt strikingly replicates the main features of the solid geology of lowland England, notably the succession of dips and scarps which swing gently across the country from north-east to south-west, only patchily covered by later glacial drift. Its southern and eastern boundary thus corresponds with the chalk escarpment of the Chilterns and its continuations; its central area with the succession of uplands and lowlands formed in older rocks – lower Greensand, Wealden clays, Middle and Upper Oolite, the Lower Oolite of the Cotswolds and, lastly, the Lias lowlands beyond them (Figure 27). One would have thought that such a correspondence would have cried out for some consideration of the environmental and agrarian factors which might have encouraged farmers in this broad tract of England to dwell in nucleated villages, and to farm their land, to varying degrees, along cooperative lines.

The sheep–corn lands

'Champion' is a problematic term, for it embraces a number of distinct landscapes. In particular, it is important to distinguish here between the open-field systems of the light lands – the wolds, downs and heaths – and those found in the clay vales. The arable lands of the latter, by the thirteenth century, generally ran all the way to the township boundaries (Hall 1995, 2). There was little woodland or pasture: these were landscapes of unrelieved arable. On the light lands, in contrast, there were often extensive areas of grazing, in the form of chalk grassland, heath or other pasture, beyond the open fields. In part this was because such land was so marginal it was not worth cultivating, but it also reflected the low fertility of the light soils more generally, which were easily leached of nutrients and in need of regular, intensive manuring. Flocks of sheep, grazed by day on the pastures (and on the fallow weeds and harvest residues), were close-folded on the arable by night in order to dung the land (Kerridge 1967, 42–51).

Geographers have long emphasised the physical constraints on the distribution of settlement in such districts. Reliable supplies of running water and good meadowland were limited to major valleys, spring lines and adjoining deposits of clay. By medieval times, at least, the broad sweeps of open chalk, limestone or sand were devoid of farms. This pattern, always present to some extent, seems to have intensified from the seventh century (Cunliffe 1972; Davison 1994; Rogerson 1995), and what Cunliffe wrote of the chalklands of the Chalton area in Hampshire in 1972 is true of many similar districts:

> The hill-top settlements belonging to the period between the fifth and the eighth centuries contrast dramatically with what we have come to accept

as the typical valley pattern of Domesday England: evidently a significant shift of settlement took place during the last quarter of the first millennium AD. (Cunliffe 1972, 5)

It is possible that this development was connected with the adoption of larger ploughs, pulled by larger teams of oxen, which needed to be adequately fed and watered; and these were certainly in widespread use by the eleventh century (Langdon 1986). Either way, as population grew loose clusters of farms developed in well-watered locations, and in the period between the ninth and twelfth centuries compact nucleations emerged, sometimes, as in parts of south Cambridgeshire, through the infilling of areas of damp commons which had originally formed the foci for settlement (Oosthuizen 1994).

Where settlements were forced to cluster in such ways any equitable division of land – whether holdings were being divided through partible inheritance, or allocated to bond tenants – could hardly take the form of enclosed and discrete blocks. The land lying close to the settlement was generally of higher value and fertility than that at a distance. This was partly because in many of these districts the land on the lower ground was naturally more fertile than the thinner and often more acid soils on the intervening uplands, and partly because the nearer land had, over the decades, received more farmyard manure than that located at a distance (something attested, for the medieval period at least, by the distribution of pottery sherds recovered by fieldwalking surveys: for example, Rogerson 1997, 26–7). More importantly, the land nearest the settlement could be reached more quickly than that lying at a distance, something which might be of critical importance at harvest time. A pattern of intermixed holdings, in the form of conveniently ploughable strips, would have been further extended as cultivation expanded. Farmers who had formerly grazed an area of heath or downland in common, and who worked together to convert it to arable, would naturally have divided it between them equitably in the form of strips (Bishop 1935).

The development of landscapes of intermixed holdings, cultivated from clusters of farmsteads, would inevitably have necessitated some degree of communal organisation of agriculture. As already noted, the heaths and downs functioned, in effect, as nutrient reservoirs, essential for keeping the light, easily leached soils in cultivation (Kerridge 1967, 42–5; 1992, 74–86). The most efficient way of manuring was to pen sheep tightly together each night in movable folds – a difficult procedure, had each cultivator been obliged to move his own small flock every day from the open pastures to a fold erected on one of his scattered strips. In addition, as Kerridge astutely commented, the farmer would also have had 'all the lambing and shearing to attend to. All this would have preoccupied him to such an extent as to leave him little time for growing cereals' (Kerridge 1992, 26). Common flocks under the control of communal shepherds were the solution (Kerridge 1992, 27), leading in turn to the adoption of various forms of communal crop rotation in order to create continuous blocks of strips under the same 'season', which could be conveniently grazed or folded in turn. Any fences or hedges that had existed were gradually neglected or removed, as the small size and large number of individual strips in a holding made these uneconomic to maintain, and grossly inconvenient for the ploughman and his team, as well as an interference to the movement of the folding flocks. Not all light land areas necessarily developed along this kind of path with the same speed: and in different districts, particular environmental and social circumstances ensured numerous variations on these broad themes. But on all light land, from the Cotswolds in the west to Breckland in the east, from the South Downs to the Yorkshire Wolds, some form of open, champion landscape had emerged, or was emerging, by the time of the Norman Conquest.

Farming the clays

This model, which I have adapted from that originally elaborated by Kerridge, has a certain appealing logic, and seems to be supported by the available archaeological and documentary evidence. But it can only explain the development of open-field landscapes in a relatively limited part of the champion belt: on its shores and islands, as it were, and to some extent within its extensions, such as the South Downs (Figure 28). In the clayland 'core' of the Midlands, where open fields were most extensive and settlement patterns most strongly nucleated, little of this argument can apply. Here there were usually far fewer constraints on the location of settlement, so that the equitable allocation of lands, or progressive division of properties, could easily have led to the spread of farms across the landscape, each set within their own ring-fence holdings. Moreover, such land was less easily leached of nutrients than the chalks and sands. Close folding was thus much less necessary, and in many cases impossible for much of the year. On these damp soils, sheep were prone to foot-rot during the winter months, and could puddle and compact the soils, so that in many Midland townships folding was restricted to the late summer and early autumn (Kerridge 1992, 77–9). The development of champion landscapes on the Midland clays was evidently the outcome of a different set of factors.

To understand what these might have been, it is necessary to describe briefly the problems which medieval farmers faced in the cultivation of the clays. Most clay soils (but not all) are more fertile than those formed in sands and chalk, and in historic times have generally turned in higher cereal yields. Where rainfall levels were high, however – above *c.*740 mm per annum – clay soils were normally leached of nutrients and lime and carried low population densities at the time of Domesday. Some clay soils in the drier east were likewise lime-deficient because of the mineral character of such parent materials as the London Clay or the Clay-with-Flints – most notably, the soils of the Hornbeam, Windsor, Batcombe and Essendon Associations (Hodge *et al.* 1984; Ragg *et al.* 1984). All these area of leached, lime-deficient clay soils were characterised in medieval times by a paucity of large villages, and by scattered farms and small hamlets, many of which were – as in the traditional interpretation of such landscapes – the result of relatively late and individualistic colonisation.

The majority of clay soils were, however, at least moderately fertile – especially those found across the Midlands, in East Anglia and much of Essex and Hertfordshire, in parts of Herefordshire and Shropshire, and in the North East. They normally carried relatively high population densities at the time of Domesday. But they needed to be farmed with care. In particular, they required systematic drainage, using ridge and furrow or some other method. In the parlance of post-medieval farmers, waterlogged land was 'cold' land, which warmed up only slowly in the spring, delaying germination and thus reducing yields (Robinson 1949, 36–7). Furthermore, waterlogged crops do not absorb nutrients well, and their root structure is poorly developed. Better drainage – somewhat paradoxically – actually increases the amount of water

FIGURE 28. Environmental factors in the distribution of 'champion' countryside: soils. (1) areas of light, sheep-corn land with limited water supplies and soils requiring regular folding. (2) areas of moderately fertile or fertile clay soil, prone to puddling and compaction and with restricted opportunities for spring cultivation (principally those of the Denchworth, Ragdale, Dunkeswick, Foggathorpe and Clifton Associations). This excludes areas of similar but less fertile, more acidic soils (such as those of the Essendon Association), and districts with more than 740 mm rainfall per annum, both of which carried low population densities in the early Middle Ages (source: Soil Survey maps of England and Wales, *Soils of Eastern England* (1984); *Soils of Southern England* (1984); *Soils of Midland and Western England* (1984); *Soils of Northern England* (1984)).

which can be taken up by the plant during the summer months, because the roots can derive moisture from a greater depth (Robinson 1949, 37).

But in addition to the problems caused by a high winter water table, clay soils are prone to puddle when wet; that is, to form a sticky mess which adheres to ploughs, harrows and other implements, and which then dries hard and brick-like. This is not merely an inconvenience to the farmer. If land is badly compacted, cereals can actually die in the seedling stage, and certainly grow slowly and produce low yields (Seymour 1996, 14–16). The aim of clay-land farmers was, and is, to encourage flocculation: to get the microscopic particles of clay to coalesce together in larger grains. Incorporating humus and lime, improving drainage, and exposing the soil to frost all encourage this process, but above all, farmers must simply try to avoid working such soils when they are wet, something which is often difficult in the spring, after long months of heavy rainfall.

All clay soils are to some extent prone to puddling but two broad types are particularly vulnerable in this respect, and need to be farmed with special care. These are the less calcareous pelosols, and the pelo-stagnogleys, soils which are clayey or silty in their upper horizons – especially those falling within the Ragdale, Denchworth, Dunkeswick and Clifton Associations (Hodge *et al.* 1984; Jarvis *et al.* 1984; Ragg *et al.* 1984). Even with modern drainage methods, cultivating such soils when wet can lead to severe problems. In the case of the Ragdale soils, for example:

> When cultivations are carried out under wet conditions, the resulting structural damage reduces the already low porosity and causes prolonged waterlogging, often to the soil surface, and the death or retardation of seedlings due to lack of oxygen. (Hodge *et al.* 1984, 295)

Problems with puddling are, in contrast, rather less serious with non-pelo-stagnogley soils, which have sandy or loamy upper horizons, such as those of the Beccles and Burlingham Associations; and with the more calcareous of the pelosols, such as those of the Hanslope Association, especially where these occur in the drier east of England. The distinction between these two broad types of soil was evidently an important one in terms of early medieval settlement and farming, for it is clear that champion countrysides were found in those reasonably populous areas in which a high proportion of the soils take the form of pelo-stagnogleys or the less calcareous pelosols. Soils of these kinds are concentrated in the Midland belt, in part because many are derived from fine-grained Jurassic clays, in part because of the particular nature of the glacial drift in this region, and in part for climatic reasons (Figure 28). Conversely, those areas of modest or high medieval population density which are dominated by non-pelo stagnogleys or calcareous pelosols were generally characterised by 'woodland' landscapes.

I noted above that in the 1930s the Orwins suggested that the need to organise joint ploughing was a major factor in the emergence of the 'Midland System'. This idea has, however, generally been rejected on the not unreasonable grounds that co-aration was practised in all districts of England. In Homans's words, in terms of plough-sharing, it was evidently 'a matter of indifference whether a villager had his land as a single parcel or in scattered strips' (Homans 1941, 81; see also Dodgshon 1979, 31–3). But the fact that regular open fields and nucleated villages tend to be associated with the kinds of clay soils most vulnerable to puddling suggests that the Orwin's suggestion has been dismissed rather too readily. Where full advantage had to be taken of every hour in which soils are suitable for ploughing or harrowing, especially in the spring months when they were most waterlogged, ploughteams needed to be assembled with particular rapidity, not least to till the land of the demesne. This was much easier where farms, plough oxen and farmers lay in close proximity, rather than scattered across the landscape. When the soils had dried out just enough to allow them to be worked without adverse effects, but further rain threatened, the time taken to gather together the beasts for the ploughteam would have been a matter of critical importance. Moreover, those who contributed to the common plough would expect some equity in the benefits they derived from it. This would be best achieved by having the lands of each holding scattered evenly across the landscape, so that they lay both near and far from the village, and embraced the full range of variations in slope, aspect, and mineralogical qualities which might determine the length of time during which they could be safely cultivated. This argument does not require, of course, that the totality of land in a township consisted of soils particularly prone to puddling and compaction: only that a significant proportion did so. Only as cultivation expanded on to these more difficult soils would these changes in landholding and settlement have become necessary. And, as in light soil districts, the emergence of landscapes of intermingled holdings would, inevitably, have obliged farmers to organise folding and the grazing of the fallows and the harvest aftermath in common, leading once again to the development of essentially communal forms of agriculture.

In some cases, the extensive and regular intermixture of holdings characteristic of champion lands may have been created at a stroke, when a village first came into existence, as bond tenants were allotted land in an equitable way. Elsewhere, open fields may have developed more gradually: at first organically, as farms were repeatedly divided by inheritance in such a way that each share comprised an equal proportion of land lying near to, and far from, the settlement; and then through planned reorganisation, as such 'organic' layouts were recast in more ordered forms. But the particularly regular arrangements of holdings – and in some cases of tofts – found in some champion villages, both on the clays and on lighter land, and their apparent relationship to the fiscal and tenurial structures of the places in question (Brown and Foard 1998, 80–6), indicates that there were other reasons why open fields, once developed, should have been thus recast. Once well-defined communities of mutually dependent farmers had come into existence, it would be natural to extend the concept of equal shares to other aspects of life, such as labour services and taxation.

Meadows and settlement

In one sense, the concept of a 'champion belt' running diagonally across the centre of Midland England is thus slightly misleading. This broad region contains two quite distinct kinds of soil – light and leached sands and chalks on the one hand, and heavy pelo-stagnogleys, and non-calcareous pelosols, on the other – which both encouraged communal farming, but for quite different reasons. This said, there were many townships whose area included soils of both types; and here, both factors may have been important. Moreover, across this same broad tract of countryside there was another, quite different, environmental circumstance which encouraged farmers to live in nucleated villages.

Hay was the principal winter fodder in medieval England, but hay meadows were not evenly scattered across the landscape. Domesday suggests that they were a particular feature of the champion Midlands (Rackham 1986, 335), but recording was evidently uneven and the first clear picture comes from the information contained in the fourteenth-century *Inquisitions Post Mortem*, as mapped by Campbell (Figure 29). In Campbell's words, meadows were in relatively short supply 'in the east and west of England', but:

> From Somerset and east Devon in the south-west to the Vale of Pickering in Yorkshire's North Riding in the north-east ... in the clay vales of this broad diagonal band of country ... meadowland was most consistently represented. Except on the wolds, few demesnes were without at least some meadow ... (Campbell 2000, 75–6)

Some champion districts – principally sheep–corn areas like the Wessex downlands – were relatively deficient in meadows, but on the whole this central belt of England was well-endowed with this resource. The reasons were topographic and environmental. Meadows were most easily created on gravel or alluvial flood plains, where hay could be obtained simply by protecting the grass in the spring and early summer from grazing livestock. The great Midland rivers – the Nene, Ouse, Welland, Trent, Severn and their principal tributaries – ran, for the most part, parallel to the dips and scarps of the main geological formations. They meandered slowly across the vales eroded into the softer rocks, and thus had broad well-watered floodplains of the required character. In most woodland districts, in contrast, meadows were more limited in area and less easy to create. In some, as across the dipslope of the Chiltern Hills and the East Anglian Heights, narrow valleys running at right angles to an escarpment provided only slender ribbons of good-quality meadow: whereas in Midland vills there was generally around an acre of meadow for every ten or fifteen of arable, in such districts the ratio might be less than half of this. On the demesne at Little Maplestead in Essex in 1338, for example, for every thirty-five acres of arable there was only a single acre of meadow; at Cressing at the same date, the ratio was 36:1 (Larking and Kemble 1857, 168); while at Writtle in 1328 it was 33:1 (Newton 1960, 26–7). Moreover, the resource was

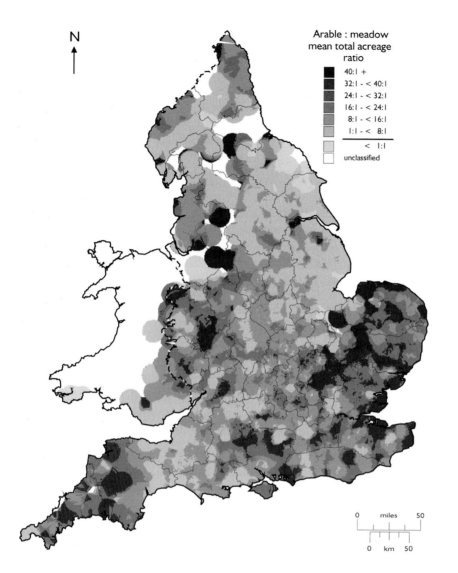

Arable : meadow
mean total acreage
ratio

40:1 +
32:1 - < 40:1
24:1 - < 32:1
16:1 - < 24:1
8:1 - < 16:1
1:1 - < 8:1
< 1:1
unclassified

FIGURE 29.
Environmental factors
in the distribution
of 'champion'
countryside: the
availability of
meadowland. The
ratio of arable to
meadowland in
England in the
early fourteenth
century, mapped
from the *Inquisitions
Post Mortem* (after
Campbell 2000,
fig. 3.06). Meadow
was generally
more abundant in
'champion' than in
'woodland' regions
(courtesy Bruce
Campbell).

often widely scattered, and in small parcels. At Great Dunmow in Essex, for example, in *c.*1250 the single acre of demesne meadow lay in two separate plots (Gervers 1996, lxxxiv).

In some regions outside the Midlands topographic circumstances ensured that good-quality meadows were in very short supply. Across much of Norfolk and Suffolk, for example, the muted topography ensured that rivers flowed sluggishly. The peaty nature of the flood-plain soils encouraged the development of fen vegetation, dominated by reeds and sedge, unsuitable for hay. In such circumstances good-quality meadows could be created through systematic embanking and drainage, but well into the nineteenth century agriculturalists bemoaned the poor state of meadowland in this district (Williamson 2003, 172–3).

Traditional hay-making was intensive in terms of both labour and equipment: labour to cut, repeatedly turn and stack the hay and carts to take it from the meadows. Pooling resources would have increased efficiency. This would have been of some significance even where, as was usually the case, the meadowland was occupied in severalty by the tenants. It would have been of particular importance when it came to the execution of labour services on the demesne meadows. Moreover, hay-making also required careful timing: 'make hay while the sun shines'. Labour had to be turned on to the meadows at precisely the right time, when the hay was in just the right condition to be cut, turned and carted. Where large reserves of meadowland existed, it made sense to live in nucleated villages. Conversely, where meadow lay in smaller, scattered parcels, or was less important in the agrarian economy, settlement could take a more dispersed form. In such circumstances, moreover, there was an incentive to retain areas of woodland and pasture, to provide grazing late into the autumn; and for peasant farms to be placed on the margins of these areas to allow more efficient livestock management. Extensive commons, large areas of woodland, isolated farms and common- and green-edge settlements were all, of course, characteristic features of the various 'woodland' landscapes.

Conclusion

Some 'woodland' districts – those located on particularly intractable clay soils – were first extensively cleared at a relatively late date, often by substantial freehold farms or sub-manors: establishments wealthy enough to maintain their own plough and team, or a substantial proportion of one, and which were thus only marginally involved in cooperative farming. Indeed, in most woodland areas the late retention of extensive woods and pastures ensured that *some* elements in the dispersed pattern of settlement originated through late assarting. But for the most part the overall characteristics of regional landscapes were related less to settlement chronology *per se* than to more complex agrarian factors. Hoskins, like others of his generation, attributed the kinds of regional variation under discussion here to ethnicity and settlement chronology, but he quoted with apparent approval the comments of Stenton, that nucleated settlements were a feature of the 'heavy lands, and, indeed, wherever there was a prospect of a steady return to cooperative agriculture' (Hoskins 1955, 54). And in the Midland belt of England, as I have argued, a range of environmental circumstances encouraged the development of communal forms of farming, and clustered settlements, to a greater extent than in the districts to the south-east and the west.

This was not necessarily because such modes of living were, given the environmental circumstances, inherently more efficient than the alternatives. Indeed, champion districts never seem to have carried the highest population densities. Nor should such landscapes be considered the inevitable consequence of the kinds of environmental circumstances I have briefly outlined.

Rather, they were the product of a particular kind of society, with a particular kind of technology: a society of small peasant farmers, holding their land on an individual basis and usually by some form of service tenancy, and each dependent on a piece of equipment – the heavy mouldboard plough – which, given the social distribution of property, could only be maintained collectively. Champion landscapes were a way of making efficient use of resources given the environmental circumstances and these specific social conditions. Outside the champion belt, similar or identical social circumstances produced a wide range of different landscapes, largely because the environmental context was different – although I would emphasise here that these landscapes were also meaningfully constituted, through conscious choices but sometimes with unforeseen results, and should not simply be regarded as backward places where the 'village moment' failed to materialise (and see Rippon, this volume).

Some historians have argued that this kind of model downplays the 'cultural dimension': 'contemporaries in some parts of the country seem to have had a notion of the proper appearance of a village, with neat rows of equally-spaced houses' (Dyer 2004). Yet such tastes and fashions did not arise out of nowhere, and in the absence of clear ethnic or cultural determinants, and given their evident association with topographic and geological patterns, it seems best to seek their origins in the real business of the medieval countryside – agriculture. But I would not wish to suggest that the inhabitants of every township in which 'champion' farming developed were best served by this particular mode of agricultural organisation. Not every township in the Midland belt contained areas of intractable clays or leached light land, or even extensive meadows. But within a district or region in which one particular way of doing things was dominant, it might well be adopted as the 'norm' even in individual places where, all things being equal, other methods of farming, or modes of settlement, would have been more convenient or efficient to lords or their tenants. The importance of this social dimension is, perhaps, made clear by the relationship between the champion belt and natural topography. As Everitt (1977) and Phythian-Adams (1987) have argued, until relatively recent times high watersheds often formed important cultural boundaries, being zones of reduced contact between neighbouring societies. It is thus noteworthy that the division between woodland and champion tends to be sharpest where it coincides with a major watershed, as along the Chiltern escarpment or the Quantock Hills (see Rippon, this volume), and more gradual and diffuse where it does not, as in western East Anglia. In this, as in so many aspects of landscape research, the distinction often drawn between the 'social' and the 'environmental' is both false and unhelpful.

CHAPTER EIGHT

Emerging Regional Variation in Historic Landscape Character: The Possible Significance of the 'Long Eighth Century'

Stephen Rippon

In the sixteenth century, Britain's was a rich and varied landscape. Settlement in the Midlands was characterised by large nucleated villages surrounded by extensive open fields – what John Leland and his contemporaries referred to as 'champion' countryside – while areas such as the south-east of England and the west of Britain had a complex mixture of more dispersed settlement patterns associated with smaller-scale common fields and large areas of closes held in severalty (the 'bosky or 'woodland' countryside of Leland and others). The origins of these villages and open fields in England's 'Central Province' have been discussed in a series of major studies (for example, Rowley 1981; Lewis *et al.* 1997; Jones and Page 2003a; 2003b; Roberts and Wrathmell 2002; Williamson 2003 and this volume), but this paper will focus on landscape change at the fringes of and beyond the village zone and consider why some areas did not develop this distinctive approach towards landscape management.

As Taylor (1983, 125) has argued, villages are in fact an aberration, not just in their limited spatial distribution but also in their relatively late appearance in the British countryside. While there were some nucleated rural settlements in late prehistoric and Roman Britain, isolated farmsteads were more common. The question of when, and why, just part of the country developed a more communal approach towards managing the landscape has been much debated, with an emerging view that it originated in the East Midlands some time around the eighth to tenth centuries, and that this approach was then adopted in adjacent areas. Various suggestions have been made as to why this 'Central Province' saw the creation of villages and open fields and these include a range of socio-economic factors related to the relationship between landed resources, an expanding economy, rising population and the structure of landownership (though it remains unclear whether it was landowners or their communities who were responsible for restructuring the landscape). It has also been argued that physical/environmental factors were important, most notably the ability of different soils to respond to the increasing demands of agriculture (see Williamson this volume). The influence of what have been called 'antecedent landscapes' – that is, the way in which the character of the Romano-British and early medieval landscape affected the nature of the later medieval countryside – has also been discussed. The focus of this paper, however, is not why villages and open fields developed in the 'Central Province', but why they did not occur elsewhere. If landscapes characterised by villages and open fields are an aberration, are the landscapes of dispersed settlement in areas such as the South West what the 'Central Province' would have looked like if villages had not been created? Were these regions beyond the Central Province somehow peripheral to the focus of landscape change in the late first millennium AD?

Unravelling the factors behind landscape replanning

A major problem in understanding why the countryside of medieval England was so varied in its character is this wide range of possible causal factors behind landscape change. Analysis at a national and regional scale clearly shows that population density alone was not a factor: there is no correlation between the 'Central Province' and the areas of highest population density in Domesday (e.g. Figure 30; Darby 1967; 1977, 87–94; Rippon 2004, 115–31; Williamson this volume). There have been various attempts at testing the correlation between other possible causal factors behind the development of villages and open fields in the 'Central Province', such as the character of the preceding countryside (e.g. Roberts and Wrathmell 2002, 19–31), the nature and drainage properties of different soils (e.g. Williamson 2003, 141–59; and this volume), and social structure and tenurial freedom (e.g. Williamson 2003, 46–52). Exploring such possible correlations at a national scale raises some fascinating possibilities but it can be difficult to untangle the various possible causal factors. Areas largely cleared of woodland by the eleventh century, for example, broadly correspond to areas of seasonally waterlogged soils seriously affected by compaction and puddling, as well as strongly manorialised parishes where all the land was owned by a single magnate or a few large owners, all of which characterise the 'Central Province' (Everitt 1985, 129; Williamson 2003 and this volume). So is there any way of untangling these various potential causes of regional variation in the character of the medieval landscape?

One way of testing whether a particular factor did indeed play a part in shaping the medieval countryside is to study places where it can be proved that certain other variables were *not* significant. One such example is coastal wetlands, such as the Somerset Levels (Figure 30) that lie towards the south-western fringes of the 'Central Province', which were reclaimed from around the tenth century when a network of settlements, roads and field systems was created that form the basis of today's historic landscape. Crucially, this episode of reclamation was occurring around the same time as the later stages of village creation in the 'Central Province', including the planning of a series

FIGURE 30.
The south-western boundary of the 'central province': (A) major features of the physical landscape and palaeoenvironmental sites referred to in the text; (B) the lack of correlation between areas with predominantly nucleated/dispersed settlement and Domesday population density.

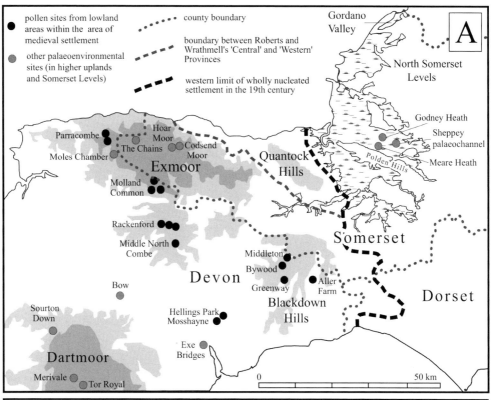

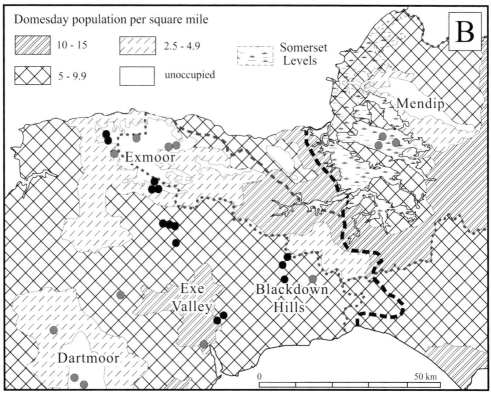

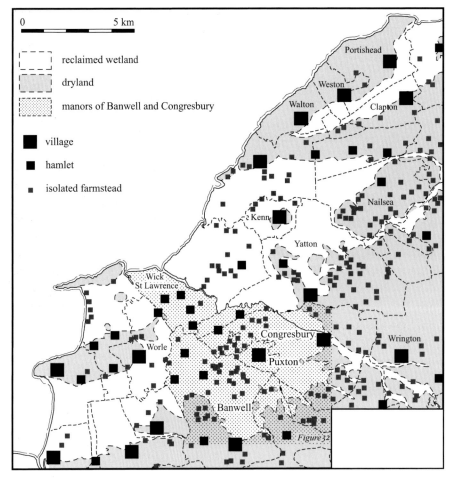

FIGURE 31.
The markedly different
nineteenth-century
settlement patterns
within a relatively
small part of north-
west Somerset, with
'Midland'-style villages
and open fields around
the Gordano valley in
the north, scattered
farmsteads and closes
always held in severalty
to the south around
Nailsea, and landscapes
characterised by
villages (e.g. Puxton),
hamlets (e.g. Wick)
and isolated farmsteads
(e.g. Congresbury
Marsh) in close
proximity on the
reclaimed North
Somerset Levels.

of nucleated villages on Glastonbury Abbey's Polden Hills estate in central
Somerset (Figure 30; Aston and Gerrard 1999; Corcos 2002). These villages
were surrounded by regularly arranged two- or three-field systems that covered most of the parish, as was the case on most of Glastonbury's Somerset
manors (and possibly one of its outlying estates, at Braunton in Devon, which
it held from AD 855 x 60 (or possibly earlier) to AD 973: Abrams 1996, 66–8;
Pearce 2004, 296–7). On the Polden Hills this reorganisation of the landscape
appears to have occurred within the context of the fragmentation of their
sixty-hide *Pouelt* estate into a series of five-hide manors, many of which have
place-names of the 'personal name + -ington' type (e.g. Cossington, Edington
and Woolavington). The same process of landscape reorganisation (the creation of villages and open fields following the fragmentation of a large estate) is
found elsewhere in Somerset – for example, around the Gordano Valley, where
a series of villages, including Clapton, Easton, Walton and Weston, each with
regularly arranged open fields, replaced a large estate of approximately fifty
hides based at Portbury (Figure 31; Rippon 1997, 136–7, fig. 34). There is also
some palaeoenvironmental support for an increasing intensity of landscape use

in central Somerset around the tenth century, when pollen sequences from Godney and Meare Heath, for example, show a marked decline in dryland trees and an increase in herbs indicative of clearance/cultivation (Beckett and Hibbert 1979, 594; Somerset County Council 1992). About the same time there was increased sedimentation in the palaeochannel of the former river Brue/Sheppey, just south of the Panborough–Bleadney Gap (Figure 30; Aalbersberg 1999, 93), and there also appears to have been an increase in alluviation in the Yeo Valley, in the south-western part of the Somerset Levels around Ilchester (Thew 1994).

Not all parts of Somerset, however, had medieval landscapes characterised by villages and open fields. In Nailsea and Yatton, for example, to the south of Gordano on the foothills that flank the North Somerset Levels, the settlement pattern was more dispersed, with a mixture of small hamlets and isolated farmsteads associated with field systems whose morphology and documentary sources suggest that they contained large areas of closes and only very small-scale open fields. So why are these adjacent landscapes so different: is it due to the physical environment (topography, soils and geology), preceding land-scape character (such as the extent of woodland clearance) or socio-economic circumstances (such as the nature of lordship and its relationship to the peas-ant/tenant community)?

Creating an historic landscape on a cleaned slate

The North Somerset Levels can be regarded as a microcosm of this wider region. In close proximity there are landscapes characterised by compact ham-lets, such as Wick St Lawrence, smaller, more loosely arranged hamlets, such as West Wick and Waywick, and areas of scattered, isolated farmsteads such as on Congresbury Marsh and in Rolstone (Figures 31 and 32). This diversity in the settlement pattern is mirrored by other facets of the landscape, such as the field systems and patterns of land holding. In some areas, such as Wick St Lawrence, a detailed survey of 1567 and estate maps of 1738–9 show that farmsteads were associated with a small number of adjacent closes (their 'home ground', amounting to between 10–50 per cent of the total land held in sev-eralty), with their remaining land scattered across the surrounding areas in what field names, other documentary sources and historic landscape analysis have shown were former open fields. In 1567, an average 17 per cent of each holding lay in surviving common fields. This is in sharp contrast to Congres-bury Marsh, where tenements consisted of large compact blocks of closes held in severalty immediately adjacent to the farmstead (amounting to between 50–90 per cent of the total land held in severalty), and with just occasional detached parcels in former common meadows and pastures some distance to the south. On average 13 per cent of each holding lay in the surviving com-mon meadows (the Dolemoors: Figure 32). A range of documentary sources shows that this striking local variation in field management and landholding can be traced back at least as far as the fifteenth century, while a programme

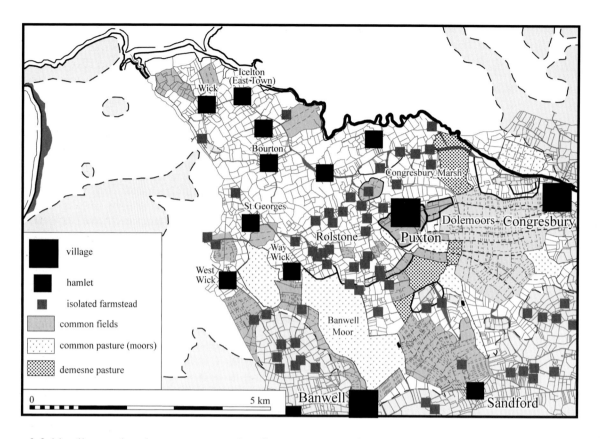

of fieldwalking, shovel test-pitting and collecting pottery from the gardens of extant houses shows that these different settlement patterns existed by the twelfth century (Rippon forthcoming). So why is there such diversity in historic landscape character within this one area, and what do detailed local studies such as these tell us about the wider issue of regional variation in landscape character?

What makes reclaimed coastal wetlands of particular value in studying the origins of the medieval countryside is that a number of the possible factors behind regional variation cannot have applied as these medieval landscapes were made on a 'cleaned slate' created during a period of early medieval flooding. We can, therefore, rule out the possibility that either soil conditions or the character of the earlier landscape influenced the form taken by the later medieval countryside as, in reclaimed wetlands such as these, the 'antecedent landscape' comprised a relatively uniform area of mudflats and saltmarshes beneath which the Roman-British land-surface was mostly buried. Following the construction of embankments along the coast and major tidal rivers from around the tenth century it was the decisions of landlords, their sub-tenants, and/or the peasant communities who colonised this newly available land that led to such marked local variation in landscape character.

In Somerset as a whole there appears to have been a tendency for settlement nucleation to occur to a greater extent on the estates of some major

FIGURE 32.
The estates of the bishops of Bath and Wells at Banwell and Congresbury. Despite being in the same ownership, when the North Somerset Levels were reclaimed a wide diversity of landscapes were created, such as the village and open fields at Puxton and the dispersed settlement pattern and enclosed fields of nearby Congresbury Marsh. This suggests that it was the sub-tenants and their communities that were responsible for deciding which type of landscape to create.

landowners, such as the abbots of Glastonbury Abbey, than on those of others, such as the bishops of Bath and Wells (Rippon 2004, 121–31). In the case of the North Somerset Levels the methodological principle established above – that, in order to understand the causal factors behind variation in the character of the medieval countryside, we need to rule out as many other potential factors as possible – can be extended into the area of social and tenurial relationships. The majority of the southern part of the North Somerset Levels (as shown on Figure 32) fell within manors (Banwell, Congresbury and Yatton) held by the same lord: the bishops of Bath and Wells. Their estates included landscapes of very different character, including areas with compact hamlets and open fields (e.g. Wick St Lawrence), loosely arranged hamlets and a few common meadows (e.g. West Wick and Waywick), and entirely dispersed settlement patterns with land arranged predominantly in closes but with detached parcels in the Dolemoors, up to 2 km to the south (e.g. Congresbury Marsh). Clearly, in this particular case, the lord of the manor appears to have exerted relatively little control over how his sub-tenants and/or the local communities chose to arrange their newly created landscapes, which is in sharp contrast to the strongly interventionist approach of the abbots of Glastonbury, seen in the planning of villages such as Shapwick.

It would appear, therefore, that around the tenth century the idea of structuring landscapes around nucleated villages and open fields had reached Somerset. The abbots of Glastonbury and their tenants were clearly enthusiastic exponents of this new approach to landscape organisation, while others, such as the bishops of Bath and Wells, adopted a far more *laissez-faire* approach. Other parts of Somerset, Wiltshire, and Dorset saw similar reorganisations though, interestingly, this was not the case in Devon and Cornwall. To the southwest of a line marked by the Blackdown and Quantock Hills the landscape was of a very different character, with more dispersed settlement patterns and a mixture of small common fields and extensive areas of closes. So why did the reorganisation of agricultural landscapes into nucleated villages and open fields not penetrate any further into the South West?

Across a watershed: landscape change beyond the Central Province in South West England

The Blackdown and Quantock Hills are a discontinuous series of uplands that divide the low-lying clay vales and wetlands of Somerset from the gently rolling hills of Devon (Figure 30). These hills not only mark the south-westerly extent of medieval landscapes characterised by nucleated villages and regularly arranged open fields, but were also a significant boundary in earlier times. They divided the land of the Durotriges to the east (as reflected in the distribution of their coins, pottery, and strongly defended hillforts containing large numbers of grain-storage pits) from Dumnonia in the west (which lacked coins, had its own distinctive ceramic tradition, and far smaller hillforts that lacked grain-storage pits: Cunliffe 1991). In the Roman period these same hills also marked the south-western edge of the Durotrigian *civitas* in the east, which was one of the most highly Romanised landscapes in Britain, as reflected in its abundance of small towns, villas, Romano-Celtic temples and durable material culture. To the west lay Dumnonia which, apart from a handful of small villas around the *civitas* capital of *Isca Dumnoniorum* (Exeter), shows very little outward signs of having adopted the trappings of Roman life (Todd 1987; Jones and Mattingly 1990; Scott 2000; Rippon 2006). So is this an example of 'antecedent landscapes' influencing the character of the medieval countryside?

It is easy to assume that the South West's landscape was simply unchanging, with the predominantly dispersed settlements and their associated pattern of mostly enclosed fields having gradually evolved from the prehistoric period. In West Penwith, at the far western end of Cornwall, this does indeed appear to have been the case, as the present pattern of small, irregularly shaped and strongly lynchetted stone-walled fields have been shown through survey and excavation to be late prehistoric and Romano-British in origin (Johnson and Rose 1982, 174; Quinnell 1986, 119–20; Herring 1993; 1994; Smith 1996). The other potential example of prehistoric field systems still surviving in use, in and around Dartmoor (Fleming 1988), can, however, be dismissed. The co-axial patterning within the historic landscape at Bittaford, to the south of Dartmoor, for example, probably results from a series of droveways extending from the South Hams up on to the moor, while elsewhere examples of the historic landscape perpetuating the line of the reaves are restricted to areas of later recolonisation and the reuse of derelict boundaries (Lambourne 2004). East of West Penwith the Romano-British and earliest medieval countryside was of a very different character to the historic landscape of today. The majority of identified settlements were enclosed by a simple univalate non-defensive ditch and/or bank enclosing an internal area of *c.*0.1 to 1.0 ha, and included a small number of oval or sub-rectangular houses (Johnson and Rose 1982; Griffith 1994; Riley and Wilson-North 2001, 65–75). A number of open settlements have also been identified (e.g. Thomas 1958; McAvoy 1980), though their true extent is difficult to establish. The Middle Iron Age open settlements at Long Range and Langland Lane in East Devon, for example, were discovered during road construction and were not identifiable on air photographs (Fitzpatrick *et al.* 1999, 7, 130–59). The scarcity of datable material culture on the Roman-British and earliest medieval rural settlements that have been excavated would also have made them almost impossible to locate through fieldwalking (e.g. Balkwill 1976; Jarvis 1976; Simpson *et al.* 1989; Horner 1993; Todd 1998; Caseldine *et al.* 2000, 65).

It is notable that while some of these late prehistoric or Romano-British settlements in the South West are associated with field systems, many are not (Silvester and Balkwill 1977; Silvester 1978a; 1978b; 1980; Griffith 1984; Simpson *et al.* 1989; Reed and Manning 2000; Quinnell 2004, 3). It is possible that while substantial enclosure ditches show up as cropmarks, lesser field boundary ditches do not, although an increasing number of large-scale excavations and watching briefs are finding no trace of Romano-British or early medieval field ditches even in the immediate vicinity of known settlement enclosures (e.g. Hayes Farm Clyst Honiton: Simpson *et al.* 1989 and CAT 2000; the A30 Exeter to Honiton improvement: FitzPatrick *et al.* 1999; and see Herring 1998, fig. 42; Johnson *et al.* 1998–9). It is possible that field boundaries were marked by banks rather than ditches (as on the limestone hills south of Newton Abbot: Phillips 1966, 12–16; Gallant *et al.* 1985; Quinn 1995), and that elsewhere these have been destroyed by weathering and ploughing, but it is clear that even those field systems which have been recorded are localised in extent and are on a different orientation to the historic landscape. There is nothing to suggest that there was a continuous fieldscape across the South West in the Romano-British and earliest medieval period; and the field systems that have been identified were of a very different character to those of the medieval period.

There is growing evidence that some at least of these small Romano-British enclosed settlements continued to be occupied into the fifth and even the sixth centuries (Hirst 1937; Guthrie 1969; Saunders 1972; Appleton-Fox 1992; Quinnell 2004, 238–42), while a number of hilltop sites were also reoccupied (Pollard 1966; Grant 1995; Gent and Quinnell 1999a, 19, 24–6; 1999b, 82). A growing body of palaeoenvironmental evidence also suggests broad continuity in the lowlands, with the maintenance of an open landscape and the continuous cultivation of cereals, albeit on a small scale (Hatton and Caseldine 1991; Caseldine *et al.* 2000; Fyfe *et al.* 2003; 2004; Hawkins 2005a; 2005b). Only on the higher uplands is there evidence for contraction. On Exmoor there was a decrease in the intensity of human activity, with a decline in arable and grassland and an increase in heather and possibly woodland around the fifth century (Moore *et al.* 1984; Francis and Slater 1990, 14). On Dartmoor there are hints of a slight decrease in the density of human activity at Merrivale and Tor Royal, although the pollen sequences at Blacka Brook and Wotter Common appear to show continuity in a predominantly pastoral landscape (Smith *et al.* 1981, 246; Gearey *et al.* 1997, fig. 5; Gearey *et al.* 2000a). On Bodmin Moor the picture is similarly varied: there is continuity in land use at Rough Tor North, but possibly slight woodland regeneration at Tresellern Marsh and Rough Tor South (Gearey *et al.* 1997; 2000b, 501). These uplands, however, lay beyond the main areas of settlement, and as early medieval place-names suggest they were probably used for transhumant grazing (Padel 1985, 127–9; Herring 1996); a decrease in the intensity of their exploitation need not suggest a widespread dislocation in the landscape elsewhere. The overriding theme in the lowland agrarian landscape between the late Roman period and the sixth/seventh centuries is, therefore, one of continuity.

It is during the fifth to seventh centuries that we get the first evidence for ownership and control of land and resources, with inscribed memorial stones, which occur across Cornwall and west Devon, with two outliers on Exmoor, implying the existence of a socially stratified elite (Pearce 1978, 24; Okasha 1993; Thomas 1994). It was presumably this elite that was responsible for maintaining contact with the Mediterranean world, reflected in the importation of late fifth- and sixth-century pottery. The greatest concentration has been found at the rocky coastal promontory at Tintagel in north Cornwall, which can best be interpreted as a 'royal citadel' (Thomas 1981; 1993; Nowakowski and Thomas 1992; Batey *et al.* 1993; Morris *et al.* 1999). Other such sites may well exist – St Michael's Mount in south Cornwall is certainly a contender (Herring 2000), along with, possibly, Burgh Island in South Devon, which lies close to the trading sites or beach markets at Bantham and Mothecombe, where ephemeral traces of occupation associated with late Roman and early medieval Mediterranean imported pottery have been recovered (Farley and Little 1968; Silvester 1981; Griffith and Reed 1998; Horner 2001). The importation of this pottery suggests that communities in the South West had something of value to exchange, and there are documentary references to English traders taking tin (presumably Cornish) to the Continent from the seventh century (Penhallurick 1986, 240). Radiocarbon dates from both Exmoor and the Blackdown Hills have also shown that iron production continued well into the post-Roman period, while at Carhampton on Exmoor an ironworking site is associated with fifth- to sixth-century Mediterranean imports (Griffith and Weddell 1996, 33; Riley and Wilson-North 2001, 112). Clearly, the fifth- to sixth-century landscape of South West England was a busy place.

All of this archaeological and palaeoenvironmental evidence is pointing to broad continuity in both society and the landscape between the fourth and the sixth centuries, but then there was a period of great change. Pottery from the Mediterranean ceased to reach eastern Dumnonia, though it is found all around other parts of western Britain (Thomas 1990). There is neither artefactual nor radiocarbon dating to suggest that Romano-British/earliest medieval settlements continued to be occupied after the sixth century, other than a few possible examples where they were reused as Christian centres (Quinnell 2004, 243). Across the South West the vast majority of Romano-British/earliest medieval enclosures and field systems are quite unrelated to the open settlements, roads and fields of the historic landscape (Padel 1985; 1999; Preston-Jones and Rose 1986; Rose and Preston-Jones 1995, figs 3.1–3.2; Herring 1998, fig. 42; Riley and Wilson-North 2001, 73–5; Turner 2003, 176–8). Even at the level of vernacular architecture we see discontinuity, with the medieval tripartite house, which dates back to the tenth/eleventh centuries at Mawgan Porth (Bruce-Mitford 1997) and possibly Gwithian (Pearce 2004, 304), standing in sharp contrast to the unicellular oval/sub-rectangular huts of the Romano-British and earliest medieval period (Preston-Jones and Rose 1986, fig. 6; Quinnell 1986, figs 3–5; 2004).

The place-names recorded in Domesday and landmarks described in the boundary clauses of tenth- and eleventh-century charters similarly suggest that the historic landscape of today has its origins before the Norman Conquest (Hooke 1994; 1999). Archaeological work in and around medieval settlements has failed to establish their origins, partly because most excavated sites are in secondary locations such as the uplands and heavy clays of the

Culm Measures, that appear to have been colonised as late as the thirteenth century (Dudley and Minter 1966; Allan 1994; Henderson and Weddell 1994; Weddell and Reed 1997). Even if sites in primary settlement locations were excavated, the lack of pre-eleventh-century pottery in Devon and disturbance to the stratigraphically earliest contexts that might potentially be radiocarbon dated, would make dating their origins difficult (Brown and Laithwaite 1993; Henderson and Weddell 1994; Brown 1998).

With so little archaeological and documentary evidence for these crucial centuries between the cessation of Roman authority and the Norman Conquest, it is to palaeoenvironmental evidence that we must turn. In Britain as a whole there are relatively few long sequences that cover the historic period and, of those we have, the majority are in upland areas (Dark 2000). These traditional sites for pollen analysis are blanket peats on the highest uplands and are of limited value in studying the medieval landscape, as they lay beyond areas that were actually settled at that time. Recent work in Devon, however, has revealed a series of palaeoenvironmental sequences from small valley mires that lay within that part of the historic landscape that was actually settled in the medieval period, such as the Rackenford area of mid Devon (e.g. Figure 33; Fyfe *et al.* 2004; Fyfe and Rippon 2004; Rippon *et al.* 2006), Molland and Parracombe in North Devon (Fyfe *et al.* 2003; 2004; Fyfe and Rippon 2004; Rippon *et al.* 2006), the Clyst Valley near Exeter (Hawkins 2005b), and the Blackdown Hills in eastern Devon (Figure 30; Hatton and Caseldine 1991; Hawkins 2005a).

These small valley mires have a relatively local catchment (of just a few square kilometres) and so will be far more sensitive to landscape change than the upland peats whose very broad catchments result in a highly generalised picture across a very wide area. With very local catchments there is obviously a danger that an individual pollen core may not be typical of the region, and so in most cases around three mires were examined in each study area. These lowland pollen sequences consistently show no significant changes in land use between the Roman and earliest medieval periods, but a major increase in cereals around the seventh/eighth centuries. Traditionally, this would have been interpreted as a simple expansion of settlement and the area of cultivation from primary to more secondary areas but if this was the case then we would expect to see a decline in woodland and rough pasture at the expense of arable. What we actually see alongside this increased cereal pollen is a substantial area of improved grassland and no decline in woodland: rather than the clearance and cultivation of new land, it appears that areas that had already been cleared were being used more intensively.

After the seventh/eighth centuries there is then very little change in the pollen record until the post-medieval period, which is significant for two reasons. Firstly, as we know that the essential fabric of the medieval landscape was in place by the tenth/eleventh centuries (see above), and as there is no change in the palaeoenvironmental record between the seventh/eighth centuries and the post-Conquest period, the origins of the medieval countryside may also date

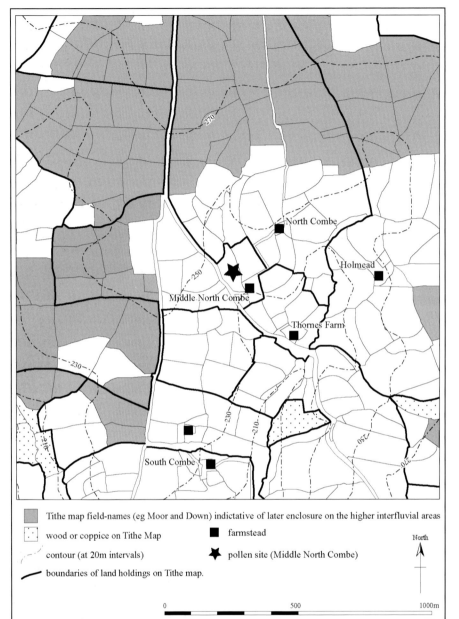

Tithe map field-names (eg Moor and Down) indicative of later enclosure on the higher interfluvial areas

wood or coppice on Tithe Map ■ farmstead

contour (at 20m intervals) ★ pollen site (Middle North Combe)

boundaries of land holdings on Tithe map.

North

0   500   1000m

FIGURE 33.
The pollen site at Middle North Combe in mid Devon. In contrast to traditional pollen sites that are in remote upland locations, this lowland peat sequence is from an area of ancient settlement and enclosure and, as such, will give a more accurate record of land use changes.

to this initial expansion of arable and improved pasture. The second reason why this continuity in the pollen record is so significant is that it is not until the fourteenth century that we have good documentary sources that describe the practice of agriculture in the South West. These sources describe a distinctive form of rotational agriculture known as convertible husbandry, in which the majority of fields were subject to alternating grain and grass crops, with a short period of cultivation (of around two to three years) followed by a long grass ley (of around six to eight years), producing a rotation of around ten years (Fox 1991; Fox and Padel 2000; Rippon *et al.* 2006). About a quarter of fields would have been cultivated in any one year, and very few fields (if any) within this core 'infield' area of intensive farming would have been permanent pasture. Documentary sources simply show that convertible husbandry existed by the fourteenth century, and that it continued into the post-medieval period. An examination of the late medieval horizons in the peat sequences therefore reveals what the pollen signature is for convertible husbandry, and as this is exactly the same as for the seventh/eighth centuries, when cereals first appear in large quantities, it would seem that this rotational system of agriculture may have developed at that time.

So what caused these changes in the landscape of South-West England around the seventh/eighth centuries? The period from around AD 680 to 830 has been described as the 'long eighth century', when southern England as a whole saw profound changes in settlement structure, architecture, the organisation of landed production and regional exchange (Hansen and Wickham 2000; Hamerow 2002, 191). This was also a turbulent period in the South West, with the eastern part of the kingdom of Dumnonia (i.e. modern Devon) being absorbed by the kingdom of Wessex in the late seventh century (Hooke 1999, 95; Pearce 2004, 252–8). There is no reason why this should have led to a sudden or synchronous replanning of the countryside, but these political changes could have initiated a period of economic expansion, innovation and change reflected in the very least by the granting of large tracts of land to the Church (e.g. King Aethelheard's grant of twenty hides at Crediton to bishop Forthhere in 739: Sawyer 1968, no. 255; Hooke 1994, 86). Could it have been these social changes that led to the gradual restructuring of the South West's landscape?

The origins of regionally distinct landscapes beyond the South West

So far we have seen that there appears to have been a significant change in the landscape of South West England around the seventh/eighth centuries, while in Somerset there appears to have been a phase of village creation (and an expansion of settlement into the coastal marshes) around the tenth century. These two periods appear to have been important across southern England. In the 'Central Province' there has been much debate over when villages and open fields were created. In Northamptonshire fieldwalking suggests that numerous scattered farmsteads associated with 'Early to Middle Saxon' pottery (fifth to ninth century), around a quarter of which are located on or adjacent to Romano-British sites, were replaced by far fewer but larger nucleated settlements that evolved into modern villages, some of which have produced 'Late Saxon' material (ninth to eleventh century: e.g. Foard 1978; Hall and Martin 1979; Taylor 1983, 116; Hall 1988; Shaw 1993; Ford 1996; Brown and Foard 2004). This process of village creation could have been a two-phase process, with the initial nucleation of settlement around a single existing focus sometime before the mid ninth century (and perhaps associated

with the fragmentation of large estates into smaller manorial holdings), followed by a reorganisation/replanning of these villages and the laying out of
their open fields around the tenth century (Brown and Foard 1998; 2004, 96).
Unfortunately, this first phase is poorly dated, but it must have been after
the early eighth century, as the scattered farmsteads that were abandoned are
associated with 'Middle Saxon' Ipswich Ware pottery (whose use extended
from around AD 720 to around AD 850: Blinkhorn 1999), but before the mid
ninth century, as they lack 'Late Saxon' pottery. The palaeoeconomic evidence
from Raunds and West Cotton also suggests broad continuity in agriculture
during the fifth to ninth centuries, with open-field farming introduced by the
tenth century (Campbell 1994).

A similar pattern of dispersed settlement associated with 'Early to Middle
Saxon' pottery being replaced around the ninth/tenth centuries by nucleated
villages associated with 'Late Saxon' pottery is also discernable elsewhere in
the East Midlands, for example in parts of Buckinghamshire (e.g. the desertion of Pennylands and origins of Great Linford: Williams 1993, 95) and
Lincolnshire (Lane 1993, 58–9; 1995, 29–31). In Leicestershire and Rutland a
dispersed scatter of small farmstead-size sites, recorded as 'Early Saxon' pottery scatters and occasional finds of 'Early to Middle Saxon' metalwork, were
similarly abandoned before the use of 'Late Saxon' pottery, the distribution of
which is restricted to medieval villages (Bowman 2004; Liddle 1996; Cooper
2000, 152; Knox 2004). In contrast to the dispersed settlement pattern on the
Lincolnshire Fens, which continued into the seventh/eighth centuries (Hayes
and Lane 1992, 215), however, fieldwalking along the fen-edge suggests that
the scatter of sites associated with 'Early Saxon' pottery was abandoned before
the use of 'Middle Saxon' pottery. In the north of the county, at Rigby Crossroads, west of Grimsby, a dispersed settlement pattern similarly appears to
have undergone nucleation around the late seventh century (Steedman 1994).
The colonisation of the nearby Norfolk Marshland also suggests that the idea
of structuring landscapes around nucleated settlements was prevalent in that
region by the Middle Saxon period. On these marshes just a single Early
Saxon site has been located, at the margins of the intertidal saltmarshes and
the freshwater backfen, which was abandoned by the eighth century (it lacked
'Middle Saxon' pottery). Soon after, a line of substantial regularly spaced settlements associated with Middle Saxon pottery, around 1–3 km apart, was
established on the higher coastal saltmarshes in what was clearly a planned/
coordinated act of colonisation based on the idea of structuring landscape
around nucleated villages, rather than isolated farmsteads (Silvester 1988; 1993;
Rippon 2000, 174).

There are also signs that there were two periods or stages of significant
landscape change elsewhere within the 'Central Province'. At Cottenham in
Cambridgeshire, for example, a loosely nucleated cluster of farmsteads dating to the seventh century was replaced around the early eighth century by
a planned and nucleated settlement adjacent to the medieval village core and
to the south of what became the manor site (Mortimer 2000). A shift in

the focus of the village led to the excavated site being abandoned in the tenth century, as was the case with several other medieval villages in the county (e.g. Willington and Fordham; Mortimer 2000). A similar process of village formation may be seen in Oxfordshire, where extensive survey and excavations within the open fields of Cassington and Yarnton have revealed an unstructured landscape of dispersed settlement associated with fifth- to seventh-century 'Early Saxon' pottery that was joined around the eighth century by a more compact and structured settlement – one that starts to have the characteristics of a village – immediately to the south of what became the church/manor complex. This period also saw significant agricultural intensification, with increased arable production, the introduction of new crops, the more intensive use of the floodplain for pasture and meadow, and the manuring of open fields that certainly existed by the tenth century when all the earlier dispersed settlements were abandoned (Hey 2004): once again, the formation of the open fields probably post-dated the initial trend towards settlement nucleation. In the Thames Valley generally there was an increase in alluviation from around the eighth/ninth centuries (Robinson 1992, 201), and the pollen sequence at Snelsmore on the nearby Berkshire Downs shows an increase in cereal cultivation around the ninth century (Waton 1982). It would appear, therefore, that landscape change, including settlement nucleation and the creation of open fields across the 'Central Province', was a prolonged process that began in some places around the seventh to ninth centuries, but was only completed around the tenth century, when some landscapes appear to have seen further restructuring.

We must avoid, however, taking a 'Midland-centric' view of landscape evolution in this period for, as we have seen in the South West, other regions were also seeing significant changes at this time. Many of the best-known excavated fifth- to seventh-century settlements lie beyond the 'Central Province', in the South East, and whilst acknowledging that none has been completely excavated, most appear to have been abandoned around the seventh or early eighth centuries. Well-known examples include Chalton (Hants), Mucking (Essex), West Stow (Suffolk) and Bishopstone (Sussex), but other cases include Fyfield/Overton Downs, Avebury and Combe Down (all in Wilts.), suggesting that this was a widespread phenomenon (see Hamerow 1991; 2002; Fowler 2000, 230; Pollard and Reynolds 2002, 183–202; McOmish *et al.* 2002). This should not, however, be seen simply as a shift in settlement location from drier soils, often on hilltops, to the valleys, as the latter were also occupied during the fifth to seventh centuries: rather than seeing a shift from one location to another, are we simply seeing a retreat from some of the more peripheral locations that communities had settled in the fifth century, and continuity elsewhere? The seventh/eighth centuries are also the period when, in East Anglia, the settlement foci that went on to become church–hall complexes came into being (Newman 1992; Moreland 2000, 86–7), during what palaeoenvironmental sequences are showing was a period of agricultural expansion. At Micklemere in Pakenham (Suffolk), for example, there was increased soil erosion within the catchment marked by a layer of mud associated with increased cereal pollen deposited around the later eighth century (Murphy 1994, 29–31), while at Hockham Mere (Norfolk) a major increase in cereals is dated to cal. AD 790–980 (Sims 1978). It appears, therefore, that the 'long eighth century' saw significant landscape changes across southern England, and that it was several centuries later that further reorganisation in, specifically, the Midlands led to the 'Central Province' emerging as a distinctive region.

Conclusion

There have recently been a series of studies into the origins of landscapes characterised by nucleated villages and open fields, but this paper has tried to take the focus away from the Midlands and to broaden discussion to include what was happening at this time beyond the 'Central Province'. There are, perhaps, four major conclusions. Firstly, we must find ways of untangling the various possible causes of regional variation in landscape character by studying areas that show significant variation in, for example, their settlement patterns and field systems, but which in certain physical or cultural ways were uniform, so ruling out a number of other possible causal factors. The second, also methodological, conclusion is that in a period for which both the archaeological and documentary sources are poor, palaeoenvironmental sequences can provide an important source of information with regards to how the landscape was being managed.

A third conclusion is that the emergence of landscapes characterised by villages and open fields was a long process, showing marked regional variation, which may have occurred in at least two stages, with a trend towards settlement nucleation preceding the formation of open fields. In parts of what became the 'Central Province' there are signs of settlement nucleation from around the eighth century, but it was only around the tenth century that fully nucleated villages and open fields emerged. Very similar landscapes were also being created at the south-western fringes of the 'Central Province' in Somerset, though this planned countryside is found alongside areas characterised by dispersed settlement. In the case of reclaimed coastal marshland, such as the North Somerset Levels, we can show that neither the natural environment nor 'antecedent landscapes' determined whether the medieval settlement pattern was nucleated or dispersed. Across Somerset these different landscapes of farmsteads, hamlets and villages were a cultural construct, and different landowners clearly adopted different strategies towards the management of their estates with some, like the abbots of Glastonbury, embracing the concept of villages and open fields and replanned their estates accordingly, while others, such as the bishops of Bath and Wells, took a less interventionist approach, leaving their sub-tenants and individual communities to create landscapes of differing structure and character.

Finally, there is the question of why the concept of villages and open fields did not extend even further into the South West (and indeed into areas such as East Anglia and the South East). It would be easy to take a Midland-centric, core–periphery view of such areas as being remote, backward and unchanging, but by looking beyond the watershed we can see that the South West had in fact seen its own period of change in how the landscape was organised around the eighth century, and that this produced a highly successful system of agriculture that turned out to be just as long-lived as that in the Midlands. Overall, therefore, the 'long eighth century' was one of profound change across southern England. There was a tendency towards the formation of more compact nucleated settlements in parts of central and eastern England, while areas in the South East and the South West also saw an intensification of agriculture that could have been associated with a physical restructuring of the countryside. In the 'Central Province' this was just the start of several centuries of change, as settlement was increasingly drawn into what eventually became our nucleated medieval villages (a process possibly encouraged by the formation of open fields), which was an approach towards landscape management that eventually spread out into areas such as central and eastern Somerset. That it spread no further south-west, however, was not because Devon and Cornwall were somehow remote and backward, but because they appear to have already developed their own regionally distinctive way of managing the landscape.

CHAPTER NINE

'Wheare most Inclosures be': The Making of the East Anglian Landscape

Edward Martin

Fifty years ago Hoskins (1955, 142) observed that 'East Anglia has a peculiar history also, as far as its landscape is concerned'. He recognised that the region had a great deal of what he termed 'ancient enclosure' which 'owes little or nothing to the enclosure commissioners'. This landscape which seemed to owe so little to the commonly accepted view of medieval agriculture had, forty years previously, perplexed Gray (1915, 387), that great scholar of English field systems, who despairingly stated that 'the early field system of few English counties is so difficult to describe as that of Essex'. Later agricultural historians preferred to think that East Anglia had once been like central England, but that 'in the woodland clays [of East Anglia] medieval field systems had been extinguished before 1650' (Holderness 1984, 205).

The Historic Field Systems of East Anglia (HFSEA) Project (2000–2005)

Since 1998 the Archaeology Service of Suffolk County Council has worked in conjunction with English Heritage on two projects to further the understanding of this difficult landscape. The first of these was an Historic Landscape Characterisation (HLC) project that was launched in Suffolk and has now been extended to five other counties in eastern England. This is creating a computer-based map of the region that analyses the landscape in terms of its current land use, but with reference to its historic origins. At the outset it was recognised that the methodology for this work relied heavily on field morphology and a follow-up project was designed to research the historic origins of the field systems of the region.

In the first half of the HFSEA project, English Heritage provided funding for the employment of Dr Max Satchell as a project officer. The supervision of the project, its completion and the interpretation of the results were undertaken by the author. Twelve detailed case studies were undertaken in a 'greater East Anglia' that included Norfolk, Suffolk, Essex, north-eastern Hertfordshire and south-eastern Cambridgeshire (Figure 34). The choice of

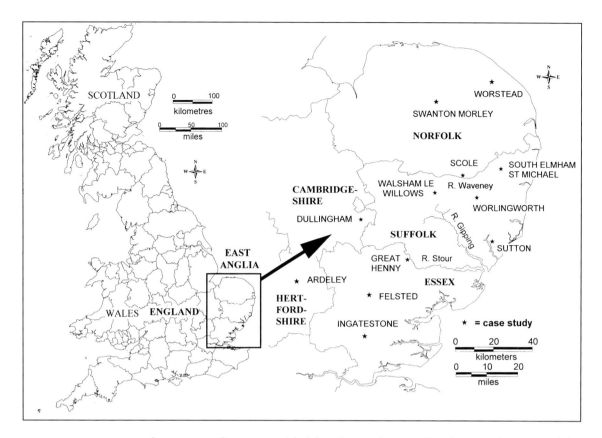

SCOTLAND

WALES   ENGLAND

EAST
ANGLIA

HERT-
FORD-
SHIRE

CAMBRIDGE-
SHIRE

DULLINGHAM ★

★ ARDELEY

INGATESTONE
★

WORSTEAD ★

★
SWANTON MORLEY

NORFOLK

SCOLE
★   ★ SOUTH ELMHAM
ST MICHAEL
WALSHAM LE   R. Waveney
WILLOWS   ★

★ WORLINGWORTH

SUFFOLK   ★ SUTTON

GREAT ★   R. Stour
HENNY

ESSEX

★ FELSTED

★ = case study

0   20   40
kilometers
0   10   20
miles

0   100
kilometres
0   50   100
miles

FIGURE 34.
Map showing East
Anglia's place within
England, and an
enlarged area showing
the location of the case
studies of the 'Historic
Field Systems of East
Anglia' Project.

the case studies was guided by the settlement 'local regions' suggested by the work of Roberts and Wrathmell (2000; 2002). In each place, the documentary and physical evidence for the medieval and later field systems was examined. The aim was to establish retrogressive links between the modern landscape and the earliest recorded farming system in each area. The detailed results of this work will be published in the project report (Martin and Satchell forthcoming).

One important general result of the project was the recognition of the importance of the regional cultivation method called 'stetch' or 'stitch' ploughing. The term derives from Old English *stycce* 'a bit, a piece', and was used in the sense of a group of furrows that combine to make a strip of ploughed land. A stetch commonly consisted of a pair of clashing furrows (called a 'head' or 'top') in the centre of the strip and three flanking furrows on each side, making eight in all (Trist 1971, 183–4; Figure 35). This technique has many similarities to the way ridge and furrow, as found in the Midlands, was formed, but the key difference is the height and permanence of the ridges. In 'classic' ridge and furrow, the ridges were high and permanent, but in stetch ploughing the ridges were low and could be 'broken' at each ploughing, simply by splitting the central head. The two methods can be described as 'high' and 'low' ridge and furrow. Stetch ploughing leaves little evidence in the form of earthworks, which has led many previous researchers

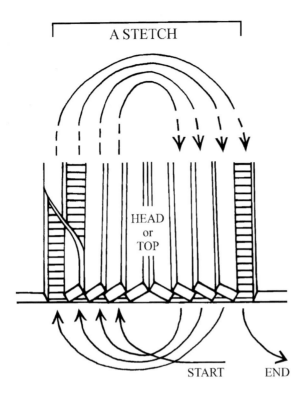

A STETCH

HEAD
or
TOP

START   END

FIGURE 35.
Diagram showing
how an East Anglian
'stetch' was ploughed
(in this case one
consisting of eight
furrows). Open
furrows were left at the
edges of each stetch to
facilitate drainage.

to believe that the region was of little value for the study of medieval field
systems. What do survive, however, are thousands of kilometres of hedges, a
high proportion of which are probably medieval, or possibly even earlier. In
the Suffolk claylands, despite twentieth-century losses, there is still an average of 4 km of hedges per square kilometre (Parker 2000). It is the pattern
of fields that is East Anglia's inheritance from its medieval farms, not ridge
and furrow earthworks.

Mapping the trends

To facilitate comparative studies between the case studies, the land in each
place was classified and quantified on the basis of a number of 'land types'
(Table 1). Land types can of course change and evolve over time, so the policy
was to envisage what could be termed the 'climax medieval' situation, where
the farming system was well developed but had not yet undergone significant
post-medieval changes.

The different percentages of the land types in each case study revealed
very significant trends. Principal amongst these was the differing importance
of common fields and 'block holdings' (block demesne and block tenements
amalgamated). High percentages of common fields were recorded in Worstead
(62 per cent), Swanton Morley (67 per cent), Scole with Frenze, Thelveton
and Thorpe Parva (altogether 56 per cent) and Dullingham (63 per cent);

TABLE 1. Land types of the Historic Field Systems of East Anglia Project.

1. Block demesne

Blocks of exclusively demesne land, including arable, pasture and farmyards, but excluding meadows, woods, parkland and strips in common fields. Subdivided into:

1.1. Core block demesne	Demesne land abutting or encompassing the hall of the manor to which it belonged. 'Core' refers to the hall–demesne relationship, not to the location within the overall settlement area.
1.2. Detached block demesne	Block demesne that was separated from the manorial hall to which it belonged.

2. Tenement blocks

Blocks of tenanted land abutting or encompassing the house and yards of individual farmsteads. Sometimes in agglomerations of several similar tenements. Included arable, pasture and farmyards, but excluded meadows, woods in severalty and common field strips.

3. Common fields

Arable land internally subdivided into unfenced strips that were held by a number of different individuals. Considerable variations were seen within this type, so it was further subdivided into:

Type 1	Archetypal system of English Midlands. Arable land in two or three large fields, subdivided into furlongs. Communal cropping and folding. All holdings, including demesne and glebe, consist of strips equally distributed across the fields. Enclosure normally effected through parliamentary acts. Ridge and furrow is a 'type-fossil'.
Type 2	Usually the dominant arable farming system within individual settlements. Number of fields very variable. Confusion in terminology between 'fields' and their subdivisions. Parliamentary acts frequently needed to end it. Sporadic ridge and furrow; stetch ploughing more usual. Sub-types:

	Type 2A	Strips belonging to individual holdings tend towards an equal distribution across the fields. Tendency to have communal cropping and folding arrangements.
	Type 2B	Strips belonging to each holding tend to be clustered in the vicinity of the holder's house. Less evidence for communal cropping and folding.

Type 3	Frequently gone by sixteenth century. Usually a minority part of the farmland – under 50 per cent of parish areas. Little evidence for communal cropping and folding. Holdings concentrated in fields nearest to farmstead to which they belong; not evenly distributed across all the fields. Impression frequently of subdivided closes rather than true common fields. Inconsistent use of terms such as field, furlong, close etc. Parliamentary acts seldom used to end this type. Stetch ploughing normal; ridge and furrow largely absent.

4. Common pasture

Grassland used for common grazing. Subdivided into:

4.1. Droves	Roadways with strips of pasture flanking one or both sides. Frequently formed links between greens or other areas of pasture.
4.2. Small greens	Areas less than 2 ha (5 acres).
4.3. Medium greens	Areas between 2 and 20 ha (5 to 49 acres).
4.4. Large greens	Areas greater than 20 ha (49 acres).
4.5. Riverside commons	Extensive areas of common pasture located beside rivers, often poorly drained. Used for animal pasture, rather than as mowing meadows.

TABLE I. *continued* Land types of the Historic Field Systems of East Anglia Project.

5. Meadow

Enclosed grassland mown for hay in summer and then used for pasturing animals. Subdivided into:

5.1. Demesne meadow	Meadow owned and exclusively used by a manorial lord.
5.2. Several meadow	Meadow held by individual tenants for their exclusive use.
5.3. Common meadow	Meadow divided into separately owned strips for hay mowing, but otherwise subject to common grazing.

6. Heath

Dry pasture characterised by grassland when on chalky soils and grassland and/or heather when on acidic soils. Mainly used for sheep grazing, or, if very poor, rabbit warrens. Subdivided into:

6.1. Several heath	Heath held by a manorial lord or a tenant for their exclusive use.
6.2. Common heath	Heath subject to common grazing.

7. Woodland

Subdivided into:

7.1. Demesne woodland	Woodland held by a manorial lord for his exclusive use.
7.2. Several woodland	Woodland held by individual tenants for their exclusive use.
7.3. Common woodland	Woodland held in common.

8. Parkland

Semi-natural areas of mixed grassland and woodland, used principally for the keeping of deer. Landscape parks established in post-medieval times were excluded.

---

moderate amounts in Walsham-le-Willows (38 per cent), Sutton (25 per cent), Great Henny (23 per cent) and Ardeley (48 per cent); low amounts in South Elmham St Michael (11 per cent) and Worlingworth (15 per cent); and none in Felsted and Ingatestone. The areas that had large amounts of common-field land lay principally to the north and west of the study area. Common fields were absent in the southernmost part of the study area, as at Felsted and Ingatestone.

Block holdings had an opposite distribution: small amounts in Worstead (6 per cent), Swanton Morley (7 per cent) and Dullingham (8 per cent); moderate amounts in Scole (25 per cent), Sutton (30 per cent), Ardeley (34 per cent), Walsham-le-Willows (44 per cent) and Great Henny (46 per cent); and large amounts in South Elmham St Michael (83 per cent), Worlingworth (76 per cent), Felsted (86 per cent) and Ingatestone (84 per cent).

In order to define further and explore these trends, the Historic Landscape Characterisation mapping was examined; the Suffolk map was concentrated upon as this was at that time the most complete and was also conveniently central to the study area. This classified the landscape into thirteen major character types and fifty-five sub-types. For the accompanying map (Figure 36), ten relevant landscape character types were selected. The original mapping was in colour and the monochrome version presented here as Figure 36 can only give an approximation of the visual contrasts, although the added 'trend lines' delineate the major changes. These lines vary in their precision because some trends are stronger than others. It should also be stressed that the HLC mapping is still very new and, as refinements are made to it, the derived boundaries may need revising in the future.

Areas defined as resulting from eighteenth-century and later enclosure

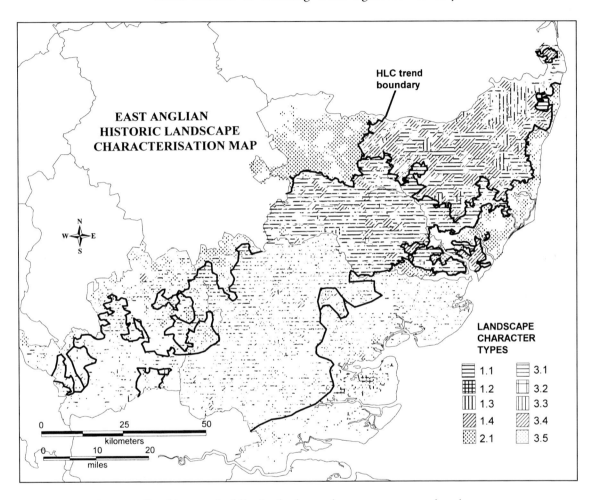

FIGURE 36.
The East Anglian
Historic Landscape
Characterisation Map
(as completed for
Suffolk, Essex and
Hertfordshire in 2003).

For this map, the following landscape character types were selected:

1.1 pre-eighteenth-century enclosure: random fields
1.2 pre-eighteenth-century enclosure: rectilinear fields
1.3 pre-eighteenth-century enclosure: long co-axial fields
1.4 pre-eighteenth-century enclosure: irregular co-axial fields
2.1 eighteenth-century and later enclosure: former common arable or heathland
3.1 post-1950 agricultural landscape: boundary loss from random fields
3.2 post-1950 agricultural landscape: boundary loss from rectilinear fields
3.3 post-1950 agricultural landscape: boundary loss from long co-axial fields
3.4 post-1950 agricultural landscape: boundary loss from irregular co-axial fields
3.5 post-1950 agricultural landscape: boundary loss from post-1700 field.
A bold 'trend' line delineates the major divisions between the types.

show a clear correlation with the parliamentary acts that specify the enclosure of common arable, as in north-west Suffolk. The areas with fields
defined as resulting from pre-eighteenth-century enclosure, however, presented more of a challenge to interpretation. The evidence from the project
suggested that they contained areas with Type 3 common fields, but were
likely also to have included areas with predominantly block holdings. Interestingly, the HLC data did suggest that two groups were present, which
had largely, but not completely, complementary distributions. Occupying most of south Suffolk up to a line just north of the River Gipping
were field systems mainly defined as 'random', in that they had no obvious axial patterning. To the north of this line, running up to the county
boundary in the north, were fields that were defined as 'long co-axial',
or 'irregular co-axial'.

By themselves, the two groups did not have obvious links to either common fields or block holdings; however, through a study of glebe or church
land a possible link was suggested. Glebe acts as a microcosm of the wider
tenurial background: where common fields are present, the glebe tends to
be in strips; where there are block holdings, the glebe also tends to be in
blocks. The compilation of glebe surveys, or 'terriers', was made obligatory
under canons of 1571 and 1604 and many still survive, providing a rapid way
of gaining an overview of landholding patterns over a wide area. A study of
early-seventeenth-century glebe terriers in West Suffolk (Dymond 2002, 82
and map 2) revealed that there was a concentration of block glebes in the
area south of the Gipping line suggested by the HLC mapping. Conversely,
common-field terminology was much more frequent in the glebes to the
north of that line. This raised the very real possibility that the 'random' field
area was linked to block holdings, and that the area with fields belonging
to the 'co-axial family' had significant associations with the Type 3 common
fields.

Another significant factor separating these two areas was their different
topographies: the area south of the Gipping line is composed mainly of sloping land, but north of the line it is mainly flat (Hoppitt 1989). This difference
had important implications for medieval farming. A slope was vitally important for arable farming in clay areas to ensure that water drained away, thus
preventing the soils from becoming waterlogged. Where the land was flat the
water tended to remain and pool, keeping the soil cold and either rotting
the seeds or adversely affecting seedlings' growth. Therefore, where plenty of
sloping land was available, arable farming was possible over a wide area and,
where there was limited sloping land, the potential for successful arable land
was limited.

In south Suffolk the abundant availability of sloping land meant that block
holdings were feasible, as most of the blocks were likely to contain some
suitable land for arable crops. But in the flat areas of north Suffolk, the
land suitable for arable farming must have been in short supply. This would
give a reason for the presence of relatively small areas of common fields – a

sharing out of the limited supply of suitable land. The case study of South Elmham St Michael bears this out. Evidence for a small area of common fields was found at the northern end of the parish, where the land slopes down to a stream. The remaining flat lands would have been more suited to the growing of grass for cattle. It comes as no surprise, then, to find that these flat lands of north Suffolk were identified in the eighteenth century as a dairying region (Young 1786, 194–5). The abundance of pasture here would also help to explain the poorly developed folding arrangements on the common fields.

Improvements to the drainage of these flat claylands, through more effective ditches, more efficient furrowing methods and, from the second half of the eighteenth century, under-draining, must have lessened the need to rely on a limited number of sloping common fields for arable crops. As their relative value lessened through the wider availability of arable land elsewhere, there would have been a tendency for them to slip out of communal use into severalty. This could well be the main reason why common fields of Type 3 disappeared without any great difficulties, and much earlier than those of Type 2. Their limited extent, combined with poorly developed communal cropping and folding arrangements, meant that there were few barriers to their conversion to severalty.

A local observer, writing *c*.1605, gives support to these deductions about the varying availability of land that was suitable for arable crops. In 'those parts inclining to the east commonly called high Suffolk [i.e. north-central and north-east Suffolk], do especially and chiefly consist upon pasture and feeding, contenting themselves onely, with so much tillage as will sattisfie their own expences'. In contrast, the 'midle parts [i.e. south-central Suffolk] although enjoying much meddow and pasture, yett far more tillage doe from thence raise their chiefest maintenance' (Hervey 1902, 29).

These farming differences find a physical expression in the distribution of timber-framed aisled barns of medieval and early post-medieval date. Aisled barns have a greater volume than normal for the storage and processing of crops, and are therefore indicative of areas where there is an emphasis on arable farming. They occur in the south-west quarter of the county, but are rare north of the Gipping (Aitkens 1999). Furthermore, most small barns, with up to three bays, are found to the north-east of the Gipping line, while those with seven or more bays are predominantly to the south of the line (Aitkens and Wade Martins 1998, map 5). The small barns would only have had a single threshing floor, but two or more occur in the larger barns.

So far the 'Gipping divide' has been explicable in terms of factors rooted in the differing topographies, but there are strong indications that it was also an important, and hitherto under-appreciated, cultural division. This is strikingly illustrated by the vernacular architecture of the region. Queen-post roofs dating from the fifteenth to seventeenth centuries have a distribution in Suffolk that almost exactly mirrors that of the dairying region mentioned

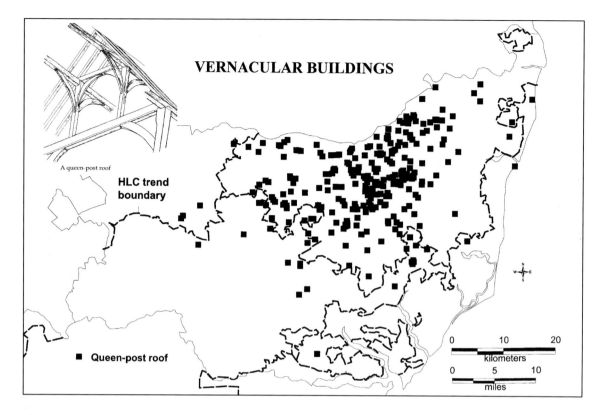

VERNACULAR BUILDINGS

A queen-post roof

HLC trend boundary

■ **Queen-post roof**

0   10   20
kilometers
0   5   10
miles

above, with very few examples south of the Gipping line (Figure 37; Colman and Barnard 1999). They are almost unknown in Essex, but common in much of Norfolk (Aitkens 1998, 45; Heywood 1998, 48). To the south of the line, in south Suffolk and Essex, their place is taken by crown-post roofs and coupled-rafter roofs (Aitkens and Wade Martins 1998, 29; Walker 1998, 9; Colman 1999). The divide also shows up in plan forms, techniques of bracing timber buildings and in the positioning of inserted sixteenth-century chimneys (Aitkens 1998, 44; Aitkens and Wade-Martins 1998, 29; Walker 1998, 9).

The 'divide', in fact, seems to be apparent in a number of culturally derived distribution patterns. One is the distribution of the term 'tye' (derived from Old English *teag*, 'a close, an enclosure') as a descriptor for a green. Although greens are widely distributed on the clayland on either side of the divide, tyes are only found to the south of it – in south Suffolk, Essex and Kent (Reaney 1935, 569; Martin 1999b). Another is the distribution of Borough English tenure (inheritance by the youngest son) which has a higher frequency to the north of the Gipping (Corner 1859; MacCulloch 1986, 31, map V).

By uniting the data derived from the HLC mapping, the case studies and parliamentary enclosure records, a new map has been created (Figure 38) showing the possible extents of the various medieval farming systems that have been discussed above. The map does not purport to be definitive, but it does provide a vehicle for debate and further research.

FIGURE 37.
The distribution of vernacular buildings with queen-post roofs in Suffolk, overlain by the HLC trend boundary (see Figure 36) (after Dymond and Martin 1999, map 82; queen-post diagram © P. Aitkens).

FIGURE 38.
The medieval farming system regions of East Anglia, as suggested by the Historic Field Systems of East Anglia Project.

Common fields, block holdings and the Viking interventions

The evidence from charters suggests that common fields were in existence in England by the mid tenth century, but their first appearance is a still a matter of debate (Hooke 1981, 58). Hall has argued for an eighth-century origin, but many other writers have preferred a more cautious ninth- or tenth-century beginning (Hall 1995, 130–1, 137; Brown and Foard 1998, 65, 76; Hooke 1998, 121; Fowler 2002, 290–1).

This period, of course, coincides with the upheavals caused by the Viking invasions and there are significant correlations between the areas with common fields and the distribution of place-names of Scandinavian origin in the region stretching from Northamptonshire northwards to Yorkshire, though not in the counties running south-westward from Oxfordshire, which lay to the south of the Danelaw boundary (Hart 1992, 7; Roberts and Wrathmell 2002, figs. 5.4 and 5.6). However, it is not a simple case of common fields being introduced by the Vikings. The available evidence indicates that in the Viking homelands, common fields first appeared slightly later than the

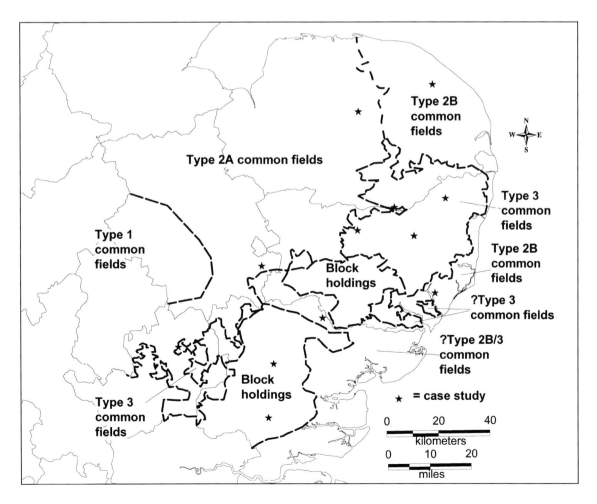

English ones. In Denmark and Sweden, common fields appeared between the late tenth century and the beginning of the twelfth (Porsmose 1987, 276; Tesch 1993, 140; Poulsen 1997, 119; Widgren 1997, 178–80).

The earliest evidence for common fields, in fact, comes from the Frankish areas of the Continent in or around the eighth century (Nitz 1988a, 249–73; Renes 1988, 164). Nitz has suggested that in south Germany common fields were introduced by the Merovingian state after the Frankish conquest, *c.* AD 743, as part of the reorganisation of the landscape for Frankish 'peasant-soldier colonists'. In his view, the origins of the system should be sought in the Frankish royal domains or those of the ecclesiastical bodies that were closely linked to the crown (Nitz 1988b, 156–7). Even in the Frankish areas there is doubt over whether 'fully developed' common-field systems were established before the tenth century (Hildebrandt 1988, 284; Verhulst 2002, 17).

Although the Anglo-Saxon Chronicle states that in AD 880 King Guthrum, after concluding a treaty with King Alfred, led his Danish army 'into East Anglia, and settled there and shared out the land', many commentators regard the evidence for a substantial influx of Scandinavian settlers as weaker here than in other parts of the Danelaw (Whitelock 1961, 50; Davis 1955; Hart 1992, 28; Williamson 1993, 107). The place-name evidence for Viking settlement in East Anglia is certainly not as strong as it is in the central and northern Danelaw, but the names are reasonably numerous in some areas (Figure 39). They are most common in Norfolk, slightly less so in north Suffolk, but markedly less in south Suffolk and Essex (Reaney 1935, xxvii–xxviii; Hart 1992, map 3.1; Williamson 1993, 109–10; Martin 1999a).

This suggestion of more Scandinavian influence in northern than in southern East Anglia finds some confirmation in a linguistic study of the differential pronunciation of an initial fricative ('f') as a voiced ('v') sound (Kristensson 1995). The isophone (or 'zone of pronunciation') for this runs across the southern end of Cambridgeshire and then across southern Suffolk to the east coast near Aldeburgh, coming close to the northern boundary of block holdings as identified in this study (Figure 38). In the area to the south the fricative was voiced, but not to the north. Kristensson has shown that the voicing of initial fricatives occurred in late Old English, but that in areas of Scandinavian influence the tendency towards voicing was 'counteracted and forestalled' (Kristensson 1995, map 14).

Hart has suggested that, although most of Essex was normally considered a part of the Danelaw, it remained in Anglo-Saxon control throughout the period of the Danish kingdom of East Anglia. From a detailed study of the Anglo-Saxon ealdormen, he has suggested that from AD 825, when the last native East Saxon king was expelled by King Egbert of Wessex, until AD 946, Essex formed, together with Surrey, Sussex and Kent, a single administrative unit subordinate to the kings of Wessex. Hart believes that the Danes only succeeded in settling the north-east corner of Essex, perhaps reaching as far south as Witham, but that the rest of Essex remained under West Saxon rule (Hart 1992, 125).

FIGURE 39. Place-name and linguistic indications of Scandinavian influence in East Anglia, overlain by the farming systems boundaries suggested by the Historic Field Systems of East Anglia Project (see Figure 38) (isophone after Kristensson 1995, map 14).

This conclusion is of great significance, because it seems to fit with the place-name and linguistic evidence. Moreover, the limited Scandinavian place-name evidence in Essex occurs in just the areas where there is some evidence for common fields, such as in the north along the Stour and in the coastal fringe. On the Suffolk coastal fringe there is again a correlation between evidence for common fields and Scandinavian place-names. In the rest of Essex and in south-central Suffolk, where there are few Scandinavian place-names, there is strong evidence for block holdings. Interestingly, in view of the political links that Hart has suggested between Essex and Kent, similar block holdings occur there too (Baker 1965).

If, as suggested, there was a link between Scandinavian settlement and common fields, how and why did they establish them in England, when as already noted, there is no evidence that the Vikings had common fields in their own homelands at this time? One significant factor may have been the Scandinavian notion of the free peasant – a man who owned and farmed his own land. Although not all Scandinavians were free men, free farmers played an important part in their society (Jones 1969, 150). Equally important,

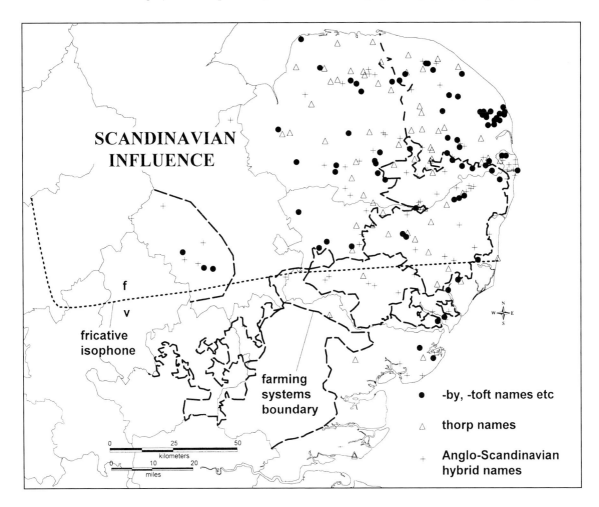

SCANDINAVIAN INFLUENCE

f
v
fricative isophone

farming systems boundary

● -by, -toft names etc

△ thorp names

+ Anglo-Scandinavian hybrid names

0   25   50
kilometers
10   20
miles

though, was the disruption that the Vikings caused to the land laws, social customs and hierarchical organisation that had previously prevailed (Hart 1992, 4). In Norfolk and Suffolk there is a very close correlation between Scandinavian place-names and high incidences of free men and sokemen in 1086, suggesting that the two were inter-related (Darby 1971, fig. 105). By contrast, the southern 'English' areas were characterised by a low proportion of both free men and Scandinavian names. This correlation suggests a possible reason why block holdings, in the south, and common fields, in the north, developed as contrasting farming systems.

In the Anglo-Saxon area of Essex, the wealth of woodland, as revealed by Domesday Book, is often seen as indicating that it was an area of late settlement. However, although woodland was certainly present on the heavier, poorly drained soils, there were substantial areas of slope soils in the valleys that probably had a history of arable cultivation stretching back into prehistory, as has been demonstrated in the area of the Stort valley at Stansted in north-west Essex (Wiltshire and Murphy 2004, 78). Finds of Roman agricultural tools and equipment are concentrated in south-east England, including Essex, making it likely that arable farming was most developed in that region during the Romano-British period (Jones and Mattingly 1990, 230, map 6.47). The distribution of Roman villas in East Anglia, and in particular those with mosaic floors, is also heavily weighted towards south Suffolk and Essex, suggesting either greater economic prosperity or a greater adoption of the Roman way of life. Either way, this would suggest a developed agricultural economy rather than an undeveloped forested region.

Palaeoenvironmental studies are not yet detailed enough to provide a clear view, but there is certainly widespread evidence for cereal crops on all soil types in Roman Essex (Murphy 1996, 175). Two sites in Essex – Mucking and Springfield Lyons – have produced evidence for early Saxon cultivation of spelt, the major wheat type of the Iron Age and Roman period (Murphy 1994, 27, 37; 1996, 177). At Springfield Lyons there is also evidence for late Saxon spelt and some emmer, suggesting continuities with Romano-British arable farming. With no apparent intervening period of common fields, it is likely that the prime agricultural land developed continuously from Iron Age and Romano-British farming practices into the block holdings seen in the early medieval period. Of particular significance are the large block demesnes of this southern region, which occupied the best arable land and contained fields that were as large as 70 ha. These invite comparison with the large demesne *culturae* of the Frankish realm in the ninth century (Verhulst 2002, 17). In physical terms these could be described as 'open' fields, but were exclusively demesne, not common fields.

In northern East Anglia, similarly, palaeoenvironmental work in the Waveney valley has shown that comparable 'prime' arable areas on the valley sides probably have a continuous cultivation history since at least the Iron Age (Wiltshire and Murphy 1999; Wiltshire forthcoming). In some cases these prime areas may be associated with co-axial field systems, but the HFSEA project's case studies suggest that the systems are not as continuous as Williamson (1987) has suggested and that some of the systems on the poorly drained clay plateaux are more likely to be late Saxon or high medieval in date (Martin and Satchell forthcoming). In this northern area, however, the period of Scandinavian rule is likely to have disrupted the established social order, making the prime arable areas available for reallocation on a more equal or 'common' basis. Thus, while the best land remained locked in block demesnes in Essex, similar land in north Suffolk and Norfolk was shared out between wider groups of peasant farmers. While some of these may have been Scandinavians, it is probable that many others were native Englishmen taking advantage of the breakdown in the social order to acquire shares of the best land. Whatever redistribution took place, there are likely to have been substantial additional changes following the English reconquest, as titles to land were either challenged or confirmed (Abrams 2001, 139). The formal arrangements of medieval common field systems may well have developed after the English reconquest and, in their final form, may owe more to Frankish concepts adopted by the English royal administration than to Viking ones. The fact that some of the earliest common fields on the Continent are associated with areas of Frankish conquest must alert us to the possibility that reorganisation after conquest may be an important factor in England too. Overall, the Viking interventions should perhaps be seen as a catalyst for change rather than a cataclysmic event, or even as fundamentally about the immigration of new people.

Conclusions

This study has shown that, as Hoskins and Gray warned, East Anglia's landscape history is complex. Part of that complexity can be understood with reference to its topography and soils, but there are also significant elements that seem to owe more to human culture than the environment. This is most clearly seen in the differential use of prime areas of arable land either as block holdings or as common fields. Factors related to the Viking interventions provide a possible explanation for the development of common fields in the northern and western parts of the region and for their appearance along the east coast and the Stour valley. This would imply a late-ninth-century date for the beginning of common fields, though the systemisation of them may in fact be a product of English royal policy in the tenth century. However, the trends towards arable expansion and the creation of large 'open' arable fields could be considerably earlier, for it is important here to stress that 'open' fields do not necessarily mean 'common' fields, as the large demesne fields of Essex and south Suffolk are variants of 'open' fields.

By disrupting the established social pattern, and by placing an increased emphasis on the more equitable sharing of the better land, the Scandinavian interventions could have triggered the development of common fields. It is not necessary to envisage a massive influx of Scandinavian immigrants, as even a small proportion might have acted as catalysts for change. Although there were undoubtedly earlier underlying cultural and environmental factors that contributed to the development of the different farming systems, it is the correlation with the Scandinavian evidence that is so thought-provoking.

No study can hope to give a definitive and unchallengeable interpretation of the historic landscape, but perhaps this study has suggested some new ways of analysing landscape evidence to enable fresh models to be developed. The emerging patterns challenge many existing views on farming systems, landscape evolution and cultural grouping and show that existing county boundaries are not necessarily the strongest cultural boundaries. The study has also shown that Sir Thomas Smith was correct when he wrote, c.1549, that Essex was one of the places 'wheare most Inclosures be' (Lamond 1893, 49).

Acknowledgements

I am grateful to Max Satchell for his contribution to the project and to my colleagues for many stimulating discussions. I would also like to thank the editors for their helpful comments on an earlier draft.

PART THREE

Landscapes of Settlement

CHAPTER TEN

Stability and Instability in Medieval Village Plans: Case Studies in Whittlewood

Mark Page and Richard Jones

Hoskins and the medieval village plan

In *The Making of the English Landscape*, Hoskins considered various issues relating to 'the shape of villages', and made the following observations:

> The variety of plan among the villages of England, besides affording one of the most delightful characteristics of the countryside, is profoundly interesting – and tantalising – to the historian of the landscape. It is interesting because he realises that this variety of forms almost certainly reflects very early cultural or historical differences, and it is tantalising for two reasons. First, because we cannot be sure that the present plan of a village is not the result of successive changes that had been completed before the earliest maps are available: we cannot be sure we know what the *original* shape was in many instances. And secondly, even if we are sure of the original shape of a village, we are not yet in a position to say – for the subject has been so little studied in this country – what the various shapes and plans mean in terms of social history. (Hoskins 1955, 60)

Many studies of the village plan have been published in the fifty years since the appearance of Hoskins's classic work. Some have challenged his assumption that village layouts changed radically over time, presenting a case for stability in plan structures over 800 or 900 years (Roberts 1977, 138; Sheppard 1966). Use has been made of nineteenth-century Ordnance Survey maps to investigate patterns of medieval settlement, thereby reinforcing the impression of continuity over change (Lewis *et al.* 1997; Roberts and Wrathmell 2000; 2002). The emphasis of much recent writing, however, has been on change, supporting Hoskins's contention that 'we cannot be sure we know what the *original* shape was' by demonstrating that village plans underwent large-scale replanning or more continuous piecemeal change over the course of the Middle Ages (Taylor 1983, 151–74; Taylor 1989a; Everson *et al.* 1991; Taylor 1997, 13–16). The earliest maps are certainly not always a reliable guide to the shape of a medieval village, especially if the settlement experienced shrinkage or desertion in the centuries following the Black Death, or was subject to rapid expansion thereafter.

The seven case studies presented in this paper, taken from the Whittlewood Forest area of north-west Buckinghamshire and south Northamptonshire, have been subject to detailed archaeological and historical investigation (Jones and Page 2003a; 2006). In each case, fieldwalking around the edge of the present village (in order to investigate possible shrinkage) was undertaken alongside test-pitting in pasture fields preserving settlement earthworks and in the gardens of houses that remain inhabited. In addition, the archaeological evidence was integrated with studies of the documentary and cartographic sources. In all seven cases, the village can be demonstrated to have expanded in the period 1000–1350 before contracting as a result of population decline between 1350 and 1550. One village – Lillingstone Dayrell (Bucks.) – was deserted in the fifteenth century and its site later occupied by a close called 'The Warren', according to a map drawn in 1611.[1] In the late thirteenth century, the village was inhabited by thirty-three households, the tenements of which lay along two parallel streets that are visible today as limestone scatters and dense concentrations of medieval pottery (Illingworth and Caley 1812–18, II, 340; Dyer 2002a, 62). Of the others, three villages retained roughly the same shape from the Middle Ages to the nineteenth century, while the plans of the remaining three were subject to more dramatic change.

Stable village plans

Nineteenth-century Ordnance Survey maps show that the village of Leckhampstead (Bucks.) comprised a number of different parts, or 'ends': Church End, Limes End, Middle End, South End, and a group of farmsteads later called Barretts End (Figure 40). This type of settlement plan has been characterised as an interrupted or irregular row (Lewis *et al.* 2001, 50–1); alternatively, it might be called a 'dispersed village'. Extensive test-pitting and fieldwalking in the parish indicates that Leckhampstead's plan has remained essentially unchanged since the eleventh century. Medieval manorial sites and regular rows of peasant houses have been identified at Church End and Weatherhead Farm (part of Barretts End), which are likely to represent the two manors of Great and Little Leckhampstead, recorded in 1279. Further earthworks and pottery scatters close to Home Farm mark another row of peasant tenements and a high-status site, possibly the residence of Adam le Vavasour, to whom part of Great Leckhampstead was subinfeudated in the late thirteenth century (Page and Jones 2003, 27–32). At Middle End no single property of status has been identified, but a further regular row of peasant houses was observed. Each of Leckhampstead's 'ends' expanded markedly in the period 1000–1350, but the settlement clusters did not fuse to create a 'polyfocal' village, as occurred at nearby Paulerspury (Northants.) (RCHME 1982, xxxix, 112–15). The settlement pattern remained dispersed, even if the 'ends' were

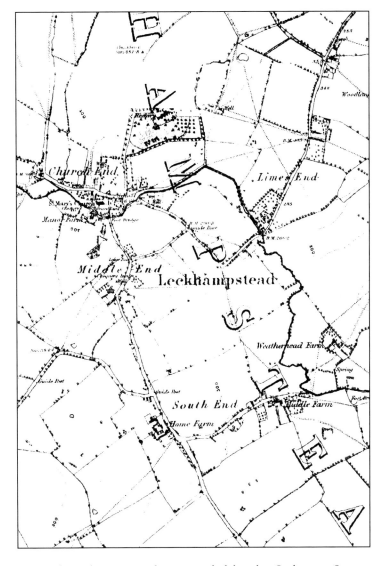

FIGURE 40.
Leckhampstead
(Bucks.) in 1889
(source: six-inch
Ordnance Survey map,
Northants. LXIV.NE).

much larger in 1350 than they were when recorded by the Ordnance Survey 500 years later. After the Black Death, settlement contracted to the scatter of isolated farmsteads depicted in the nineteenth century, except at Church End, where a cluster of houses survived. Nevertheless, these farmsteads preserved the framework of 'ends' at Leckhampstead which has persisted from the Middle Ages to the present day.

Similarly, at Silverstone (Northants.), both nineteenth-century Ordnance Survey maps and an early-seventeenth-century estate map show that the village was made up of three distinct parts: the largest comprised the area around the church and the roads radiating from it; the other two parts were (and are) called West End and Cattle End (Figure 41). The three 'ends' surrounded, and in places encroached upon, a large open space, formerly an area of common field, called Woodcrafts on an estate map of *c.*1608.[2]

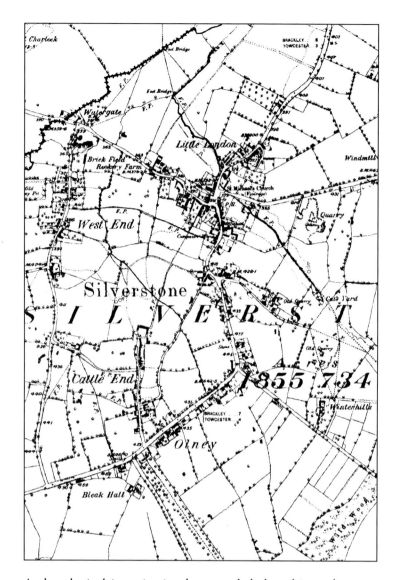

FIGURE 41.
Silverstone
(Northants.) in 1892
(source: six-inch
Ordnance Survey map,
Northants. LX.NW).

Archaeological investigation has revealed that this settlement pattern was of long-standing. Rows of houses along High Street (leading south from the church) and West End were laid out after 1100, while Cattle End developed following woodland clearance in the thirteenth century. The now lost Wood End, named in fifteenth-century manorial court rolls, may have comprised a group of tenements to the south of West End which was subsequently deserted.[3] Despite late medieval contraction and twentieth-century infilling, the village plan at Silverstone has remained essentially unaltered for more than 700 years (Jones and Page 2003b).

The shape of the village of Whittlebury (Northants.) has also remained largely unchanged since the thirteenth century. The present-day village may be classified as a regular row, a plan also depicted on the *c.*1608 estate map. The village assumed this form after 1250 when the southern extension was laid out, following earlier development to the south and east of the church, which lay within the enclosure of an Iron Age hillfort (Jones and Page 2001, 20–5).

At Leckhampstead, Silverstone and Whittlebury, village plans depicted on maps of the seventeenth and nineteenth centuries can, therefore, be demonstrated to have formed in the Middle Ages and remained largely unaltered despite medieval growth and contraction, and subsequent developments in more recent times. The original shape of these villages was preserved over many centuries, displaying remarkable stability in structure and layout. From the eleventh century or earlier, Leckhampstead and Silverstone were characterised by a relatively dispersed pattern of settlement, while Whittlebury was marked by a more nucleated appearance. The origins of these villages in the period after AD 850, and the reasons for their differing plans, have been explored elsewhere; briefly, they evolved from pre-existing settlements (which we call 'pre-village nuclei'), rather than from the abandonment of outlying hamlets and farmsteads (Jones and Page 2006). The explanation for the subsequent resilience of their layouts may be that they were not subject to large-scale replanning by lord or community at one point in time. Thus, in all three villages, the provision of additional rows of tenements in the centuries before 1350, although clearly planned, did not disrupt the existing framework of the settlement structure. Nor did subsequent contraction lead to the complete disappearance of the earlier form, as occurred at Lillingstone Dayrell (see above). By contrast, in several nearby villages, plans were subject to a much greater degree of change during the Middle Ages.

Unstable village plans: Akeley and Lillingstone Lovell

The present-day village of Akeley (Bucks.) is notable for its clustered appearance, a result of twentieth-century infilling. In the nineteenth century, Ordnance Survey maps depicted two regular rows of houses, separated by an area of open ground but joined by a short road called Church Hill, running south-east from the church (Figure 42). In the Middle Ages, however, this road almost certainly did not exist, and settlement clustered around the church on the north side of the open space, and close to the manor house on the south. These two parts were known as Church End and South End, according to a survey of 1623.[4] The open space may be called a 'green', and served as an area of both arable and pasture. Occupation on the south side of the green was more sporadic than on the north side, and was largely abandoned after 1350. This may have been the occasion for a reorganisation of the village plan. A combination of archaeological, documentary and architectural evidence suggest that the plots in South End were quickly cleared and the land converted to pasture, while in Church End houses were constructed, the crucks of which in some cases still survive (Woodfield *et al.* 2005, I). Medieval Akeley was thus a polyfocal village, the two areas of settlement on either side of the green possibly fusing at its south-western corner as a result of expansion before the Black Death, before separating thereafter, leaving the manor house virtually

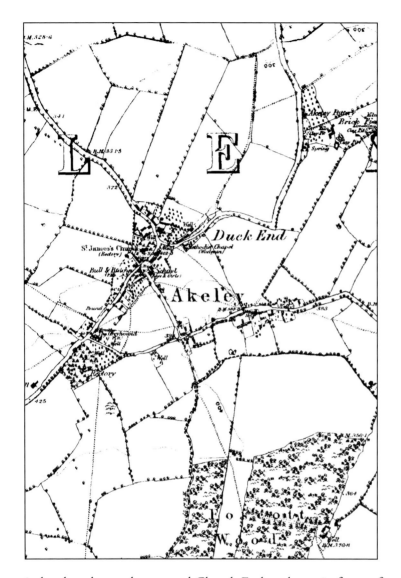

FIGURE 42.
Akeley (Bucks.) in
1889 (source: six-inch
Ordnance Survey map,
Northants. LXIV.NE).

isolated to the south-east, and Church End as the main focus of settlement in the village. In more recent times, the two 'ends' have gradually come together again through Church Hill traversing the green to create the present nucleated plan.

The nineteenth-century Ordnance Survey map of Lillingstone Lovell (Bucks.; formerly a detached part of Oxfordshire) depicts a loosely nucleated village comprising two main elements (Figure 43): first, a regular row of about a dozen houses fronting on to a stream, known today as Brookside; and secondly, about 100 m west of Brookside, a parallel row called Church Lane, on the western side of which, at the T-junction with the main road through the village, lies the parish church of St Mary the Virgin. Houses lie both to the north of the church, along Church Lane, and to its west, along the main street. The modern manor house is located about 1.5 km to the north-east of

Lillingstone Lovell
Early focus and zones of expansion 1100-1250

▨ Settlement areas
— C19 boundaries

0   100   200m

N

Lillingstone Lovell
Reorganization and expansion post-1250

▨ Settlement areas
▨ Manorial complex
— C19 boundaries

0   100   200m

N

MANORIAL COMPLEX

FIGURE 43.
The origins and
development of
Lillingstone Lovell
(Bucks.), 1100–1900.

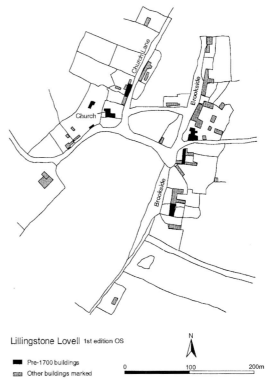

Lillingstone Lovell 1st edition OS

■ Pre-1700 buildings
▨ Other buildings marked

0   100   200m

N

the church. An earlier manor house, Lillingstone Hall, lies 500 m to the south. A number of post-medieval farmsteads are scattered throughout the parish.

The village of Lillingstone Lovell was subject to at least two phases of reorganisation during the Middle Ages. As Hoskins (1955, 60) suspected, these may be related to changes in the social history of the settlement. The origins of the medieval village appear to lie in the area around the church, from which pottery dating to the late tenth century has been recovered. The church itself is of interest. There are architectural indications of an early-eleventh-century construction date, most notably the presence on the north side of a side chapel or porticus-like structure with a narrow entrance from the nave, suggesting an ecclesiastical site of some importance, perhaps with authority over the surrounding area (Barnwell 2004, 8–10). It may be significant that in the later Middle Ages, Lillingstone Lovell was known as Great or *Magna* Lillingstone; its neighbour, Lillingstone Dayrell, as Little or *Parva* Lillingstone. The church remained the focus for the growth of settlement in the immediate post-Conquest period. Pottery sherds dating to about 1100 mark out an area which was occupied at this date of 5–8 acres (2–3 ha), to the north of the church.

Domesday Book records two manors in Lillingstone Lovell in 1086. An original estate of five hides held by the king had been split in half; each of the new manors comprised two ploughlands and woodland measuring ten furlongs by five. A recorded population of four – three villeins and a bordar – lived in one manor, while seven households – five villeins, a bordar and a slave – resided in the other. There is no evidence to suggest that these eleven families lived anywhere other than in the area around the church, although the precise location of their homesteads cannot be determined. The principal axis of the settlement was probably Church Lane which, at this time, formed just one section of an important cross-country route. Even today, footpaths can be followed northwards for 5 km from Church Lane to Pury End and Paulerspury (Northants.). Likewise, to the south of the church, geophysical survey has detected the continuation of the route, which probably ran for 3 km roughly parallel to the present road to Akeley.

In the 150 years after 1100, archaeological evidence suggests the growth of four main zones of occupation. This expansion (the precise sequence of which is unclear) forms the first phase in the reorganisation of the medieval village. First, the area immediately to the east of the church was occupied; earthworks can still be seen there today. Secondly, the eastern side of the stream was colonised. Two separate blocks of tenements can be identified, to the south of the modern houses. Thirdly, a group of tenements was laid out on the western side of the stream. Finally, a now obscured area of occupation probably lay to the south of the church, where the southern continuation of Church Lane crossed two roads running parallel to the present main village street.

These developments are likely to be related to a growth of population and the subdivision of one of the Domesday manors. The eleven households recorded in Domesday Book increased nearly fourfold in the 200 years to the

Hundred Rolls inquiry of 1279. There may have been 190 people living in the village at this time. One of the Domesday manors remained intact and was held in 1279 by Margaret Dansey, who gave her name to the village before the Lovells acquired the manor in the fourteenth century. The other Domesday manor was divided in half during the twelfth century and the two lords, like Margaret Dansey, were almost certainly resident in the village in 1279 (Page and Jones 2003, 34–6). The location of their manor houses are not known and we cannot attribute particular parts of the village to the properties of individual lords. But the planned extension of the village, in discrete blocks on either side of the brook, may have owed something to the wish of these three lords to demarcate separate areas of ownership. Furthermore, analysis of visible plot sizes in Lillingstone Lovell reveals no clear pattern; the width of messuages was either 20 m (66 feet or 4 perches) or 30 m (99 feet or 6 perches). This may reflect the social structure of the village at the time of the Hundred Rolls, with the larger plots occupied by villeins each holding half a virgate, and the smaller plots by tenants holding cotlands.

In the fourteenth century, Margaret Dansey's manor was divided into two parts, called Overend and Netherend.[5] This change may be related to the second phase in the reorganisation of the village. In the field to the south of the church are the well-preserved earthworks of a large manorial complex which was probably built in the late thirteenth century. Geophysical surveys and the evidence from test-pitting appear to indicate the foundations of a manor house, barns, dovecote, watermill and five interlinked fishponds (Page and Jones 2003, 32–4). The insertion of this manorial complex into the village plan was almost certainly accompanied by the diversion of the main street through the village on to its present course, forced northwards towards the church in order to avoid the manor. At the same time, the continuation of Church Lane southwards to Akeley was probably cut off and replaced by the surviving parallel path to the east. Any tenants who lived along these roads must have been forcibly removed and their houses cleared. Their removal seems to be linked to the infilling of the row on the eastern bank of the stream and its extension both to the north and south, developments which can be dated to the period 1250–1350. On the eve of the Black Death, therefore, the village of Lillingstone Lovell had reached its most developed state. A large manorial enclosure, perhaps belonging to the Lovell family, lay at its heart, next to the church, to the north, south and east of which were situated blocks of peasant tenements, linked to each other by lanes.

Finally, a brief afterword on the shrinkage of the village. The plague and its effects devastated Lillingstone Lovell, as it did so many other settlements. The abandonment of the manorial site and many of the peasant houses was almost certainly complete before 1450, as revealed by the scarcity of late medieval pottery fabrics. Further contraction followed, but it is probable that the village had assumed something like its present form by the time the various manors of Lillingstone Lovell were united in the possession of Nicholas Wentworth in 1545.

Unstable village plans: the two villages of Wicken

At Wicken (Northants.), nineteenth-century maps show the village to be a straggling affair exhibiting few signs of cohesion (Figure 44). It was made up of four principal components set around the northern and western sides of an eye-shaped loop formed by the road system. On the north-western edge of the village was Manor Farm and the church of St John. Open ground separated these from a double row of cottages to the south-east, which formed the main core of the village, and a second group of cottages and larger farms which lay to the south-west. The final element was a less regular grouping of cottages which lay isolated along the road to Leckhampstead. This is broadly the plan depicted on an estate map of 1717, the intervening years seeing only piecemeal additions and the occasional loss of individual cottages.[6] It is also a plan which we can recognise today, the only major changes being the replacement of Manor Farm with a small housing estate, and developments along the back lane and in the area of the old quarry. For nearly 300 years, therefore, the cartographic evidence attests to relative stability in the village plan, an impression supported by a survey of the standing buildings, which revealed the fragmentary survival of pre-1700 fabric in sixteen properties spread across all four parts of the settlement (Woodfield *et al.* 2005, XII).

A combination of evidence, however, suggests that this view of the permanence of the village plan is misleading. The maps themselves carry evidence for the loss of significant buildings: field-names on the 1717 map, such as 'The Old Church Yard' and 'Dove House Close', lie between the south-western cluster and the cottages south of the brook; and the tithe map appears to show

FIGURE 44. The origins and development of Wicken (Northants.), 900–1900.

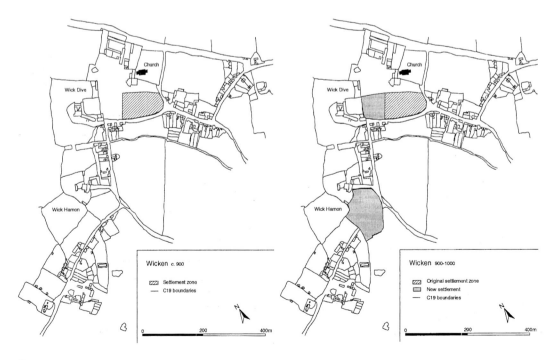

isolated fishponds on the southern side of the Leckhampstead Road. On the ground, there are areas of settlement earthworks in 'Dove House Close' and the western half of the central loop, as well as to the north of the brook in the area immediately south and west of the church. These fill the gaps, lending more coherence to the village plan; Wicken loses its polyfocal aspect and adopts a more nucleated appearance.

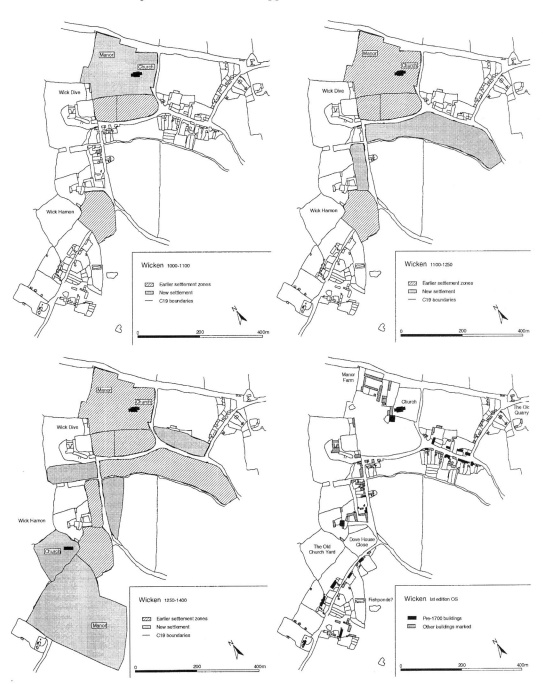

Yet the maps do not reveal the process by which this change in the village plan took place. Are we looking at internal shift? Do the southern fishponds mark the location of an earlier capital messuage which shifted north to the Manor Farm site? Does the old churchyard likewise indicate that the church migrated northwards? Or are we looking at settlement shrinkage, the loss of elements of the village plan before the first maps were produced? A single village containing more than one manor is far from unusual: divided lordship was a common experience in many communities. But why two churches? The answer is that we are looking not at one village, but at two. By 1066 Wicken was split between the manor of Wick Dive, to the north of the brook, and Wick Hamon, to the south. Given their proximity and shared beginnings (despite the pluralisation of the name Wicken, which might be taken to imply more than one *wic* or specialised farm, place-name scholars would argue that the settlement began as a single entity), it was perhaps inevitable that close ties should exist between the two. In the mid thirteenth century Wick Hamon was a chapelry, probably dependent upon the church of Wick Dive, but by 1278 Wick Hamon had been granted its own parochial status, the parish boundary also following the brook. To all intents and purposes, then, the manors and their associated villages were independent of one another throughout the Middle Ages. In fact, the manors would only be reunited in single ownership by Richard Woodville of Grafton in 1449, and the parishes unified by John Spencer of Althorp in 1587, after which the church of St James, Wick Hamon, was allowed to decay (Riden 2002, 413, 423, 432, 435). The 1717 map of Wicken thus depicts a villagescape whose origins were little more than 100 years old.

The development of Wick Dive and Wick Hamon can, however, be traced with some accuracy, revealing the often complex and divergent paths each followed in the adoption of their eighteenth-century plans. Wick Dive is the older of the two villages and almost certainly the original *wic*, a primacy which is borne out in the ecclesiastical superiority it held over its neighbour. There is a complete absence of evidence for any activity before AD 850, the nascent settlement occupying a virgin site immediately south of the church. In its earliest phases, the occupied zone remained small. After AD 950 there are the first signs of growth, as Wick Dive expanded westwards. At the same time, the first indications of settlement in Wick Hamon appear in the area immediately east of its church. Absence of any contemporary material from within the central loop suggests that this was reserved as an area of pasture. The radial road network which converges on this open space might indicate its use as a central collecting ground for livestock driven in from the wider landscape and offers the possibility that animal husbandry may have been the principal function of the *wic*.

In the post-Conquest period, both villages continued to expand. Little is known about growth in Wick Hamon, except that it remained outside the central loop. By 1100 the function of this area had changed, having been brought into cultivation. The need for more arable land may have its origins in the division of the earlier *wic* estate, the manor of Wick Hamon no longer being able to draw on the resources of a more extensive territory, and thus being forced to turn to more localised provisioning. The degradation of the central loop is also seen in Wick Dive, where a regular row of peasant tenements, sharing a common street frontage of 30 m (99 feet or 6 perches), was laid out in a single planned phase in the interior of the loop around 1100. There are also signs that the manorial complex north-west of the church had been established by the early twelfth century. The history of Wick Dive up to the eve of the Black Death was characterised by expansion. Although the precise chronology of events cannot be teased from the archaeological evidence for lack of closely dated pottery, it seems that the southern row was extended to the east, the northern row was newly established, and a short row south of the rectory was laid out between 1250 and 1350. Expansion in Wick Dive was thus modular; existing units were preserved and new units were added, but the integrity of the village plan remained unaltered.

This contrasts strongly with the contemporary sequence of events in Wick Hamon. In the 1240s a capital messuage was built on the southern side of the Leckhampstead Road. Whether this replaced an earlier manor located elsewhere in the village is not known. Although largely founded on arable land outside the village, it may have necessitated the clearance of a number of peasant dwellings on its northern fringes. The site of the manor house may be represented by a scatter of pottery recovered from the field to the south of the present houses. If so, the house appears to have been framed by the two fishponds shown on the tithe map, and separated by them from the manorial farm, of which the dovecote and malthouse have been excavated in a garden to the north. A dovecote is mentioned in an extent for William son of Hamon in 1248, presumably referring to the structure found during the excavation (Page and Jones 2003). William had held the manor since the early thirteenth century and should almost certainly be identified as the architect of this new complex. Seigniorial interest in Wick Hamon extended well beyond the manorial buildings and its effect on the villagescape was even more profound than that identified at Lillingstone Lovell. William may have founded the chapel, first mentioned in 1218 (Riden 2002, 432), and he probably also created the deer park, its pale running directly south of the proposed manor house site, which would thus have enjoyed views into the park's interior. The origins of the line of the Leckhampstead Road might also be found in the establishment of this park forcing the old route, which ran directly south from the village, to be diverted to the north. This was also the point when settlement colonised the central loop, with what appears to be a regular row of tenements laid out either to accommodate a rising population or those displaced by the building of the manorial complex. In Wick Hamon, then, manipulation of the village plan was total and changes were effected rapidly, in contrast to the more steady development of its neighbour.

From the mid fourteenth century both villages began to contract. By the mid fifteenth century the manorial complex at Wick Hamon had been completely abandoned, in contrast to Wick Dive, which continued to function as the capital messuage for the amalgamated manors. In both Wick Hamon and Wick Dive there were significant losses within the peasant tenement rows, both contracting to perhaps half of their previous extent, broadly in line with current estimates of population decline. Moreover, the villages began to fragment into the parts mapped in the eighteenth century.

Conclusions

Modern research methods, in particular the integration of archaeological evidence (derived from both deserted and surviving areas of settlement) with documentary and cartographic sources, now enable village plans to be accurately reconstructed at each stage of their development, removing the uncertainty that inevitably surrounded the subject fifty years ago. At Akeley, Lillingstone Lovell and Wicken, evidence has been found to demonstrate that village plans experienced not only progressive change in their growth and contraction, but also radical alteration at various moments in their history, changes that are hidden from view in their earliest eighteenth- or nineteenth-century depictions. In the case of these three villages, therefore, reliance upon Ordnance Survey maps to investigate the pattern of medieval settlement is undoubtedly misleading. By contrast, greater continuity in village layout between the Middle Ages and the nineteenth century can be demonstrated at Leckhampstead, Silverstone and Whittlebury. On this basis, Hoskins's assumption that village plans changed substantially over time may be correct in about half of England's surviving villages, thus challenging the reconstruction of medieval settlement patterns based solely on the use of the earliest available maps. Our ability to trace the village plan back to its origins may mean that the subject is no longer tantalising, but it is all the more interesting; for with certainty comes the opportunity to address why different communities chose to adopt different village models, the question which lies at the heart of the Whittlewood research from which these case studies have been taken.

Notes

1. Buckinghamshire Record Office (BRO), D22/22/5.
2. Northamptonshire Record Office (hereafter NRO), Map 4210.
3. NRO, XYZ 1390, mm. 1, 2d, 9, 21.
4. New College, Oxford, 4467.
5. PRO:TNA, SC2 155/19.
6. NRO, Map 5692.

Acknowledgements

The research for this paper was funded by the Arts and Humanities Research Council as part of a five-year project, 'Medieval settlements and landscapes in the Whittlewood area'. The authors are grateful to Christopher Dyer, Mark Gardiner and Stephen Rippon for their advice and encouragement during the project.

CHAPTER ELEVEN

Reaching Beyond
The Clearances: Finding the
Medieval – Based Upon Recent
Survey Work by RCAHMS
in Strath Don, Aberdeenshire

Piers Dixon

The agricultural improvements of the eighteenth and nineteenth centuries swept away the medieval and post-medieval settlement pattern of hamlets called townships, or *touns* in Scots, and replaced them with improved farm-steadings. A recent study has emphasised the concomitant migration of the rural population to the manufacturing towns and rural villages, a process involving considerable social dislocation (Devine 1994) for which one recent authority has coined the term 'lowland clearances' (Aitchison and Cassell 2003). My title echoes this in order to emphasise the degree of change from the post-medieval period that has occurred in the lowlands of Aberdeenshire and the difficulties inherent in researching medieval settlement.

This paper is based upon recent fieldwork and documentary research by the Royal Commission on the Ancient and Historical Monuments of Scotland (RCAHMS) in Strath Don, Aberdeenshire (Figure 45). The Strath Don survey encompassed a large part of Aberdeenshire, including the watershed of the Don and some adjacent areas. It is bounded by the Cairngorms on the west and the sea at Aberdeen on the east, covering an area of some 2000 square kilometres. The fieldwork focused primarily on abandoned sites of all periods up to and including the twentieth century. However, the author has also examined the topography of many occupied settlements in order to seek evidence for continuity from before the agricultural improvements of the eighteenth and nineteenth centuries. Prior to the Poll Tax (1696) there are no comprehensive sources of settlement evidence for Aberdeenshire, and topographic and settlement evidence becomes increasingly patchy the earlier one goes. This situation is compounded by the almost complete absence of settlement remains that are demonstrably medieval, as opposed to post-medieval. This makes any reconstruction of the medieval settlement pattern a difficult process, particularly as the modern landscape of Strath Don is largely a result of the agricultural changes of the later eighteenth and early nineteenth centuries, modified by the twentieth-century trends of mechanisation and afforestation. It comprises scattered farms and enclosed fields occupying lowland vales, locally called howes, fringed with ranges of hills, now often clad with conifer plantations. The few villages were usually planted by improving landlords during the eighteenth and nineteenth centuries to provide a place for the labour-force to live (e.g. Echt, Rhynie, Monymusk and Alford), as were the numerous smallholdings or crofts. This rural settlement pattern was well established by the time it was depicted on the Ordnance Survey first edition six-inch maps of Aberdeenshire (OS 1869–70).

Touns, cottars and crofts

Topographical descriptions of settlement dating from the twelfth to the fifteenth centuries are rare, and most contemporary sources use the Latin terms *villa de* or, more frequently, *terra de*, in effect referring to the unit of land belonging to a farm. From the fifteenth century, however, topographical details are mentioned more frequently and the suffix *toun* is often applied to the name of the settlement of the farm (giving rise to many of the modern place-names ending in *-ton*). Here the tenant or tenants of the farm resided, thus giving rise to the descriptive term *fermtoun*. Such settlements usually formed the nucleus of a township, though *kirktouns* were a special case at the ecclesiastical focus of the parish (e.g. Kirktoun of Rayne). The *fermtouns* were only one element in the overall settlement pattern that emerged in the late medieval period. At least three other forms of settlement are identifiable: *milltouns*, *cottowns* (or *cottertouns*) and individual crofts; this increases to four if manorial sites are also included.

These terms reflect recognisable groups in the rural population which played a part in the evolution of the nucleated settlements that dominated the settlement pattern across Aberdeenshire. The estate mill, for instance, was an essential element in the pattern of rural settlement, its position dictated by a suitable source of water. In some cases this could be found adjacent to an existing *toun*, as at Clatt, but in others it lay some distance away, as at Mill of Leslie. Where it was separate, it sometimes developed the status of a farm in its own right, either as a croft (e.g. Fetternear in 1511: Innes 1845, 364–7), or a *fermtoun*, as at Milton of Noth.

Cottars, in contrast, form the unseen class of rural medieval Aberdeenshire, essentially being sub-tenants who barely appear in documentary records. The Poll Tax returns of 1696, however, indicate their frequency in the late seventeenth century. By and large, they depended on their labour for their livelihood, but some were able to keep a cow and hold small plots in the cultivated lands of the township, as can be seen at Monymusk in the eighteenth century (Hamilton 1945, xxv). The frequent occurrence of *cotts*, *cottowns* or *cottertouns* on estate maps suggest that many cottars resided in separate settlements because of their status. Examples of *cottertouns* are shown on estate maps near Mains of Leslie,[1] and near Newbigging by Clatt,[2] while two deserted buildings that are shown adjacent to the *'Affleck intown'* field on a map of Essie are annotated *'old stances of cottertoun'*.[3]

Eighteenth-century estate maps reveal the fourth component in the settlement pattern, the individual croft. In contrast to the landless cottar, the crofter held a separate small farm with its own steading, but was generally a dependent sub-tenant of the farmer, rather than an independent farmer in his own right. For example, Simon Ley's Croft near Mains of Leslie is identified on estate maps,[4] while at Newseat in Rhynie, John Cruikshank's Croft is one of several farmsteads that held small pieces of arable on the fringes of the *toun* fields.[5] The dependent status of these crofters may be seen in the documentation relating to the Duke of Gordon's estates in Rhynie and Essie,[6] the Leslie estate[7] and the Monymusk estate (Hamilton 1945, xxvi). Indeed, of seventeen crofts shown on the Leslie estate maps of 1758, only four are still occupied (e.g. Temple Croft). As dependencies, the land occupied by these crofts could be reincorporated in the farm at the end of the tenancy, which would then see their demise as separate entities. At the beginning of the nineteenth century, old croft land was described as infield by the Board of Agriculture report for Aberdeenshire (Keith 1811, 171, 231–2), which matches the status of the croft land in the estate surveys.[8] This suggests that crofts were not a form of long-lived settlement so much as a method of intake by which new land was broken in by a crofter under beneficial terms. Evidence of this practice can be probably be detected at Garbet, near Craigs of Longley, where four crofts were established in 1686, apparently as additions to the existing *toun*.[9] However, no settlements are depicted at Garbet on the estate plan of 1776,[10] by which time the lands of Garbet had reverted to outfields belonging to the nearby Boganclogh Farm (Figure 46).

On this evidence, the croft was a dynamic element in the Aberdeenshire rural economy in the post-medieval period, and it should perhaps be placed in the wider context of the expanding settlement pattern at that time, rather than regarded as a medieval form of settlement. Nevertheless, such an impression may simply reflect the difficulties of finding evidence to push back this component of the settlement pattern for, without direct documentation, they are easily overlooked. The earlier documented examples tend to be where crofts were leased directly from the landlord rather than held by sub-tenants. This is why these particular crofts appear in the rentals, whereas those occupied by sub-tenants are unlikely to be documented. The croft of Auchleck or Affleck, for example, is listed as part of the grant of Lesmoir to James Gordon in 1537 (Bulloch 1907, 166). Others are recorded at Fetternear, in the bishop of Aberdeen's rental of 1511, which lists fourteen crofts including ones attached to a brewery, a smithy and a mill (Innes 1845, 364–7). The earliest reference to a croft dates from 1310, when Ade Chapelane, a burgess of Aberdeen, sold his croft called 'le Spyttalhillis' (Innes 1845, 40). At face value this may be evidence that crofts were also components of the medieval settlement pattern,

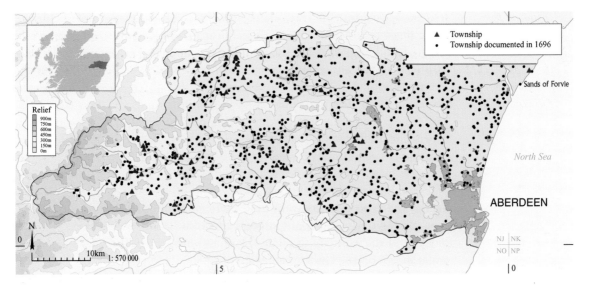

Relief
900m
750m
600m
450m
300m
150m
0m

▲ Township
• Township documented in 1696

Sands of Forvie

North Sea

ABERDEEN

N

0

10km 1: 570 000

NJ | NK
NO | NP

| 5

| 0

but this particular croft and some other late medieval holdings of the burgesses may be facets of the royal burgh's developing hinterland rather than a
more general feature, especially since crofts do not appear anywhere else in
the documentary sources until the sixteenth century.

Whatever their origins, relatively few *touns* retain their pre-improvement
layout today, and many of them have been replaced by single farms. Nevertheless, examination of the handful of *touns* that are still occupied, those that
appear on eighteenth-century estate maps and the abandoned examples surviving in the margins shows that there are two characteristic types. The first
type comprises row villages which exhibit some evidence of planning in the
common alignment of house-plots (see below); while the second is made up of
what are termed here 'clustered townships'. The layout of a clustered township
is apparently haphazard, comprising a group of houses and yards without a
single dominant street, or any rows of yards. Belhinnie, Belnacraig and Kirkton of Oyne are surviving examples and others, such as Upper Coullie, Little
Collieston, Craich, Dalmadilly, Upperton and Pitcandlich, survived in this
form as late as the Ordnance Survey first edition six-inch map (OS 1869–70),
but by far the majority are known only from pre-improvement estate maps
of the late eighteenth century (Figure 45). Clustered townships, which are
found throughout Strath Don, from Lochans in Glen Carvie in the west to
Little Collieston near the coast at Slains in the east, are part of a much wider
distribution extending along the eastern fringes of the Highlands (RCAHMS
and HS 2002, 55–7).

Yet even in clustered townships elements of order may be found. This is to
be seen in the common alignment of the houses and yards, typically employing a major axis with a secondary one at right angles, which is often mainly
north to south or east to west. The use of these major axes is well illustrated on
estate maps at townships like Auchline in Clatt[11] or Upper Coullie in Monymusk.[12] These *touns* are amongst the larger examples, but the same tendency

FIGURE 45.
Map of the *touns*
listed in the Poll Tax
return of 1696, and
clustered townships
recorded by RCAHMS
in the Strath Don
Survey. The inset is a
location map of the
RCAHMS survey area
(Crown Copyright:
RCAHMS).

is in evidence at smaller *touns* comprising no more than two or three yards and a few houses, such as Edderlick[13] or Brae of Scurdargue in Rhynie.[14] It can also be seen in the archaeological remains of several of the *touns* that have been recorded in the course of the survey, such as Newton Wood, Lynardoch in Glenernan (Figure 47), and Garbet near Craigs of Longley (Figure 46).

New burghs and planned villages

The origins of planned villages are obscure, but the foundation of royal and baronial burghs in the late twelfth and early thirteenth centuries provides a context for the creation of this type of settlement. Indeed, the foundation of a burgh at Inverurie by David, earl of Huntingdon, the brother of King William, and the construction of the motte and bailey castle, known as the Bass of Inverurie, together with the royal foundation of a burgh and a castle (Castlehill) at Kintore, and the port and burgh of Newburgh by Alexander Comyn, were part of the Anglo-Norman settlement of the area, providing alternative administrative and market centres to the royal burgh of Aberdeen. Their economic success, however, was overshadowed by Aberdeen and there is little archaeological evidence to reveal their character at this time. The excavators of the deserted burgh of Rattray, further north in Aberdeenshire, have argued that while many small burghs have often been assumed to have been trading centres, they in fact served as little more than agricultural

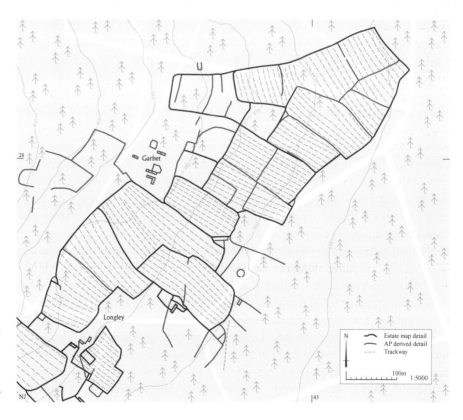

FIGURE 46.
The *toun* of Garbet and isolated buildings that may be the crofts recorded in 1686. This plan is based upon an estate map of Garbet of 1776 (National Archives of Scotland, Register House Plan No. 2257) and features transcribed from an RAF vertical air photograph (Crown copyright: RCAHMS).

markets (Murray and Murray 1993), while Carter has argued that they should be viewed as components of lordship (Carter 1999, 657ff).

Whatever the case, medieval burgh foundations are typified by rows of adjoining burgage plots, or tofts, each of a similar breadth and depth (Colman 2004, 283). The plots fronted a street or market place, and were granted to burgesses to build their houses and conduct their business, as at Aberdeen (Dennison *et al.* 2002, 17–19). Inverurie has a roughly triangular market place at the north end of its high street, which is lined by properties of similar size, as depicted on the Ordnance Survey first edition six-inch map (OS 1869–70). The grant of a toft in the burgh of Inverurie to Robert of Billingham confirms that properties of this sort existed here by 1185 (Stringer 1985, 225). Confirmation of the layout of the burgh, however, does not come until the late fifteenth century, when records show that it was parcelled into properties distributed in the Upper and Lower Roods, lying to the west and east of the high street respectively (Davidson 1878, 118–19; Carter 1999, 657). This gives a *terminus ante quem* for the laying out of the burgh, which is most likely to have occurred at its foundation by Earl David in the late twelfth century, since there is no obvious subsequent occasion for it to have been executed (Carter 1999, 657). In the mid seventeenth century Robert Gordon depicts Inverurie as two rows of houses on either side of a north–south street,[15] a layout that more or less matches the present high street.

Rows of yards or *tofts* were not, however, the sole preserve of burgh planning. Indeed, they may also be found in rural settlements, as is plain from eighteenth-century estate maps, indicating an element of planning and suggesting similar a period of origin to that of the burghs. Row layouts typify medieval villages in southern and eastern Scotland, as well as many parts of England and Europe (e.g. Roberts and Glasscock 1983; Dixon 1998; Lewis *et al.* 2001, 172–7). In Scotland, the archaeology, such as it is, suggests that there were indeed planted row settlements appearing in the twelfth and thirteenth centuries, but the lordship context is more complex. The excavated medieval settlement at Springwood Park Kelso in Roxburghshire appears to have been part of a planned village of the twelfth to fourteenth centuries that was replanned twice (Dixon 1998), presumably by the native Anglian lords of Maxwell, while Rattray, a possession of the incoming Comyns from the early thirteenth century, was laid out along a street between the motte and the church. Its status as a medieval burgh is uncertain, and it may have been essentially a rural settlement and port that acquired burghal status at the end of the medieval period (Murray and Murray 1993).

The introduction of row villages to the north-east may be attributed to the influx of a new class of Flemish or Anglo-Norman landholders (Lynch 1991, 56–9; Stringer 1985, 80–103), including the reformed monasteries, during the twelfth and thirteenth centuries. In the lordship of the Garioch (Figure 48), a number of Anglo-Norman and Flemish incomers were granted land in return for service to Earl David of Huntingdon in the late twelfth century (Stringer 1985, 30ff). While some of these grants were of old holdings with names of

Gaelic origin, such as Bourtie, Durno, Ardoyne, Leslie and Resthivet, others were probably new settlements. The names of these settlements typically combine the name of the founder with the English suffix *toun*, or, as it appears in Latin in the charters, *villa*. In the Garioch such names include Williamstoun in Culsalmond, Glanderstoun in Kennethmont, Johnstoun and Courtistoun in Leslie, and Inglistoun near Keithhall (Stringer 1985, 83ff). Duncanstone (*Duncanstoun)* in Leslie parish appears to be another example, although it is not documented until the fifteenth century. The thirteenth-century form of Flinder in Kennethmont, *Flandres*, is thought to be descriptive of its origin as a Flemish foundation (Alexander 1952, 278).

The original forms of these settlements are not known for certain, but those that make their appearance on eighteenth-century estate plans appear to be row villages, where a row comprises three or more adjacent yards, usually laid out along a street. Indeed, row villages are quite common on these maps, particularly in the Garioch. Estate maps of 1758 for the Leith Hall estate of Leslie, for example, depict Duncanstone (Figure 49), Old Leslie, Old Flinder and Christkirk as villages with one or more rows of yards arranged along one or more streets.[16] Elsewhere there are single short rows of yards, as at Bogs of Leslie[17] or Belnagauld (Gaelic *Baile na gall*, town of the strangers: Alexander 1952, 170) in Glencarvie.[18] Another short row of yards aligned from north to south on a map of the Monymusk estate in 1774 is labelled as the site of the ruins of Delab.[19] Relatively few of these row villages are still occupied, but examples include Duncanstone (Figure 50), Kirkton of Daviot, Kirkton of Rayne, and Balhalgardy. The main distribution of these modern survivals and of those depicted on estate maps falls in the Garioch (Figure 48), but a few isolated examples lie in Mar, such as Blairdaff and Tillyfourie near Monymusk,[20] and Torries near Tough.[21]

In Strath Don at least, the general coincidence of the distribution of row villages with estates where incomers were given land in the Garioch tends to support the idea that many of these settlements were laid out in the twelfth or thirteenth century (Figure 48). This must be treated with some caution, however, for there are some row villages that were probably founded when *touns* were split in the post-medieval period (see below). One of these is Little or New Flinder, which is depicted on two successive pre-improvement estate plans of 1758 and 1797[22] relating to Leith Hall as two short rows on either side of a street. This raises the question as to whether there was any material or chronological difference between the short rows that have been recorded and the fully developed street layout of the larger examples. It may simply be the size of the population and the resources available to a *toun* that dictated whether it developed a formal layout along a street. It should also be borne in mind that a short row depicted in the eighteenth century may have resulted from the shrinkage of a larger village following the post-medieval dispersal of settlement.

A second phase of burgh foundations from the late fifteenth century provided further occasions when planned villages might have been created.

Known as burghs of barony, these gave commercial benefits to the baronial
landlord, and continued to be created up until the early eighteenth century.
Few of these developed into significant settlements, but at some the elements
of a planned village combined with burgh architecture, such as a market
cross, or a *tolbooth* (Scots for a town hall), betray their mixed commercial
and agricultural origins. Indeed, the settlement of the burgh of barony was
often little more than a township with market rights where some of the tenants had a special tenurial status as burghers, as at Clatt in 1511 (Innes 1845,
360–4). As such, the element of planning detectable in some of them may
indicate that any burgh architecture was an addition to an earlier planned
village. For example, the layout of Oldmeldrum, erected as a burgh in 1671

FIGURE 47.
An aerial view of
the earthworks of
the deserted *toun* of
Lynardoch. Note the
co-axial arrangement
of houses and
yards, the successor
shepherd's house
and the reverse-S rig
(Crown copyright:
RCAHMS, SC961127).

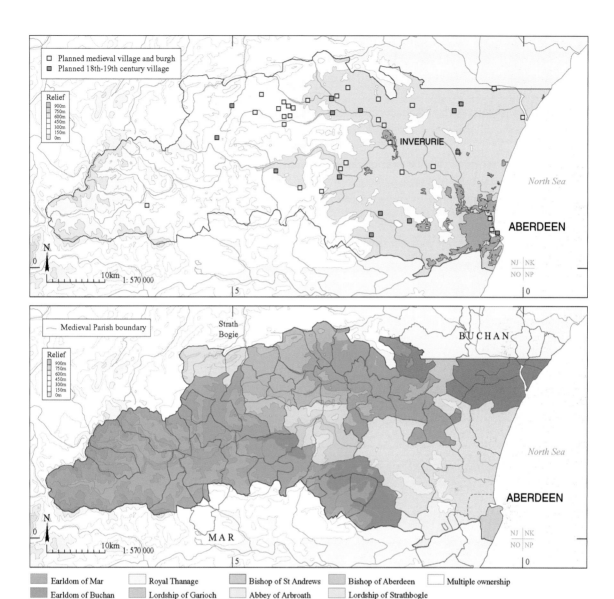

- ☐ Planned medieval village and burgh
- ☒ Planned 18th-19th century village

Relief
- 900m
- 750m
- 600m
- 450m
- 300m
- 150m
- 0m

INVERURIE

North Sea

ABERDEEN

NJ | NK
NO | NP

N

0

10km   1: 570 000

5

0

— Medieval Parish boundary

Strath
Bogie

BUCHAN

Relief
- 900m
- 750m
- 600m
- 450m
- 300m
- 150m
- 0m

North Sea

ABERDEEN

NJ | NK
NO | NP

N

0

10km   1: 570 000

MAR

5

0

| ▨ Earldom of Mar | ☐ Royal Thanage | ▨ Bishop of St Andrews | ▨ Bishop of Aberdeen | ☐ Multiple ownership |
| ▨ Earldom of Buchan | ▨ Lordship of Garioch | ▨ Abbey of Arbroath | ▨ Lordship of Strathbogle | |

FIGURE 48.
Map of the
distribution of planned
villages and the pattern
of lordship *c*.1185 in
the Strath Don Survey
area. Compare the
area of the lordship
of Garioch with the
distribution (Crown
copyright: RCAHMS).

(Pryde 1965), displays clear signs of its planned origins, comprising four rows of narrow properties fronting a rectangular market square, on the west side of which stood the tolbooth (OS 1869–70). Clatt (erected in 1501: Pryde 1965) may once have had a similar plan to Oldmeldrum, if on a smaller scale, but appears at first sight more like a clustered township. In the late eighteenth century, it comprised over thirty houses and twenty yards clustered around the church, with streets leading out on the four quarters.[23] Between the roads, short rows of yards framed the central space of the village, which was occupied by the churchyard, the market cross to the south-east of the church,[24] and a number of small houses and yards, occupying what was once, perhaps, the market square. The characteristic toft-rows are also apparent at the post-medieval burgh foundations of Old Rayne in 1498 and Insch in 1677 (Pryde 1965). Of these, Old Rayne has an extant market cross in a small square at the junction of two streets that lead off at right angles to one another, lined by house-plots, while the site of the bishop's palace lies at the far end of the street leading to the north. Insch, a classic example of a street village, has no burgh architecture, unless the widening of the street between the church and the crossroads at the centre of the village marks the location of the market place, while the intimate relationship of the settlement with agriculture is evident from an estate map of Insch, which shows that the tenants in the village held scattered blocks of land in the surrounding fields in runrig fashion.[25]

Changes in the settlement pattern during the post-medieval period: settlement expansion, dispersal and township splitting

Despite these indications of planning, whether medieval or post-medieval in origin, it is clear from an analysis of estate maps and documentary sources that the pre-improvement settlement pattern was subject to certain processes of change during the post-medieval period that obscure the medieval settlement pattern. Two particular trends can be detected, one involving the

FIGURE 49.
An estate plan of Duncanstone planned village in 1797. Note the reverse-S strip fields and runrig division of land (copyright: National Trust for Scotland, Leith Hall MS).

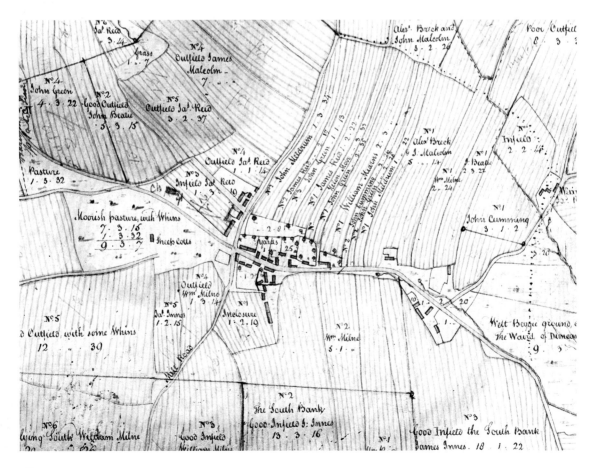

splitting or dispersal of large *touns* into two or more smaller settlements, and the other the expansion of settlement into marginal land. These trends are also part of a wider pattern of change in the settlement pattern of Scotland from the fifteenth century onwards (Dodgshon 1981, 195; Dixon 2003, 53). In the mid seventeenth century Gordon of Straloch attributed the changes that had occurred in the settlement pattern during his lifetime to the expansion of arable land and the demands of efficiency:

> Here also I desire to warn my reader that though our kingdom is, generally speaking, populated with few villages, paucity of inhabitants must not be inferred. The reason of this state of matters is as follows. Husbandmen eager for tillage thought from the very first that they were restricted in villages, and that, when they had so many neighbours, too little provision was made for agriculture; for at first the districts were divided into village settlements. To each of these so much of the arable land was allotted as could be tilled with four ploughs. These sections of lands were called in the ancient language *daachs* [i.e. davachs], which signifies village allotments. In many places in the higher districts the boundaries still remain, though the homesteads have been separated. But when the woods had been cut down four ploughs were no longer sufficient. Wide extent of bounds was inimical to agriculture, so that the proprietors, dividing the fields, set limits for each farmer according to his means, in such a way that the homesteads were continuous but not contiguous. I remember seeing instances of this in my early years. The farmers abandoned their villages and removed each to his own possession, where any vein of more fertile soil attracted him. Here the home was fixed, and so it remains at the present day. (Mitchell 1907, 272–3)

To Gordon, writing in the mid seventeenth century, the pattern of settlement was a relatively recent creation, in which the proliferation of new settlements following the division of farms had led to a general dispersal of settlement and desertion of medieval villages. But this is also supported by many of the names of townships in the Poll Tax returns, which are prefixed with Upper and Nether, Easter and Wester, Old and New, or Meikle and Little (Stuart 1844). Such naming protocols not only imply the splitting of existing townships, but also that the old village site probably continued in use in these instances. The 'old' prefixes in the Poll Tax yield the locations of some thirty villages in Strath Don that are potentially medieval in origin, such as Old Flinder or Old Leslie, though in every case they continued in occupation until the improvements. Examples of late medieval desertions, however, are rare, but the remains of Forvie, which were uncovered in excavations beside the church in the Sands of Forvie, may be one (Figure 45).[26] Here the reason for its final loss may be related to sand-blow rather than any economic trends, but the evidence for the date of its abandonment is equivocal, since there was still a taxable community at Forvie in 1696 (Stuart 1844), despite the excavator's description of finding medieval pottery associated with the stone foundations of the buildings.

FIGURE 50.
Air photograph of
the planned village
of Duncanstone from
the south-west (Crown
copyright: RCAHMS,
SC 976824).

The main period of *toun*-splitting dates to the sixteenth and seventeenth centuries, but one of the earliest examples of the dispersal of farms within a township in Strath Don is at Pitfoddel in Petercoulter, where it had certainly occurred by 1430 (Robertson 1857, 264), while at Knockinblewis in Chapel of Garioch it had happened by 1511 (Paul 1984, No. 3600). On the Gordon estates of Rhynie and Essie, Merdrum was divided before the early sixteenth century (Paul 1984, No. 3599), while Noth and Forest were split into Old and New during the seventeenth century (see Gordon rentals: Harrison 2001b, 18). During the following 150 years many other farms and crofts were established, and are depicted on the estate maps of 1776.[27] Similar developments can be paralleled in Clatt parish where the number of settlements increased threefold between the rental of 1511 (Innes 1845, 360–4) and the late-eighteenth century estate maps.[28] The Poll Tax returns serve as the most obvious index of the dispersal, or division of *touns*. The proportion of places prefixed Old and New, Over and Nether, Little and Meikle, or Easter and Wester account for 20 per cent, and rise to 28 per cent when Mains farms are included (Stuart 1844).

As indicated earlier, the process of *toun*-splitting reflects two trends in the settlement record. On the one hand it is a manifestation of the expansion of

Finding the
Medieval – Based
Upon Recent Survey
Work by RCAHMS
in Strath Don,
Aberdeenshire

settlement within the framework of existing townships, but on the other it reflects settlement spreading into marginal areas that were previously unoccupied. A rental of the Earldom of Mar preserved in the Exchequer Rolls (Burnett 1882, 459–60) suggests that Skellater, lying just above the mouth of Glen Ernan on the north side of upper Strath Don, and the Orde opposite it on the south, just above the mouth of Glen Conrie, mark the upper limit of settlement in 1451. Documentary evidence suggests that the expansion of settlement beyond this into the upper reaches of the Strath took place in the sixteenth century, though a note of caution should be sounded with such a statement, for there is no extant documentation for any individual settlements in the parish of Invernochty until the fifteenth century. That the head of the valley was managed differently may be seen from the grant of a hunting forest at Corgarff in the early sixteenth century, tacit recognition not only that it was unsettled, but that there was sufficient woodland for the deer. Corgarff Castle is said to have originated as a hunting lodge of the Earl of Mar (*Stat. Acct.* xiii 1794, 182), and the tower is first recorded in the sixteenth century, when it was occupied by members of the Forbes of Towic family. Gordon of Straloch's map of the area around Corgarff[29] depicts the area as woodland and it is not until General Roy's map in the mid eighteenth century (1747–55) that any settlement above Corgarff is recorded, although the relatively large taxable populations recorded for Castletown of Corgarff and Allargue on the other side of the Strath in the Poll Tax return (Stuart 1844) suggest an expansion of settlement was underway in the late seventeenth and early eighteenth centuries.

Eighteenth- and nineteenth-century settlement reorganisation and agricultural improvements

The eighteenth century saw the beginning of a reformation of the rural landscape of Strath Don, led by lairds who improved their home farms and the parks of their country houses. Sir Archibald Grant of Monymusk was one of the foremost in the process of the reorganisation of landed estates during the eighteenth century (Hamilton 1945). As well as planting trees extensively, he encouraged new rotations of crops that abolished the infield–outfield division of land by using legumes and turnips, the construction of enclosures and the clearance of stone, the intake of new land, and the removal of sub-tenants in order to create uniform farming units. However, it was not until the turn of the nineteenth century that landlords and tenant farmers throughout the lowlands invested in major improvements, including the building of new steadings and the enclosure of fields.

The effects of these changes, particularly the removal of sub-tenants during the later eighteenth century, are reflected in a widespread decline in the rural population of Aberdeenshire. If Old Machar, which formed part of the expansion of Aberdeen, is excluded, there was a general decrease in the rural population of Strath Don of about 5,000 persons between 1755 and the 1790s

(Keith 1811, 604–5). Some of the ministers' reports in the Statistical Account explain the decline as a product of the amalgamation of small farms and crofts, as at Bourtie and Oyne (*Stat. Acct.* ix 1793, 434; xv 1795, 105), while in Strathdon, Clatt and Auchindoir parishes they attribute it to emigration for work in the manufacturing industries of the towns (*Stat. Acct.* xiii 1794, 171ff; viii 1793, 535; xii 1794, 490ff).

This decline in the rural population is manifested in a retreat of settlement from the margins and the loss of the less economically viable small tenants. This may be illustrated by an analysis of the Gordon estates of Rhynie and Essie, which include upland terrain. A series of estate maps of 1776 depict abandoned settlements in both upland and lowland contexts, ranging from small townships to crofts and *cottertouns*. In several instances detached outfields are shown where previously documented settlements had already disappeared, such as at Garbet and Stonerives, whose lands had been absorbed by the adjacent townships of Boganclogh and New Merdrum respectively.[30] The amalgamation of farms that was taking place in the upland fringe was also taking place across the lowlands and continued on the Duke of Gordon's estates at Rhynie after the 1770s. Some settlements disappeared altogether, like Longley, Gulburn Croft, Howtoun and Smithston, while others became settlements for labourers of the nearby improved farms, as at Raws and Bogs of Noth (Harrison 2001b, 26). A similar process is also evident in the late eighteenth and early nineteenth centuries in the north part of the lowland parish of Clatt, an area transferred from John Forbes of Newe to the Leith Hall estate in the course of the same period. Here a number of crofts, small farms and cottages were cleared in the process of reorganising the farms.[31]

This sort of evidence for the amalgamation and reorganisation of farms, and the removal of sub-tenants, crofters and cottagers, is not only widespread across Strath Don, but it is also documented throughout the north-eastern counties of Aberdeenshire, Kincardineshire and Banffshire (Gray 1976). Indeed, it is also a feature of the improvements that occurred in central and southern Scotland in the second half of the eighteenth century. The difference in the north-east is the way in which the surplus labour force that these changes created was managed. In the southern and central parts of Scotland, some went to manufacturing and industrial enterprises, while many others moved to the rural villages (Devine 1994, 146–57). In the north-east, old rural burghs like Inverurie provided some scope for manufacturing, but most emigration from the countryside went to Aberdeen. Rural labour, therefore, had to be secured in other ways. Some landowners sought to secure their workforce by planting villages with allotments for each of the tenants, a good example being Rhynie on the duke of Gordon's estate, but the solution that was a speciality of the north-east involved the creation of a new class of crofter. Unlike most of their predecessors before the improvements, these crofters held their smallholdings directly of the landowner. These were already becoming a reality in the 1790s and are mentioned in the *Statistical Accounts*. In Kemnay, for instance, there were '*a good many small parcels of land, which we call crofts, held immediately of* the proprietor' (*Stat. Acct.* xii 1794, 205). The reasons for this development are not hard to find, for the Napoleonic Wars had raised fears about the possibility of revolution. Because few crofts were big enough to provide for a family, the crofters were obliged to labour for wages on the farms. This not only tied the crofters to the estates, but also cooled any rising discontent about the loss of their former status as sub-tenants and crofters of pre-improvement farms. It also enabled landowners to invest in the improvement of former common pasture at little direct outlay. The new crofts were predominantly small, taking in less than 20 ha (50 acres), and the basic cottages only provided accommodation for the family and a cow (Gray 1976). In economic terms, these new smallholdings were marginal, and this has led to the demise of many of them. In some cases the ruins have survived and have been recorded during the survey of Strath Don, but others have been simply swept away or replaced by improved farms in the late nineteenth century.

Other processes led to the complete clearance and desertion of pre-improvement *touns*. In particular, many lairds invested in the emparkment of land around country houses and the creation of Mains farms. The clearance of settlements to make way for new parks is a more familiar aspect of the improvement history of England (Beresford and Hurst 1971, 45), but it also forms part of the history of rural improvement in Scotland. Several instances have been recorded in Strath Don. In Glen Ernan, for example, the process of improvement of individual farms in *c.*1790 went hand in hand with the creation of the policies around the houses at Edinglassie and Inverernan. This led to the clearance of several *touns*, at Edinglassie, Haughton, Braeside and Coul (Harrison 2001a, 44), and at Inverernan the eponymous *toun* and Camasour. In the lowlands several settlements suffered this same fate: for example, the *toun* of Earlsfield was taken in to the policies of Leith Hall between 1758 and 1797 and a steading of the same name erected on an entirely new site.[32] This means that it cannot be assumed that a modern farm with the same name as a pre-improvement *toun* occupies the same site.

While there is no evidence in Strath Don for large-scale clearance events affecting whole glens, as happened elsewhere in highland Aberdeenshire (RCAHMS 1995), a few small-scale clearances occurred, apparently to make way for sheep. One such was at Delnadamph, where the clearance of the south side of the Strath, which included several small *touns* near Inchmore and an unnamed *toun* to the east of the shooting lodge (since demolished), was probably carried out to establish a sheep station at Inchmore and only latterly the shooting estate. Likewise, on the Gordon estates the *toun* of Boganclogh was cleared by 1822 to make way for a sheep farm held directly by the Duke of Gordon.[33] Here a new improved steading was built at the site of the *toun*, but no enclosed fields were laid out, since they were not needed. A similar clearance was carried out at Lynardoch in Glen Ernan, probably by Forbes of Newe, in which the *toun* and its dependencies (Caldens) were removed. A shepherd's house was eventually built on the site (Figure 47; Harrison 2001a, 50), but the grazing was held directly by the estate until the 1870s.

Conclusions

The settlement pattern of Strath Don has been in a constant state of flux since the medieval period, with periods of expansion and contraction as well as agricultural improvement. The earliest period of expansion is represented by the documented *villa* of Anglo-Norman and Flemish immigrants of the twelfth and thirteenth centuries in the lordship of the Garioch. This, and the evidence of estate maps for planned villages, present a *prima facie* case for the planting of villages and burghs in the medieval period. It begs the question of the origin of the clustered township as the unplanned element in the settlement pattern. Its widespread distribution throughout Aberdeenshire and the eastern fringe of the highlands suggests that this was a typical settlement form in the eastern lowlands of Scotland. There is clearly more work to be done here, but the idea of planned villages imposed on an existing pattern of settlement in the twelfth and thirteenth centuries is an attractive one, if simplistic. Indeed, the concept of planned villages is one that recurs right up until the estate village in the nineteenth century. The establishment of crofts in the late medieval and post-medieval periods was, it appears, as important an engine of settlement expansion as township splitting in Strath Don. Its reinvention on the margins of the improved farmland in the nineteenth century is a local solution to the labouring problem that is unique to the north-east of Scotland, and represents the final phase of settlement expansion.

Notes

1. National Archives of Scotland (hereafter NAS), Register House Plans (hereafter RHP) 5199, Plans of the estates of Leslie belonging to John Leith Esq., 1758, no. 4.
2. NAS, RHP 14753, Plan of the estate of Knockespock and Terpersie belonging to James Gordon of Moorplace, 1745–1760.
3. NAS, RHP 2256, Plan of Essie and Lesmoir in the lordship of Huntly, property of the Duke of Gordon, 1776.
4. NAS, RHP 5199, Plans of the estates of Leslie belonging to John Leith Esq., 1758, no. 4.
5. NAS, RHP 2261, Plan of Scurdargue and Newseat in the lordship of Huntly, property of the Duke of Gordon, 1776.
6. NAS, Crown Estate Records for the Duke of Gordon's estates (hereafter CR8), item 163.
7. NAS, RHP 5199, Plans of the estates of Leslie belonging to John Leith Esq., 1758, nos 1–13.
8. NAS, RHP 5199, Plans of the estates of Leslie belonging to John Leith Esq., 1758, nos 1–13.
9. NAS, Sheriff Court Records for Aberdeenshire, SC1/60/31.
10. NAS, RHP 2257, Plan of Garbet and Boganclogh in the lordship of Huntly, property of the Duke of Gordon, 1776.
11. NAS, RHP 14753, Plan of the estate of Knockespock and Terpersie belonging to James Gordon of Moorplace, 1745–1760.
12. Lady Grant MS, Monymusk House, Aberdeenshire, Plan of the Lands and Barony of Monymusk belonging to Sir Archibold Grant, 1774.

13. NAS, RHP 5199, Plans of the estates of Leslie belonging to John Leith Esq., 1758, no. 11.
14. NAS, RHP 2261, Plan of Scurdargue and Newseat in the lordship of Huntly, property of the Duke of Gordon, 1776.
15. National Library of Scotland (hereafter NLS), Gordon MS 32 Formarten and part of Marr and Buquhan by Robert Gordon of Straloch, c.1636–52.
16. NAS, RHP 5199, Plans of the estates of Leslie belonging to John Leith Esq., 1758, nos 2, 3, 7 and 9.
17. NAS, RHP 5199, Plans of the estates of Leslie belonging to John Leith Esq., 1758, no. 5.
18. Aberdeen University Library, MS 2769/I/131/6, Plan of Glen Carvy and Bunzeach, 1766.
19. Lady Grant MS, Monymusk House, Aberdeenshire, Plan of the Lands and Barony of Monymusk belonging to Sir Archibold Grant, 1774.
20. Lady Grant MS, Monymusk House, Aberdeenshire, Plan of the Lands and Barony of Monymusk belonging to Sir Archibold Grant, 1774.
21. NAS, RHP 232, Plan of Kincraigie Estate, Tough, 1769.
22. NAS, RHP 5199, Plans of the estates of Leslie belonging to John Leith Esq., 1758, no. 1; National Trust for Scotland (hereafter NTS), Leith Hall MS, A Survey of the lands of Leith Hall, 1797.
23. NAS, RHP 14753, Plan of the estate of Knockespock and Terpersie belonging to James Gordon of Moorplace, 1745–1760.
24. Royal Commission on the Ancient and Historical Monuments of Scotland (hereafter RCAHMS), NJ52NW18, may be consulted via Canmore at www.rcahms.gov.uk.
25. NTS, Leith Hall MS, A Survey of the lands of Leith Hall, 1797.
26. RCAHMS, NK02NW 1.
27. NAS, RHP 2254, Plan of part of the Lordship of Huntly lying within the parishes of Rhynie, Essie and Gairtly. Property of the Duke of Gordon, 1776.
28. NAS, RHP 14753, Plan of the estate of Knockespock and Terpersie belonging to James Gordon of Moorplace, 1745–1760; NAS, RHP 260/2, Plan of the property of Capt. John Forbes of Newe in Clatt parish, c.1771.
29. NLS, Gordon MS 27, Strath Don by Robert Gordon and James Gordon, c.1636–52.
30. NAS, RHP 2257, Plan of Garbet and Boganclogh in the lordship of Huntly, property of the Duke of Gordon, 1776; NAS, RHP 2259, Plan of New Merdrum in the lordship of Huntly, property of the Duke of Gordon, 1776.
31. Compare NAS RHP 260/2, Plan of the property of Capt. John Forbes of Newe in Clatt parish, c.1771, and Ordnance Survey first edition for Aberdeenshire 1869–70 of Clatt parish.
32. NAS, RHP 5198, Plans of the estates of Leith Hall belonging to John Leith Esq., 1758; NTS Leith Hall MS, A Survey of the lands of Leith Hall, 1797.
33. NAS, CR8, item 66.

Acknowledgements

I should like to thank Stratford Halliday, Alex Hale and Jack Stevenson for reading and commenting on the paper, Ian Parker and Kevin Macleod for the drawings and Tahra Duncan for preparing the digital images. I should also thank all those others from the Royal Commission on the Ancient and Historical Monuments of Scotland who worked on the survey of Strath Don, on which this paper is based. The ideas expressed herein are entirely my own.

CHAPTER TWELVE

The Origins and Persistence of Manor Houses in England

Mark Gardiner

The problem of the origins of manors has been examined by a number of historians since Aston (1958) wrote on the subject almost half a century ago. Indeed, Aston himself revisited the problem and provided a 'postscript' or, more accurately, a commentary, to his earlier work some twenty-five years after its first publication (Aston 1983). Since that time many important contributions have been made by, among others, Blair (1994), Dyer (1996a), Faith (1997) and Hooke (1988). Much of this more recent work has tended to stress the importance of the fragmentation of estates during the tenth and eleventh centuries, in which areas of land from large estates were either granted to fiefs or to lessees in return for services. There was an overwhelming tendency for the lands which were granted to specific individuals or for a period of lives, typically for three lives, to become heritable. These developments were once seen as 'centrifugal', to use Dyer's phrase, by which power passed from great lords to their tenants who established control over their fiefs (Dyer 1980, 48). More recent work has tended to regard the changes as managerial. Great lords who had little knowledge of, or control over, activities in the fields were supplemented by lesser lords who were on the spot and exercised a tighter rein on agricultural matters (Harvey 2004).

Landscape historians and archaeologists have contributed little to the discussion of the origin of manors, even though archaeological evidence has been drawn upon by others. Archaeology cannot readily identify the abstract forces leading to manorial formation, but it may be able to recognise the physical evidence resulting from their operation, in particular the emergence of the manor house within the landscape. It may seem rather reductive to try to trace the development of a fundamental and complex institution such as the manor through its buildings, but a moment's reflection will suggest that this is not entirely unreasonable. Manorial buildings were the embodiment of the manor, in physical, symbolic and fiscal terms. For example, the mid-eleventh-century will of Thurstan son of Wine describes his two manors at Shouldham in Norfolk as 'the estate at the north hall' and 'the estate at the middle hall' (Whitelock 1930, 80, ll. 10.19). Likewise, we can confidently assume that when an agreement was made to relinquish land in return for the west hall at Winterton, it was not just one building that was expected in return, but also the estate associated with it (Whitelock 1930, 96, l.1–2). Thus, the manor buildings, and specifically the hall, were used as a metonym for the whole manor. The same sort of usage is evident in Domesday Book. When the Domesday commissioners wished to indicate that there was a manor, they used the expression *ibi est una aula* ('there is a hall there'). And where a manor had been split between two thegns as, for example, at King's Clere (Hants), Domesday Book notes that there were two halls (Munby 1982, 23, 22). The manor hall could also be used to represent the organisation of the manor. Where a manor had been farmed out (or leased) to villeins, Domesday Book recorded '*non est ibi aula*', to show that it was not of normal type and there was no demesne (Munby 1982, 3, 17). However, the Domesday manor is a difficult thing to define, as Maitland (1897, 119–20) observed long ago. The Domesday commissioners' essential interest in the manor hall was not with it, either as a building or as a symbol; it had a more practical side. The *aula* was simply the place at which geld was collected by the king and, except for that, it may have differed little from many other similar farms (Palmer 1987, 153; Faith 2004, 78).

It seems that it may be possible for us to use manorial buildings as they were used by people in the past – to represent manorial organisation. But we need to hesitate for a minute before we accept the simple equation that a manor house equals a manor. Most demesnes in the period before 1200 were run not by the major lords and their officials, but by others. These might have been either tenants who had the land in dependent tenure – in other words, feudal tenants – or those who held it by lease for a period of time. We may question how much the lord would wish to invest in the construction of buildings on a demesne which was to be worked by others, and whether the tenants, particularly if they were lessees for a short period, would wish to spend more than the minimum effort to maintain such buildings. If the demesne was leased not to a single farmer, but to a group of villagers, there is the further issue of whether there would have been a single manorial farmstead at all, or whether, as Domesday Book appears to suggest in a small number of entries, there might be no central hall and no manorial buildings. Some later evidence reinforces this point. The demesne of Grittleton (Wilts.) was leased from at least the late twelfth century by the 'men of the vill', or, more probably, by the wealthy among them. When the manor was taken in hand again by Glastonbury Abbey during the mid thirteenth century, a survey found that it had only a hall and granary. This contrasts with the other leased manors of the abbey, which had the usual array of buildings found on a *curia* (Stacy 2004, 121).

The first problem which needs to be confronted is how it is possible using landscape or archaeological evidence to distinguish the manorial buildings from any other farmstead. There is no infallible means of identifying manorial sites, but it is possible to use a number of indicators to suggest the status of the buildings. Rarely can any one provide a certain identification, but taken together they do allow us to determine whether it is likely the site was seigniorial.

Character of buildings

We might expect the typical manorial *curia* or farmstead to contain not only a hall and chamber, but also numerous other buildings, including a brewhouse and bakehouse, and also barns and granaries, although these last two are sometimes difficult to distinguish from other buildings in the archaeological record. An analysis of the utensils and equipment recorded in List B of the eleventh-century document known as *Gerefa*, ostensibly a guide to a reeve on how to run the lord's farmstead, suggests that these were ordered according to their location in the buildings of the *curia*. The list suggests that there were separate buildings for the kitchen, dairy, granary, buttery, spence (for the storage of dry goods) and brewhouse or bakehouse (Gardiner 2006). Blair (1993, 5–11) has shown that some manorial *curiae* were arranged around courtyards or, alternatively, with the domestic buildings in a single row or 'long range'. Excavations in Northamptonshire have identified examples of long ranges at Raunds Furnells and West Cotton, and further such groups of buildings occur at Ellington, Sulgrave and Brooklands (see Appendix for references).

Manorial appurtenances

Mills and dovecotes were typically associated with manorial sites in the late Middle Ages and we might expect them to have been so before 1200, although the evidence is less clear (Holt 1988, 37–8). Those mills whose valuations were included in Domesday Book were evidently held by manorial lords; mills held by tenants may not have been listed. Maitland (1897, 144) suggested that the fractions of mills recorded in Domesday Book might indicate, at least in some cases, that they had been erected at the expense of tenants of the vill. The siting of mills was dictated by the suitability of a watercourse or, at the end of the period considered here, an elevated position for a windmill. A mill would not necessarily have been located near to the manor house, but a number of mills served only the hall, as Domesday Book indicates. For example, the entry for Boarhunt (Hants) records that there was one mill worth 42d, which evidently ground the tenants' corn, and another for the needs of the manor hall (Munby 1982, 21, 1). Dovecotes, too, could be situated anywhere, but normally they were placed within the *curia*, if only to ensure the security of the birds from thieves. Purpose-built structures for keeping doves are found from at least the late twelfth century (Round 1913, 214–15). The right to keep doves was a seigniorial prerogative, but it was sometimes extended by lords to clergy. The dovecotes of the latter were generally located within the church itself and so are hardly likely to be confused with manorial settlements (McCann 2000, 29).

Proximity to the church or presence of a chapel

These are not invariable indicators of manorial status, for lords were not the only ones to found churches; groups of peasants also did so. Equally, we must be aware that rectilinear churchyards have four sides and they may be abutted on one side or more by peasant houses. However, the conjunction of manor house and church is sufficiently common that it would be foolish to ignore it as a potential indicator (Morris 1989, 259–61, 268–74).

Nature of finds

We might expect that the finds from a manorial site would be rather different from those from houses of their peasants. A bell found at Cogges (Oxon), for example, is thought to have been for hunting dogs which, given the clear association of lordship and hunting, is likely to indicate the presence of a manorial settlement (Blair and Steane 1982, fig. 28, no. 4; Gillingham 1995). The bone chess pieces found at West Cotton bespeak a leisured life, which we might associate with a lord rather than peasants (Windell *et al.* 1990, 28). Another chess piece has been found at Bradford Bury, near Milton Keynes (Mynard 1994, 33–5). Equally, the Romanesque stone voussoirs from Harding's Field, Chalgrove (Oxon) can have only come from a high-status building, and provide evidence for the presence of a manor here in the later twelfth century (Page *et al.* 2005, 117). The nature of the bone assemblage may also indicate high-status settlement. The bones of some species of wild birds are found most commonly on elite sites, while the discovery of remains of goshawks in excavations at Puxton (Somerset) suggests a manorial building in which hunting birds were kept (Sykes 2004; Stephen Rippon pers. comm.). On the other hand, the pottery on seigniorial sites seems to have been little different to that found around the houses of their peasants (Brown 1997, 92–3).

Place-names

Place-names may provide an indication of the status of a site. The name 'Manor Farm' is an obvious example, but 'Bury' or 'Burystead' may also suggest the presence of a *curia*. These latter names are from the Old English *burh*, which in this instance was applied to an enclosed manor house (Williams 1992, 222–3). However, the *burh* element is applied quite widely for many different types of sites, particularly those with an enclosure, as the discussion in the *Vocabulary of English Place-Names* indicates (Parsons and Styles 2000, *s.v.*). Excavations at Bradford Bury have confirmed that this was indeed the site of a manor house (Mynard 1994, 1–59).

Documentary evidence

Written sources, and particularly those before 1200 which are considered here, may confirm the presence of a manorial site, but rarely locate its position precisely.

Yet, even with these wealth of possible indicators, it is sometimes still difficult to be certain about the identification of the status of a site. This is particularly true if the excavation has been restricted in area so that the range and character of buildings cannot be determined. One of the issues which has become evident on three sites which have been extensively excavated is the question of the persistence of the status of the settlement. Manorial sites might be superseded by peasant farmsteads, as happened at West Cotton,

Raunds Furnell and the South Manor site at Wharram Percy. Equally, it is possible that peasant farmsteads could be transformed into manorial *curiae*, although no examples have been recognised, unless this happened at North Elmham (Wade-Martins 1980a, 151). It is also necessary to question the validity of dating evidence from excavation. Many of the sites listed below may have had earlier origins than those suggested by excavation. It is very easy to imagine that the substantial stone footings of the thirteenth century are the earliest evidence of occupation and thus ignore the underlying deposits. For example, we know nothing of the 'sleeper trenches' which were noted beneath the early-thirteenth-century buildings at Weaverthorpe Manor (Yorks.: Brewster 1972, 115). Similarly, excavations at Fulmer (Bucks.) found a house built in the later thirteenth century, though it had evidently been constructed on the site of earlier occupation. Little was found of that activity until the site was stripped for gravel extraction when a line of substantial pits, from an earlier building, was glimpsed (Farley 1982, 49). Even when substantial extensive remains have been uncovered, they may not be readily datable. It is rarely possible to date sites more closely than fifty years on the evidence of ceramics and, in many cases, even that degree of precision is not possible. The final issue which needs to be confronted before we consider the pattern of evidence is whether the archaeological results are representative. The manor houses discussed here have all been excavated, but that does not mean that all these sites were abandoned. We cannot write off all these examples as 'failed' manors; they were not places which were ultimately unsuccessful and therefore atypical of manorial sites as a whole. A significant number of the excavations took place next to, and in some cases even within, buildings which were the successors of manor houses. All the sites listed in the Appendix were established before 1200. Numerous events may have occurred in the succeeding eight hundred years which led to their abandonment. There is no reason, therefore, to think that the sites collected here are not typical.

The foundation of manor houses

A total of forty-five sites of probable manorial status established in England before 1200 have been identified from a survey of excavation reports (Appendix). The dates of foundation have been noted and also the date of abandonment, if it was before 1500. The dates have been expressed to the nearest half-century, although in some cases that has required making a judgement from the evidence presented in the excavation report. The total number of sites is not enormous, and is certainly not large enough to use for detailed statistical purposes, but it is sufficient to give an indication of general patterns in the foundation of *curiae* and of their persistence. In particular, there is limited evidence from the ninth century and there are considerable problems in dating these sites with any precision. Few inferences can be drawn about these early sites.

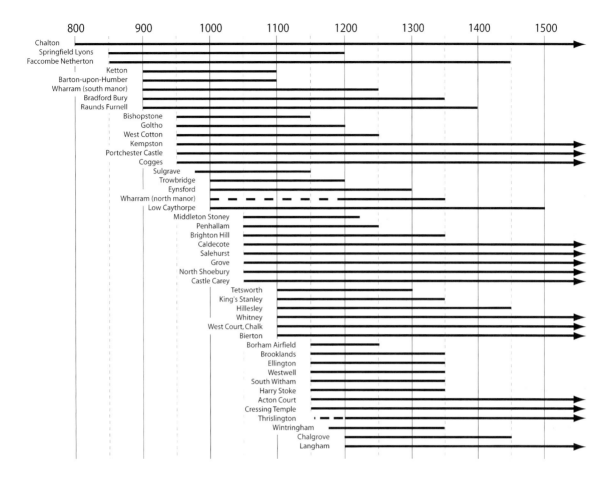

FIGURE 51.
Diagram showing the
period of occupation of
English manor-house
sites founded before
1200, arranged by date
of inception.

A simple glance at the results (Figure 51) shows that manorial sites were established in approximately equal numbers, given the limitations of dating and the quantity of evidence, in every century from the tenth to the twelfth (Table 2). Recent studies of manorialisation have emphasised the importance of the tenth and early eleventh centuries in particular (Dyer 2002b, 30–3). A number of processes seem to have operated at that time, all of which resulted in the formation of the manors of the type which are only revealed in full detail in the thirteenth century, when there is a greater abundance of documents. It is widely agreed that one of the processes in this period was the division of large estates into smaller elements, sometimes leading to the foundation of separate manors. This was the period, for example, when the long, strip-like townships came into existence on the Oxford Chilterns, on the Berkshire and Surrey Downs and in the Vale of Rother in Sussex (Blair 1991, 30–4; Blair 1994, 133; Gardiner 1984, 81–2; Hooke 1988). Each township developed to include a variety of the different types of terrain, but whether this was the result of a planned division or was driven by long-standing farming practice which required a variety of land types is uncertain.

Approximate date of manor house construction	Number
900	5
950	7
1000	3
1050	8
1100	6
1150	9
1200	3

TABLE 2. Chronology of the construction of manor houses to 1200.

An alternative to permanent grants was to lease areas of land to tenants. Whereas in the ninth century leases were often contracted for a single life, by the tenth these were frequently for a period of three lives (Kelly 2000, cxlix; Lennard 1959, 167). The problem lords had to guard against was that a lease for a period of lives might lead to the establishment of an hereditary fief. The original arrangement of a tenancy for a limited term might either be overlooked by the lord or disputed by the occupiers, leading to the permanent alienation of manors. It was this loss of lands which led to the compilation of Hemming's Chartulary by the church of Worcester (Dyer 1996a, 177; King 1996, 116). Yet, in spite of the problems of leasing lands for extended periods, the practice continued through the eleventh and twelfth centuries, and some leases were renewed for successive generations of the same family (Lennard 1959, 174). Under these conditions, the lessees might well decide that it was worthwhile investing in the construction of manorial buildings on 'their' lands.

A third process leading to the formation of new manors was partible inheritance. The operation of this is apparent from Domesday Book, which reveals that many vills had been divided in recent years between heirs. Thames Ditton, for example, was divided on the death of Leofgar between his three sons (Wood 1975, 5, 27). Partible inheritance did not necessarily result in the physical division of lands, which might be held in parage or joint lordship. Two brothers had divided the manor of Shalford in Surrey before 1066 and had separate houses, perhaps meaning that they ran their different demesne farmsteads, but might nevertheless have maintained a single court for the manor (Wood 1975, 5, 27). Lands, even when they were divided, might be subsequently amalgamated, as numerous Domesday entries show. However, the complete tenurial separation of the lands of the manor must have been the most common outcome of division by partible inheritance. An example has been traced at Acton (Somerset) where the division of the manor, implied by the entry in Domesday Book, led to the establishment of two discrete manors, each with its own manor house, neither of which was on the site of the original (Manco 1996).

A fourth process was the grouping of separate lands to form entirely new manors. This is best documented in monastic chartularies, where it is possible to trace how religious houses through donation, purchase and exchange were able to accumulate lands within a locality, and might seek to form them into a single lordship, paying rents resolute to the superior lord. The Templar preceptories of Cressing (Essex) and South Witham (Lincs.) seem to have been established as manor sites in this way (Ryan 1993, 11; Mayes 2002). However, it is unlikely that the practice was confined to religious bodies and secular lords might do the same, though this is rarely documented in the period before 1200.

We should, however, be cautious about assuming that all newly established manorial complexes indicate the foundation of a new manor. In some cases, the site of the manor house may have moved and therefore the new *curia* was simply replacing an older one. Elsewhere, the demesne may have been leased to a group of tenants and, as suggested above, agricultural work might have been managed from their farmsteads. In that case, would there have been a manor house at all? The manor court, if indeed there was such a thing at this period (for which see Evans 2004, 159), could have been held in the open air, as hundred courts generally were, and did not require a building. However, by the early twelfth century the implication of *Leges Henrici Primi* seems to have been that lords would have held hallmote (manorial) courts, and the very name implies that these were held within the hall (Faith 1997, 255).

The abandonment of manor houses

A second issue which emerges from a consideration of the sites listed in the Appendix is the impermanence of manorial settlements. Only one third of the manors founded before 1200 persisted in the same spot until 1500 (Figure 52). It has already been argued that this is not a result of a biased sample; archaeologists have not only been digging on the sites of failed manors, but also in and around the sites occupied by the standing buildings of former manors. During the two centuries between 1000 and 1200 there were very considerable changes in the structures of lordship. Attention has already been drawn to the fragmentation of estates during the tenth and eleventh centuries, but the Norman Conquest also led to a very considerable change in the patterns of lordship. Earlier work had suggested that the lands of Anglo-Saxon lords were 'inherited' by the Normans, who essentially preserved the estate structure under new lordship (Sawyer 1985). More recent studies have reversed this view and shown that the English estates were entirely torn apart and reconfigured under Norman lords (Fleming 1991, 107–44). The impact of this reorganisation is demonstrated in the way in which the value of such estates declined, suggesting that there was considerable economic disruption produced by the tenurial revolution (Fleming 1991, 123–4). The practical effects on the ground are hard to envisage, but are likely to have included the removal of some *curiae* and the new construction of others. Yet against this we must

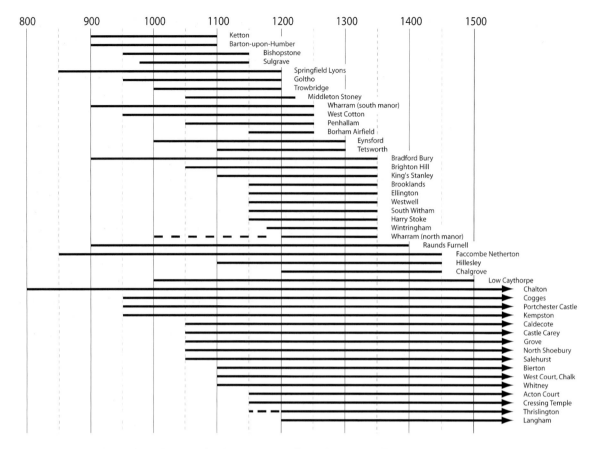

| 800 | 900 | 1000 | 1100 | 1200 | 1300 | 1400 | 1500 |

Ketton
Barton-upon-Humber
Bishopstone
Sulgrave
Springfield Lyons
Goltho
Trowbridge
Middleton Stoney
Wharram (south manor)
West Cotton
Penhallam
Borham Airfield
Eynsford
Tetsworth
Bradford Bury
Brighton Hill
King's Stanley
Brooklands
Ellington
Westwell
South Witham
Harry Stoke
Wintringham
Wharram (north manor)
Raunds Furnell
Faccombe Netherton
Hillesley
Chalgrove
Low Caythorpe
Chalton
Cogges
Portchester Castle
Kempston
Caldecote
Castle Carey
Grove
North Shoebury
Salehurst
Bierton
West Court, Chalk
Whitney
Acton Court
Cressing Temple
Thrislington
Langham

set the archaeological evidence, which does not reflect this view of the tenurial disruption following the Conquest: not a single desertion has been identified from the late eleventh century.

The Norman tenurial revolution was a particular instance of very rapid change in the structure of lordship. Changes were, however, taking place throughout the later medieval period as lands were sold or leased or divided or merged. We have already seen the impact of this in the division of the manor of Acton, which led to the foundation of two new *curiae* and the abandonment of one other. Wharram Percy (Yorks.) provides an instance of the merging of two manors. The site of the South Manor was abandoned in 1254 when the Chamberlain family sold their manor to the Percys. Thereafter, the combined manors were administered from the North Manor site (Beresford and Hurst 1990, 45–7; cf. Stamper and Croft 2000, 198–203). Behind this general pattern of manorial change, a number of particular factors emerge. Figure 52 shows excavated manorial sites arranged, this time, according to their date of abandonment. The mean period of occupation for manorial sites established in both the tenth and eleventh centuries was a little under three hundred years, but sites first occupied in the twelfth century had an even shorter average period of occupation – about two hundred years. Even if we allow for the limitations of the data – the small size of the sample and the

FIGURE 52.
Diagram showing the period of occupation of English manor-house sites founded before 1200, arranged by date of abandonment.

poor dating evidence – there does appear to be a real difference here. One of the reasons for the desertion of *curiae* was that the enclosed or fortified sites of the eleventh and twelfth centuries no longer remained suitable in later periods. Some of these were the ditched *burhs* or enclosures of the pre-Conquest and immediate post-Conquest period. Others were smaller rural castles founded after the Conquest, what might be termed manorial castles. They may have provided status and security for their inhabitants in the eleventh and twelfth century, but their restricted enclosures could have proved to be unsuitable for the larger *curiae* of the thirteenth century, and the manor house was re-established elsewhere. Alternatively, the timber-and-earth castles of the twelfth century may no longer have been a statement of prestige in the thirteenth, when most such buildings would have been of stone. The site at Castle Carey (Somerset) was first occupied just before or shortly after the Norman Conquest, when a ringwork was constructed. That was replaced in the early twelfth century by a motte and bailey castle on a slightly different alignment. It was adapted in turn during the early thirteenth century to form the site of a manor house, set within a new enclosure and in a slightly different position (Leach and Ellis 2004). The sequence of events at Middleton Stoney, Goltho, Sulgrave and Trowbridge was similar, to the extent that *curiae* within the castle enclosures were either replaced by ones outside, or the earlier site was abandoned entirely.

Approximate date of manor house desertion	Number
1100	2
1150	2
1200	4
1250	4
1300	2
1350	10
1400	1
1450	3

TABLE 3. Chronology of the desertion of manor houses founded before 1200.

Around 1350 there was a notable increase in the desertion or relocation of manorial sites (Table 3), the most likely reason for which was the impact of demesne leasing in the second half of the fourteenth century. Estates sought to maximise their income by leasing their demesnes for fixed rents to farmers, much as they had before 1180. It had the benefit of providing a fixed income for the lord during a period of economic instability. If a farmer could be found who would lease the whole demesne, including the *curia*, then there would be little change. Demesne leases often required lessees to maintain buildings, although lords might also provide money or materials to assist in this work (for example, Du Boulay 1966, 227–8). However, greater changes would occur if the demesne land was leased without the manorial farmstead, or the demesne was divided up and leased to a number of tenants. In both circumstances the buildings might find no further use and no longer be maintained. For example, the demesne at Hanbury (Worcs.) was let in parcels in 1407 and, as the land was worked from the lessees' farms, the *curia* fell into disuse (Dyer 1991, 54). At Wardington (Oxon), the site of the manor house had been replaced for similar reasons by cottages for tenants by the mid fifteenth century (Le Patourel 1991, 832).

Conclusions

It is sometimes assumed in studies of landscape history that the manorial *curia* was a fixed feature in the otherwise changing landscape of the high and later Middle Ages and the early modern period. Villages and field patterns might be recast, but the sites of the church and the manor house remained the same. That view of the manor house as an ancient feature of the countryside which both reflected and represented the antiquity of the family which occupied it might be crudely characterised as the *Victoria County History* perspective on the past (particularly as represented in the volumes published before the First World War). The study of the archaeological evidence has shown that such a view is not supportable. Assumptions about families and the persistence of manorial settlements have been projected backwards from more recent times. A late medieval lord would usually possess many manors, and no single manor house would be the family seat and represent the lineage in the way that gentry houses came to do in the eighteenth and nineteenth centuries. The absence of sentiment about the antiquity of buildings or sites meant that *curiae* might be readily created or removed as circumstances required.

Those particular circumstances which led to the creation and removal of manor houses were both tenurial and economic. Patterns of tenure may be likened to the pieces in a child's kaleidoscope: though the elements remained the same, they might be rearranged in numerous different configurations. Consequently, manor houses were established and abandoned as the lands were bought or sold or inherited over the generations and organised into different patterns of lordship. The changing economics of estate management also produced transformations in the manorial *curia*. Manors were taken in hand and cultivated directly particularly from the 1180s until some point generally during the late fourteenth or early fifteenth century. During that period of direct management, investment in buildings, and especially agricultural buildings, had the potential to produce a substantial return through a reduction in the wastage of crops and in more efficient practices. The benefits to the lord in spending considerable sums in buildings before and after this period of 'high farming' are less obvious, and their responses were very mixed. From the 1460s onwards manor farmhouses in Hampshire were constructed either by the lords or by the lessees who sought buildings to reflect their status (Roberts

2003, 211–14), but elsewhere, as noted above, manorial farmsteads might be allowed to fall down or were demolished.

This paper has sought to emphasise that manor houses did not have a single origin, but multiple origins. They were established in considerable numbers in the tenth century, as we might have expected from documentary sources, but also in the eleventh and twelfth, and new manor houses continued to be founded in later centuries as patterns of lordship and agricultural needs changed. Archaeology, with its particular capacity to reveal long-term change, can provide an insight into the growth and persistence of these symbols of lordship.

Acknowledgements

Part of the archaeological evidence was collected during a project on timber buildings in the period 900–1200, funded by the Leverhulme Trust. I am indebted to Emily Murray for her assistance on that project and also to Chris Dyer, Ros Faith and Stephen Rippon for their valuable comments on a draft of this paper.

Appendix. Excavated manorial sites established before 1200.

Name of site	Start date	End date (if before 1500)	Publication reference
Manor Fm, Chalton, Hants.	800		Cunliffe 1973; Hughes 1984
Springfield Lyons, Essex	850	1200	Buckley and Hedges 1987
Faccombe Netherton, Hants.	850	1450	Fairbrother 1990
Barton-upon-Humber, Lincs.	900	1100	Rodwell and Rodwell 1982; Bradley 2002
Ketton, Northants.	900	1100	Ian Meadows pers. comm.
Wharram Percy (south manor), Yorks.	900	1250	Stamper and Croft 2000
Bradford Bury, Bucks.	900	1350	Mynard 1994
Raunds Furnell, Northants.	900	1400	Cadman and Foard 1984; Dix 1987
West Cotton, Northants.	950	1250	Windell *et al.*1990; Chapman in prep.
Goltho, Lincs.	950	1200	Beresford 1987; Hodges 1988; Everson 1988
Bishopstone, Sussex	950	1150	Thomas 2005
Cogges, Oxon.	950		Blair and Steane 1982
Portchester Castle, Hants.	950		Cunliffe 1975

Name of site	Start date	End date (if before 1500)	Publication reference
Kempston, Beds.	950		Crick and Dawson 1996
Sulgrave, Northants.	975	1150	Davison 1977
Trowbridge, Wilts.	1000	1200 (for inner bailey)	Graham and Davies 1993
Eynsford, Kent	1000	1300	Rigold 1972; Horsman 1988
Low Caythorpe, Yorks.	1000	1500	Coppack 1974
Middleton Stoney, Oxon.	1050	1220	Rahtz and Rowley 1984
Penhallam, Cornwall	1050	1250	Beresford 1974
Brighton Hill, Hants.	1050	1350	Fasham *et al.* 1995
Caldecote, Herts.	1050		Beresford 1978
Castle Carey, Somerset	1050		Leach and Ellis 2004
Grove, Beds.	1050		Baker 1997
North Shoebury, Essex	1050		Wymer and Brown 1995
Salehurst, Sussex	1050		Gardiner *et al.* 1991
Tetsworth, Oxon.	1100	1300	Robinson 1973
King's Stanley, Gloucs.	1100	1350	Heighway 1989
Hillesley, Avon	1100	1450	Williams 1987
Bierton, Bucks.	1100		Allen 1986
West Court, Chalk, Kent	1100		Moore 1999
Witney, Oxon.	1100		Allen and Hiller 2002
Boreham Airfield, Essex	1150	1250	Clarke 2003
Brooklands, Surrey	1150	1350	Hanworth and Tomalin 1977
Ellington, Hunts.	1150	1350	Tebbutt *et al.* 1971
Westwell, Kent	1150	1350	Westman 1999
South Witham, Lincs.	1150	1350	Mayes 2002
Harry Stoke, Avon	1150	1350	Young 1995
Acton Court, Gloucs.	1150		Rodwell and Bell 2004
Cressing Temple, Essex	1150		Robey 1993
Wintringham, Hunts.	1175	1350	Beresford 1977
Thrislington, Co. Durham	before 1200		Austin 1989
Wharram Percy (north manor), Yorks.	1000–1200	1350	Rahtz and Watts 2004b
Lagham, Surrey	1200		Ketteringham 1984
Chalgrove, Oxon.	1200	1450	Page *et al.* 2005

PART FOUR

Perceived and Ritual Landscapes

'Powerhouses' of the Wolds Landscape: Manor Houses and Churches in Late Medieval and Early Modern England

Briony McDonagh

This paper presents preliminary results from a project which investigated the geographical relationships between manors, churches and rural settlements in the Yorkshire Wolds in the late medieval and early modern period. This is, of course, a well-researched theme, and a number of commentators have remarked on the relationship between manors, churches and settlements in the medieval period (Roberts 1987; Morris 1989; Daniels 1996). Such scholars have typically examined the origins of manor–church–settlement relationships in the pre-Conquest period, and their development in the period after 1066, but they have generally paid less attention to questions about the continued meaning of these relationships in the later medieval and early modern period. It is precisely this theme that this paper seeks to explore, paying particular attention to what the geographical relationships between manors, churches and settlements might reveal about the ways power was articulated through the landscape in the period before *c.*1600. The research draws on theories adopted, developed and critiqued within historical and cultural geography, which argue that space, territory and landscape can be conceived as mediums through which social relations are produced and reproduced (Schein 1997; Mitchell 2005). Yet, with a few notable exceptions, geographers have generally applied these theories to studying modern, rather than medieval, landscapes. Similar theoretical perspectives are also evident amongst both historians and archaeologists, who have increasingly attempted to theorise the interconnections between space, social meaning and power in *medieval* contexts (Graves 1989; Saunders 1990; Giles 2000; Altenberg 2003). However, such research has typically focused on architecture, rather than the spatial arrangement of buildings in the landscape. As a response, this paper attempts to combine these new theoretical insights with more traditional methodologies for analysing and mapping settlement form, in order to examine how settlement morphology was implicated in the practices of power in late medieval and early modern England.

The empirical research for this paper was undertaken in the Yorkshire Wolds, low chalk hills which run in a broad arc through the historic East Riding of Yorkshire (Figure 53). The medieval and early modern landscape was one of tightly nucleated villages, large hamlets and open fields (Harris 1961, 14, 20; Roberts and Wrathmell 2000, 47). Before the parliamentary enclosures of the mid eighteenth century, the Wolds were essentially 'all champion', as one seventeenth-century observer noted (cited in Harris 1961, 18). There were few hedges and trees between the fields and the vast common pastures of the thriving sheep–corn economy. The population density was relatively low, except in the villages of the southern and eastern dipslope. Some of those villages were included within the survey, principally because while the settlements themselves stand in the Hull Valley, the parishes stretch westwards towards the Wolds.

The study uses documentary, cartographic and standing buildings sources, in combination with visual, landscape and place-name evidence, in order to reconstruct the settlement morphology of the Yorkshire Wolds. Only those buildings and features whose site could be determined in the period before c.1600 are included in the survey. In other words, the study was primarily concerned to use medieval and sixteenth-century evidence for the relationship

FIGURE 53.
The historic East Riding of Yorkshire and the Yorkshire Wolds.

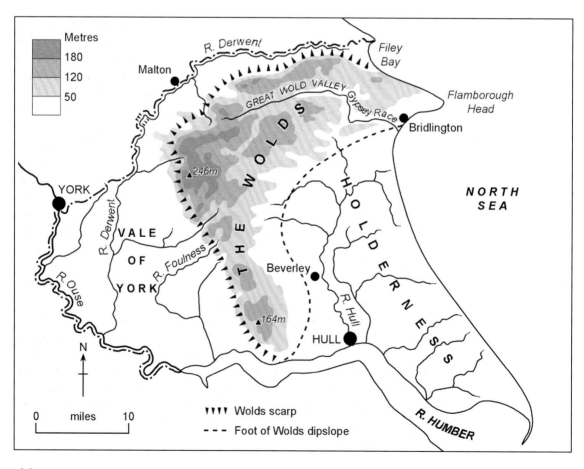

between manor, church and settlement, rather than assuming that later evidence necessarily reflected earlier settlement morphologies. A series of maps were produced recording the reconstructed settlement morphology of individual villages (for example, see Figure 54 below), in addition to parish-by-parish summaries of the key sources for determining the location of manor, church and settlement. The maps are spatial representations of settlement form across the period 1400–1600, and they tend to show all the features for which one can determine a location. Importantly, they are not necessarily 'snapshots' of the landscape at a single, identifiable point in time, though I have tried to be sensitive to changes in settlement form. Using the maps, the villages were then categorised according to whether the manor house and church were integrated within, peripheral to, or isolated from the settlement. The results presented here explore the geographical relationships between manor, church and village in the case of twenty-eight manor houses whose site can be determined in the period before *c.*1600.

Manor–church–settlement relationships in the Yorkshire Wolds

Manor houses in the Yorkshire Wolds, as in other parts of the country, were commonly located in close proximity to churches. In 57 per cent of the sample the manor house stood on a site next to the parish church. This equates with a slim majority of the sample, so that the most common spatial relationship between manor and church was that where the two buildings stood adjacent, either within the settlement or on its periphery. For the benefit of this paper, these sites have been classified as Type 1 sites. In some Wolds villages, the church was integrated within the manorial enclosure, as at Harpham and Weaverthorpe. In these cases, the church stood either within or abreast of the ditch encircling the manorial complex. These are what might be termed 'manor–church complexes'. In other instances, the manor house and church were sited in adjoining plots, so that the two buildings typically stood within 50 and 200 m of each other. Manor house and church might be sited either within the settlement, as at Sledmere, or on its periphery, as at Burton Agnes. The Type 1 site at Burton Agnes is shown in Figure 54. Burton Agnes, in the eastern Wolds, stands five miles south-west of Bridlington. It was a relatively large village of fifty-five households in 1506 (*CIPM* 1898–1955, 66). The medieval church of St Martin stood *c.*50 m west of the twelfth-century manor house, itself on the northern periphery of the settlement.

Peripheral manor houses were also found on sites *not* adjacent to churches. Fourteen per cent of the villages in the sample may be classified as Type 2 sites, where the manor house and church were both peripheral to the settlement though, rather than being adjacent as in the first category, they were remote from one another. Depending on the size and form of the settlement, the manor house and church might stand between 600 and 850 m apart, and were located at opposite extremes of either long, linear settlements or large, agglomerated villages.

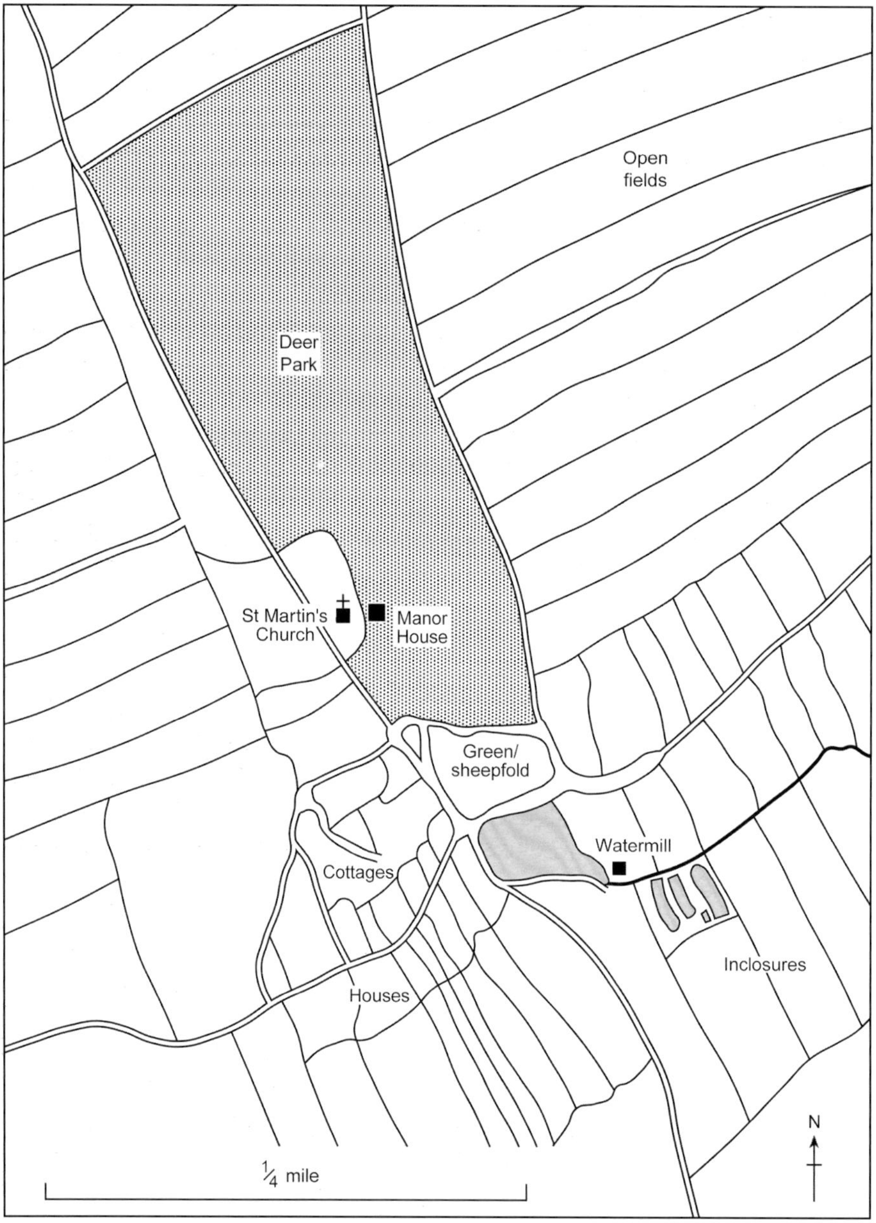

FIGURE 54.
Type 1 site: Burton
Agnes in the later
medieval period.

The Type 2 site at Nunburnholme is shown in Figure 55. Nunburnholme, in the west-central Wolds, was a medium-sized village, with around thirty houses in the mid sixteenth century. The manor house and parish church stood at opposite ends of the long, linear settlement. The church of St James, which contains Norman fabric, occupied the most westerly toft in the village, and a manorial survey of 1563 (transcribed in Morris 1907, 234–42) reveals the manor house to have stood some 750 m north-east of the church, next to the village green and the site of the dissolved nunnery.

Manor houses at Carnaby, Etton and Hunmanby, like that at Nunburnholme, were all found adjacent to settlements to which the church was also peripheral, but not adjacent to the manor. At least two, and possibly three, of these parishes were multi-manorial. That is, in the late medieval and early modern period two or more manor houses stood within or close by the villages. At Etton, Hunmanby and possibly also Carnaby, one manor house stood in close proximity to the parish church at one end of the settlement, whilst another manor house stood at the opposite end of the village. This may also have been the case at South Cave, although the evidence for the site of the second manor (West Hall) comes from a mid-eighteenth-century map and has therefore been excluded from the analysis above.[1] Such multi-manorial parishes were relatively common in the Yorkshire Wolds, as they also were in parts of Lincolnshire and Nottinghamshire (Morris 1989, 230).

At Type 3 sites, the manor house was remote from both church and settlement. Eighteen per cent of the Wolds settlements included in the sample can be categorised as Type 3 sites. The church was typically integrated within the settlement, and the manor house stood between 500 and 1500 m from the church and village. In all but one case, the manor house was sited within a deer park.

Bishop Burton (Figure 56) is located three miles west of Beverley in the southern Wolds. Like Burton Agnes, it was relatively large village with around fifty houses and cottages in the mid sixteenth century (Allison 1979, 7).[2] Here the medieval church stood within the village, just south of the green, while the manor house stood some 700 m north-west of the church and settlement, isolated within the deer park.

There were no instances in the study area where both manor house and

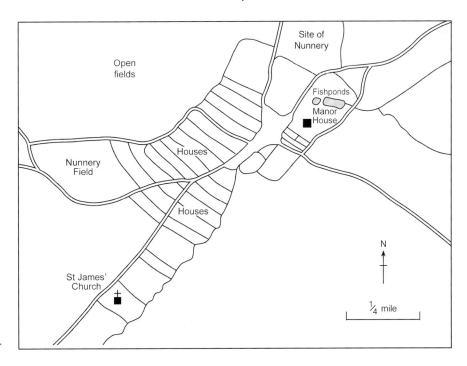

FIGURE 55.
Type 2 site:
Nunburnholme *c*.1563.

189

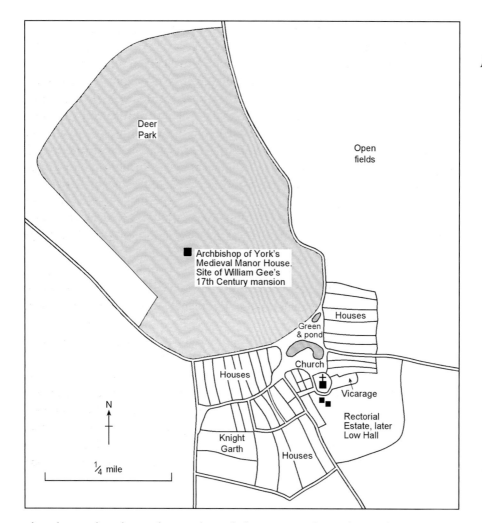

Deer
Park

Open
fields

■ Archbishop of York's
Medieval Manor House.
Site of William Gee's
17th Century mansion

Houses

Green
& pond

Church

Houses

N

Vicarage

Rectorial
Estate, later
Low Hall

Knight
Garth

Houses

¼ mile

FIGURE 56.
Type 3 site: Bishop
Burton in the later
medieval period.

church stood within a deer park, and thus remote from the settlement. Such
isolated manor–church groupings are a common landscape feature in other
parts of the country, for example in Essex (Rodwell and Rodwell 1977, 94–125),
Suffolk (Dymond 1968, 29) and Cleveland (Daniels 1996, 109). Yet, if isolated
churches were largely unknown in the Wolds, manor houses were not uncom-
monly found outside villages, as, for example, at Bishop Burton, Leconfield
and Hunmanby. Alongside a small number of park lodges, isolated farmsteads
and monastic granges, manor houses were one of the few landscape elements
to produce a more dispersed pattern of settlement in a landscape otherwise
characterised by nucleated villages and hamlets.

While both isolated and integrated manor houses were a significant presence in the Wolds landscape, peripheral sites were by far the most common
location for manor houses, with 68 per cent of manor houses located on the
edge of a settlement. The proportion of peripheral churches was also high,
accounting for 65 per cent of the sample. Such peripheral manor houses and
churches were more common in the Yorkshire Wolds than in other parts of

England. For example, Daniels (1996, 107) found that seven out of fifty-seven churches in his Tees Valley study area were adjacent (peripheral) to the settlement. Similarly, Rodwell and Rodwell (1977, 94–125) record only twenty-nine examples out of a total of 204 settlements in the archdeaconry of Colchester (Essex) of churches in peripheral locations, thirteen of which were grouped with a manor house. Not only was proximity the most common spatial relationship between manor and church, and peripherality the most common manor–settlement and church–settlement relationship, but proximity and peripherality frequently occurred together, so that in fourteen out of twenty-eight cases (50 per cent), manor and church stood together at the periphery of a settlement. Comparison with other studies suggests that such peripheral manor–church groupings are more common in the Wolds than elsewhere in the country. Daniels (1996, 104–5) cites only two examples in Cleveland, accounting for only 3.5 per cent of his sample.

So having mapped the geographical relationships between manor houses, parish churches and settlements, the paper has identified and classified three common morphological patterns found in the Yorkshire Wolds – Type 1, 2 and 3 sites. The second part of this paper considers how the morphological patterns described above can be best explained. In particular, I want to draw attention to the way in which the geographical relationships between manors, churches and settlements might have been conceived, understood and given meaning, especially in the later medieval and early modern period. I also want to highlight some of the ways in which the geographical relationships between buildings might be caught up in the practices by which social meaning and political power were constituted. As in the paper so far, I will focus in particular on ideas of proximity and peripherality, the two most common spatial themes uncovered within the Wolds sample, although the project as a whole explores the meaning(s) of other spatial forms.

Proximity

Commentators have typically interpreted the close proximity of manors and churches as a result of planning, in particular signalling that such churches were founded in the pre- or immediately post-Conquest period as private chapels for the use of the lord and his family (Dymond 1968, 29; Blair 1988, 8; Morris 1989, 249–50). Such churches were built on sites 'to suit [the lord's] own convenience' (Morris 1989, 250), and hence stood adjacent to the manor house of their founder. The so-called 'promotion law' written by Archbishop Wulstan of York (1002–23) recognised church ownership as one of the key criteria making a man worthy of being called a thegn, and the only surviving visual representation of a pre-Conquest manor depicts the church adjacent to the hall (Williams 1992, 226–7, 232–3). Moreover, Norman castles, like Anglo-Saxon *burhs*, were commonly sited close to churches (Morris 1989, 261; Pounds 1991, 12; Speight 1993, 158–68; Creighton 2005, 111). Of the Yorkshire castles listed by Speight (1993, 275–8), 74 per cent stood within a quarter of a mile (*c*.400 m) of the parish church. Of these, Speight defined 35 per cent as adjacent to the church, and identified a further 15 per cent where the church lay within or adjacent to the castle bailey or was located within a larger pre-Norman structure in which the castle was also sited.

Speight (1993, 158, 161) asserts that most castles post-date the adjacent churches; that is, the castles were founded next to the churches, rather than vice versa. Morris (1989, 258) suggests that the origins of such castle–church complexes often pre-date the Norman Conquest and, in some cases, Norman lords certainly fortified the residences of their Anglo-Saxon forerunners. For example, late Anglo-Saxon halls lie beneath the Norman mottes or ringworks at Sulgrave (Northants.), Goltho (Lincs.) and Trowbridge (Wilts.), as well as the eleventh-century manorial site at Raunds (Northants.; Davison 1977; Morris 1989, 268, 270; Creighton 2005, 117). Morris (1989, 258) further underlines the depth of history at some sites, suggesting that in some places existing mounds, including barrows, were developed into mottes. This layering of the landscape is complex and the chronology difficult to unpick, especially where excavation has yet to be undertaken. In other places, castles were apparently built without reference to Anglo-Saxon residences and may represent an unprecedented intrusion into the landscape. Yet their builders still chose sites next to churches. Speight has argued that 'when the Normans entered an area, the quickest means to establish control was to throw up a castle close to a Saxon church ... and by doing so take over the hub of the local community' (Speight 1993, 158). By siting castles next to pre-existing churches, Norman lords might 'harness ... the power of the church' (Speight 1993, 161), thereby promoting the 'Normanisation' of the landscape. In such cases, the Norman builders of castles may have deliberately made reference to older forms of landscape organisation, particularly to the close proximity of churches and pre-Conquest centres of seigniorial power. Thus, even where castles do not directly overlie Anglo-Saxon *burhs*, the Norman builders of castles may have modelled their complexes on Anglo-Saxon precedents.

Much the same may be said of non-fortified manorial residences, whose owners might draw on both the Anglo-Saxon *burh* and Norman castle–church complexes as models. We see this at Weaverthorpe, in the northern Wolds: St Andrew's church was probably a patronal foundation of the early twelfth century (Brewster 1972, 126), and stood directly west of the twelfth-century manor house, straddling the bank of the manorial enclosure. The church and hall were on a near-axial alignment, a relationship also noted at several Anglo-Saxon sites including Sulgrave (Northants.), where the early eleventh-century hall was aligned on the same axis as the church's west door (Davison 1977, 113). The church at Weaverthorpe might be interpreted as a gate-block or strong-point within the defensive earthwork, similar to the church towers within *burh* walls and hedges discussed by Williams (1992, 234). Churches in analogous positions have been identified in both pre-Conquest and Norman contexts; for example, at Repton (Derbys.), Thetford (Norfolk) and Castle Camps (Cambs.) (Morris 1989, 261). Yet if the complex at Weaverthorpe represented a planned imposition in the landscape similar to those found elsewhere in the Anglo-Saxon period, it almost certainly post-dated the Norman Conquest. Excavation revealed no evidence for occupation during the Saxon period, and the silting of the ditch below the Staxton Ware horizon may indicate a period of abandonment before the construction of the church in the early twelfth century (Brewster 1972, 119). As such, the manorial complex and patronal church at Weaverthorpe would be appear to modelled on pre-Conquest modes of landscape organisation, though the enclosure itself was not preceded by an Anglo-Saxon thegnly residence.

The later medieval period

In the twelfth century manorial lords were encouraged to grant away ownership of churches to monasteries (Pounds 1991, 12). Yet ownership of a church continued to be an important metaphor for status, as is evidenced by a number of practices. For example, many castle chapels were established as a response to the church reforms of the twelfth century, with the consequence that '[p]atronage of a castle chapel [came] to resemble that of a parish church at an earlier date' (Pounds 1991, 13). Another possibility, available to a wider section of society and increasingly common in the thirteenth and fourteenth centuries, was to found a chantry within a parish church and thereby satisfy 'in a way acceptable to the Church, the deep-rooted desire for a religious establishment under private control which, in its grosser forms, had been stamped out by the reforms of the twelfth century' (Colvin 2000, 172). Moreover, by siting a manor house in close proximity to a parish church a manorial lord might imply ownership of that church, and thereby draw a parallel between his manorial complex and other higher-status manors and castles with private chapels.

In the Wolds, manorial lords continued to emphasise the spatial and symbolic relationships between manor houses and parish churches. Even at sites where the close spatial relationship between manor and church may have first emerged in the pre-Conquest period, the relationship between manor and church might be consciously revived in the twelfth and thirteenth centuries. At Burton Agnes, Roger de Stuteville built a new manor house on a conspicuous site next to the parish church in *c*.1170, probably soon after he acquired the manor (Allison 1974, 107). At Harpham, in the north-east Wolds, the St Quintin family constructed a moat around their manorial complex sometime before the late thirteenth century. The parochial chapel was included within the moat, even though the available evidence suggests that it had neither been founded by, nor was ever owned by, the occupants of the manor house. Interestingly, the moat is first mentioned in 1297 and it is possible that it was constructed soon after the manor changed hands in *c*.1199 (Allison 1974, 224).[3] The construction of the moat seems to have allowed the St Quintins to make a strong territorial claim for the ownership of the chapel. The moat functioned to draw a distinction between the manorial complex, including the chapel, and the settlement. It would seem that in building the house and moat, the St Quintins were trying to imply ownership of what was legally a public space (the church). At both Harpham and Burton Agnes, therefore, new lords of the manor seem to have tried to consolidate their position and status by emphasising the visual and symbolic links between their manor houses and the parish church.

Patronage of the church was another means by which this could be achieved. Many of the Wolds churches had chantry chapels annexed to them in the fourteenth century which were used as private mortuary chapels for the burial of the lords of the manor and their family. Such chapels were often founded as part of wider building campaigns, which might extend and embellish both the parish church and the manor house. At Harpham, the construction of the chantry chapel founded by William St Quintin in 1340 was part of a wider programme of embellishment which lasted throughout much of the fourteenth century and included the rebuilding of the tower by William's wife, Joan, in c.1374 (*CPR* 1898b, 454; *CPR* 1914, 407). Much the same thing had happened at Burton Agnes in the early decades of the fourteenth century, when the north aisle was rebuilt by Sir Roger de Somerville and the chantry established, and again c.1500, when the chapel was moved into a new annex, the tower rebuilt and the clerestorey added under the patronage of Sir Walter Griffith (d. 1531) and his mother, Lady Agnes (*CPR* 1898a, 29; Raine 1884, 287). In such cases, the church might seem to the common people more like the private funerary chapel of the lord of the manor than a space for the parishioners. Embellishment and refenestration programmes, chantry chapels and the continuing intercessionary prayers which would have taken place next to tombs, all functioned to imply space was private and manorial, rather than public and communal.

The visual and symbolic links between manor and church might be further emphasised by adopting similar architectural forms, particularly where phases of expansion in the church were paralleled within the manor house. For example, at Burton Agnes, a large traceried window was inserted in the west wall of the manor house, probably in the fifteenth century (Wood 1981, 10). Little of it now remains, but it was undoubtedly very similar to the east window of the church's south aisle, which it directly overlooked. It would appear as if the medieval house and the church utilised common architectural forms and motifs; in other words, they shared architectural codes, a practice which was at least partially dependent on proximity of the two buildings.

The early modern period

Just as the twelfth-century lords of Burton Agnes and Harpham seem to have been keen to build on sites next to the churches, later landowners also sought to maintain the spatial relationship between the manor house and church. Manor houses were built and rebuilt on sites next to churches in the sixteenth century, despite changes in ownership and function. The medieval hall of *c.*1170 at Burton Agnes was replaced by a much larger house in 1610. The new hall was built on an adjacent site, 100 m east of the church, and the medieval hall retained as service quarters. Much the same thing seems to have happened at Sewerby (in Bridlington parish), and at Londesborough the medieval house was rebuilt on the same site in 1587. The new owners of manorial estates at Boynton, Burton Fleming, Ganton, Lockington and South Cave East Hall built their grand new houses on the sites of the medieval halls, thereby consciously or unconsciously preserving the close spatial relationship between manor and church. The later sixteenth century was, of course, a period of increased social mobility and, with the exception of South Cave, these estates were purchased by esquires or gentlemen, rather than by knights. Sites in close proximity to parish churches may have been particularly attractive to purchasers, especially those attempting to set themselves up as gentry. Just as Norman castles were built next to pre-existing churches in order to 'harness ... the power of the church' (Speight 1993, 161), later medieval and early modern landowners might deliberately emphasise the spatial relationships between manor and church in order to associate themselves with the knightly class of landowners who had held these estates before them.

Whilst those moving up the social hierarchy sought to appropriate the trappings of gentility, the more established gentry also perceived the need to assert and defend their status. As such, the new and old gentry alike invested in grand new houses, the architectural form of which proclaimed their wealth and gentility (Girouard 1978, 3; Cooper 1999, 3; Emery 2005). Moreover, by siting these houses close to churches landowners could stress their role as pious patrons of the church and benevolent lords to their tenants, thereby working to produce or reproduce their social status and political power.

Peripheral sites

Commentators have offered a number of suggestions to explain peripheral locations, particularly those of churches. These include morphological explanations, such as settlement shift or contraction (Beresford 1973, 578) and the late manorialisation of a region (Grant and Bigmore 1974, 11). However, given the early dates of evidence from the study area, neither theory is really convincing in the Wolds context. Other commentators have argued that peripheral and isolated sites are particularly characteristic of the later medieval and early modern period. Williamson and Bellamy (1987, 62) have suggested that houses were increasingly relocated in the later medieval period, first to peripheral locations adjacent to their parks in the thirteenth and fourteenth centuries, and later into isolated parkland settings. Lasdun (1991, 24) dates the emergence of houses in parkland settings more precisely, arguing that the trend first appeared in the second half of the fifteenth century, and was more fully realised around the middle of the sixteenth century. Lasdun (1991, 24) and Williamson and Bellamy (1987, 61–2) attribute this movement to an increased desire for privacy, also evident in the withdrawal of the lord from the hall and the increased popularity of private dining rooms and sleeping chambers.

The manor houses at Wharram Percy have been cited as an example of this process (for example, by Roberts 1977, 146). Yet the North Manor, originally believed to be a mid-thirteenth-century rebuilding of the South Manor on a site outside the village nucleus (Beresford and Hurst 1976, 121, 142), may actually have been coexistent with the South Manor from as early as 1086 (Beresford and Hurst 1990, 47; Rahtz and Watts 2004a, 2). Two manors were recorded at Domesday (Roffe 2000, 2), and later documentary evidence seems to support the notion that there were two manor houses in the village in the twelfth and thirteenth centuries (Beresford 1979, 17–20). It is unclear from the documentary sources whether the Percy or the Chamberlain family held the North Manor before 1254, but Roffe (2000, 3) suggests that the South Manor house may have been built to serve the Percy family's new estate at Wharram, probably acquired between 1166 and 1176–7, although they perhaps held other land in the vill before that date. Importantly for this paper, the South Manor site was seemingly abandoned soon after 1254, not because the lord wished to relocate his manor to the periphery of the settlement, but because the Chamberlain and Percy estates had been united (Beresford 1979, 18) and there was no longer any need for two manor houses.

Whether a high-status Anglo-Saxon site underlies the earthworks of the North Manor complex, as Richards (1992) has speculated, remains open to debate. While excavation has revealed good evidence for high-status occupation of the South Manor site in the Anglo-Saxon and Anglo-Scandinavian periods (Richards 1997), the pre-Conquest history of the North Manor site has proved more elusive. Excavation suggests that the North Manor may have occupied the site of a Romano-British farm (Milne 2004, 23) and Anglo-Saxon settlement has been identified within the vicinity of the North Manor (Richards 1992, 93; Milne 1992, 5; Milne 2004, 35). Yet Milne (2004, 35) remains cautious, noting that the features excavated at the North Manor could represent *either* a pre-Conquest manorial complex *or* peasant houses later overlain by part of the manorial enclosure. However, whatever future excavations may reveal about the pre-Conquest history of the site, it seems that the North Manor probably occupied a site peripheral to the settlement from the eleventh or twelfth century onwards, if not earlier.

Evidence from elsewhere in the Wolds also suggests that manor houses occurred on peripheral sites throughout the medieval and early modern period. The houses at Weaverthorpe, Sherburn and Burton Agnes stood on peripheral sites by the late twelfth century, if not before. Manor houses on peripheral sites existed at Etton and Harpham by *c.*1300, while at Scorborough, Londesborough, Ganton and South Cave (East Hall) manor houses were built or rebuilt on sites peripheral to settlements in the sixteenth century. Moreover, it is possible to demonstrate a similar range of dates for the construction of isolated manor houses. In the Wolds, manor houses were located outside villages from at least the early fourteenth century. The Archbishop of York's manor house at Bishop Burton seems to have been isolated within his park some 700 m north-west of the parish church since the fourteenth century, if not earlier. At Leconfield, the Percy's manor house was on a site 700 m south-west of the church from at least 1308 (*CPR* 1894, 144), and a messuage called *Le Burlyn* is mentioned in Hunmanby parish in 1303, when it was described as 'lying without the town'.[4] Although these houses may previously have been sited within or close by settlements, any such movement significantly pre-dates the later medieval or sixteenth-century trend noted by Lasdun (1991) and Williamson and Bellamy (1987).

This last example may be considered in greater detail. Gilbert de Gant's motte and bailey castle at Hunmanby lay directly west of the church. The castle was probably destroyed in the civil wars of the twelfth century, and the capital messuage inherited by the Tattershalls from the Gants, and mentioned together with the house called *Le Burlyn* in 1303, was probably its replacement. The 1303 reference seems to imply that the capital manor lay within the town, and the manor house probably occupied a site close to the castle and the church on the western periphery of the settlement, while the house called *Le Burlyn*, which was described as having a hall and kitchen in 1316, lay in an area of early enclosures 1.5 km east of the town.[5] The manor house was seemingly in disrepair by the early fourteenth century. In 1303, it was described as 'having no dovecote, orchard or herbage' and was worth only a quarter of its 1298 value.[6] It is perhaps no coincidence that the house outside the settlement called *Le Burlyn* was mentioned for the first time in the same year that the main manor is recorded as being in disrepair. The Tattershall family may have resided at *Le Burlyn* rather than the capital manor previously occupied by the Gants. Yet if the Tattershall family did indeed chose to reside at a house isolated from the settlement, the occupation of the manor house was short-lived; after the death of Robert de Tattershall in 1306, the estate was divided between a number of co-heirs, each of whom held a moiety of the house called *Le Burlyn*, although it seems unlikely that any of them ever resided there (Allison 1974, 231).

The movements of manor houses in the period *c.*1400–1600 do not con-form well to Lasdun's (1991) and Williamson and Bellamy's (1987) notion of a progression between integrated, peripheral and isolated sites. For example, at Carnaby, the medieval manor house which stood at the southern periphery of the settlement may have been abandoned or demolished in favour of a sixteenth-century hall closer to the centre of the village (*CIPM* 1938, 181; Le Patourel 1973, 111; Allison 1979, 127).[7] At Flamborough, the Constable family were forced to abandon their medieval manor house when Robert Constable was attainted and executed for his involvement in the Pilgrimage of Grace in 1537. In 1593/4, his grandson, another Robert Constable, was living in a capital messuage or tenement described as 'at the south end' of Flamborough, and known as 'South Hall' by 1699.[8] The house stood *c.*275 m south of the church, but still peripheral to the village, just as the fourteenth-century castle had been.

Elsewhere in the Wolds, peripheral manor houses continued to occupy the same sites throughout the medieval and early modern period. Burton Agnes and Londesborough have been mentioned above, and at Etton, the manor house of the de Etton and the Langdale lords of the manor occupied the site, and possibly even the building, which had belonged to the Knight's Templars in the thirteenth and early fourteenth centuries. A Latin charter of 1323 confirms a grant by Laurence de Etton to his son Nicholas, and describes how the capital messuage and adjoining croft 'formerly were of the Templars of Jerusalem, in the same place' (cited in Hall 1932, no. 33).

Peripheral sites were perhaps important to the owners of manor houses because they allowed manorial lords to imply a physical, and by implication social, distinction between the manorial complex and the village. The Anglo-Saxon *burh* may again provide a model, for at least some pre-Conquest church–manor complexes were peripheral to settlements. Discussing the late ninth- and early tenth-century site at Raunds (Northants), Creighton (2005, 113) noted that 'excavation has revealed the manorial site and adjacent propriety church to have lain perpendicular to one another within linked embanked and ditched enclosures on higher ground than the rest of the settlement, from which the complex was deliberately segregated'. The proximity of manor and church, and their physical separation from the village, reinforced the perceived differences between the manorial complex and the wider settlement, that is, between the feudal lord and the peasants; a distinction which Saunders (1990, 187) noted was also represented architecturally. In Anglo-Saxon and later medieval England alike, social hierarchy could be produced and reproduced through spatial morphology.

In lower-lying areas, the spatial and social distinction between manor and village, lord and villagers, might again be emphasised by the construction of a moat. Moats were constructed around peripheral manor houses at Carnaby and Harpham, on the southern dipslope of the Wolds, and at Scorborough in the Hull Valley, though for geological reasons they were less common on the chalk of the high Wolds (Le Patourel 1973, 7). Where the church lay inside the manorial ditch or was enclosed within the moat, it might allow the manorial lord to imply ownership of the church. Conversely, incorporating a church within a manorial enclosure might function to refigure manorial space as public, communal space. Manor houses were not private spaces in the modern sense of the term; manorial courts were often held in manor houses, and tenants might have gone to them in order to pay rent or attend seasonal feasts, like those held by the earl of Northumberland on his Yorkshire estates in the 1520s (Girouard 1978, 25).

By placing the church and churchyard within or close by the manorial complex, as at Harpham, manorial space might come to be appropriated for other events. As Dymond (1999) has demonstrated, medieval churchyards were communal spaces in which villagers often celebrated the patron saint's day, played games, drank ale and danced. In the use of such churchyards for activities concerned with village identity and parish fundraising, we can begin to see the complex interaction and overlapping of manorial, church and village space that might have occurred in some places.

Conclusions

Whilst recognising the diversity of manor–church–settlement relationships evident in the Yorkshire Wolds, this paper has demonstrated that, as in other parts of England, manor houses and churches in the Wolds were commonly sited in close proximity. Moreover, such manor houses and churches were commonly found on the periphery of settlements, so that in 50 per cent of the sample manor and church stood together at the edge of a village. In many places in the Yorkshire Wolds, peripherality to the settlement and proximity to the church seem to have worked together to imply ownership of the church and separateness from the settlement. While the lord of the manor might constitute or maintain his power through the architecture of his manor house or his patronage of the church, these practices were themselves caught up in and partially dependent on the spatial relationships between manor, church and settlement.

For Girouard (1978), country houses were 'powerhouses'. Not only did property ensure economic and political security by providing a population who would labour or fight for their patron, but the house itself functioned as 'visible evidence of … wealth' (Girouard 1978, 3), as well as of intelligence, pedigree and the right of its owner to rule. Much the same can be said of churches. The paper has discussed manor houses and parish churches in this context, and suggested some of the ways power might have operated through such buildings. More generally, the argument of the paper is that buildings not only *reflected* the status, wealth and lineage of their owners and patrons, but also provided sites through which social status and political power could be actively *negotiated* and maintained.

This leads on to two related assertions. First, the spatial relationships between manors, churches and settlements which existed in the period 1400–1600 are not simply the outcome of earlier processes. In particular, the close proximity of manors and churches evident in the Yorkshire Wolds, and noted elsewhere by Morris (1989, 248–74) and others, is not solely a result of pre-Conquest practices of church foundation. Rather, the spatial, as well as the visual and symbolic, relationships between manors, churches and settlements were actively produced and reproduced in the later medieval and early modern period through a variety of practices which included investing in tombs and chantries, adopting parallel architectural forms within the church and manor house and rebuilding manor houses on the same sites. Second, in contrast to traditional accounts of the rural landscape which have understood the transition from late medieval to early modern society as a period of radical change that engendered 'the emergence of a wholly new socio-economic and spatial order' (Campbell 1990, 72), evidence from the Yorkshire Wolds suggests potential continuities between the medieval and early modern landscape.

Rather than manor houses being progressively relocated first to peripheral and later to isolated sites, as Lasdun (1991) and Williamson and Bellamy (1987) suggested, this paper has demonstrated that manor houses often maintained their sites throughout the medieval and early modern period. Yet this is not to suggest that these landscapes were somehow set apart from power relations. Continuity with the past was one of the means by which manorial lords and other landowners might assert their ancestry, wealth and status. If, as cultural geographers have argued, the landscape 'remains permanent only to the degree it is continually reproduced' (Mitchell 2003, 240), then we must recognise that continuity, as much as change, may signal that landscapes and buildings were caught up in the practices by which meaning was (re)produced and power constituted in late medieval and early modern England.

Notes

1. Hull University Library (hereafter HUL), DDBA/4/31.
2. Public Record Office: The National Archives (hereafter PRO:TNA), SC6/Hen VIII/7158; HUL, DDGE/3/23.
3. HUL, DDSQ/5/1.
4. East Riding of Yorkshire Archive and Record Service (hereafter ERYARS), DDHU 9/4.
5. ERYARS, DDHU 9/7.
6. ERYARS, DDHU 9/3 and 9/4.
7. PRO:TNA, C 54/921 m 3.
8. ERYARS, DDX22/2 and 22/3; ERYARS, IA/64.

Acknowledgements

I would like to acknowledge the support offered to me by Professor Mike Heffernan and Professor Charles Watkins, both at the School of Geography, University of Nottingham, and the Arts and Humanities Research Council, who fund the project. I would also like to thank Chris Lewis and Elaine Watts for their help in preparing the figures.

CHAPTER FOURTEEN

Medieval Designed Landscapes: Problems and Possibilities

Robert Liddiard

Reconsidering designed landscapes

It is legitimate to say that in 1955, when *The Making of the English Landscape* was published, the subject of 'medieval designed landscapes' did not exist. Although Hoskins and his contemporaries were fully aware of the existence of gardens during the medieval period, it was assumed that these were small, enclosed spaces that lacked the scale and sophistication of their post-medieval counterparts. Certainly, the idea that during the Middle Ages the environs of the noble residence were consciously manipulated in order to improve the visual setting of great buildings did not enter into Hoskins's pioneering work: for landscape historians of this period, the landscaping of the area around the mansion in order to enhance the visual effect of the whole was a phenomenon that emerged in England only during the sixteenth century (Hoskins 1955, 126). The suggestion that medieval men and women did not, or could not, conceive of the countryside in anything other than functional terms remained influential in writing on high-status landscapes for many decades; the scattered nature of landholding, attitudes to private property and a perceived lack of appropriate sensibilities all ensured that 'the aesthetic manipulation of the countryside was not to begin until after the close of the Middle Ages' (Williamson 1988, 261).

The rather austere picture of medieval magnates, both secular and ecclesiastical, existing within the bounds of purely utilitarian residences has now, of course, been subject to much revision and reinterpretation. Pioneering studies of documentary sources have revealed extensive references to garden design in the centuries prior to the Renaissance (Harvey 1981). Landsberg (1995) has drawn attention to a triumvirate of medieval features: the small, enclosed garden, or *herber*, the larger orchard-type garden, and the park-like garden known as the little park or pleasure park, all of which are found at both secular and ecclesiastical residences. Gardens of *herber* type and their associated orchards and pleasure parks are all now attested archaeologically. Here, the significance lies not so much in the idea that such features have never been encountered before, or that archaeology has confirmed the documentary sources; rather, it lies in a new understanding that the spatial arrangement and embellishment of structures around a residence in order to make it pleasurable to look at, and to accommodate more than simply utilitarian functions, sets such landscapes apart from the manorial countryside of medieval England. This new appreciation that the creation of parks to provide a sylvan backdrop to residences, the construction of lakes and approach drives, and the use of ornamental planting all took place in the Middle Ages as well as in the post-medieval period has ensured that the term 'medieval designed landscape' – leaving aside for a moment what this definition might actually mean – is now accepted among researchers. The aim of this paper is to highlight some of the key findings of the most recent scholarship and then offer some observations on the problems and possibilities that this work has presented.

The role of field survey

Archaeological field survey has dramatically increased our understanding of the nature of medieval pleasure grounds. Perhaps the principal finding has been that, in addition to the small, enclosed, *herber*-type gardens, often depicted in manuscript illustrations, more substantial and elaborate gardens existed, like that at Somersham Palace (Cambs.; Taylor 1989b), where Taylor has demonstrated the sophistication of the elite landscape of the bishops of Ely. The episcopal buildings sat within a complex landscape of several components: the village of Somersham was relocated in order to provide an approach drive that was itself flanked by two substantial ponds; this drive gave access to a moated area that enclosed the palace and its associated garden; two larger gardens lay to the south, comprising raised terraces, ponds and a moated enclosure that probably contained a summer house; and the two gardens were bisected by another raised causeway that gave access to the palace's associated deer park. The park lay on rising ground and would have provided spectacular views over the whole residential complex. Somersham is not unique, and similar examples have been identified at other episcopal sites, such as Nettleham (Lincs.; Everson *et al.* 1991) and Cawood (Yorks.; Blood and Taylor 1992).

The rigorous study of the field archaeology of medieval high-status landscapes has, however, achieved far more than simply expanding our knowledge of relict garden features. Analyses such as those by Everson and Taylor cited above demand an awareness of the importance of the contemporary association between great buildings and their surroundings, rather than any modern construction. The possible disjuncture between modern and medieval interpretations is seen perhaps most obviously in the field of castle studies which, for many decades, heavily influenced by a military determinism, was predisposed to interpret the environs of buildings as killing grounds. At Kenilworth, for example, the heritage tour invokes this approach to the ruined castle: it is, apparently, the modern equivalent of a burnt-out Iraqi tank (Johnson 2002, 160). While this particular metaphor provides a modern context for the buildings, it is quite different to the original arrangement, where the residential structures were provided with formal gardens that were integrated with a wider landscape of water and parkland. An appreciation of the original contexts of these buildings is a necessary precursor to identifying and understanding the notions of power that were being projected by such schemes. Thus, at Clarendon Palace (Wilts.), Edward II's works on the enlargement of the park can be directly related to his plans for a parliament there in 1317, the king clearly desiring a suitable setting for a major political event not long after his disastrous expedition against the Scots (Richardson 2005).

An awareness of the contemporary relationship between residence and surroundings encourages the interpretation of landscape features at medieval high-status sites as the remains of pleasure grounds. While this statement may not be particularly profound, it is worth repeating because, as Everson has observed (Everson and Williamson 1998, 143), there is an important 'conceptual leap' that has to take place before this basic point can be appreciated. The implications, once this theoretical leap has been taken, are considerable, as it opens up enormous potential for identifying new sites and reinterpreting recorded sites in a different context. Again, the ramifications for castle studies in particular are significant. The notion that the considerable effort often expended on surrounding all, or part of, the main site with water was concerned not with inhibiting the effectiveness of siege engines, but with providing a suitable image and setting for the buildings, reveals much about seigniorial attitudes to the environment and lordly power in the landscape (Figure 57).

The conclusions reached by landscape historians about medieval pleasure grounds also have clear implications for the chronology of landscape design in England, at least in terms of that conceived by Hoskins. While there can be no doubt now that landscape design did not begin in the sixteenth century, the origins of medieval landscapes are, currently, obscure. One achievement has, however, been to push the origins of design back as far as the twelfth century. Although somewhat enigmatic in their nature, documentary descriptions or vignettes such as that of St Hugh of Lincoln, who described Stow Palace in Lincolnshire as being 'delightfully surrounded by woods and ponds', are suggestive (Everson 1998, 32–3). So too are licences to crenellate that include, from the early thirteenth century onwards, parks, ponds and other seigniorial appurtenances listed alongside the royal 'permission' to fortify buildings; these clearly refer to a long-established tradition of residential surroundings. This tradition is outlined explicitly in the famous description by Gerald of Wales in 1188 of Manorbier Castle (Pembs.), which is so rich in detail that it 'cannot be recalled too often':

> The castle called Maenor Pyrr … is excellently well defended by turrets and bulwarks, and is situated on the summit of a hill, extending on the western side towards the sea-port, having on the north and south a fine fishpond hard by its walls, as conspicuous for its grand appearance as for the depth of its waters. On the same side is a beautiful orchard, bounded by a vineyard and elsewhere by a wood, remarkable for its projecting rocks and by the

FIGURE 57.
Saltwood Castle,
Kent. The remains of a
former pond adjacent
to the castle, with a
retaining dam in the
distance. Such features
are now interpreted
as ornamental, rather
than a response to the
possibility of attack.

height of its hazel trees ... between the castle and the church, by the site of a very large lake with a mill, there follows down the valley a rivulet of never failing water ... (Coulson 2003, 127)

The image of, in this case, a castle in its contemporary setting, underscores not only the aesthetic of the twelfth century but also suggests that part of the meaning of the residential surroundings was constructed from the surrounding landscape. Manorbier also serves as a reminder that designed landscapes are not only to be found in lowland England, where they first attracted archaeological attention, but exist across the British Isles. Indeed, it now seems apparent that the best-preserved examples are to be found in upland areas, places often characterised as militarised or border landscapes that might be thought to lack such residential planning. Again, the potential of the study of designed landscapes to give broader insights into social history is underlined; perhaps the most relevant example is that of Ireland, where the existence of such landscapes directly contradict earlier assumptions about lordship and ethnicity, and raises doubts about broader 'conflict' models of Irish historiography (O'Keeffe 2004).

Recent years have thus seen a move away from questions of recording and recognition, that characterised the early 1990s, towards those concerning the place of designed landscapes in medieval society. But it is worth reiterating the enormous strides that have taken place and appreciating that there is now an acceptance of the basic idea that medieval high-status residences were routinely (perhaps invariably) surrounded by pleasure grounds which were constructed in a way not dissimilar to that of the post-medieval period. Thus, to give one example, in a recent survey of Odiham Castle (Hants), the landscape context occupies a central part of the investigation and there is almost an expectation that aesthetic manipulation of the landscape at a site of this status was the norm (Brown 2004).

The scale of design and the design threshold

At present, it is only possible to speculate about the scale of landscape design in medieval England. No list of sites has been compiled, but known examples currently number in the region of 100 sites, a total that includes monastic houses, secular and ecclesiastical palaces, and castles (Christopher Taylor pers. comm.). While any attempt to calculate the number of designed landscapes which existed in the medieval period is clearly a task for the future, it is possible, on the basis of work already undertaken, to offer some informed speculation on numbers of sites.

The considerable amount of fieldwork already undertaken across the country has established the characteristics of those high-status residences where designed landscapes are often found. Ravensworth (Yorks.) is a case in point; the castle of the FitzHugh family exhibits many of the elements now considered typical of medieval designs (Figure 58; Everson 2003). The residential building was surrounded by a mere, which was itself provided with walks; a large terraced garden lay to the north; and the whole ensemble was surrounded

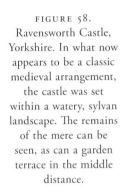

FIGURE 58.
Ravensworth Castle, Yorkshire. In what now appears to be a classic medieval arrangement, the castle was set within a watery, sylvan landscape. The remains of the mere can be seen, as can a garden terrace in the middle distance.

by a park. The settlement of Ravensworth was shifted closer to the castle, providing a suitably elaborate entrance to the whole complex. While, as noted above, the total number of designed landscapes is not known, it is possible to establish approximate totals for numbers of castles, such as Ravensworth, and thus, *a priori*, for numbers of associated landscapes. The same operation can be undertaken for ecclesiastical palaces and monastic houses.

For the purposes of this paper a preliminary list of known examples of designed landscapes was produced and then compared with published lists of medieval baronies, castles, monastic houses and palaces (Sanders 1960; Knowles and Hadcock 1971; King 1983; Thompson 1998). As would be expected, those places where designed landscapes had already been identified were also to be found on the longer lists of castles, monasteries and palaces. To the list of known designed landscapes were added those sites where, in all probability, one might reasonably expect to find evidence of landscape design, but where systematic survey has not taken place. Where possible, these were checked against relevant publications and SMR records in order to ascertain the existence of parks, ponds or other features. Although this undertaking was in no way systematic, it is nonetheless instructive that large numbers of places where full-scale survey has yet to be attempted do in fact exhibit suggestive references to what are, in all probability, designed landscapes. This would include the episcopal manor of Pucklechurch (Gloucs.), described by Leland as 'a parke and a goodly lordshipe', and Marwell (Hants), where the bishop's house overlooked an artificial lake set within a park (Roberts 1988).

Even allowing for marginal cases, a national figure of 1,000 sites is easily obtained. As a comparison, a further list of sites was complied for one relatively well-studied county, Norfolk. This yielded twenty-two sites, a total which, if multiplied by the fifty-two pre-1974 counties of England and Wales, would again result in a figure of more than 1,000. While this is, as the author freely admits, a crude analysis, it does represent the first attempt to quantify the scale of landscape design in medieval England and Wales and, while a four-figure total might seem high, it does bear comparison with the several thousand possible sites postulated for the sixteenth and seventeenth centuries.

If the figure of over 1,000 medieval designed landscapes is in any way close to the historical reality then this would carry with it several implications. Firstly, landscape design was as widespread in the Middle Ages as in later historical periods, an idea with implications for the inspiration of early Tudor pleasure grounds and elite landscapes often considered to be 'Renaissance' in origin. Secondly, this would mean that, at present, only approximately 10 per cent of sites are currently adequately understood, underlining the scale of the task for the future in terms of recording. Thirdly, a necessarily speculative exercise in attempting to quantify the extent of landscape design in the Middle Ages brings into focus a important issue, which we might call the 'design threshold': at what stage does the landscape of a residence exhibit evidence of deliberate design? This question is also raised by studies of estate centres of relatively minor status that have revealed the care with which the configuration of manor house, church and associated manorial appurtenances were spatially organised. Yet we would, probably quite correctly, be reluctant to call the small fiefs at places such as Lavendon (Bucks.), with its careful arrangement of lordly appurtenances, a 'designed landscape', with the connotations of status that the term implies (Brown and Everson 2005). The same could be said of Horsford Castle in Norfolk, a sub-barony of the honour of Eye in Suffolk (Liddiard 2000). The castle is that of Walter of Caen, a follower of William Malet, and probably dates from very soon after the Conquest. Here we see the familiar conjunction of castle, water feature and parkland, but at what stage a landscape like that at Horsford moves from being associated simply with economic exploitation to acquiring an aesthetic significance is a moot point.

Yet this is a question that field archaeology is well placed to answer in due course. The range of optical techniques and design features used to engineer desired effects in gardens of the post-medieval period are well known and their deployment at medieval garden sites can easily be tested. At Somersham, for example, Taylor (1989b) has highlighted the linear arrangement of fishponds that corrected the effects of perspective when viewed, although it remains to be seen how frequently such methods were used elsewhere. When it is considered that the vast majority of designed landscapes await thorough investigation, it becomes clear that the question of the design threshold cannot be answered at present, but the problem is a meaningful one and certainly warrants further investigation.

The complexity of design

As outlined above, questions over the extent of landscape design in the Middle Ages await full investigation. The same is also true of our understanding of the chronological development of medieval pleasure grounds. While the complexity of some lordly enterprises is not in any doubt, the existence of distinctive 'styles' of landscape that changed over time, as in the post-medieval period is, as yet, less certain.

It may be instructive at this point to discuss what is still probably the best-known medieval designed landscape, that at Bodiam Castle in Sussex. The 'battle for Bodiam' now occupies a specific place in historiography, and is notorious for kick-starting a serious debate over the military role of the castle, but analysis of the site also opened up to a wide audience the idea that landscape design existed in England prior to the Renaissance (Taylor *et al.* 1990). Since the 1990s, however, Bodiam has too often been held up (including by this author) as a typical medieval designed landscape. This is, in fact, not the case: continued field survey has demonstrated that, rather, Bodiam is simply one example among a multiplicity of styles.

Bodiam Castle is very much rooted in its own chronological place in English landscape history, exhibiting the well-known preference at the time for placing the main building within a watery landscape. Probably the closest parallel to Bodiam is Shirburn Castle (Oxon, 1377), which, both in terms of its

FIGURE 59.
Middleham Castle,
Yorkshire: view of the
castle from the garden.
The southern range
was rebuilt in the
early fifteenth century,
probably the time
when the garden was
constructed.

architecture and the surrounding landscape, suggests similar intent on the part of the builder, or possibly even that the two castles shared the same designer. The architectural design of Bodiam and Shirburn lends itself to comparison with other sites, such as Castle Bolton (Yorks.) and Nunney (Somerset), of the late fourteenth century, a group of castles that are often discussed together in major narratives (Brown 1976).

The social background of those men responsible for these buildings is often invoked in explaining the form of these castles. Most were 'new men' who had made their fortunes from administration and the protracted war with France. Against a background of an unpopular foreign war and social unrest in a society still dealing with the effects of plague, the particular military style of their buildings represented their triumphant, but also selfishly defiant, entry into the higher reaches of aristocratic society. It is therefore of interest that at Bodiam Sir Edward Dallyngrigge chose a particular design that ensured the castle seemed to float on water and which was approached in a highly elaborate way. Although 'water castles' continued to be built into the fifteenth century, sites such as Bodiam and Shirburn belong very much to their own place in time and explanations for their designs need to be sought in the complex character and chronological context of the site.

To a large extent, the links that need to be made in order to assess fully the significance of a landscape like that at Bodiam can only be provided by detailed local and regional surveys. A pressing task is the collation of more site 'biographies' in order to gain, as far as possible, a clearer idea of the chronology of landscape design in the medieval period. Although the range of features, such as ponds or parks, that could be combined in medieval designs are well known, it remains difficult, but vitally important, to gain some idea of what constituted a designed landscape at any given point, and how this changed over time.

The overarching problem in such an analysis, however, is the difficulty of accurately dating designed landscapes. In the majority of cases only an educated guess on the basis on documentary sources or the identification of a likely creator provides an approximate date for a landscape. At Kilpeck Castle (Hereford), for example, the landscape comprised a garden enclosed by two raised banks, one of which formed a dam for an ornamental lake. This dam also formed part of a walk where a visitor could look back over the lake and garden to the castle in the background. No archaeological date for this complex has so far been forthcoming, but a date prior to the fourteenth century is implied by the decline of Kilpeck after the Black Death and by documentary references to gardens and ponds in the late thirteenth century (Whitehead 2001, 232). Despite these difficulties, however, there are some examples where a landscape of probable medieval date remains fossilised.

FIGURE 60.
Raglan Castle,
Monmouthshire: view
of the castle park, with
the 'wild' landscape of
the Black Mountains
in the distance.

A particularly well-dated example has been found at Bassingbourn (Cambs.) where, in spite of the poor condition of the site, the garden, probably that of John Tiptoft, has been dated to *c*.1460 (Oosthuizen and Taylor 2000). This is of some importance, not simply as one of the earliest possible 'Renaissance' gardens recognised, but also in that it provides a firmly dated example to which other sites can be compared. Only when such comparative work is

undertaken will Bassingbourn's novelty or, possibly, its lack of it, be appreciated. The trend-setting design at Bassingbourn is perhaps suggested by the more conservative example at Middleham Castle (Yorks.) where Moorhouse (2003) has recorded an extensive landscape of ponds and terraces that represent the early-fifteenth-century pleasure ground of Ralph, fourth Earl Neville, or Joan Beaufort, his wife. Here, the rebuilding of the castle's south range was intimately connected with the landscape beyond (Figure 59). The private chambers overlooked a series of ponds and, in turn, a series of garden terraces cut into the sloping ground away from the castle. Incorporated into the design was an earlier ringwork and bailey that was reused probably as some kind of platform, from which a guest could look back to the castle below. Whether the antiquity of the ringwork was fully understood and deliberately reused as a garden feature, possibly as a statement of continuity, is a tantalising possibility. While the recording of 'fossilised sites' will aid the search for a typology of medieval garden sites, it is also important to remember that the archaeological remains at most sites will be of many phases and it almost goes without saying that landscapes with complex histories have complex meanings.

The meaning of design

While the continued recording of medieval designed landscapes remains an important and still under-performed process, attention has now shifted to assessing the function and meaning of landscape design within medieval society. The clear implication of the results of field survey is that there was a strong set of ideas about residence in the Middle Ages that found expression in the environment of the elite mansion. The need at present is to tease these ideas out carefully if we are to understand the distinctiveness of the designs of this period and also avoid simplistic statements that simply link landscape design to status. It may well be the case that social climbers may have desired a residence that had been choreographed in a particular way in order to demonstrate rank, but the real issues are how was this achieved and why it may have been deemed appropriate in the first place.

The possible meanings that underpinned such landscapes are now relatively well rehearsed: several authors have discussed the seigniorial, symbolic and religious significance of elite residences. Gilchrist (1999, 111), for example, has explored the cultural meanings bound up in the perception of gardens as places of recreation and paradise, but also as well-defined feminine spaces associated with sexual encounters. The role of elite landscapes in advertising a command of resources has also received much attention. The harsh realities of food production are at the heart of the much-quoted description of Owain Glen Dwr's residence at Scyarth (Denbighshire), where the reader is invited to partake in the lord's landscape of plenty, as opposed to that of dearth outside (Liddiard 2005, 116–17). Although literary and documentary sources have contributed to the study of designed landscapes, field survey has helped reveal the ideals towards which landscape designers were striving. Of considerable interest is the use of the park to provide a suitable backdrop to great buildings. At a range of sites across the county, the choreography between park and residence is being revealed by field survey.

The environment of the park was, of course, emblematic of aristocratic rank, but the actual configuration of some parks could be highly inventive. In some cases there was evidently a concern to make the park look bigger than was actually the case. At Framlingham (Suffolk), the line of the pale ran over the skyline until it was no longer possible to see it from the castle, at which point it abruptly stopped. This was clearly an attempt to make the park appear to continue on indefinitely. Such visual illusions were also be created in different regions. At Restormel (Cornwall), Herring (2003) has drawn attention to the isolation of the castle within its attendant park, creating the appearance for those in the river valley below that the castle sat within unbounded parkland. The secure, private, environment of parks provided an opportunity for lords to create a seemingly boundless sylvan landscape with unlimited resources – as close to an earthly paradise as was possible within the working agricultural countryside.

Where geography allowed, there is also some suggestion that the ordered landscape of the park and residence was deliberately contrasted with wilder countryside. At Ludgershall Castle (Wilts.), a park enhanced the setting of the castle, but here a distant view of Salisbury Plain was also included in the vista (Everson *et al*. 2000). A similar scheme is seen at Raglan Castle, where the main park occupies rising ground away from the castle and is framed by the Black Mountains in the distance (Figure 60). Literary sources from the period suggest that moorland or mountainous landscapes were unpleasant places characterised by disorder and ungodliness, and haunted by evil spirits – places where heroes frequently entered the underworld for encounters with mythical creatures (Van Emden 1984).

The ideal of creating a residence from which one could, and should, take pleasure is also evidenced in the idea that there was a correct way to approach and experience an elite landscape. One early example of a pleasurable approach concerns the visit in 1123 of Henry I to Ranulf the Chancellor's Castle at Berkhamstead (Herts.). Henry I was a monarch who seems to have inspired genuine fear on the part of his nobles and Ranulf was no doubt anxious to ensure the correct protocol. The chronicler Henry of Huntingdon related the events as the party neared the end of their journey:

> Now as he [Ranulf] was conducting the king on the way to giving him hospitality, and had reached the very top of the hill from which his castle could be seen, in his exaltation of mind he fell from his horse, and a monk rode over him. He was so badly injured by this that after a few days his life ended. (Greenway 1996, 471)

This incident, while unfortunate for Ranulf, throws light on the aesthetic landscape of, in this case, the twelfth century. Interestingly, this event implies that hospitality was not something that began at the castle gate, but rather in the wider countryside, and it may not be without importance that adjacent to Berkhamstead Castle was a large deer park. But the terminology used by Henry of Huntingdon also suggests that there is more of significance here; namely that the ensemble of residence in its setting could be appreciated for its own sake.

The theme of a correct entry to the residence is also one that finds a different expression in an ecclesiastical context. In an unattributed twelfth-century description of Clairvaux Abbey (France), it is the metaphorical qualities of water that bring civilisation to the otherwise barren landscape in which the monastic house is situated (Matarasso 1993). The valley in which Clairvaux sits is something of a wilderness and part of the monks' labour was to destroy the briars that inhibited the growth of trees. The precinct wall divided this unordered, hostile landscape from the ordered environment of the monastic house, with the civilising agent being water from the river Aube, which entered the monastery via a series of channels. It was the water that sustained all aspects of life in the house, supplying the raw material for the orchards, meadows, tanneries and monastic buildings. Once the channels returned the water to the river, the landscape reverted to one of wilderness. This description of Clairvaux neatly dovetails with the picture of monastic houses provided by archaeology, but it is the metaphor of the stream as the giver of life and the impression given of Paradise and Eden on earth that is perhaps most vivid.

FIGURE 61.
Leeds Castle, Kent.
A medieval designed
landscape, but
one layered with
complex cosmological
significance.

Such documentary descriptions are of great importance, as they underline the fact that in a world where symbolism and ritual was of everyday significance, the landscape could embody cultural meanings that are barely apparent today. This idea is echoed by Michelson's analysis of Leeds Castle in Kent (Giovanna Michelson pers. comm.). The visually pleasing aspects of the site make Leeds a popular visitor attraction today, and the conjunction of water and parkland were obviously intended to appeal to royal sensibilities in the late thirteenth century (Figure 61). There was far more to this landscape than lordship and status, however, as the circuitous route through the park and into the castle was probably linked to wider ideas of medieval cosmography and microcosm; the location of the castle at the centre of its ordered, watery, sylvan landscape echoed Jerusalem's placing at the centre of the Universe. The multiplicity of cultural associations that this particular castle could sustain is also pointed up by the description of at least one room in the castle as the 'Gloriette', a term that evoked a literary-inspired sense of the exotic (Ashbee 2004). It is ideas such as these that open up much larger themes for discussion and suggest that far more complex ideas underpin medieval landscape design than have hitherto been apparent.

Conclusion: the problems of definition

A discussion of what might be termed 'ritual' landscapes of the Middle Ages raises issues of methodology and of the correct definition of terms, particularly what is meant by medieval landscape 'design'. It is instructive here to consider the historiographical evolution of the subject, which has a bearing on how we study these complex landscapes. The 'discovery' of medieval designed landscapes was largely fuelled by the results of field survey, rather than being the logical result of a body of theory: when 'garden archaeology' was found at sites that were unquestionably medieval in date, the traditional view of the origins of landscape design needed reappraisal (Taylor 2000). Thus, ideas about designed landscapes have been pushed further and further back chronologically by the results of fieldwork. To some extent it could be argued that interpretations of medieval landscapes are largely derived from our understanding of seventeenth- and eighteenth-century ideas of landscape design whereas, in the medieval world, conceptions of landscape may have been very different. This may be underlined by the fact that the term 'design' is sixteenth-century, and not medieval in date; in fact, it is derived from a Dutch word originally meaning 'to mark out' (Liddiard 2000, 10).

It is, therefore, at least worth pointing out that the term 'designed landscape' is in fact only very loosely defined. While those examples of medieval date are clearly concerned at some level with aesthetics, the issue of where we draw the line between production and aesthetics, and between designed and non-designed, is for the future. The literary depictions of medieval landscapes that mention ponds, parks and pleasure grounds also eulogise productive fields, bountiful rivers, settlements and barns – structures that, currently, might not be included in the term 'designed landscape'. It may be the case that the current trend to discuss post-medieval high-status landscapes in terms of the 'estate' might also be applicable to medieval landscapes. This said, the examples of Leeds and Clairvaux would suggest there are some intriguing ritual aspects to these landscapes that, currently, are hidden from view. Discussion of ritual and ritual landscapes have largely been the preserve of prehistorians and anthropologists in recent years; it might be the case that medievalists can learn as much about their landscapes from prehistorians as they can from garden archaeologists (Tilley 1994; Bradley 1996).

Whatever methodological approaches are adopted, the challenge now is to interpret the landscapes of the Middle Ages within the context of the society that created them and its attendant systems of belief and visual imagery. But no matter what the approach, it is incumbent on medievalists to stress the contributions of their period to the wider history of landscape design. Not to do so risks the development of a teleological argument that sees medieval designed landscapes simply as the precursors to later parks and gardens. Such an approach would undoubtedly inhibit the study of the individuality of landscape design in this period.

Acknowledgements

I should like to thank Paul Stamper for including this paper in a highly stimulating session at the Leicester conference and Paul Everson and Christopher Taylor for many fruitful discussions on this topic.

CHAPTER FIFTEEN

St Leonard's at Kirkstead, Lincolnshire: The Landscape of the Cistercian Monastic Precinct

Paul Everson and David Stocker

In recent correspondence, the eminent garden historian Mavis Batey recalled her good fortune in attending Hoskins's extra-mural lectures in Oxford in the early 1950s. She describes how she 'greatly profited by his *wide-angled lens approach* to historic landscapes'. This paper, a contribution to the theme of buildings in the landscape, also attempts a 'wide-angled lens approach', drawing part of its argumentation from the wider landscape in which an individual building sits and also using that understanding of the wider landscape to inform our discussion of the building itself. We seek to show that a study of St Leonard's chapel at Kirkstead raises the question of peripheral chapels in Cistercian precincts – a topic which has been dealt with too simplistically in the past and for which we suggest a landscape approach is especially revealing. We hope Hoskins himself might have approved.

The chapel of St Leonard at Kirkstead in Lincolnshire is located on the east side of the River Witham, some 4 km upstream from Tattershall, and near the Witham's confluence with the River Bain and the Kyme Eau. This merging of waterways marks the transition of the Witham from valley to open fenland landscape (Stocker and Everson 2003, fig. 17.1). Locally, St Leonard's is situated on the south side of the precinct of the Cistercian abbey of Kirkstead, the layout of which survives clearly as much-illustrated earthworks of exceptional quality (e.g. Knowles and St Joseph 1952, 126–7; Wilson 1982, 28–9; Platt 1984a, 225; Platt 1984b, 197; Aston 1993, 98–9); and, along with one tall finger of masonry from the south transept of the abbey's conventual church, it constitutes the principal architectural survival from that abbey.

This is an exceptionally stylish building of early thirteenth-century date (Figure 62). Its detailing, of the highest quality, is consistent throughout and dates from the 1220s or 1230s, having clear connections with contemporary work at Lincoln Cathedral (Parker 1846; Pevsner and Harris 1989, 417–18; further independent architectural records, also made before the chapel's wholesale reordering, include Spring Gardens 1878, pls 63–66 (drawings made in 1872 by J. Norton), Spring Gardens 1890, pl. 8 (drawings made by A. Hartshorne in 1882

FIGURE 62.
Engraved general
view of St Leonard's
Kirkstead from the
north-west (source:
Parker 1846, plate VI).

and published in Hartshorne 1883), and *The Builder*, 1 March 1912, 239 and facing 258 (Arthur Cates Prize drawings by J. B. F. Cowper)). It was St Leonard's architectural quality that underpinned efforts to ensure its preservation in the nineteenth century, most notably through publication of J. H. Parker's *Architectural Description* in 1846 with splendid engraved plates, because it formed (as Parker urged) a model for new churches 'in the hilly districts of this and other agricultural counties' (Parker 1846, 11).

In the modern literature and by competent authorities St Leonard's is consistently characterised as a *capella ante portas* to Kirkstead Abbey (e.g. Knowles and St Joseph 1952, 126; Gilyard-Beer 1959, 38; Pevsner and Harris 1964, 287–8; Owen 1971, 18, pl. VI; Platt 1984a, 156–7; Pevsner and Harris 1989, 417–18; Coppack 1998, 108; Robinson 1998, 134; Bond 2004, 228–9). A recent review of the building type has reiterated the assessment (Hall 2001, 68–74). That this cannot be an adequate explanation of its function, however, has been demonstrated by a recent site survey, combining ground survey of earthworks and aerial-photographic transcription of plough-levelled features (Jecock *et al.* 1994). This revealed the layout of the principal conventual buildings in the south part of an enclosure, organised around the main cloister and with further monastic buildings to its east and south-east, with water supplies servicing them, as expected. But it also identified the foundations of a gatehouse in the north boundary of the ditched enclosure, which now contains the inner core of the precinct. This is probably an inner gatehouse, a common feature of Cistercian layouts, since the order's regulations placed great emphasis on the reserved status of the conventual buildings, from which seculars were wholly excluded (Fergusson 1990). Valuable recent work at Stoneleigh (Warks.) has shown that, as the points of transition from one zone to another, each gatehouse had an emblematic significance that could be reflected in its architecture (Ramey 2004). It seems there was no answering gatehouse on the south side of the ditched enclosure, however, even though the Kirkstead precinct may have been laid across a pre-existing routeway from north to south. This is also to be expected as it is unthinkable that seculars might have had through transit immediately adjacent to a Cistercian cloister (Fergusson and Harrison 1999, 164–6).

The location of the abbey's gatehouse, then, is firmly established facing north, and lies where one would expect in relation to the innermost portion of the layout of the monastery. It also sits logically relative to local routeways in the wider landscape (Figure 63). The abbey was certainly approached from the north, via a short road – 'Abbey Lane' – that sprang at right angles off the ancient east–west cross-valley causeway (Stocker and Everson 2003). The outer precinct boundary in that direction must have enclosed the prominent array of fish-breeding ponds, which sit into an embayment marked by the five-metre contour. In the north-east, at least for as long as it lies on the hard land above the five-metre contour, the boundary may be marked by the continuous, curving boundary of the field east of the fish ponds, which has an earthwork embankment. This alignment is extended south of the lane by a drain, but cropmarks reveal a good corner to the south-east between an east and a south side, which lies coherently with cropmarks marking the south boundary further west. The west side of the precinct coincides with the edge of firm land towards the Witham at about the five-metre contour and is shadowed by curvilinear lengths of sill drain, which return eastwards into the embayment below the fish ponds. We might conjecture that the monastery's main outer gatehouse therefore lay at the north-west corner of the hard land created by the array of fish ponds. A mid-thirteenth-century agreement describes following the east–west highway across the Witham 'as far as the stone cross which is at the end of the causeway which comes from the gate of the abbey' (Owen 1971, 58, citing Foster 1920, 171–2). That causeway might perhaps be the ditched line of Abbey Lane – which would place the gatehouse at the crossing of the stream latterly known as 'The Sewer', near to Old Hall and Old Hall Farm – or, perhaps more plausibly, the crossing of the embayment to the corner of the fishponds. There may even have been three gatehouses here, between any of which may have stood the structure known as *Gaythusbrigg* (i.e. gatehouse bridge) in the agreement. But whatever the details, St Leonard's is clearly unrelated to this public approach; it is clearly not *ante portas*.

What, then, was St Leonard's relationship with the abbey? Now that we can appreciate that it lay on the reserved or quiet side of the precinct, a discrete function might be suggested, such as an infirmary chapel. Cropmarks show that the building lay in a separate enclosure that formed part of the precinct's southern boundary, and this might support conjecture along these lines. But counter-arguments rule out this idea quite decisively. As an infirmary chapel, the building we see should have been physically attached to a hall, of which there is no sign. Even had the hall been timber, a major arch would have been necessary to allow patients in the hall to see or hear mass performed in the chapel. There is no sign of any such conjunction with a hall of any material, in any direction.

Could it have been a parish church, perhaps established before the abbey

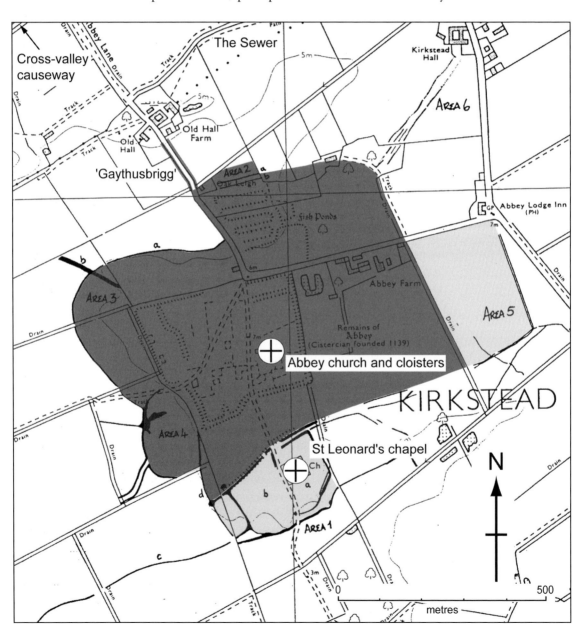

relocated here in the mid-twelfth century? Arguments that St Leonard's was parochial during the Middle Ages figured in the legal wrangling surrounding its transition, in the early nineteenth century, from a nonconformist to an Anglican place of worship. The principal evidence adduced was archaeological, including the presence of a supposedly medieval font (Parker 1846, 10–11). Unfortunately this object, still within the chapel, is clearly a recycled medieval mortar. In fact, there are no medieval references to a parochial institution here. Its rather unusual post-Dissolution history as an extra-parochial and donative chapel confirms this non-parochial standing. The chapel is first documented at the end of the seventeenth century and in the eighteenth century, when it was used by a nonconformist congregation and a resident dissenting incumbent through the initiative of Daniel Disney, an enthusiastic Presbyterian, who acquired the Kirkstead estate through his wife Katherine née Clinton (Parker 1846, 9–11; Warren 1919; Stell 2002, 212–13).

So, finding three suggestions for the building's function – a *capella ante portas*, an infirmary chapel or a parish church – unsatisfactory, what can we learn from its architectural form? A brief description of its principal features is necessary (Figure 64), though this is not the place to catalogue the fabric's miserable vicissitudes between its transfer to the Church of England in 1812 and its major reordering on the eve of the Great War (e.g. Parker 1846; Anon. 1857–8, lxx–lxxi; 1913–14a, lxxi; 1913–14b, 1–2; Trollope 1875–6, 157–8; Walter 1899, 248–50).

St Leonard's is a simple three-bay rectangular structure, oriented east–west and lit laterally by pairs of lancets in each bay and by a triple lancet array in the east wall. It is vaulted throughout, with the east bay having an additional transverse rib and a historiated vaulting boss depicting the *Agnus Dei* (Figure 64(b)). This additional decoration suggests there was an altar in this east bay, served also by the piscina in the south wall. Nicholson's drawing of the interior (Parker 1846, pl. VII), without fixtures and fittings, envisages a dais or altar step occupying the eastern half of the east bay. Photos in the National Monuments Record of the building cleared during its restoration just before the First World War show neither clear evidence for this, however, nor any survival of original paving.

There is a substantial space above the vault, which is now lit by a new window in the modern wooden west gable that supports the present steep-pitched roof. This replaces the tiled, hipped roof that covered the building through much of the nineteenth century, which in turn replaced a thatched predecessor belonging to its phase as a nonconformist chapel. It seems likely that stone gables supported the original roof, and thus the vault space might originally have been adequately lit by upper windows to east and west. That it was not redundant space, but rather accommodation integral to the original function of the building, is demonstrated by the integral vice, an original feature in the turret on the building's north-west corner. The upper parts of this turret survive in their original state and demonstrate that the stair rose only into the vault space and did not terminate in a pinnacle with access to the parapet.

FIGURE 63.
St Leonard's Kirkstead in the context of the interpreted plan of the abbey precinct (after Jecock *et al.* 1994, appendix 4, fig. 1).

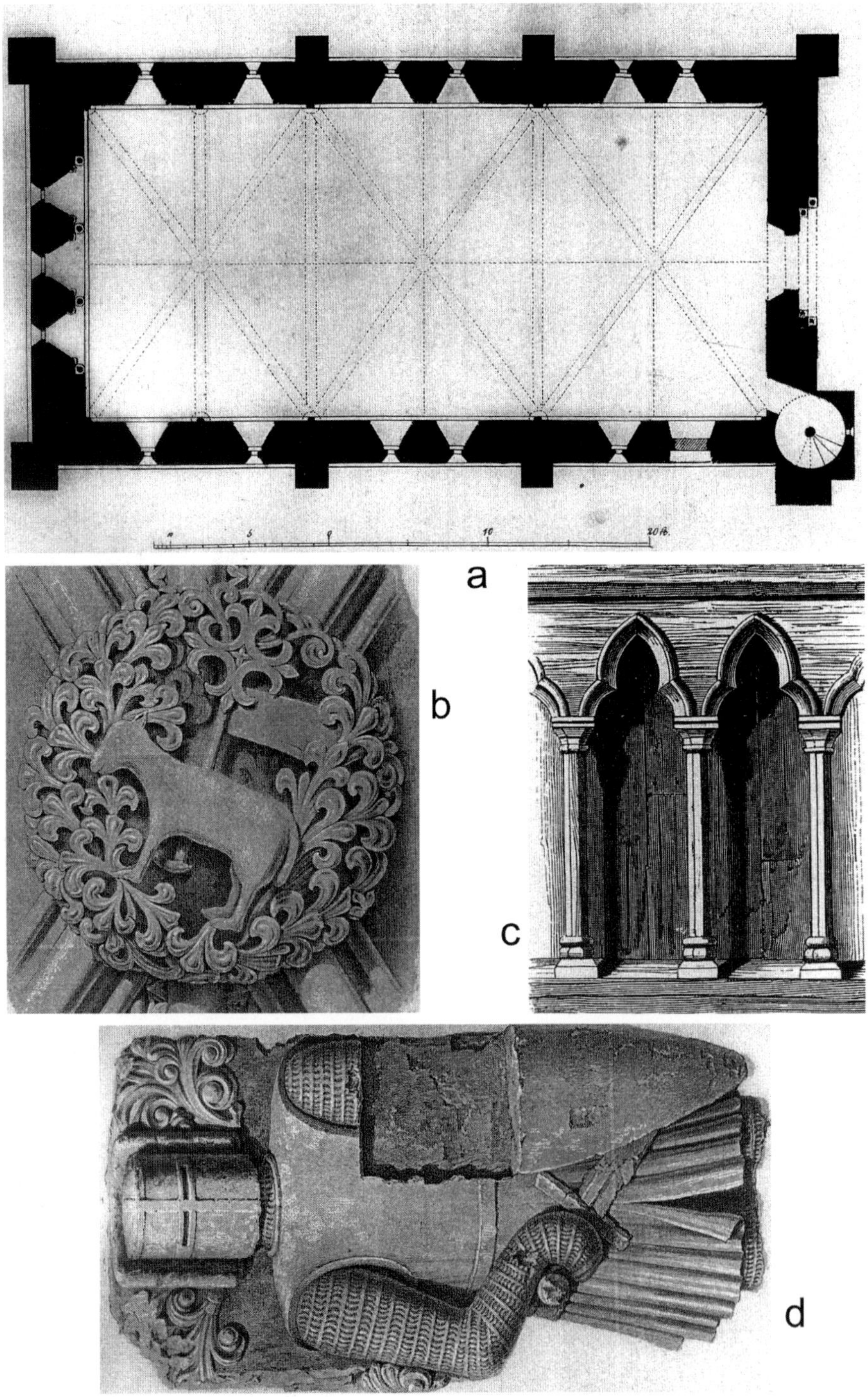

FIGURE 64.
Architectural details
from St Leonard's
Kirkstead: (a) plan;
(b) eastern vault boss;
(c) section of wooden
screen; (d) effigy
(source: Parker 1846, 19
and plates I, V).

Next to the stair turret, in the west bay of the north wall, there a second
original doorway, in addition to the main west door in the western façade
(Figure 64(a)). It is now blocked, presumably because its purpose no longer

had a place in the post-medieval uses of the building as a public place of worship – nonconformist, then Anglican. The specific location of both these features – the vice and the north doorway – is significant in that it demonstrates that those who serviced this chapel had access to the whole interior. It was a unity. They were not confined to a liturgical arena in the east bay, as might have been expected had this been a parochial chapel or other public ecclesiastical structure. Had that been the case, the secondary doorway might then have occurred in the east bay.

A factor in distracting our attention and undermining our grasp of that original unity of space today is the wooden screen, which currently divides the interior into a two-bay nave and one-bay chancel, facilitating the current parochial use. In itself a notable survival, with polygonal shafts and simple pointed trefoiled arches (Figure 64(c)), it might well – as Pevsner and others have noted – be contemporary with the building (Pevsner and Harris 1989, 418; for antiquarian notice of these screen fragments, see Hartshorne 1883; Sympson 1889–90, 198–9, 209; Jeans 1891, 91). But it was made up as late as the early twentieth century from bits recovered from pews inherited from the nonconformist chapel, when its fittings were finally swept away (photos in NMR). That woodwork might not even have come from Kirkstead at all, when the nonconformist chapel was fitted out in the late seventeenth or eighteenth centuries; even if it did, there is no reason to presume that the medieval screen from which it derived came from this building rather than from some other part of the monastery. Indeed, it was most likely a gift of the patron, Daniel Disney, or his appointed minister; perhaps after one or more stages of recycling in secular use in the considerable intervening period since the Dissolution.

So the building's layout tells us of a chapel function employing a single internal space, with an altar occupying the eastern bay. It was serviced by staff who might also occupy accommodation integral with the building above the vault and who could enter and leave it by a northern doorway towards the conventual buildings. These staff, presumably ordained priests (whether monks or not), circulated throughout the building; they were not confined to the eastern end. The landscape considerations demonstrate that seculars probably approached the chapel from the south, on something less than a main road, rather than from the north. In fact, that route comes only to this building. The chapel, therefore, had limited, privileged access. Such personages approached through its showy west façade, which might itself have evoked aspects of the cathedral at Lincoln. Yet, sited on the monastic boundary, it was in that respect positioned at an interface between the secular and the religious world.

The foundation of an independent chapel is not apparently documented at Kirkstead. But what sounds like a closely analogous case is well documented at another Cistercian house: Meaux in east Yorkshire. The Meaux Chronicle records the foundation of a chapel in 1238 'near the monastery' at the instigation of Sir Peter Mauley, whose wife Isabella had requested burial within the monastic precinct (Dugdale 1826, 388, 395 (no. XII, from the abbey's Register));

Bond 1867, 59–61; the case is discussed by Cassidy-Welch 2001, 238). The result – clearly a negotiated one and involving a very substantial endowment of land – was a detached chapel that was to be maintained by the monks of Meaux and serviced at their expense by two secular priests and two clerks, who were to say a mass for the dead, the hours, and a mass for the virgin daily, as well as a mass for the anniversary of Isabella's death. This was a detached chantry chapel. Part of the negotiation surrounding the institution was undoubtedly about its location, for it is described as 'capella beatae Mariae prope pontem qui est in bosco'.

This type of institution relates closely to shifts in religious thought, and specifically to the promotion of ideas about purgatory and prayers for the dead given a liturgical impetus by Pope Innocent III, d. 1216; the Cistercians played a significant role in developing and promulgating *exempla* illustrating the concept of purgatory, notably in the thirteenth century (see generally Le Goff 1984 and especially 174–5, 295–6, 300–10, 324–6; Sayers 1994, 19–20; Fergusson and Harrison 1999, 164–6; Cassidy-Welch 2001, 217–41). The Cistercians came under particular pressure not simply to accommodate seculars burial within their precincts, but even more problematically to sustain an ever-increasing volume of suffrages and commemorations. The General Chapter ruled broadly in 1217 that seculars could be buried in Cistercian monasteries, but, though numbers of altars grew in a manner confirmed by the archaeological record of monastic churches, increasingly commemorations were bundled together into periodic intercessions for the dead. One way, evidently, for influential patrons to maintain their individuality and assert their special relationship to a monastery was to institute a detached chantry, like that of the de Mauleys at Meaux.

Interestingly, the documentation for Meaux reveals a second example of such an institution, which exhibits even more clearly the salient characteristics in such cases and the potential complexities and compromises involved in reaching a satisfactory resolution. In 1316 Richard de Otringham, rector of Shelford (Cambs.), sought the foundation and maintenance of a chantry of seven priest-monks, in return for very extensive gifts of lands and property to Meaux. The negotiated outcome was the creation of a chantry at Beverley supported by a secular priest; while the bulk of the foundation – for six priest-monks – was transferred to the very threshold of the abbey, *ad capellam extra portas monasterii* (Bond 1867, 294–7; Dugdale 1826, 388, 395 (nos IX, XI)). But the process, according to the Meaux Chronicle, spread over a generation or more. Remarkably, the chantry was originally instituted at Ottringham in Holderness, some 14 miles (22.5 km) from Meaux, and lasted in that form for twenty-four years; but it was regarded as irregular and scandalous. The abbey finally secured the donor's agreement, and the support of the diocesan, to move the chantry and to build a chapel for it 'in some other convenient place outside the precinct and the boundary of the monastery', and they allotted the income from their churches at Nafferton and Skipsea to achieve this. So finally, after thirty years at Ottringham, the chantry's monk-priests were recalled to the abbey and the chantry's routine was reinstituted, under the instruction of the cantor, *extra portas*. But that was not the end. For, eleven years later, Abbot Adam set out, by again applying for licence from the archbishop, to secure the removal of this chantry to a new stone chapel over the very entrance of the great gate of the monastery, whose construction he had set in train. Apparently to underpin the move, the abbey obtained additional gifts of land at Ottringham from the heirs of the original donor (most satisfactorily completing their tenure of the barony of Ottringham) and special royal licence in respect of *mortmain*; but it appears that the project remained unfulfilled.

This tale of the Otringham chantry at Meaux shows how fluid the arrangements for establishing chantries around the periphery of a Cistercian monastery might be, especially if in their first form they did not conform to the requirements of the order's statutes. An abbey might prove to be more dogmatic in its wishes, more tenacious, and institutionally more long-lived than the seculars with whom they dealt. And the physical form and location of the building housing the chantry institution might change.

Topographically, the location of both these chapels lay peripheral to the Meaux precinct (Figure 65). The de Mauley chantry was *prope pontem qui est in bosco*. It is known – and was apparently famous in its time – that a part of the precinct at Meaux was full of ash trees, and known as 'the wood', until they were cleared in 1396–9 (Bond 1868, 354). In the fourteenth century the chaplain of the chapel in the woods had a chamber in the abbey's outer court, from which he was removed in the 1390s (Bond 1868, 226). Butler draws on this documentation in glossing the survey of Meaux undertaken by the Royal Commission on the Historical Monuments of England in 1980, and published in an interpreted form (Butler 1985), and identifies this wood as the north-east enclosure of the precinct, which is full of ridging, and an earthwork within it as the de Mauley chapel. There are uncertainties about this identification, driven as it is – like so much else said in interpreting the site at Meaux – by this abbey's rich documentary record, with little regard to the field archaeology. In fact, it is most improbable that the chantry's location is marked by the small moat, known as 'Chapel Close' on Ordnance Survey mapping, since that cuts through the ridging and evidently relates to a post-Dissolution ornamental layout occupying the precinct. Nevertheless, against the far north-east boundary of the enclosure and abutting the precinct boundary there is a rectangular earthwork of a stone-founded building oriented east–west and measuring about 18 m by 8 m in plan. The field remains may suggest a subsidiary structure at the west end of its south side. It seems to have stood in a small plot measuring about 36 m by 28 m, whose relationship to the ridging within the enclosure is not now clear. This foundation is marked on early Ordnance Survey sheets and identified as 'Chapel (site of)' (Ordnance Survey six-inch map of 1851; twenty-five-inch map of 1910). Perhaps it is this that Butler and others identify as the de Mauley chantry. Its location at the outer, roadside edge of an outer enclosure adjoining the core area of the monastery certainly parallels the configuration at Kirkstead and makes it a plausible candidate for

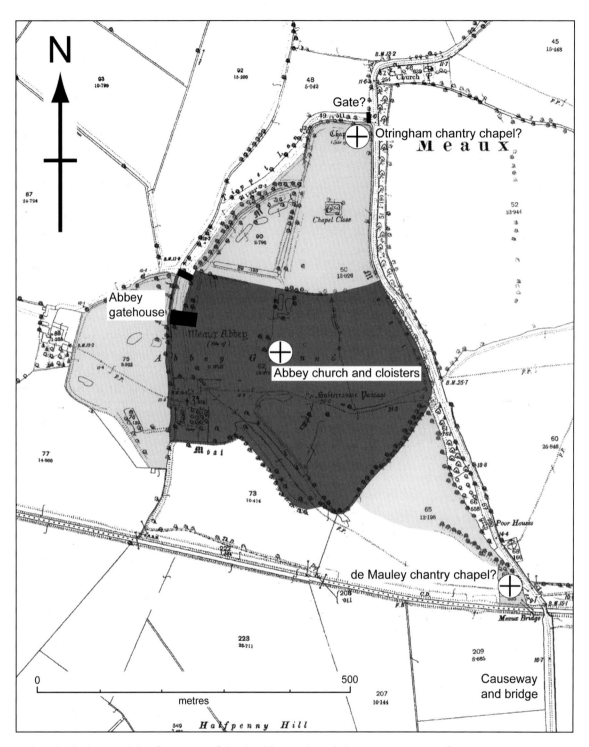

a detached chantry. The footprint of the building, though large, is not out of scale with St Leonard's. But its size may make it a more plausible candidate for the later and well-staffed Otringham foundation rather than the de Mauley chapel. And it may have lain adjacent to a monastic gate, since it seems likely that there was such a barrier at the eastern end of Tippet's Lane, which until the later nineteenth century went nowhere other than to the site of the abbey's inner gatehouse and probably therefore lay 'within' rather than 'outside' the monastery – acting like an extended outer 'chimney' between gates.

The association of the de Mauley chapel with a bridge may also suggest that it lay elsewhere. *The* bridge at Meaux is quite clearly that at the south-east of the precinct – a causeway and later 'Meaux Bridge' – which negotiates the substantial valley drained by the east–west arm of the Holderness Drain (Figure 65). Here, too, a strip of woodland separates the routeway from the precinct boundary as it climbs from the bridge, and there was a group of buildings at the woodland's south end (now removed) including a poor house and a nonconformist chapel that might signal a traditional location for an institutional presence (Ordnance Survey six-inch map of 1851). More importantly, this side of the precinct also has a substantial, ditched outer enclosure appended to the core precinct, in the extreme south-eastern corner of which were formerly a couple of small closes against the roadside. They thereby sat on the end of the cross-valley causeway and bridge, in the way that the de Mauleys' 'chapel of St Mary near the bridge' might be expected to do, in a prominent public location but visually connected – in a manner somewhat similar to St Leonard's at Kirkstead – with the claustral side of the abbey located on the high point of the local topography to the north-west. The de Mauleys' desire to associate their chapel with the abbey's bridge may have had an additional and particular significance beyond merely describing its physical location. The motif of a perilous bridge of access to paradise is persistent in the visionary literature surrounding the concept of purgatory (Le Goff 1984, 19, 35, 36, 94–5, 109, 111, 188, 196, 297).

The two locations on the north-east and south-east periphery at Meaux suit well, on topographical and archaeological grounds, the documented detached chantry chapels. They are not clustered at the main abbey gatehouse, as has perhaps been too readily assumed (Butler 1985; and see new work reported briefly by Foster 2001–2). Instead we are looking at a broader, more diversely populated monastic landscape, in which chantries lie away from that crowded arena, typically at the outer edge of outer enclosures of the monastic precinct, and commonly include – at least as founded – residential accommodation for their priests. Both of these possible chapel sites, however, are at the interface between the secular and religious worlds, rather than – as scholars might perhaps presume to have been patrons' intentions in creating a chantry – at locations in or adjacent to the monastic church. In the earlier case this might relate to Isabella's sex, since Cistercians forbade females access. In practice though, a physically liminal location might have a particular appropriateness for an institution created to accommodate the negotiated transition between life and death (Cassidy-Welch 2001, 217–41).

It is not uncommon to encounter detached chapels – unlocated topographically and uncertain in function – within the records of Cistercian houses. A

FIGURE 65.
Interpreted plan of
Meaux Abbey, near
Hull, Yorkshire East
Riding, showing the
context of documented
chantry chapels.

good example, also in Lincolnshire, occurs at Revesby Abbey. Here, three chapels with known dedications, which were evidently not simply altars within the monastic church, are referred to (Owen 1975, 20). St Laurence *ad portas* was plausibly a *capella ante portas* in the normal sense, like those at Tilty, Merevale, Thame, Rievaulx or Hailes, and, like them, was probably succeeded by the later parish church of the same dedication on a site at the landward entrance to this fen-edge precinct. Chapels of St Aldred and St Cithe, however, are unlocated except in lying 'near the old wood'. If that was Shire Wood, north-west of the core abbey precinct, then these chapels might both have been positioned on the east–west through road across from the wood and on the edge of enclosures that formed the larger monastic precinct. At Sawley (Lancs., formerly Yorks.), too, the local name of St Mary's Well within the notable run of presumably monastic closes lying against the north-east precinct boundary might signal a detached chapel of this type. Its location on the private side of the monastery, its view over the conventual complex, and its external access would be typical, though no certain building foundation has been identified in recent survey work (Hunt *et al.* 2005).

There is increasing evidence from the fourteenth and fifteenth centuries for burial of seculars and the endowment of chantries at Cistercian as at other monastic houses, as, for example, at Sawley in 1376; though it seems not to have been brought together and grants typically lack the detail found at Meaux, resulting in automatic presumptions that such chapels were founded in or adjacent to the conventual church (Coppack *et al.* 2002, 25 citing Whitaker 1878, 57 and suggesting a site to the north of the abbey church). Nevertheless, the will of Sir Thomas Bourchier in 1512 provides good documentation of the endowment of a precisely similar institution to those at Meaux or Kirkstead – a detached chapel – at Boxley, near Maidstone in Kent, by one of the leading families of south-eastern England in the early sixteenth century (Cave-Browne 1892, 35). In fact, Boxley enables us to cite at least one other instance of a peripherally located chapel that had a chantry function and where the fabric survives. That is the chapel of St Andrew (Figure 66; see Lampreys 1834, 62 and Surtees 1883 for passing notice in antiquarian literature; Cave-Browne 1892, 30–1 for a drawn view from the south-west; Newman 1969, 149 (where it is called Sandling Post Office) and DoE 1984, 32 for descriptions). It was apparently converted to a secular dwelling in the later sixteenth or early seventeenth century by extending and rebuilding its west end, wrapping that extension round its south side, and inserting a central stack and first floors. But it originally comprised a rectangular stone chapel – probably of two squarish bays internally – plus an annexe against the south side of the chapel's east end, whose structural form and precise footprint are unknown but which seems likely to have been a two-storeyed lodging block. It is uncertain whether a timber-framed, two-storey eastern extension is pre- or post-Reformation. Measuring about 8 m by 5 m, the core chapel is smaller and far less elaborate in detailing than St Leonard's at Kirkstead. Its timber roof, moulded tie beam and wooden cornice all suggest a fifteenth-century

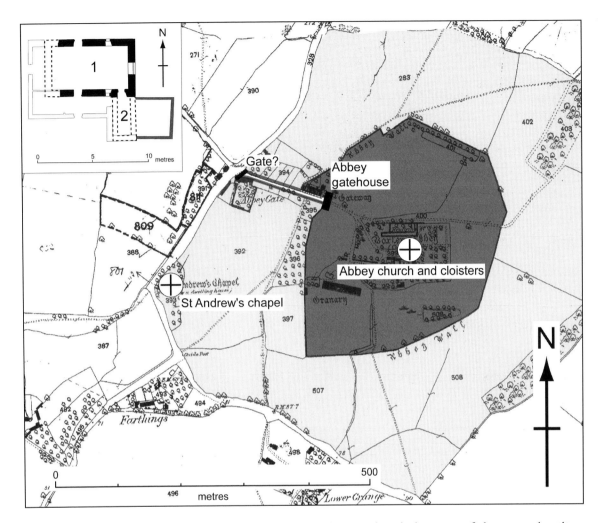

Labels on map: Gate? · Abbey gatehouse · Abbey church and cloisters · St Andrew's chapel

FIGURE 66.
Interpreted plan of
Boxley Abbey, near
Maidstone, Kent,
showing the context
of the chapel of
St Andrew. Inset:
simplified diagram
of the plan of the
medieval chapel:
1 chapel; 2 two-storey
residential block; later
accretions omitted.

date, which conforms with the late medieval character of the stone detailing of doors and windows. There are opposed north and south doors midway in the present building, which would have stood closer to the chapel's west end. This may suggest that (as at Kirkstead) the priests had access to the whole structure and not solely to a liturgical eastern arena, whereas seculars had circumscribed access from the west.[1] This chapel is directly documented only at the end of the fifteenth century (Hussey 1911, 222). Whether the foundation could have been earlier, perhaps thirteenth-century, requires a study of the complex building fabric that is beyond the scope of this paper.

St Andrew's at Boxley exhibits a number of critical features that are common to our exploration of chapels on the periphery of Cistercian precincts. It clearly has residential facilities for the priests in a two-storey annexe that is the equivalent of the roof space at Kirkstead. It is located away from the abbey gatehouse. This is true even if there was an extended 'chimney' and outer gate at the roadside, as seems probable topographically (Figure 66). It is also located prominently and publicly at a junction of through routes, and near to where there is a bridging of local watercourses. Furthermore, like the chapels at Kirkstead and Meaux, within the monastic landscape it stands against the outer edge of a peripheral zone of large enclosures that abut the core precinct. If St Andrew's chapel were a thirteenth-century foundation, it would match St Leonard's and the de Mauley chapel in timing for this rather elaborate type of chantry foundation as well as in its other characteristics.

The Meaux and Boxley chapels, we suggest, indicate the type of institution represented by our chapel at Kirkstead, but several further surviving details there give the proposal a more specific focus. Most significant is the remains of a knight's effigy (Figure 64(d)), which was dug up in a reflooring, having been used – face down – as part of the pavement. Crossley dates this monument *c.*1240 and Kemp *c.*1250 (Crossley 1921, 208, 236; Kemp 1980, 44; see also Hartshorne 1883). The foliage around the head is so close to that in the chapel's architecture as to make the two probably contemporary. The effigy has traditionally been identified with Robert de Tateshale 2, d. 1212, who obtained the right to found the market at Tattershall, essentially founding a new town and certainly thereby transforming that settlement (for a fuller consideration of these linkages with the lordship of Tattershall, see Everson and Stocker forthcoming). But an alternative, more suitable to the style-critical dating, is Robert de Tateshale 3, *c.*1201 to 1249, who married Mabel, heiress of Hugh d'Albini earl of Sussex, and twice (in 1230 and 1239) received licence to crenellate his castle at Tattershall and so develop the family caput and consolidate its standing. Perhaps the effigy is actually of the father, with the institution of the chantry being the son's work. We might envisage the chapel with its principal furnishing, a big table tomb bearing the effigy placed centrally within the two western bays, thereby allowing good circulation. The de Tateshales, of course, were hereditary patrons of Kirkstead Abbey.

A second distinctive detail is the west window of *vesica piscis* form. It functions not so much to illuminate the chapel generally but quite specifically to light the western bays where we suggest the de Tateshale monument formed the centrepiece. Its presence and size so much exercised Parker and his contemporaries – because of the uncomfortable way it was thought to sit within its blank arcade – that they thought it might be a secondary insertion. But close (as we might say, archaeological) examination of the fabric produced a report that was long, circumspect, and firmly in the negative. It is an original feature (Parker 1846, 12–14). The decision to use this unusual shape of window may relate directly to the building's function as a chantry chapel. The *vesica piscis* is, after all, the shape of the 'mandorla', which occurs iconographically in a limited number of contexts, typically with apocalyptic themes. It is most likely to have housed a depiction of Christ in Judgement in stained glass, which would be an appropriate iconography for the function we have envisaged for St Leonard's. A rarer but attractive alternative, however, would be the Assumption of the Virgin, for the St Mary was taken as their special patron by the Cistercians and dedicatee of all the Order's houses (Boase 1962, 8–14; Marks 2004, 148 for discussion of the iconography of the Assumption and its devotional occurrences). Examples of the Assumption in oval mandorlas in stained glass survive from the first decade of the fourteenth century (Newton 1979, 31, 1d, 16c and d; also illustrated and discussed in Alexander and Binski 1987, 212–13), though they are more common in the fifteenth century, including a local example of *c.*1410–30 at Wrangle in Lincolnshire (Hegbin-Barnes 1996, 363; and see, for example, Pevsner 1962, 145–7 (glazing at East Harling, Norfolk, given in memory of the two husbands of Anne Harling); RCHME 1981, 8b and pl. 55 (York, Holy Trinity Goodramgate), 19a (York, St Denys)). There is even an early sixteenth-century Cistercian example in the gatehouse chapel at Merevale Abbey memorialising Thomas Skevington, former monk at Merevale, abbot of Beaulieu and bishop of Bangor (Marks 1986, 221–3; Austin 1998, 49, 51–2, 74–5). The unusually narrow paired lancets of the side walls of the building, which might plausibly have contained grisaille glass and therefore produced a relatively ill-lit internal space (Marks 1986, 213–17; see also the comments of Sarah Brown in Austin 1998, 1), would have tended to emphasise the effect of this west window. On sunny afternoons it would have thrown a shaft of light on to the monument, touching the effigy with the image of intercession and promised redemption.

While architectural considerations and the parallels at Meaux and Boxley carry us to the functional interpretation of St Leonard's as a chantry chapel, the best evidence for this identification with the de Tateshales is actually the building's topographical location and landscape context (Figure 67). Its setting, in a close forming the south boundary of the precinct of Kirkstead, is a location of privileged access on the secluded side of the complex. Coming from the south, only the lords of Tattershall would appear to have had unfettered access, as the chapel stands only a few hundred metres north of their hunting park that swept round the north side of their caput, essentially from the Witham to the Bain. As the exclusive reserve of the de Tateshales, the park's presence between the abbey and the town of Tattershall will have discouraged direct popular access to the monastery from this direction. The de Tateshales themselves will have relished this approach to 'their' abbey directly from their new castle by way of their own hunting grounds. It is a context appropriately reflected in the dedication to St Leonard (Everson and Stocker forthcoming). Taking this route, they would have breasted the low rise now occupied by Old Abbey Farm and seen ahead of them, we suggest, the family chantry chapel across a shallow valley as if on an island, with the extensive structures of the abbey beyond. It was a view that few others saw, dominated by the cloistral complex and the bulk of the conventual church – a close approach to the intimate heart of the monastery.

St Leonard's and other examples discussed here might thus be thought to establish a new archaeological site type or component within the landscape of Cistercian monasteries, and an important variation on the ways in which lordly patronage was expressed (Astill and Wright 1993). But probably more

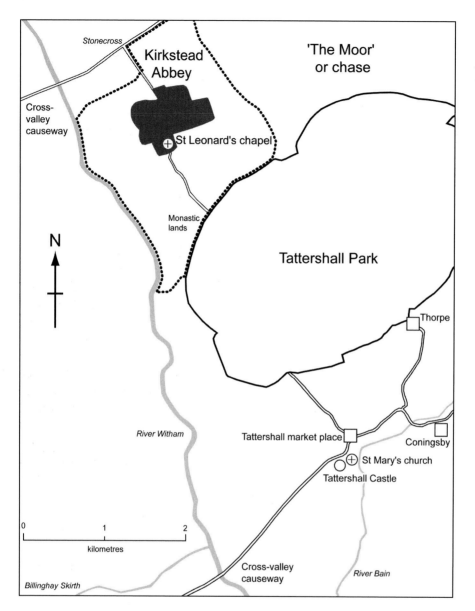

Stonecross

Kirkstead Abbey

'The Moor' or chase

Cross-valley causeway

St Leonard's chapel

Monastic lands

N

Tattershall Park

Thorpe

River Witham

Tattershall market place

Coningsby

St Mary's church

Tattershall Castle

0   1   2

kilometres

Cross-valley causeway

River Bain

Billinghay Skirth

FIGURE 67.
Kirkstead, Lincolnshire: wider landscape plan.

importantly, both conceptually and in landscape terms, this discussion begins to explore the nature of the monastic precinct boundary as a zone, permeable in different circumstances and to different degrees (Figures 63, 65 and 66), rather than as the hard line in the landscape traditionally conceived in archaeological thinking.

Note

1. Our understanding of the building's phases draws on a short RCHME report, plus photographs taken in 1996 in the NMR, reference BF008609.

CHAPTER SIXTEEN

Conclusions: The Future
of Medieval Landscape Studies

Stephen Rippon and Mark Gardiner

Fifty years on from Hoskins's seminal study of the making of the English landscape there is an ever-increasing interest in the history of both the rural countryside and urban and industrial areas. There are now two excellent journals that have landscape archaeology and history as their focus (*Landscape History* and *Landscapes*), and the subject is now widely taught in universities at both undergraduate and postgraduate level. So where is the study of the medieval landscape going?

There have been great advances in our techniques of landscape research since Hoskins, including the use of extensive aerial and ground survey; the technique of fieldwalking was unheard of in the 1950s. Archaeological techniques for the examination of landscape have been added to the battery of methods used by historians. The earlier archaeological approach towards studying the medieval landscape understandably focused on deserted sites that are amenable to survey and excavation, but recently this been balanced by projects that have investigated still-occupied settlements, for example through the excavation of small test-pits. Examples include the villages of Shapwick (Aston and Gerrard 1999) and the Whittlewood area (Jones and Page 2003a; 2006; and this volume), and the hamlets and farmsteads of the North Somerset Levels (Rippon forthcoming). These projects have also started to date other elements of the historic landscape, such as trackways and furlong boundaries, and this use of archaeological survey and excavation to examine the origins of still-functioning features of the countryside looks set to become increasingly common.

Other elements of the medieval and later landscape that continue in use today are ecclesiastical, domestic and agricultural buildings. Britain has a long history of standing building recording and this was another of Hoskins's interests; he was the originator of the idea of a 'Great Rebuilding' of rural houses in the late sixteenth and early seventeenth centuries (Hoskins 1953). A major advance since the 1950s has been the growing realisation that the development of rural housing sufficiently robust to have survived until today took place much earlier than Hoskins and his contemporaries appreciated (Dyer 1986; Currie 1988). This has allowed the excavated remains of buildings to be compared with standing structures, and instead of seeing the two as different types – one ephemeral and poorly built, the other enduring and the result of substantial investment of materials – the evidence from excavated and standing buildings are now compared with increasing frequency (Wrathmell 2002). Indeed, recent dendrochronological programmes are showing that the traditional dating of vernacular buildings, based on typology, date stones and documentary sources, may be a little on the conservative side and that in some regions a significant number of our farmsteads and cottages have late medieval origins (Penoyre and Penoyre 1999). There remains, however, a stubborn divide between those who study vernacular architecture, and scholars of the wider landscape, and a challenge for the future must be the closer integration of these two disciplines.

Another area of research into the medieval landscape in which there is a need for closer integration with archaeology and history is the study of field- and place-names. This has moved beyond the stage of simply cataloguing names and establishing their etymologies, and studies such as that by Gelling and Cole (2000), for example, have suggested that place-name elements were used in very precise ways to describe specific landscape features. Although this has been examined in detail by these authors, the implications of the use of such names remain to be considered. In particular, it seems that it may well be possible to use names as a guide to the way in which the landscape was perceived. This may be illustrated with a simple example. Many years ago Gelling (1978, 124) observed that topographical names were generally earlier than habitative ones. As we might expect, the natural landscape and its features was more important to occupants early in the medieval period and only later were the names of places derived from the names of their occupants or tenants. This shift seems to have taken place in the tenth century, a period, as we have noted above, that seems to have been formative in the crystallisation of the physical fabric of the countryside in many areas. More detailed studies of place-names are now required which link them not only to the topography of the landscape, but past perceptions of the environment.

Dendrochronology is just one example of the growing use of science in the study of the medieval landscape. Another group of techniques that are transforming our understanding of the countryside are those concerned with palaeoenvironmental analysis. Long sequences of sediments that have built up over the course of the past two millennia, such as peat bogs and valley floodplains, contain within them a record of changing climate, natural vegetation and human land use, and these are enhancing and, in some cases, transforming our appreciation of the medieval countryside. When Hoskins was writing, for example, it was widely believed that there was widespread woodland regeneration following the social and economic trauma of the Roman withdrawal from Britain. In recent decades a number of pollen cores have indeed shown that some of the more physically 'marginal' areas of Britain did see a decrease in the intensity of landscape use, reflected in some scrub and woodland regeneration. In lowland areas, by contrast, this was not usually the case, and locating more palaeoenvironmental sequences from these areas must be a priority for future research (Dark 2000; Fyfe and Rippon 2004; Rippon *et al*. in press).

Since the 1950s there have also been great advances in the study of palaeoenvironmental assemblages from settlements, notably in the form of the plant and animal remains that reflect the agrarian economy. This material has particular significance for our understanding of peasant farming, which seldom appears in the documentary record, and for understanding the economic links between the countryside, the producer of food, and towns – increasingly important consumers of rural produce. A recent work has looked at the principles of how the links between town and hinterland might be studied, while a further volume has considered the details of the connection in the late medieval period (Perring 2002; Giles and Dyer 2005).

As described above, another major theme in landscape research that has emerged in recent decades has been the study of the 'historic landscape' – the present pattern of fields, roads and settlements – that in areas which were not transformed by Parliamentary Enclosure has the potential to be of medieval, or earlier, origin. Several papers in this volume have discussed the long history of research into the plans of both towns and villages, while Roberts and Wrathmell (2000; 2002) have recently characterised the nineteenth-century settlement pattern of England, identifying a 'Central Province' of predominantly nucleated settlement, with areas of more dispersed settlement to the south-east and the west. This must broadly reflect the areas of 'champion' and 'woodland' landscape recorded by topographical writers from the sixteenth century, yet the origin of this marked regional variation in landscape character remains unclear. In England, Scotland and Wales there are currently separate programmes of historic landscape characterisation that are attempting to map systematically local and regional variation in the character of our countryside, though again based on nineteenth-century and later sources. Underlying all this work is a crucial issue that has all too often not received the attention that it deserves: the nineteenth century is the first occasion for which we have comprehensive cartographic coverage of our country, but just how far back can we project these patterns? In this volume, Page and Jones have shown that in one study area, around half of the nineteenth-century village plans are significantly at variance to their medieval forms, and there is a desperate need elsewhere to test the models derived from historic landscape characterisation through fieldwork (for example, see Rippon forthcoming).

The subject of industry is barely mentioned in the present volume, and indeed, with the exception of mining and quarrying, industrial processes are rarely thought to have had a significant impact on the medieval landscape. If, however, we include the production of timber, firewood and charcoal (Galloway *et al*. 1996; Foard 2001), processing sites such as watermills and windmills (Langdon 2004), and transport routes, including both roads and their bridges (Harrison 2004) and canals (see papers in Blair forthcoming), then it is apparent that industry had an important effect on the landscape. To these examples may also be added the areas that were set aside for the production of specialist goods, including salt (Rudkin and Owen 1960; Rippon 2000), reeds for thatching (Bailey 1989, 152) and rabbits for their fur (Bailey 1989, 129–35). The distinctive landscapes of horse studs (Moorhouse 2003, 332–4), sheep cotes (Dyer 1996b) and fishing sheds (Fox 2001) might also be added to this list, though studies of such landscapes are generally still in their infancy.

We noted in the Introduction that there was a growing awareness among medieval archaeologists and historians of the way in which people in the past had perceived the landscape. We have only recently started to realise the extent to which designed landscapes were being created in the medieval period (for example, see Liddiard's paper in this volume), and the developing interest in how people in the past experienced their environment reflects a concern about similar matters in prehistory that is of longer standing. For the historic period, it is possible to use not only the evidence of the landscape itself, but also written and oral sources to understand how people perceived the world around them (Rose 2004, 108–12). The possibility of using place-names in this way has already been mentioned, but another source of evidence is the rich record of folklore that is often is related to specific places. Phythian-Adams (2000, 134–42) has shown the way in which the currency of stories defines 'topographies of superstition', or areas of land in which the action of folktales are set. There are, however, problems in the use of folk legends in this way. Folklore represents itself as being timeless, and indeed it is often difficult to determine when stories originated and even when they had wide currency. We also need to consider how to relate folk stories to the wider aspects of life. Do they have wider implications for the behaviour of groups within the landscape? This still needs to be investigated.

There is, perhaps, one further aspect of medieval landscape research upon which we should reflect. As was mentioned earlier, landscape archaeology and history is now widely taught in British universities at both undergraduate and postgraduate level, and television programmes such as Time Team have done an enormous amount to raise the profile of archaeology as a whole, including the study of landscape. Hoskins and his contemporaries were also able to enthuse the public with the excitement of landscape research through university extra-mural education, though this has now sadly declined in many places. While this is not the place to engage in a political debate over government funding policies that have made so many universities close down their Extra Mural/Continuing Education/Lifelong Learning Departments, it is important that we seek new avenues through which to educate and enthuse the wider public about the importance of our historic environment. In the South West, for example, the Devon Archaeological Society now provides a series of courses, taught by former University Lifelong Learning tutors, and such ventures will be crucial if we are to maintain interest in our discipline. We have, therefore, a number of challenges that must be addressed in order to ensure a healthy future for research into the medieval landscape. One of the characteristic features of past research has been the synergy between archaeology, history and historical geography, and this must continue. In particular we must strive for a closer integration of field archaeology, local history, the study of standing buildings, place-names, and industrial sites, and palaeoenvironmental evidence. Some old debates, such as the origins of regional variation in landscape character, remain to be resolved, while new fields of research, such as the study of the ways in which past communities may have perceived their environment, are only just beginning. Much has been achieved since Hoskins raised our awareness of the history and complexity of the landscape, and it is to be hoped that the next half-century will be as rewarding.

Contributors

....

Dr Oliver Creighton is Lecturer in Archaeology at the University of Exeter. His research interests include medieval landscapes, castle studies and town walls. His two most recent books are *Castles and Landscapes: Power, Community and Fortification in Medieval England* and (with R. A. Higham) *Medieval Town Walls: An Archaeology and Social History*.

Dr Piers Dixon is an Operations Manager in Survey and Recording with the Royal Commission on the Ancient and Historic Monuments of Scotland and has interests in rural settlement, GIS and historic landscapes. He has worked on a variety of excavation and survey projects in northern England and Scotland. He has published the results of his excavations on both sides of the border, as well as a book entitled *Puir Labourers and Busy Husbandmen* (2002).

Paul Everson has recently retired from English Heritage. As a field archaeologist, his interests include aspects of church archaeology and monastic, garden and settlement studies, but especially their interrelationships within the landscape. Recent publications are on the post-Dissolution conversion of Lewes Priory, and (with Abby Hunt) on industry and the sublime in early modern gardens.

Dr Mark Gardiner is Senior Lecturer in Archaeology at Queen's University Belfast. He is currently working on a study of the cultural history of the medieval house and has recently completed an examination of the development of timber buildings in the period 900–1200 (with Emily Murray). He is a co-author of *The South-East to AD 1000*.

Dr Nick Higham is Professor of Early Medieval and Landscape History in the School for Arts, Histories and Cultures, University of Manchester. His principal research interests focus on the medieval landscape of north-west England and on the Anglo-Saxon period. Recent publications include: *A Frontier Landscape: The North West in the Middle Ages* (2004).

Dr Richard Jones is Lecturer in Landscape History at the University of Leicester. His research interests include medieval rural settlement, farming and non-farming landscapes, and the use of manure in the Roman and medieval periods. He is co-author (with Dr Mark Page) of *Medieval Villages in an English Landscape: Beginnings and Ends* (2006).

Dr Robert Liddiard is Lecturer in Landscape History at the University of East Anglia. His research interests include high-status buildings, landscape design before the Renaissance and the impact of lordship on the medieval countryside. Among his recent publications are *Castles in Context: Power, Symbolism and Landscape* (2005). He is currently editing a book on the medieval deer park.

Dr Keith Lilley is Lecturer in Human Geography at Queen's University Belfast. His publications include *Urban Life in the Middle Ages 1000–1450* (2002), as well as papers on medieval urban landscapes and geographical techniques combining morphological analysis and GIS. He is currently completing his second book, *City and Cosmos*.

Dr Chris Lloyd is Lecturer in Geography at Queen's University, Belfast. His research interests include spatial data analysis, historical geography, archaeology and remote sensing. He has published a variety of journal articles and book chapters on spatial analysis in the physical and social sciences.

Briony McDonagh is a researcher at the School of Humanities, University of Hertfordshire. Her thesis focused on manor houses, churches and settlements in the late medieval and early modern period, particularly in reference to the landscapes of the Yorkshire Wolds.

Edward Martin is an archaeological officer with Suffolk County Council. He has undertaken a wide range of archaeological work and landscape history, including a study of field systems in East Anglia for English Heritage. He co-edited *An Historical Atlas of Suffolk* (third edition, 1999).

Dr Mark Page is Assistant Editor of the Victoria County History of Oxfordshire. Previously he was a research fellow at the Centre for English Local History, University of Leicester, where he worked on the Whittlewood Project. He is co-author of *Medieval Villages in an English Landscape: Beginnings and Ends* (2006).

Dr Stephen Rippon is Reader in Landscape Archaeology at the University of Exeter. His main research interests are the development of the British and north-west European landscape during the Roman and medieval periods, and has published books on *The Gwent Levels* (1996), *The Severn Estuary* (1997), *The Transformation of Coastal Wetlands* (2000), and *Historic Landscape Analysis* (2004).

Dr Brian K. Roberts is a historical geographer and Professor Emeritus at the University of Durham. His studies *The Making of the English Village*, *Landscapes of Settlement*, *Region and Place* (with Stuart Wrathmell), and a forthcoming study, *Village Plans in Northern England and Beyond, AD 900–1250*, emphasise the role of maps as research tools rather than mere illustrations of research.

Contributors

Canon Dr Terry Slater is Reader in Historical Geography at the University of Birmingham and Honorary Lay Canon of Birmingham Cathedral. His research interests are in medieval urban topography and medieval town planning. He is the editor of *Towns in Decline* (2000) and is currently editing *An Historical Atlas of Warwickshire* (2006).

David Stocker currently works for English Heritage. Although many of his publications are concerned with aspects of church archaeology, they also include books and articles on many aspects of English archaeology, architectural history and conservation. His most recent works form part of collaborative studies of Lincoln and of the English colleges of Vicars Choral.

Dr Steve Trick currently works for the Centre for Archaeological Fieldwork, Queen's University, Belfast. He recently completed his PhD on early agricultural settlement in southern Romania. His research interests include landscape theory and the use of GIS to study human sensory perception in the past.

Dr Tom Williamson is Reader in Landscape History at the University of East Anglia. He has written widely on landscape archaeology, agricultural history, and the history of landscape design. His recent books include *The Transformation of Rural England: Farming and the Landscape 1700–1870* (2002), *Shaping Medieval Landscapes* (2003), *Chatsworth: A Landscape History* (with John Barnatt, 2005) and *The Archaeology of Rabbit Warrens* (2006).

Bibliography

Aalbersberg, G. (1999) *The Alluvial Fringes of the Somerset Levels*, unpublished PhD thesis, University of Exeter.

Abrams, L. (1996) *Anglo-Saxon Glastonbury: Church and Endowment*, Boydell Press, Woodbridge.

Abrams, L. (2001) 'Edward the Elder's Danelaw' in eds N. J. Higham and D. H. Hill, *Edward the Elder, 899–924*, Routledge, London, 128–43.

Aitchison, P. and Cassell, A. (2003) *The Lowland Clearances: Scotland's Silent Revolution 1760–1830*, Birlinn, Edinburgh.

Aitkens, P. (1998) 'Mid-Suffolk houses, 1250–1530' in eds D. F. Stenning and D. D. Andrews, *Regional Variation in Timber-Framed Building in England and Wales Down to 1550*, Essex County Council, Chelmsford, 40–6.

Aitkens, P. (1999) 'Aisled barns' in eds D. Dymond and E. Martin, *An Historical Atlas of Suffolk*, 3rd edn, Suffolk County Council, Ipswich, 176–7.

Aitkens, P. and Wade Martins, S. (1998) *The Farmsteads of Suffolk: A Thematic Survey*, unpublished report for English Heritage.

Alexander, J. and Binski, P. eds (1987) *Age of Chivalry. Art in Plantagenet England 1200–1400*, Royal Academy of Arts, London.

Alexander, W. M. (1952) *The Place-Names of Aberdeenshire*, Spalding Club, Aberdeen.

Allan, J. (1994) 'Medieval pottery and the dating of deserted settlements on Dartmoor', *Proceedings of the Devon Archaeological Society* 52, 141–7.

Allen, D. (1986) 'Excavations in Bierton, 1979. A Late Iron Age 'Belgic' settlement and evidence for a Roman villa and a twelfth to eighteenth century manorial complex', *Records of Buckinghamshire* 28, 1–120.

Allen, T. G. and Hiller, J. (2002) *The Excavation of a Medieval Manor House of the Bishops of Winchester at Mount House, Witney, Oxfordshire*, Oxford Archaeological Unit, Oxford.

Allison, K. J. ed. (1974) *The Victoria History of the Counties of England. A History of the County of York East Riding Volume II Dickering Wapentake*, Oxford University Press for the Institute of Historical Research, London.

Allison, K. J. ed. (1979) *The Victoria History of the Counties of England. A History of the County of York East Riding Volume IV Harthill Wapentake, Hunsley Beacon Division*, Oxford University Press for the Institute of Historical Research, London.

Altenberg, K. (2003) *Experiencing Landscapes: A Study of Space and Identity in Three Marginal Areas of Medieval Britain and Scandinavia*, Lund Studies in Medieval Archaeology 31, Almqvist and Wiksell, Stockholm.

Anon. (1857–8) 'The report', *Associated Architectural Societies Reports and Papers* 4, lxv–lxxviii.

Anon. (1877) 'Extent of burgages, lands, etc, assigned for the castle of Beaumaris', Supplement to *Archaeologia Cambrensis* 1, xiv–xix.

Anon. (1913–14a) 'The report', *Associated Architectural Societies Reports and Papers* 32, lxx–lxxx.

Anon. (1913–14b) 'Churches etc. visited by the Society from Woodhall Spa on 25th and 26th June 1913', *Associated Architectural Societies Reports and Papers* 32, 1–20.

Appleton-Fox, N. (1992) 'Excavations at a Romano-British round: Reawla, Gwinear, Cornwall', *Cornish Archaeology* 31, 69–123.

Armi, C. Edson (1983) *Masons and Sculptors in Romanesque Burgundy*, Pennsylvania State University Press, University Park and London.

Arrowsmith, P. (1997) *Stockport: A History*, Stockport Metropolitan Borough Council, Stockport.

Ashbee, J. A. (2004) ''The chamber called *Gloriette*': living at leisure in thirteenth- and fourteenth-century castles', *Journal of the British Archaeological Association* 157, 17–40.

Astill, G. G. (2000) 'General survey, 600–1300' in ed. D. M. Palliser, *The Cambridge Urban History of Britain, I, 600–1540*, Cambridge University Press, Cambridge, 27–49.

Astill, G. G. and Wright, S. M. (1993) 'Perceiving patronage in the archaeological record: Bordesley Abbey' in ed. M. Carver, *In Search of Cult: Archaeological Investigations in Honour of Philip Rahtz*, Boydell, Woodbridge, 125–37.

Astill, G. G., Hirst, S. and Wright, S. M. (2004) 'The Bordesley Abbey project reviewed', *Archaeological Journal* 161, 106–58.

Aston, M. (1993) *Know the Landscape: Monasteries*, Batsford, London.

Aston, M. and Bond, J. (1976) *The Landscape of Towns*, Dent, London.

Aston, M. and Gerrard, C. (1999) '"Unique, Traditional and Charming". The Shapwick Project, Somerset', *Antiquaries Journal* **79**, 1–58.

Aston, T.H. (1958) 'The origins of the manor in England', *Transactions of the Royal Historical Society* fifth series **8**, 59–83.

Aston, T.H. (1983) 'A postscript' in eds T.H.Aston, P.R.Coss, C.C.Dyer and J.Thirsk, *Social Relations and Ideas: Essays in Honour of R.H.Hilton*, Cambridge University Press, Cambridge, 26–43.

Atkins, P., Simmons, I.G. and Roberts, B.K. (1998) *People, Land and Time*, Arnold, London.

Austin, D. (1989) *The Deserted Medieval Village of Thrislington, Co Durham: Excavations 1973–74*, Society for Medieval Archaeology monograph **12**, Society for Medieval Archaeology, London.

Austin, J.D. (1998) *Merevale Church and Abbey. The Stained Glass, Monuments and History of the Church of Our Lady and Merevale Abbey, Warwickshire*, Brewin, Studley.

Bailey, M. (1989) 'The concept of the margin in the medieval English economy', *Economic History Review* second series **42**, 1–17.

Baker, A.R.H. (1965) 'Some fields and farms in medieval Kent', *Archaeologia Cantiana* **53**, 152–74.

Baker, A.R.H. (1973) 'Field systems of southeast England' in eds A.R.H.Baker and R.A.Butlin, *Studies of Field Systems in the British Isles*, Cambridge University Press, Cambridge, 377–429.

Baker, E. (1997) 'Grove: royal manor, alien priory cum grange – or lost minor palace' in eds G.de Boe and F.Verhaeghe, *Military Studies in Medieval Europe*, Papers of the Medieval Europe Brugge 1997 conference **11**, Instituut voor het Archeologisch Patrimonium, Zellik (Belgium), 227–36.

Baker, N.J. and Holt, R. (2004) *Urban Growth and the Medieval Church. Gloucester and Worcester*, Ashgate, Aldershot.

Baker, N.J. and Slater, T.R. (1992) 'Morphological regions in English medieval towns' in eds J.W.R.Whitehand and P.J.Larkham, *Urban Landscapes – International Perspectives*, Routledge, London, 43–68.

Balkwill, C.J. (1976) 'A Roman site at Okehampton', *Proceedings of the Devon Archaeological Society* **34**, 89–92.

BaRAS (1995) *Archaeological Excavation at the Portwall and Ditch*, BaRAS report **198/1996**, Bristol and Region Archaeological Services, Bristol.

BaRAS (2000) *Archaeological Excavation of a Medieval Watergate at Temple Quay, Bristol, 2000*, BaRAS report **677/2000**, Bristol and Region Archaeological Services, Bristol.

Barlow, F., Biddle, M., von Feilitzen, O. and Keene, D.J. eds (1976) *Winchester Studies I. Winchester in the Early Middle Ages: An Edition and Discussion of the Winton Domesday*, Clarendon Press, Oxford.

Barnwell, P. (2004) *The Whittlewood Project: Notes on the Medieval Churches*, unpublished report deposited with the Archaeology Data Service.

Barron, C.M. (2004) *London in the Later Middle Ages: Government and People 1200–1500*, Oxford University Press, Oxford.

Batey, C., Sharpe, A. and Thorpe, C. (1993) 'Tintagel Castle: archaeological investigations of the steps area 1989–1990', *Cornish Archaeology* **32**, 47–66.

Beaumont, W. (1872) *Annals of the Lords of Warrington*, 1, Chetham Society old series **86**.

Beckett, S.C. and Hibbert, F.A. (1979) 'Vegetational change and the influence of prehistoric man in the Somerset Levels', *New Phytologist* **83**, 577–600.

Beresford, G. (1974) 'The medieval manor of Penhallam, Jacobstow, Cornwall', *Medieval Archaeology* **18**, 90–145.

Beresford, G. (1977) 'Excavation of a moated house at Wintringham in Huntingdonshire', *Archaeological Journal* **134**, 194–286.

Beresford, G. (1978) 'Excavations at the deserted medieval village of Caldecote, Hertfordshire – an interim report', *Hertfordshire's Past* **4**, 3–14.

Beresford, G. (1987) *Goltho: The Development of an Early Medieval Manor c. 850–1150*, English Heritage archaeological report **4**, Historic Buildings and Monuments Commission, London.

Beresford, M.W. (1957) *History on the Ground*, Lutterworth Press, London.

Beresford, M.W. (1967) *New Towns of the Middle Ages, Town Plantation in England, Wales and Gascony*, Lutterworth, London.

Beresford, M.W. (1973) 'Isolated or ruined churches as evidence for population contraction' in ed. J.Schneider, *Économies et Sociétés au Moyen Âge: Melanges Offerts à Édouard Perroy*, Publications de la Sorbonne, Paris, 573–80.

Beresford, M.W. (1979) 'Documentary evidence for the history of Wharram Percy' in eds D.D.Andrews and G.Milne, *Domestic Settlement 1: Areas 10 and 6*, Society for Medieval Archaeology monograph **8**, Society for Medieval Archaeology, London, 5–25.

Beresford, M.W. (1984) *Time and Place: Collected Essays*, London, Hambledon Press.

Beresford, M.W. and Hurst, J.G. (1971) *Deserted Medieval Villages: Studies*, Lutterworth Press, London.

Beresford, M.W. and Hurst, J.G. (1976) 'Wharram Percy: a case study in microtopography' in ed. P.H. Sawyer, *Medieval Settlement: Change and Continuity*, Edward Arnold, London, 114–44.

Beresford, M.W. and Hurst, J.G. (1990) *Wharram Percy Deserted Medieval Village*, Batsford, London.

Beresford, M.W. and St Joseph, J.K.S. (1958) *Medieval England: An Aerial Survey*, Cambridge University Press, Cambridge.

Beresford, M.W. and St. Joseph, J.K.S. (1979; 2nd edn) *Medieval England: An Aerial Survey*, Cambridge University Press, Cambridge.

Bishop, T.A.M. (1935) 'Assarting and the growth of the open fields', *Economic History Review* **6**, 26–40.

Blair, J. (1988) 'Introduction: from minster to parish church' in ed. J. Blair, *Minsters and Parish Churches: The Local Church in Transition 950–1200*, Oxford University Committee for Archaeology, Oxford, 1–19.

Blair, J. (1991) *Early Medieval Surrey: Landholding, Church and Settlement before 1300*, Alan Sutton, Stroud.

Blair, J. (1993) 'Hall and chamber: English domestic planning 1000–1250' in eds G. Meirion-Jones and M. Jones, *Manorial Domestic Buildings in England and Northern France*, Society of Antiquaries, London, 1–21.

Blair, J. (1994) *Anglo-Saxon Oxfordshire*, Alan Sutton, Stroud.

Blair, J. (2000) 'Small towns 600–1270' in ed. D.M. Palliser, *The Cambridge Urban History of Britain, I, 600–1540*, Cambridge University Press, Cambridge, 245–70.

Blair, J. ed. (forthcoming) *Water Transport and Management in Medieval England*, Oxford University Press, Oxford.

Blair, J. and Steane, J.M. (1982) 'Investigations at Cogges, Oxfordshire 1978–81: the priory and the parish church', *Oxoniensia* **47**, 37–125.

Blinkhorn, P. (1999) 'Of cabbages and kings: production, trade, and consumption in Middle-Saxon England' in ed. M. Anderton, *Anglo-Saxon Trading Centres: Beyond the Emporia*, Cruithne Press, Glasgow, 4–23.

Blood, N.K. and Taylor, C.C. (1992) 'Cawood: an archiepiscopal landscape', *Yorkshire Archaeological Journal* **64**, 83–102.

Boase, T.S.R. (1962) *The York Psalter in the Library of the Hunterian Museum, Glasgow*, Faber, London.

Bocchi, F. (1997) *Bologna e i suoi Portici. Storia dell'Origine e dello Sviluppo*, Grafis, Bologna.

Boeminghaus, D. (1976) *Stadtbesichtigungen. Dargestellt am Beispiel Duderstadt*, Krämer, Stuttgart.

Boerefijn, W. (2000) 'Geometry and medieval town planning: a contribution to the discussion', *Urban Morphology* **4**, 25–34.

Bond, E.A. ed. (1867) *Chronicon Monasterii de Melsa*, Rolls Series **43**, pt 2, Longmans, London.

Bond, E.A. ed. (1868) *Chronicon Monasterii de Melsa*, Rolls Series **43**, pt 3, Longmans, London.

Bond, J. (1987) 'Anglo-Saxon and medieval defences' in eds J. Schofield and R. Leech, *Urban Archaeology in Britain*, Council for British Archaeology research report **61**, Council for British Archaeology, London, 92–115.

Bond, J. (2004) *Monastic Landscapes*, Tempus, Stroud.

Bonney, M. (1990) *Lordship and Urban Community: Durham and its Overlords 1250–1540*, Cambridge University Press, Cambridge.

Bowman, P. (2004) 'Villages and their territories part II: The southeast Leicestershire survey' in eds P. Bowman and P. Liddle, *Leicestershire Landscapes*, Leicestershire Museums Archaeological Fieldwork Group monograph **1**, Leicestershire Museums Archaeological Fieldwork Group, Leicester, 120–36.

Bradley, J. (2002) 'Excavations at Barrow Road, Barton-on-Humber, 1999–2000', *Lincolnshire History and Archaeology* **37**, 5–20.

Bradley, R. (1987) 'Time regained: the creation of continuity', *Journal of the British Archaeological Association* **140**, 1–17.

Bradley, R. ed. (1996) *Sacred Geography*, supplement to *World Archaeology* **28** (2).

Bradley, R. (2000) *An Archaeology of Natural Places*, London, Routledge.

Brewster, T.C.M. (1972) 'An excavation at Weaverthorpe Manor, East Riding, 1960', *Yorkshire Archaeological Journal* **44**, 114–33.

Britnell, R.H. (1993) *The Commercialisation of English Society 1000–1500*, Cambridge University Press, Cambridge.

Britnell, R.H. (2004) *Britain and Ireland 1050–1530*, Oxford University Press, Oxford.

Brodt, B. (1997) *Städte ohne Mauern. Stadtentwicklung in East Anglia im 14, Jahrhundert*, Veröffentlichungen des Deutschen Historischen Instituts in London, Paderborn.

Brooks, N.P. and Whittington, G. (1977) 'Planning and growth in the medieval Scottish burgh: the example of St Andrews', *Transactions of the Institute of British Geographers* new series **2**, 278–95.

Brown, D. (1997) 'Pots from houses', *Medieval Ceramics* **21**, 83–94.

Brown, G. (2004) 'Odiham Castle, Hampshire', *Archaeological Investigation Report Series* **17/2004**, English Heritage, Swindon.

Brown, R.A. (1976) *English Castles*, Batsford, London.

Brown, S. (1998) 'Recent building recording and excavations at Leigh Barton, Churchstow, Devon', *Proceedings of the Devon Archaeological Society* **56**, 5–108.

Brown, S. and Laithwaite, M. (1993) 'Northwood Farm, Christow: an abandoned farmstead on the eastern fringes of Dartmoor', *Proceedings of the Devon Archaeological Society* **51**, 161–84.

Brown, T. and Everson, P. (2005) 'Earthworks at Lavendon', *Records of Buckinghamshire* **45**, 45–64.

Brown, T. and Foard, G. (1998) 'The Saxon landscape: a regional perspective' in eds P. Everson and T. Williamson, *The Archaeology of Landscape: Studies Presented to Christopher Taylor*, Manchester University Press, Manchester, 67–94.

Brown, T. and Foard, G. (2004) 'The Anglo-Saxon period' in ed. M. Tingle, *The Archaeology of Northamptonshire*, Northamptonshire Archaeological Society, Northampton, 78–101.

Bruce-Mitford, R. (1997) *Mawgan Porth: A Settlement of the Late Saxon Period on the North Cornish Coast. Excavations 1949–52, 1954 and 1974*, English Heritage archaeological report **13**, English Heritage, London.

Bucher, F. (1972) 'Medieval architectural design methods, 800–1560', *Gesta* **11**, 37–51.

Buckley, D. G. and Hedges, J. D. (1987) *The Bronze Age and Saxon Settlements at Springfield Lyons, Essex: An Interim Report*, Essex County Council occasional paper **5**, Essex County Council, Chelmsford.

Bulloch, J. M. ed. (1907) *The House of Gordon*, vol. 2, New Spalding Club, Aberdeen.

Burnett, G. ed. (1882) *The Exchequer Rolls of Scotland 1437–54*, Edinburgh.

Butler, R. (1985) 'Meaux Abbey (TA 092395)', *Archaeological Journal* **141**, 46–8.

Büttner, H. and Meissner, G. (1981) *Bürgerhäuser in Europa*, Kohlhammer, Leipzig.

Cadman, G. and Foard, G. (1984) 'Raunds: manorial and village origins' in ed. M. L. Faull, *Studies in Late Anglo-Saxon Settlement*, Oxford University Department for External Studies, Oxford, 81–100.

Campbell, B. M. S. (1981) 'Commonfield origins – the regional dimension' in ed. T. Rowley, *The Origins of Open-Field Agriculture*, Croom Helm, London, 112–29.

Campbell, B. M. S. (1990) 'People and Land in the Middle Ages, 1066–1500' in eds R. A. Dodgshon and R. A. Butlin, *An Historical Geography of England and Wales*, Academic Press, London, 69–121.

Campbell, B. M. S. (2000) *English Seigniorial Agriculture, 1250–1450*, Cambridge University Press, Cambridge.

Campbell, G. (1994) 'The preliminary archaeological results from Anglo-Saxon West Cotton and Raunds' in ed. J. Rackham, *Environment and Economy in Anglo-Saxon England*, Council for British Archaeology research report **89**, Council for British Archaeology, York, 65–82.

Carter, S. P. (1999) 'The burgh of Inverurie, Aberdeenshire: archaeological evidence from a medieval lordship' *Proceedings of the Society of Antiquaries of Scotland* **129**, 649–61.

Carver, M. (1987) *Underneath English Towns. Interpreting Urban Archaeology*, Batsford, London.

Caseldine, C. J., Coles, B. J., Griffith, F. M. and Hatton, J. M. (2000) 'Conservation or change? Human influence on the mid-Devon Landscape' in ed. R. A. Nicholson and T. P. O'Connor, *People as Agents of Environmental Change*, Symposia of the Association for Environmental Archaeology **16**, Oxbow, Oxford, 60–9.

Cassidy-Welch, M. (2001) *Monastic Spaces and their Meanings: Thirteenth-Century English Cistercian Monasteries*, Medieval Church Studies **1**, Brepols Turnhout.

CAT (2000) *Hayes Farm, Clyst Honiton, nr. Exeter, Devon: Archaeological Evaluation Phase 1 (1999)*, Cotswold Archaeological Trust Report **001127**, Cotswolds Archaeological Trust, Cirencester.

Cataldi, G., Formichi, F., Merlo, A. and Visentin, L. (2003) 'Pienza, a planned vicus transformed in a town', in ed. A. Petrucciolli, M. Stella and G. Strappa, *The Planned City?*, Proceedings of the ISUF International Conference, Uniongrafica Corcelli Editrice, Bari, 104–9.

Cave-Browne, J. (1892) *The History of Boxley Parish*, privately printed, Maidstone.

Chapman, A. (in prep.) *Raunds, West Cotton: A Study in Settlement Dynamics*.

Cherry, G. C. (1994) *Birmingham. A Study in Geography, History and Planning*, Wiley, Chichester.

CIPM (1898–1955) *Vol. 3: Henry VII*, HMSO, London.

CIPM (1904–in progress), HMSO, London.

CIPM (1938) *Vol. 12: 39–43 Edward III*, HMSO, London.

Clarke, R. (2003) *A Medieval Moated Settlement and Windmill: Excavations at Boreham Airfield, Essex 1996*, East Anglian Archaeology occasional paper **11**, Essex County Council, Chelmsford.

Coldstream, N. (2003) 'Architects, advisers and design at Edward I's castles in Wales', *Architectural History* **46**, 19–36.

Colman, R. (2004) 'The archaeology of burgage plots in Scottish medieval towns: a review', *Proceedings of the Society of Antiquaries of Scotland* **134**, 281–324.

Colman, S. (1999) 'Crown-post roofs' in eds D. Dymond and E. Martin, *An Historical Atlas of Suffolk*, 3rd edn, Suffolk County Council, Ipswich, 178–9.

Colman, S. and Barnard, M. (1999) 'Raised-aisled halls and queen-post roofs' in eds D. Dymond and E. Martin, *An Historical Atlas of Suffolk*, 3rd edn, Suffolk County Council, Ipswich, 180–1.

Colvin, H. (2000) 'The origin of chantries', *Journal of Medieval History* **26**, 163–73.

Conzen, M.R.G. (1960) *Alnwick, Northumberland: A Study in Town-Plan Analysis*, Institute of British Geographers publication **27**, Institute of British Geographers, London.

Conzen, M.R.G. (1968) 'The use of town plans in the study of urban history' in ed. H.J.Dyos, *The Study of Urban History*, Edward Arnold, London, 113–30.

Conzen, M.R.G. (1972) 'Geography and townscape conservation', in ed. J.W.R.Whitehand, *The Urban Landscape: Historical Development and Management. Papers by M.R.G.Conzen*, Institute of British Geographers special publication **13**, Institute of British Geographers, London, 75–86.

Conzen, M.R.G. (1988) 'Morphogenesis, morphological regions and secular human agency in the historic townscape, as exemplified by Ludlow' in eds D.Denecke and G.Shaw, *Urban Historical Geography: Recent Progress in Britain and Germany*, Cambridge University Press, Cambridge, 253–72.

Cooper, N. (1999) *The Houses of the Gentry 1480–1680*, Yale University Press, New Haven.

Cooper, N.J. (2000) *The Archaeology of Rutland Water*, Leicestershire Archaeological monograph **6**, University of Leicester Archaeological Services, Leicester.

Coppack, G. (1974) 'Low Caythorpe, East Yorkshire – the manor site', *Yorkshire Archaeological Journal* **46**, 34–41.

Coppack, G. (1998) *The White Monks: The Cistercians in Britain 1128–1540*, Tempus, Stroud.

Coppack, G., Hayfield, C. and Williams, R. (2002) 'Sawley Abbey: the architecture and archaeology of a smaller Cistercian abbey', *Journal of the British Archaeological Association* **155**, 22–114.

Corcos, N. (2002) *The Affinities and Antecedents of Medieval Settlement: Topographical Perspectives from Three of the Somerset Hundreds*, British Archaeological Reports British series **337**, Archaeopress, Oxford.

Corner, G.R. (1859) 'On the custom of Borough English', *Proceedings of the Suffolk Institute of Archaeology* **2**, 227–41.

Coulson, C.L.H. (2003) *Castles in Medieval Society*, Oxford University Press, Oxford.

Courtney, P. (2005) 'Urbanism and "feudalism" on the periphery: some thoughts from marcher Wales' in eds K.Giles and C.Dyer, *Town and Country in the Middle Ages: Contrasts, Contacts and Interconnections, 1100–1500*, Society for Medieval Archaeology monograph **22**, Maney Publishing, Leeds, 65–84.

CPR (1894) *Edward II vol.1: AD 1307–1313*, H.M.S.O., London.

CPR (1898a) *Edward II vol.2: AD 1313–1317*, H.M.S.O., London.

CPR (1898b) *Edward III vol.4: AD 1338–1340*, H.M.S.O., London.

CPR (1914) *Edward III vol.15: AD 1370–1374*, H.M.S.O., London.

Creighton, O.H. (2005) *Castles and Landscapes: Power, Community and Fortification in Medieval England*, Equinox, London.

Creighton, O.H. (forthcoming) 'New light on medieval town defences in England, Wales and Gascony', *Château Gaillard, Etudes de Castellologie Medievale* **22**.

Creighton, O.H. and Higham, R.A. (2005) *Medieval Town Walls: An Archaeology and Social History*, Tempus, Stroud.

Crick, J. and Dawson, M. (1996) 'Archaeological excavations at Kempston Manor, 1994', *Bedfordshire Archaeology* **22**, 67–95.

Crossley, F.H. (1921) *English Church Monuments AD 1150–1550*, Batsford, London.

Cunliffe, B.W. (1972) 'Saxon and medieval settlement patterns in the region of Chalton, Hampshire', *Medieval Archaeology* **16**, 1–12.

Cunliffe, B.W. (1973) 'Manor Farm, Chalton, Hampshire', *Post-Medieval Archaeology* **7**, 31–59.

Cunliffe, B.W. (1975) *Excavation at Portchester Castle II: Saxon*, Reports of the Research Committee of the Society of Antiquaries of London **33**, Society of Antiquaries, London.

Cunliffe, B. (1991; 3rd edn) *Iron Age Communities in Britain*, Routledge, London.

Cunliffe-Shaw, R. (1958) 'Two fifteenth-century kinsmen: John Shaw of Dukinfield, mercer, and William Shaw of Heath Charnock, surgeon', *Transactions of the Lancashire and Cheshire Historical Society* **110**, 15–30.

Currie, C.R.J. (1988) 'Time and chance: modelling the attrition of old houses', *Vernacular Architecture* **19**, 1–9.

Daniels, R. (1996) 'The church, the manor and the settlement: the evidence from the Tees Valley, England', *Ruralia* **1**, Prague Institute of Archaeology, Prague, 102–14.

Darby, H.C. (1967) 'The south-western counties' in ed. H.C.Darby, *The Domesday Geography of South-West England*, Cambridge University Press, Cambridge, 348–92.

Darby, H.C. (1971; 3rd edn) *The Domesday Geography of Eastern England*, Cambridge University Press, Cambridge.

Darby, H.C. (1977) *Domesday England*, Cambridge University Press, Cambridge.

Dark, P. (2000) *The Environment of Britain in the First Millennium AD*, Duckworth, London.

Davidson, Rev. J. (1878) *Inverurie and The Earldom of the Garioch: A Topographical and Historical Account of the Garioch from the Earliest Times to the Revolution Settlement*, Edinburgh.

Davis, R.H.C. (1955) 'East Anglia and the Danelaw', *Transactions of the Royal Historical Society* fifth series **5**, 23–39.

Davis, R.H.C. (1968) 'An Oxford charter of 1191 and the origins of municipal freedom', *Oxoniensia* **33**, 53–65.

Davison, A. (1990) *The Evolution of Settlement in Three Parishes in South East Norfolk*, East Anglian Archaeology **49**, Norfolk Archaeology Unit, Dereham.

Davison, A. (1994) 'The field archaeology of Bodney, and the Stanta extension', *Norfolk Archaeology* **42**, 57–79.

Davison, B.K. (1977) 'Excavations at Sulgrave, Northamptonshire 1960–76: an interim report', *Archaeological Journal* **134**, 105–114.

Denecke, D. (1979) *Göttingen. Materialien sur Historischen Stadtgeographie und zur Stadtplanung*, E.Goltze KG, Göttingen.

Dennison, P., Ditchburn, D. and Lynch, M. eds (2002) *Aberdeen before 1800: A New History*, Tuckwell Press, East Linton.

Devine, T.M. (1994) *The Transformation of Rural Scotland: Social Change and the Agrarian Economy, 1660–1815*, Edinburgh University Press, Edinburgh.

Diel, J. (1981) *Die Tiefkeller im Bereich Oberlinden*, Stadt und Geschichte Neue Reihe des Stadtarchivs Freiburg i. Br. **2**, Schillinger, Freiburg.

Dix, B. (1987) 'Raunds area project', *Northamptonshire Archaeology* **21**, 3–30.

Dixon, P.J. (1998) 'A rural medieval settlement in Roxburghshire: excavations at Springwood Park, Kelso 1985–6', *Proceedings of the Society of Antiquaries of Scotland* **128**, 671–751.

Dixon, P.J. (2003) 'Champagne country: a review of medieval settlement in lowland Scotland' in ed. S.Govan, *Medieval or Later Rural Settlement in Scotland: 10 Years On*, Historic Scotland, Edinburgh, 53–64.

Dodd, A. (2003) *Oxford before the University: The Late Saxon and Norman Archaeology of the Thames Crossing, the Defences and the Town*, Thames Valley Landscapes monograph **17**, Oxford Archaeological Unit, Oxford.

Dodgshon, R.A. (1979) *The Origin of British Field Systems: An Interpretation*, Academic Press, London.

Dodgshon, R.A. (1981) *Land and Society in Early Scotland*, Clarendon Press, Oxford.

Dodgson, J.McN. (1970) *The Place-Names of Cheshire*, vols 1 and 2, English Place-Name Society **44**, **45**, Cambridge University Press, Cambridge.

DoE (1984) *List of Buildings of Special Architectural and Historic Interest. Borough of Maidstone, Kent (Parishes of Bearsted, Bicknor, Boxley, Bredhurst, Detling, Hucking, Stockbury and Thurnham)*, Department of the Environment, London.

Dolgner, D. and Roch, I. (1987) *Stadtbaukunst im Mittelalter*, Bauwesen, Berlin.

Downham, C. (2003) 'England and the Irish-Sea Zone in the eleventh century', *Anglo-Norman Studies* **26**, 55–73.

Du Boulay, F.R.H. (1966) *The Lordship of Canterbury: An Essay on Medieval Society*, Nelson, London.

Duby, G. (1968) *Rural Economy and Country Life in the Medieval West*, Edward Arnold, London.

Dudley, D. and Minter, M. (1966) 'The excavation of a medieval settlement at Treworld, Lesnewth, 1963', *Cornish Archaeology* **5**, 34–58.

Duffy, C. (1979) *Siege Warfare. The Fortress in the Early Modern World 1494–1660*, Routledge, London.

Dugdale, W. (1826) *Monasticon Anglicanum*, vol.5, Longman, London.

Dunsford, H. and Harris, S.J. (2003) 'Colonisation of the wasteland in County Durham, 1100–1400', *Economic History Review* **56**, 34–56.

Dyer, C.C. (1980) *Lords and Peasants in a Changing Society: The Estates of the Bishopric of Worcester, 680–1540*, Cambridge University Press, Cambridge.

Dyer, C.C. (1986) 'English peasant buildings in the later Middle Ages (1200–1500)', *Medieval Archaeology* **30**, 18–45.

Dyer, C.C. (1989) ''The retreat from marginal land': growth and decline of medieval rural settlement', in eds M.Aston, D.Austin and C.Dyer, *The Rural Settlements of Medieval England*, Blackwell, Oxford, 45–58.

Dyer, C.C. (1991) *Hanbury: Settlement and Society in a Woodland Landscape*, Department of English Local History occasional paper, fourth series **4**, Leicester University Press, Leicester.

Dyer, C.C. (1996a) 'St Oswald and 10,000 West Midland peasants' in eds N.P.Brooks and C.Cubitt, *St Oswald of Worcester: Life and Influence*, Leicester University Press, London, 174–93.

Dyer, C.C. (1996b) 'Sheepcotes: evidence for medieval sheep farming', *Medieval Archaeology* **39**, 136–64.

Dyer, C.C. (2000) 'Small towns 1270–1540' in ed. D.M. Palliser, *The Cambridge Urban History of Britain, I, 600–1540*, Cambridge University Press, Cambridge, 505–37.

Dyer, C.C. (2002a) 'Whittlewood: revealing a medieval landscape', *Current Archaeology* **182**, 59–63.

Dyer, C.C. (2002b) *Making a Living in the Middle Ages: The People of Britain 850–1520*, Yale University Press, New Haven.

Dyer, C.C. (2003) 'The archaeology of medieval small towns', *Medieval Archaeology* **47**, 85–114.

Dyer, C.C. (2004) Review of Williamson, *Shaping Medieval Landscapes*, *Landscape History* **26**, 131–2.

Dyer, C.C. (2005) 'Making sense of town and country' in eds K.Giles and C.Dyer, *Town and Country in the Middle Ages: Contrasts, Contacts and Interconnections, 1100–1500*, Society for Medieval Archaeology monograph **22**, Maney Publishing, Leeds, 313–21.

Dymond, D.P. (1968) 'The Suffolk landscape' in ed. L.M.Munby, *East Anglian Studies*, Heffer, Cambridge, 17–47.

Dymond, D.P. (1999) 'God's disputed acre', *Journal of Ecclesiastical History* **50**, 464–97.

Dymond, D.P. (2002) 'The parson's glebe: stable, expanding or shrinking?' in eds C.Harper-Bill, C.Rawcliffe and R.G.Wilson, *East Anglia's History. Studies in Honour of Norman Scarfe*, Boydell, Woodbridge, 73–91.

Elrington, C.R. ed. (1979) *The Victoria County History of the County of Oxford, 4, City of Oxford*, Oxford University Press for the Institute of Historical Research, Oxford.

Emery, A. (2005) 'Late medieval houses as an expression of social status', *Historical Research* **78**, 140–61.

Epstein, S.R. ed. (2001) *Town and Country in Europe, 1300–1800*. Cambridge University Press, Cambridge.

Evans, R. (2004) 'Whose was the manorial court' in ed. R.Evans, *Lordship and Learning: Studies in Memory of Trevor Aston*, Boydell, Woodbridge, 155–68.

Everitt, A. (1977) 'River and wold: reflections on the historical origins of regions and *pays*', *Journal of Historical Geography* **3**, 1–19.

Everitt, A. (1985) *Landscape and Community in England*, Hambledon Press, London.

Everson, P. (1988) 'What's in a name? 'Goltho', Goltho and Bullington', *Lincolnshire Archaeology and History* **23**, 93–9.

Everson, P. (1998) '"Delightfully surrounded with woods and ponds": field evidence for medieval gardens in England' in ed. P.Patterson, *There by Design*, RCHME, London, 32–8.

Everson, P. (2003) 'Medieval gardens and designed landscapes' in ed. R.Wilson-North, *The Lie of the Land: Aspects of the Archaeology and History of Designed Landscapes in the South West of England*, Devon Gardens Trust, Exeter, 24–33.

Everson, P. and Stocker, D. (forthcoming) 'Masters of Kirkstead' in ed. J.McNeill, *King's Lynn and the Fens*, Transactions of the British Archaeological Association 2005 Conference, Maney, Leeds.

Everson, P. and Williamson, T. (1998) 'Gardens and designed landscapes' in eds P.Everson and T.Williamson, *The Archaeology of Landscape*, Manchester University Press, Manchester, 139–65.

Everson, P., Brown, G. and Stocker, D. (2000) 'The earthworks and landscape context' in ed. P.Ellis, *Ludgershall Castle, Excavations by Peter Addyman, 1964–1972*, Wiltshire Archaeology and Natural History Society monograph **2**, Wiltshire Archaeology and Natural History Society, Devizes, 97–115.

Everson, P.L., Taylor, C.C. and Dunn, C.J. (1991) *Change and Continuity: Rural Settlement in North-West Lincolnshire*, HMSO, London.

Fairbrother, J.R. (1990) *Faccombe Netherton: Excavations of a Saxon and Medieval Manorial Complex*, British Museum occasional paper **74**, British Museum, London.

Faith, R.J. (1997) *The English Peasantry and the Growth of Lordship*, Leicester University Press, London.

Faith, R.J. (2004) 'Cola's *tûn*: rural social structure in late Anglo-Saxon Devon' in ed. R.Evans, *Lordship and Learning: Studies in Memory of Trevor Aston*, Boydell, Woodbridge, 63–78.

Farley, M. (1982) 'Excavations at Low Farm, Fulmer, Bucks: II, the medieval manor', *Records of Buckinghamshire* **24**, 46–72.

Farley, M.E. and Little, R.I. (1968) 'Oldaport, Modbury', *Proceedings of the Devon Archaeological Society* **26**, 31–6.

Fasham, P.J., Keevill, G. and Coe, D. (1995) *Brighton Hill South (Hatch Warren): An Iron Age Farmstead and Deserted Medieval Village in Hampshire*, Wessex Archaeology report **7**, Trust for Wessex Archaeology, Salisbury.

Fehring, G. (1991) *The Archaeology of Medieval Germany, An Introduction*, Routledge, London.

Fergusson, P. (1990) '' Porta patens esto': notes on early Cistercian gatehouses in the north of England' in eds E.Fernie and P.Crossley, *Medieval Architectural and Intellectual Context: Studies in Honour of Peter Kidson*, Hambledon, London, 47–60.

Fergusson, P. and Harrison, S. (1999) *Rievaulx Abbey*, Yale University Press, New Haven.

Fitzpatrick, A., Butterworth, C.A. and Grove, J. (1999) *Prehistoric and Roman Sites in East Devon: The A30 Honiton to Exeter Improvement DBFO Scheme, 1996–9*, Wessex Archaeology, Salisbury.

Fleming, A. (1988) *The Dartmoor Reaves*, Batsford, London.

Fleming, R. (1991) *Kings and Lords in Conquest England*, Cambridge University Press, Cambridge.

Fletcher, R. (1997) *The Barbarian Conversion: From Paganism to Christianity*, Henry Holt, New York.

Foard, G. (1978) 'Systematic fieldwalking and the investigation of Saxon settlement in Northamptonshire', *World Archaeology* **9**, 357–74.

Foard, G. (2001) 'Medieval woodland, agriculture and industry in Rockingham Forest, Northamptonshire', *Medieval Archaeology* **45**, 41–95.

Ford, S. (1996) 'The excavation of a Saxon settlement and a Mesolithic flint scatter at Northampton Road, Brixworth, Northamptonshire', *Northamptonshire Archaeology* **26**, 79–108.

Foster, C. (2001–2) 'Recent work at Meaux Abbey', *Church Archaeology* **5** and **6**, 92–8.

Foster, C.W. ed. (1920) *Final Concords of the County of Lincoln, Vol II*, Lincoln Record Society **17**.

Fowler, P. (2000) *Landscape Plotted and Pieced: Landscape History and Local Archaeology in Fyfield and Overton, Wiltshire*, Reports of the Research Committee of the Society of Antiquaries of London **64**, London.

Fowler, P. (2002) *Farming in the First Millennium AD. British Agriculture Between Julius Caesar and William the Conqueror*, Cambridge University Press, Cambridge.

Fox, H. S. A. (1991) 'Farming practice and techniques, Devon and Cornwall' in ed. E. Miller, *The Agrarian History of England and Wales, 3, 1348–1500*, Cambridge University Press, Cambridge, 303–23.

Fox, H. S. A. (2001) *The Evolution of the Fishing Village: Landscape and Society along the South Devon Coast, 1086–1550*, Leopard's Head Press, Oxford.

Fox, H. S. A. and Padel, O. (2000) *The Cornish Lands of the Arundells of Lanherne, Fourteenth to Sixteenth Centuries*, Devon and Cornwall Records Society **41**.

Francis, P. D. and Slater, D. S. (1990) 'A record of vegetational and land use change from upland peat deposits on Exmoor part 2: Hoar Moor', *Proceedings of the Somerset Archaeological and Natural History Society* **134**, 1–26.

Friedman, D. (1988) *Florentine New Towns: Urban Design in the Late Middle Ages*, MIT Press, Cambridge, Mass.

Friedman, D. (1992) 'Palaces and the street in late-medieval and Renaissance Italy', in eds J. W. R. Whitehand and P. J. Larkham, *Urban Landscapes. International Perspectives*, Routledge, London, 69–113.

Friedman, D. and Pirillo, P. eds (2004) *Le Terre Nuove*, Biblioteca Storica Toscana **44**, Olschki, Florence.

Fyfe, R. M. and Rippon, S. J. (2004) 'A landscape in transition? Palaeoenvironmental evidence for the end of the 'Romano-British' period in South West England' in eds R. Collins and J. Gerrard, *Debating Late Antiquity in Britain AD 300–700*, British Archaeological Report British series **365**, Archaeopress, Oxford, 33–42.

Fyfe, R. M., Brown, A. G. and Rippon, S. J. (2003) 'Mid- to late-Holocene vegetation history of greater Exmoor, UK: estimating the spatial extent of human-induced vegetation change', *Vegetation History and Archaeobotany* **12**, 215–32.

Fyfe, R. M., Brown, A. G. and Rippon, S. J. (2004) 'Characterising the late prehistoric, 'Romano-British' and medieval landscape, and dating the emergence of a regionally distinct agricultural system in south west Britain', *Journal of Archaeological Science* **31**, 1699–714.

Gallant, L., Luxton, N. and Collman, M. (1985) 'Ancient fields on the South Devon limestone plateau', *Proceedings of the Devon Archaeological Society* **43**, 23–37.

Galloway, J. A. (2005) 'Urban hinterlands in later medieval England' in eds K. Giles and C. Dyer, *Town and Country in the Middle Ages: Contrasts, Contacts and Interconnections, 1100–1500*, Society for Medieval Archaeology monograph **22**, Maney Publishing, Leeds, 111–30.

Galloway, J. A., Keene, D. and Murphy, M. (1996) 'Fuelling the city: production and distribution of firewood and fuel in London's region, 1290–1400', *Economic History Review* new ser. **49**, 447–72.

Gardiner, M. F. (1984) 'Saxon settlement and land division in the western Weald', *Sussex Archaeological Collections* **122**, 75–83.

Gardiner, M. F. (2006) 'Implements and utensils in *Gerefa*, and the organization of seigneurial farmsteads in the High Middle Ages', *Medieval Archaeology* **50**, 260–7.

Gardiner, M. F., Jones, G. and Martin, D. (1991) 'The excavation of a medieval aisled hall at Park Farm, Salehurst, East Sussex', *Sussex Archaeological Collections* **129**, 81–97.

Gearey, B. R., Charman, D. J. and Kent, M. (2000a) 'Palaeoecological evidence for the prehistoric settlement of Bodmin Moor, Cornwall, southwest England. Part I: the status of woodland and early human impacts', *Journal of Archaeological Science* **27**, 423–38.

Gearey, B. R., Charman, D. J. and Kent, M. (2000b) 'Palaeoecological evidence for the prehistoric settlement of Bodmin Moor, Cornwall, southwest England. Part II: land use changes from the Neolithic to the present', *Journal of Archaeological Science* **27**, 493–508.

Gearey, B. R., West, S. and Charman, D. J. (1997) 'The landscape context of medieval settlement on the southwestern moors of England. Recent palaeoenvironmental evidence from Bodmin Moor and Dartmoor', *Medieval Archaeology* **41**, 195–209.

Gelling, M. (1978) 'The effect of man on the landscape: the place-name evidence in Berkshire' in eds S. Limbrey and J. G. Evans, *The Effect of Man on the Landscape: The Lowland Zone*, CBA research report **21**, Council for British Archaeology, London, 123–5.

Gelling, M. and Cole, A. (2000) *The Landscape of Place-Names*, Shaun Tyas, Stamford.

Gent, H. and Quinnell, H. (1999a) 'Excavations of a causewayed enclosure and hillfort on Raddon Hill, Stockleigh Pomeroy', *Proceedings of the Devon Archaeological Society* **57**, 1–76.

Gent, H. and Quinnell, H. (1999b) 'Salvage recording on the Neolithic site at Haldon Belvedere', *Proceedings of the Devon Archaeological Society* **57**, 77–104.

Gervers, M. ed. (1996) *The Cartulary of the Knights of St John of Jerusalem in England Part 2: Primara Camera, Essex*, Records of Social and Economic History new series **23**, British Academy, Oxford.

Gilchrist, R. (1995) *Contemplation and Action: The Other Monasticism*, Leicester University Press, London.

Gilchrist, R. (1999) *Contesting the Past: Gender and Archaeology*, Routledge, London.

Giles, K. (2000) *An Archaeology of Social Identity: Guildhalls in York* c. *1350–1630*, British Archaeological Reports British series **315**, John and Erica Hedges, Oxford.

Giles, K. and Dyer, C. ed. (2005) *Town and Country in the Middle Ages: Contrasts, Contacts and Interconnections, 1100–1500*, Society for Medieval Archaeology monograph **22**, Maney Publishing, Leeds.

Gillingham, J. R. (1995) 'Thegns and knights in eleventh-century England: who was then the gentleman?', *Transactions of the Royal Historical Society* sixth series **5**, 129–53.

Gilyard-Beer, R. (1959) *Abbeys. An Introduction to the Religious Houses of England and Wales*, HMSO, London.

Girouard, M. (1978) *Life in the English Country House: A Social and Architectural History*, Yale University Press, New Haven.

Gooder, E., Woodfield, C. and Chaplin, R. (1966) 'The walls of Coventry', *Transactions of the Birmingham Archaeological Society* **81**, 88–138.

Graham, A. H. and Davies, S. M. (1993) *Excavations in Trowbridge, Wiltshire, 1977 and 1986–1988*, Wessex Archaeology report **2**, Trust for Wessex Archaeology, Salisbury.

Grant, E. G. and Bigmore, P. G. (1974) 'Rural Settlement in Norfolk' in eds E. G. Grant and P. G. Bigmore, *Rural Settlement in Norfolk*, Middlesex Polytechnic Historical Geography Research Group, Middlesex, 1–18.

Grant, N. (1995) 'The occupation of hillforts in Devon during the late Roman and post-Roman periods', *Proceedings of the Devon Archaeological Society* **53**, 97–108.

Graves, C. P. (1989) 'Social space in the English medieval parish church', *Economy and Society* **18**, 297–322.

Gray, H. L. (1915) *English Field Systems*, Harvard University Press, Cambridge, Mass.

Gray, M. (1976) 'North-east Agriculture and the labour force 1790–1875' in ed. A. A. Maclaren, *Social Class in Scotland: Past and Present*, Donald, Edinburgh, 86–104.

Greene, P. (1989) *Norton Priory: The Archaeology of a Medieval Religious House*, Cambridge University Press, Cambridge.

Greenway, D. ed. (1996) *Henry Archdeacon of Huntingdon, Historia Anglorum*, Oxford University Press, Oxford.

Griep, H.-G. (1985) *Kleine Kunstgeschichte des Deutschen Bürgerhauses*, Wissenschaftliche Buchgesellschaft, Darmstadt.

Griffith, F. M. (1984) 'Roman military sites in Devon: some recent discoveries', *Proceedings of the Devon Archaeological Society* **42**, 11–32.

Griffith, F. M. (1994) 'Changing perceptions of the context of prehistoric Dartmoor', *Proceedings of the Devon Archaeological Society* **52**, 85–99.

Griffith, F. M. and Reed, S. J. (1998) 'Rescue recording at Bantham Ham, South Devon, in 1997', *Proceedings of the Devon Archaeological Society* **56**, 109–31.

Griffith, F. M. and Weddell, P. (1996) 'Ironworking in the Blackdown Hills: results of recent survey' in ed. P. Newman, *The Archaeology of Mining and Metallurgy in South West Britain*, Peak District Mines Historical Society/Historical Metallurgy Society, Matlock, 27–34.

Griffiths, D. (2001) 'The North-West Frontier' in eds N. J. Higham and D. H. Hill, *Edward the Elder, 899–924*, Routledge, London, 167–87.

Guthrie, A. (1969) 'Excavations of a settlement at Goldherring, Sancreed, 1958–1961', *Cornish Archaeology* **8**, 5–39.

Hall, D. (1982) *Medieval Fields*, Shire, Prices Risborough.

Hall, D. (1988) 'The late Saxon countryside: villages and their fields' in ed. D. Hooke, *Anglo-Saxon Settlements*, Blackwell, Oxford, 99–22.

Hall, D. (1995) *The Open Fields of Northamptonshire*, Northamptonshire Record Society **38**.

Hall, D. and Martin, P. (1979) 'Brixworth, Northamptonshire – an intensive survey', *Journal of the British Archaeological Association* **132**, 1–6.

Hall, D., Wells, C. E. and Huckerby, E. (1995) *The Wetlands of Greater Manchester*, North West Wetlands Survey **2**, Lancaster Imprints, Lancaster.

Hall, J. (2001) 'English Cistercian gatehouse chapels', *Cîteaux* **52**, 61–92.

Hall, T. W. (1932) *Etton, an East Yorkshire Village, Time 1170 to 1482*, J. W. Northend, Sheffield.

Hallam, E. M. (1986) *Domesday Book Through Nine Centuries*, Thames and Hudson, London.

Hamerow, H. (1991) 'Settlement mobility and the 'Middle Saxon Shift': rural settlements and settlement patterns in Anglo-Saxon England', *Anglo-Saxon England* **20**, 1–17.

Hamerow, H. (2002) *Early Medieval Settlements*, Oxford University Press, Oxford.

Hamilton, H. ed. (1945) *Selections from the Monymusk Papers (1713–1755)*, Scottish History Society third series **39**, Scottish Historical Society, Edinburgh.

Hansen, I. L. and Wickham, C. ed. (2000) *The Long Eighth Century: Production, Distribution and Demand*, Brill, Leiden.

Hanworth, R. and Tomalin, D. J. (1977) *Brooklands: Weybridge: The Excavation of an Iron Age and Medieval Site, 1964–5 and 1970–71*, Surrey Archaeological Society research report **4**, Surrey Archaeological Society, Guildford.

Harland, J. (1856–62) *Mamecestre*, 3 vols, Chetham Society old series, **53**, **56**, **58**.

Harris, A. (1961) *The Rural Landscape of the East Riding of Yorkshire, 1750–1850: A Study in Historical Geography*, Oxford University Press, London.

Harris, B. and Ryan, G. (1967) *An Outline of the Law Relating to Common Land*, Sweet and Maxwell, London.

Harris, R. (1993) 'The Jew's House and the Norman House', in ed. M. Jones, *Lincoln Archaeology 1992–93*, Fifth Annual Report of the City of Lincoln Archaeology Unit, City of Lincoln Archaeology Unit, Lincoln, 24–8.

Harrison, D. (2004) *The Bridges of Medieval England. Transport and Society 400–1800*, Clarendon Press, Oxford.

Harrison, J. (2001a) *Glenernan: A Report for the RCAHMS*, unpublished, RCAHMS, Edinburgh.

Harrison, J. (2001b) *Rhynie and Essie: A Report for RCAHMS*, unpublished, RCAHMS, Edinburgh.

Hart, C. (1992) *The Danelaw*, Hambledon Press, London.

Hartshorne, A. (1883) 'On Kirkstead Abbey, Lincolnshire, Kirkstead Chapel, and a remarkable monumental effigy there preserved', *Archaeological Journal* 40, 296–302.

Harvey, J. (1981) *Medieval Gardens*, Batsford, London.

Harvey, P. D. A. (2004) 'The manorial reeve in twelfth-century England' in ed. R. Evans, *Lordship and Learning: Studies in Memory of Trevor Aston*, Boydell, Woodbridge, 125–38.

Haslam, J. ed. (1984) *Anglo-Saxon Towns in Southern England*, Phillimore, Chichester.

Haslam, J. (1988) 'Parishes, churches, wards and gates in eastern London' in ed. J. Blair, *Minsters and Parish Churches: The Local Church in Transition 950–1200*, Oxford University Committee for Archaeology, Oxford, 35–43.

Hatton, J. M. and Caseldine, C. J. (1991) 'Vegetation change and land use history during the first millennium AD at Aller Farm, East Devon as indicated by pollen analysis', *Proceedings of the Devon Archaeological Society* 49, 107–14.

Hawkins, S. (2005a) *Vegetation History and Land-Use Change in the Blackdown Hills, Devon, U.K.*, unpublished report, Community Landscapes Project, University of Exeter.

Hawkins, S. (2005b) *Vegetation History and Land-Use Change in the Clyst Valley, Devon, U.K.*, unpublished report, Community Landscapes Project, University of Exeter.

Hayes, P. P. and Lane, T. W. (1992) *The Fenland Project Number 5: Lincolnshire Survey, the South West Fens*, East Anglian Archaeology 55, Heritage Trust of Lincolnshire, Sleaford.

Hegbin-Barnes, P. (1996) *The Medieval Stained Glass of the County of Lincolnshire*, CVMA Great Britain Survey catalogue, 3, Oxford University Press, Oxford.

Heighway, C. (1989) 'Excavations near the site of St George's church, King's Stanley', *Glevensis* 23, 33–42.

Henderson, C. G. and Weddell, P. J. (1994) 'Medieval settlement on Dartmoor and in West Devon: the evidence from excavations', *Proceedings of the Devon Archaeological Society* 52, 119–40.

Herring, P. (1993) 'Examining a Romano-British boundary at Foage, Zennor', *Cornish Archaeology* 32, 17–28.

Herring, P. (1994) 'The cliff castles and hillforts of West Penwith in the light of recent work at Maen Castle and Treryn Dinas', *Cornish Archaeology* 33, 40–56.

Herring, P. (1996) 'Transhumance in medieval Cornwall' in ed. H. Fox, *Seasonal Settlement*, University of Leicester, Leicester, 35–43.

Herring, P. (1998) *Cornwall's Historic Landscape: Presenting a Method of Historic Landscape Characterisation*, Cornwall Archaeology Unit, Truro.

Herring, P. (2000) *St Michael's Mount, Cornwall: Reports on Archaeological Works, 1995–1998*, Cornwall Archaeological Unit, Truro.

Herring, P. (2003) 'Cornish medieval deer parks' in ed. R. Wilson-North, *The Lie of the Land: Aspects of the Archaeology and History of Designed Landscapes in the South West of England*, Devon Gardens Trust, Exeter, 34–50.

Hervey, F. ed. (1902) *Suffolk in the 17th Century. The Breviary of Suffolk by Robert Reyce, 1618*, John Murray, London.

Hewitt, H. J. (1967) *Cheshire under the Three Edwards*, Cheshire Community Council, Chester.

Hey, G. (2004) *Yarnton: Saxon and Medieval Settlement and Landscape, Results of Excavations 1990–96*, Oxford Archaeology, Oxford.

Heywood, I., Cornelius, S. and Carver, S. (1998) *An Introduction to Geographical Information Systems*, Longman, London.

Heywood, S. (1998) 'From aisles to queen posts: medieval timber framing in Norfolk' in eds D. F. Stenning and D. D. Andrews, *Regional Variation in Timber-Framed Building in England and Wales Down to 1550*, Essex County Council, Chelmsford, 47–50.

Higham, N. J. (1986) *The Northern Counties to AD 1000*, Longman, London.

Higham, N. J. (1988) 'The Cheshire burhs and the Mercian frontier to 924', *Transactions of the Antiquarian Society of Lancashire and Cheshire* 85, 193–221.

Higham, N. J. (1993) *The Origins of Cheshire*, Manchester University Press, Manchester.

Higham, N. J. (1997) 'Patterns of patronage and power: the governance of late Anglo-Saxon Cheshire' in eds J. C. Appleby and P. Dalton, *Government, Religion and Society in Northern England, 1000–1700*, Sutton, Stroud, 1–13.

Higham, N. J. (2000), 'The Tatton Park project, part 2: the medieval estates, settlements and halls', *Journal of the Chester Archaeological Society* 75, 61–133.

Higham, N.J. (2004) *A Frontier Landscape: The North West in the Middle Ages*, Windgather Press, Macclesfield.

Hildebrandt, H. (1988) 'Systems of agriculture in central Europe up to the tenth and eleventh centuries' in ed. D. Hooke, *Anglo-Saxon Settlements*, Blackwell, Oxford, 275–90.

Hindle, B.P. (1990) *Medieval Town Plans*, Shire Publications, Princes Risborough.

Hirst, F.C. (1937) 'Excavations at Porthmeor, Cornwall, 1933, 1934 and 1935', *Journal of the Royal Institute of Cornwall* 24, appendix II.

HMSO (1958) *Royal Commission on Common Land 1955–8*, Cmnd. 462, HMSO, London.

Hodge, C., Burton, R., Corbett, W., Evans, R. and Scale, R. (1984) *Soils and their Uses in Eastern England*, Soil Survey of England and Wales, Harpenden.

Hodges, R. (1988) 'The Danish contribution to the origin of the English castle', *Acta Archaeologica* 59, 169–72.

Holderness, B.A. (1984) 'East Anglia, the Home Counties and south-east England' in ed. J. Thirsk, *The Agrarian History of England and Wales, 5.1, 1640–1750, Regional Farming Systems*, Cambridge University Press, Cambridge, 197–338.

Holdsworth, P. (1983) 'The Anglo-Saxon period' in ed. M. Morris, *Medieval Manchester: A Regional Study*, Greater Manchester Archaeological Unit, Manchester, 6–16.

Holt, R. (1988) *The Mills of Medieval England*, Blackwell, Oxford.

Homan, W.M. (1949) 'The founding of New Winchelsea', *Sussex Archaeological Collections* 88, 22–41.

Homans, G.C. (1941) *English Villagers of the Thirteenth Century*, Harvard University Press, Cambridge, Mass.

Homans, G.C. (1953) 'The explanation of English regional differences', *Past and Present* 42, 18–34.

Hooke, D. (1981) 'Open-field agriculture – the evidence from pre-conquest charters of the West Midlands' in ed. T. Rowley, *The Origins of Open Field Agriculture*, Croom Helm, London, 39–63.

Hooke, D. (1988) 'Regional variation in southern and central England in the Anglo-Saxon period and its relationship to land units and settlement' in ed. D. Hooke, *Anglo-Saxon Settlements*, Blackwell, Oxford, 123–51.

Hooke, D. (1994) *The Pre-Conquest Charter-Bounds of Devon and Cornwall*, Boydell Press, Woodbridge.

Hooke, D. (1998) *The Landscape of Anglo-Saxon England*, Leicester University Press, London.

Hooke, D. (1999) 'Saxon conquest and settlement' in eds R. Kain and W. Ravenhill, *Historical Atlas of South-West England*, Exeter University Press, Exeter, 95–104.

Hooke, D. ed. (2001) *Landscape – The Richest Historical Record*, Society for Landscape Studies supplementary series 1, Society for Landscape Studies, Amesbury.

Hope-Taylor, B. (1977) *Yeavering: An Anglo-British Centre of Early Northumbria*, HMSO, London.

Hoppitt, R. (1989) 'A relative relief map of Suffolk', *Transactions of the Suffolk Naturalist's Society* 25, 80–85.

Horner, W.S. (1993) 'A Romano-British enclosure at Butland Farm, Modbury', *Proceedings of the Devon Archaeological Society* 51, 210–15.

Horner, W.S. (2001) 'Secrets of the sands', *Devon Archaeological Society Newsletter*, May 2001, 1, 8–9.

Horsman, V. (1988) 'Eynsford Castle: a reinterpretation of its early history in the light of recent excavations', *Archaeologia Cantiana* 105, 39–57.

Hoskins, W.G. (1943) 'The reclamation of waste in Devon, 1550–1800', *Economic History Review* first series 13, 80–92.

Hoskins, W.G. (1953) 'The rebuilding of rural England, 1570–1640', *Past and Present* 4, 44–59.

Hoskins, W.G. (1955) *The Making of the English Landscape*, Hodder and Stoughton, London.

Hoskins, W.G. (1967) *Fieldwork in Local History*, Faber, London.

Howell, C. (1983) *Land, Family and Inheritance in Transition: Kibworth Harcourt 1280–1700*, Cambridge University Press, Cambridge.

Hughes, M. (1984) 'Rural settlement and landscape in late Saxon Hampshire' in ed. M.L. Faull, *Studies in Late Anglo-Saxon Settlement*, Oxford University Department for External Studies, Oxford, 65–79.

Hughes, M. (1994) 'The fourteenth-century French raids on Hampshire and the Isle of Wight' in eds A. Curry and M. Hughes, *Arms, Armies and Fortifications in the Hundred Years War*, Boydell, Woodbridge, 121–43.

Hume, A. (1863) *Ancient Meols: Or some Account of the Antiquities found near Dove Point, on the sea-shore of Cheshire*, J.R. Smith, London.

Hunt, A., Pollington, M., Dunn, C. and Pearson, T. (2005) 'Sawley Abbey, Sawley, Lancashire: a Cistercian monastic precinct and post-medieval landscape', *Archaeological Investigation Report Series* 17/2005, English Heritage, Swindon.

Hussey, A. (1911) 'Chapels in Kent', *Archaeologia Cantiana* 29, 217–58.

Illingworth, W. and Caley, J. ed. (1812–18) *Rotuli Hundredorum*, 2 vols, Record Commission, London.

Innes, C.N. ed. (1845) *Registrum Episcopatus Aberdonensis. Ecclesie Cathedralis Aberdonensis Regesta Que Extant in Unum* 1, Spalding Club, Aberdeen.

Jarvis, K. (1976) 'The M5 Motorway and the Peamore/Pocombe Link', *Proceedings of the Devon Archaeological Society* 34, 41–72.

Jarvis, R. A., Bendelow, V. C., Bradley, R. I., Carroll, D. M., Furness, R. R., Kilgour, I. N. L and Ling, S. J. (1984) *Soils and their Uses in Northern England*, Soil Survey of England and Wales, Harpenden.

Jeans, G. E. (1891) 'Rood screens in Lincolnshire (with additions by C. Moor and E. M. Sympson)', *Lincolnshire Notes and Queries* 2, 90–92.

Jecock, H. M., Tuck, C. and Winton, H. (1994) *Kirkstead Abbey, Lincolnshire: Incorporating Monastic Precinct, Fishponds, and Air Photographic Transcription*, unpublished RCHME reports in NMR.

Johnson, D. A., Moore, C. and Fasham, P. (1998–9) 'Excavation at Penhale Round, Fraddon, Cornwall', *Cornish Archaeology* 37–8, 72–120.

Johnson, M. (2002) *Behind the Castle Gate: From Medieval to Renaissance*, Routledge, London.

Johnson, N. and Rose, P. (1982) 'Defended settlement in Cornwall – an illustrated discussion' in ed. D. Miles, *The Romano-British Countryside*, British Archaeological Reports British series 103, British Archaeological Reports, Oxford, 151–207.

Jolliffe, J. E. A. (1926) 'Northumbrian institutions', *English Historical Review* 41, 1–42.

Jones, B. and Mattingly, D. (1990) *An Atlas of Roman Britain*, Blackwell, Oxford.

Jones, G. (1969) *A History of the Vikings*, Oxford University Press, Oxford.

Jones, M. J., Stocker, D. and Vince, A. (2003) *The City by the Pool: Assessing the Archaeology of the City of Lincoln*, Oxbow, Oxford.

Jones, R. and Page, M. (2001) 'Medieval settlements and landscapes in the Whittlewood area: interim report 2001–2', *Medieval Settlement Research Group Annual Report* 16, 15–25.

Jones, R. and Page, M. (2003a) 'Characterising rural settlement and landscape: Whittlewood Forest in the Middle Ages', *Medieval Archaeology* 47, 53–83.

Jones, R. and Page, M. (2003b) 'Medieval settlements and landscapes in the Whittlewood area: interim report 2003–4', *Medieval Settlement Research Group Annual Report* 18, 37–45.

Jones, R. and Page, M. (2006) *Medieval Villages in an English Landscape: Beginnings and Ends*, Windgather Press, Macclesfield.

Kalanke, K. L. and Kuchen, M. (1982) *Braunschweig, vom Wik zur Regionalstadt*, J. H. Meyer, Braunschweig.

Kalinowski, W. (1972) 'Poland', in ed. E. A. Gutkind, *International History of City Development VII: Urban Development in East-Central Europe: Poland, Czechoslovakia and Hungary*, The Free Press, New York, 1–108.

Keene, D. (1985) *Survey of Medieval Winchester*, Winchester Studies 2, Oxford University Press, Oxford.

Keith, G. S. (1811) *A General View of the Agriculture of Aberdeenshire*, Board of Agriculture, Aberdeen.

Kelly, S. E. (2000) *Charters of Abingdon Abbey, Part 1*, Anglo-Saxon Charters 7, Oxford University Press, Oxford.

Kemp, B. (1980) *English Church Monuments*, Batsford, London.

Kermode, J. (2000a) 'The greater towns 1300–1540' in ed. D. M. Palliser, *The Cambridge Urban History of Britain, I, 600–1540*, Cambridge University Press, Cambridge, 441–65.

Kermode, J. (2000b) 'Northern Towns' in ed. D. M. Palliser, *The Cambridge Urban History of Britain, I, 600–1540*, Cambridge University Press, Cambridge, 657–80.

Kerridge, E. (1967) *The Agricultural Revolution*, Allen and Unwin, London.

Kerridge, E. (1992) *The Common Fields of England*, Manchester University Press, Manchester.

Ketteringham, L. L. (1984) 'Excavations at Lagham Manor, South Godstone, Surrey (TQ364481)', *Surrey Archaeological Collections* 75, 235–49.

King, D. J. C. (1983) *Castellarium Anglicanum*, Kraus, New York.

King, V. (1996) 'St Oswald's tenants' in eds N. P. Brooks and C. Cubitt, *St Oswald of Worcester: Life and Influence*, Leicester University Press, London, 100–16.

Kissock, J. (1997) '"God made nature and men made towns": post-Conquest and pre-Conquest villages in Pembrokeshire', in ed. N. Edwards, *Landscape and Settlement in Medieval Wales*, Oxbow, Oxford, 123–37.

Klockow, H. (1964) *Stadt Lippe – Lippstadt*, Volksbank Lippstadt, Lippstadt.

Knowles, D. and Hadcock, R. (1971) *Medieval Religious Houses in England and Wales*, Longman, London.

Knowles, D. and St Joseph, J. K. (1952) *Monastic Sites from the Air*, Cambridge University Press, Cambridge.

Knox, R. (2004) 'The Anglo-Saxons in Leicestershire' in eds P. Bowman and P. Liddle, *Leicestershire Landscapes*, Leicestershire Museums Archaeological Fieldwork Group monograph 1, Leicestershire Museums Archaeological Fieldwork Group, Leicester, 95–104.

Koster, E. (1998) 'Urban morphology and computers', *Urban Morphology* 2, 3–10.

Koter, M. and Kulesza, M. (1999) 'The plans of medieval Polish towns', *Urban Morphology* 3, 63–78.

Kristensson, G. (1995) *A Survey of Middle English Dialects 1290–1350: The East Midland Counties*, Lund University Press, Lund.

Lambourne, A. (2004) *'According to the Logic of the Landscape': A Critical Examination of the Significance of the Dartmoor Reaves for the Wider Devon Landscape of Today*, unpublished MA dissertation, University of Exeter.

Lamond, E. ed. (1893) *A Discourse of the Common Weal of this Realm of England*, Cambridge University Press, Cambridge.

Lampreys, S.C. (1834) *A Brief Historical and Descriptive Account of Maidstone and its Environs*, Brown, Maidstone.

Landsberg, S. (1995) *The Medieval Garden*, British Museum, London.

Lane, T.W. (1993) *The Fenland Project Number 8: Lincolnshire Survey, the northern fen-edge*, East Anglian Archaeology **66**, Heritage Trust of Lincolnshire, Sleaford.

Lane, T.W. (1995) *The Archaeology and Developing Landscape of Ropsley and Humby, Lincolnshire*, Lincolnshire Archaeology and Heritage reports series **2**, Heritage Lincolnshire, Sleaford.

Lang, J. (2000) 'Monuments from Yorkshire in the age of Alcuin' in eds H.Geake and J.Kenny, *Early Deira: Archaeological Studies of the East Riding in the Fourth to Ninth centuries AD*, Oxbow, Oxford, 109–119.

Langdon, J. (1986) *Horses, Oxen, and Technological Innovation*, Cambridge University Press, Cambridge.

Langdon, J. (2004) *Mills in the Medieval Economy: England, 1300–1540*, Oxford University Press, Oxford.

Larking, L.B. and Kemble, J.M. eds (1857) *The Knights Hospitallers in England: being the Report of Prior Philip de Thame to the Grand Master, Elyan de Villanova*, London.

Lasdun, S. (1991) *The English Park: Royal, Private and Public*, Andre Deutsch, London.

Lauret, A., Malebranche, R. and Séraphin, G. (1988) *Bastides. Villes Nouvelles du Moyen-Age*, Éditions Milan, Toulouse.

Lavadan, P. and Hugueny, J. (1974) *L'Urbanisme au Moyen Age*, Arts et Métiers Graphiques, Paris.

Le Goff, J. (1984) *The Birth of Purgatory*, University of Chicago Press, Chicago.

Le Patourel, H.E.J. (1973) *The Moated Sites of Yorkshire*, Society for Medieval Archaeology monograph **5**, Society for Medieval Archaeology, London.

Le Patourel, H.E.J. (1991) 'Rural buildings in England and Wales: England' in ed. E.Miller, *The Agrarian History of England and Wales, 3, 1348–1500*, Cambridge University Press, Cambridge, 820–90.

Leach, P. and Ellis, P. (2004) 'Roman and medieval remains at Manor Farm, Castle Carey', *Somerset Archaeology and Natural History* **147**, 81–128.

Lebon, J.H.G. (1952) *The Evolution of Our Countryside*, Dennis Dobson, London.

Lennard, R.V. (1959) *Rural England 1086–1135: A Study of Social and Agrarian Conditions*, Oxford University Press, Oxford.

Lewis, C., Mitchell-Fox, P. and Dyer, C. (1997) *Village, Hamlet and Field: Changing Medieval Settlements in Central England*, Manchester University Press, Manchester.

Lewis, C., Mitchell-Fox, P. and Dyer, C. (2001; 2nd edn) *Village, Hamlet and Field: Changing Medieval Settlements in Central England*, Windgather Press, Macclesfield.

Lewis, C.P. (1991) 'An introduction to the Cheshire Domesday' in eds A.Williams and G.H.Martin, *The Cheshire Domesday*, Alecto, London, 1–25.

Lewis, E.A. (1912) *The Mediaeval Boroughs of Snowdonia*, Henry Sotheran, London.

Lewis, J. (2000) *The Medieval Earthworks of the Hundred of West Derby: Tenurial Evidence and Physical Structure*, British Archaeological Reports British Series **310**, Archaeopress, Oxford.

Leyland, M. (1994) 'The origins and development of Durham Castle' in eds D.Rollason, M.Harvey and M.Prestwich, *Anglo-Norman Durham 1093–1193*, Boydell, Woodbridge, 407–24.

Liddiard, R. (2000) *Landscapes of Lordship: The Castle and the Countryside in Medieval Norfolk*, British Archaeological Reports British series **309**, J. and E.Hedges, Oxford.

Liddle, P. (1996) 'The archaeology of Anglo-Saxon Leicestershire' in ed. J.Bourne, *Anglo-Saxon Landscapes in the East Midlands*, Leicestershire Museums Arts and Records Service, Leicester, 1–10.

Lilley, K.D. (1998) 'Taking measures across the medieval landscape: aspects of urban design before the Renaissance', *Urban Morphology* **2**, 82–92.

Lilley, K.D. (1999) 'Urban landscapes and the cultural politics of territorial control in Anglo-Norman England', *Landscape Research* **24**, 5–23.

Lilley, K.D. (2000a) 'Mapping the medieval city: plan analysis and urban history', *Urban History* **27**, 5–30.

Lilley, K.D. (2000b) ''Non urbe, non vico, non castris': territorial control and the colonization and urbanization of Wales and Ireland under Anglo-Norman lordship', *Journal of Historical Geography* **26**, 517–31.

Lilley, K.D. (2001a) *Urban Life in the Middle Ages 1000–1450*, Palgrave, Basingstoke.

Lilley, K.D. (2001b) 'Urban planning and the design of towns in the Middle Ages: the Earls of Devon and their 'new towns'', *Planning Perspectives* **16**, 1–24.

Lilley, K.D. (2004) 'Cities of God? Medieval urban forms and their Christian symbolism', *Transactions of the Institute of British Geographers* new series **29**, 296–313.

Lilley, K.D., Lloyd, C. and Trick, S. (2005a) *Mapping Medieval Townscapes: A Digital Historical Atlas of King Edward I's 'New Towns' of England and Wales*, Archaeology Data Service, York (online via www.ads.ac.uk).

Lilley, K.D., Lloyd, C., Trick, S. and Graham, C. (2005b) 'Analysing and mapping medieval urban forms using GPS and GIS', *Urban Morphology* **9**, 5–15.

Lilley, K.D., Lloyd, C. and Trick, S. (2005c) 'Mapping medieval urban landscapes: the design and planning of Edward I's new towns of England and Wales', *Antiquity* **79**, number 303, Project Gallery # 3 (http://antiquity.ac.uk/ProjGall/lilley/).

Lowther, P., Ebbatson, L., Ellison, M. and Millett, M. (1993) 'The city of Durham: an archaeological survey', *Durham Archaeological Journal* **9**, 27–119.

Lynch, M. (1991) *Scotland: A New History*, Barrie and Jenkins, London.

McAvoy, F. (1980) 'The excavation of a multiperiod site at Carngoon Bank, Lizard, Cornwall, 1979', *Cornish Archaeology* **19**, 31–62.

McCann, J. (2000) 'Dovecotes and pigeons in English law', *Transactions of the Ancient Monument Society* **44**, 25–50.

MacCulloch, D. (1986) *Suffolk and the Tudors, Politics and Religion in an English County 1500–1600*, Oxford University Press, Oxford.

McOmish, D., Field, D. and Brown, G. (2002) *The Field Archaeology of the Salisbury Plain Training Area*, English Heritage, London.

Maitland, F.W. (1897) *Domesday Book and Beyond: Three Essays in the Early History of England*, Cambridge University Press, Cambridge.

Manco, J. (1996) 'Iron Acton: a Saxon nucleated village', *Transactions of the Bristol and Gloucestershire Archaeological Society* **113**, 89–96.

Manley, J. (1987) 'Cledemutha: a late Saxon burh in north Wales', *Medieval Archaeology* **31**, 13–46.

Marks, R. (1986) 'Cistercian window glass in England and Wales' in eds C. Norton and D. Park, *Cistercian Art and Architecture in the British Isles*, Cambridge University Press, Cambridge, 211–27.

Marks, R. (2004) *Image and Devotion in Late Medieval England*, Sutton, Stroud.

Martin, D. and Martin, B. (2004) *New Winchelsea, Sussex: A Medieval Port Town*, Heritage Marketing and Publications, Great Dunham.

Martin, E. (1999a) 'Place-name patterns' in eds D. Dymond and E. Martin, *An Historical Atlas of Suffolk*, 3rd edn, Suffolk County Council, Ipswich, 50–1.

Martin, E. (1999b) 'Greens, commons and tyes' in eds D. Dymond and E. Martin, *An Historical Atlas of Suffolk*, 3rd edn, Suffolk County Council, Ipswich, 62–3.

Martin, E. and Satchell, M. (forthcoming) *Wheare most Inclosures be. East Anglian Fields: History, Morphology and Management*, East Anglian Archaeology.

Mason, D.J.P. (1975) 'Chester: Lower Bridge Street', *Cheshire Archaeological Bulletin* **3**, 40–1.

Mason, D.J.P. (1976) 'Chester: the evolution of its landscape', *Journal of the Chester Archaeological Society* **59**, 14–23.

Mason, D.J.P. (1985) *Excavations at Chester, 26–42 Lower Bridge Street, the Dark Age and Saxon Periods*, Chester City Council, Chester.

Matarasso, P. (1993) *The Cistercian World, Monastic Writings of the Twelfth Century*, Penguin, London.

Mayes, P. (2002) *Excavations at a Templar Preceptory, South Witham. Lincolnshire 1965–67*, Society for Medieval Archaeology monograph **19**, Society for Medieval Archaeology, Leeds.

Meckseper, C. (2004) 'Recenti ricerche sulle città di nuova fondazione in ambito tedesco al tempo degli Hohenstaufen' in eds D. Friedman and P. Pirillo, *Le Terre Nuove*, Biblioteca Storica Toscana **44**, Olschki, Florence, 3–26.

Meinig, D.W. (1979) 'Reading the landscape, an appreciation of W.G. Hoskins and J.B. Jackson' in ed. D.W. Meinig, *The Interpretation of Ordinary Landscapes*, Oxford University Press, New York, 195–244.

Middlebrook, S. (1968) *Newcastle upon Tyne – Its Growth and Achievement*, S.R. Publishers, Wakefield.

Miller, K. (1984a) 'Beverley town defences', *Archaeological Journal* **141**, 21–2.

Miller, K. (1984b) 'Beverley, North Bar', *Archaeological Journal* **141**, 23–5.

Miller, K., Robinson, J., English, B. and Hall, I. (1982) *Beverley: An Archaeological and Architectural Survey*, HMSO, London.

Milne, G. (1992) 'Site 39' in eds G. Milne and J.D. Richards, *Wharram: A Study of Settlement on the Yorkshire Wolds, VII. Two Anglo-Saxon Buildings and Associated Finds*, York University Archaeological Publications **9**, University of York, York, 5–12.

Milne, G. (2003) *The Port of Medieval London*, Tempus, Stroud.

Milne, G. (2004) 'Site 45' in eds P.A. Rahtz and L. Watts, *Wharram: A Study of Settlement on the Yorkshire Wolds, IX. The North Manor Area and North-West Enclosure*, York University Archaeological Publications **11**, University of York, 19–35.

Mitchell, Sir A. ed. (1907) *Geographical Collections Relating to Scotland, Made by Walter Macfarlane*, vol. 2, Scottish History Society, Edinburgh.

Mitchell, D. (2003) 'California living, California dying: dead labour and the political economy of landscape' in eds K. Anderson, M. Domosh, S. Pile and N. Thrift, *Handbook of Cultural Geography*, Sage, London, 233–48.

Mitchell, D. (2005) 'Landscape' in eds D. Atkinson, P. Jackson, D. Sibley and N. Washbourne, *Cultural Geography: a Critical Dictionary of Key Concepts*, I.B. Taurus, London, 49–56.

Moore, P. (1999) 'Excavations at the site of West Court manor house, Chalk', *Archaeologia Cantiana* **119**, 353–67.

Moore P.D., Merryfield, D.L. and Price, M.D.R. (1984) 'The vegetation and development of blanket mires' in ed. P.D.Moore, *European Mires*, Academic Press, London, 203–35.

Moorhouse, S. (2003) 'Anatomy of the Yorkshire Dales: decoding the medieval landscape' in eds T.G.Manby, S.Moorhouse and P.Ottaway, *The Archaeology of Yorkshire: An Assessment at the Beginning of the Twenty-First Century*, Yorkshire Archaeological Society occasional paper 3, Yorkshire Archaeological Society, Leeds, 293–362.

Moreland, J. (2000) 'The significance of production in eighth-century England' in eds I.L.Hansen and C.Wickham, *The Long Eighth Century: Production, Distribution and Demand*, Brill, Leiden, 69–104.

Morgan, P. ed. (1978) *Domesday Book 26: Cheshire*, Phillimore, Chichester.

Morris, A.E.J. (1979) *History of Urban Form*, Longman, Harlow.

Morris, C.D., Batey, C.E., Brady, K., Harry, R., Johnson, P.G. and Thomas, C. (1999) 'Recent work at Tintagel', *Medieval Archaeology* 43, 206–15.

Morris, M. ed. (1983) *Medieval Manchester: A Regional Study*, Greater Manchester Archaeological Unit, Manchester.

Morris, M.C.F. (1907) *Nunburnholme: Its History and Antiquities*, John Sampson, York.

Morris, R. (1989) *Churches in the Landscape*, Dent, London.

Mortimer, R. (2000) 'Village development and ceramic sequence: the middle to late Saxon village at Lordship Lane, Cottenham, Cambridgeshire', *Proceedings of the Cambridge Antiquarian Society* 89, 5–33.

Munby, J. ed. (1982) *Domesday Book 4: Hampshire*, Chichester, Phillimore.

Murphy, P. (1994) 'The Anglo-Saxon landscape and rural economy: some results from sites in East Anglia and Essex' in ed. J.Rackham, *Environment and Economy in Anglo-Saxon England*, Council for British Archaeology research report 89, Council for British Archaeology, York, 23–39.

Murphy, P. (1996) 'Environmental archaeology' in ed. O.Bedwin, *The Archaeology of Essex. Proceedings of the 1993 Writtle Conference*, Essex County Council, Chelmsford, 168–80.

Murray, J.C. and Murray, H.K. (1993) 'Excavations at Rattray, Aberdeenshire. A Scottish deserted burgh', *Medieval Archaeology* 37, 109–218.

Mynard, D.C. (1994) *Excavations on Medieval Sites in Milton Keynes*, Buckinghamshire Archaeological Society monograph series 6, Buckinghamshire Archaeological Society, Aylesbury.

Nevell, M. (1991) *Tameside 1066–1700*, Tameside Metropolitan Borough Council, Manchester.

Newman, J. (1969) *Buildings of England, North East and East Kent*, Penguin, Harmondsworth.

Newman, J. (1992) 'The late Roman and Anglo-Saxon settlement pattern in the Sandlings of Suffolk' in ed. M.Carver, *The Age of Sutton Hoo: The Seventh Century in North-Western Europe*, Boydell Press, Woodbridge, 25–38.

Newton, K.C. (1960) *Thaxted in the Fourteenth Century*, Essex Records Office, Chelmsford.

Newton, P.A. (1979) *The County of Oxford: A Catalogue of Medieval Stained Glass*, CVMA Great Britain Survey catalogue 1, Oxford University Press, London.

Nitz, H.-J. (1988a) 'Settlement structures and settlement systems of the Frankish central state in Carolingian and Ottonian times' in ed. D.Hooke, *Anglo-Saxon Settlements*, Blackwell, Oxford, 249–73.

Nitz, H.-J. (1988b) 'Introduction from above: intentional spread of common-field systems by feudal authorities through colonization and reorganization', *Geografiska Annaler* 70B (1), 156–7.

Nitz, H.-J. (2001) 'Medieval towns with grid plan and central market place in east-central Europe: origins and diffusion in the early thirteenth century', *Urban Morphology* 5, 81–102.

Nowakowski, J.A. and Thomas, C. (1992) *Grave News from Tintagel: An Account of a Second Season of Archaeological Excavation at Tintagel Churchyard, Cornwall, 1992*, Cornwall Archaeological Unit, Truro.

Okasha, E. (1993) *Corpus of Early Christian Inscribed Stones of South-West Britain*, Leicester University Press, London.

O'Keeffe, T. (2004) 'Were there designed landscapes in medieval Ireland?', *Landscapes* 5, 52–68.

Oosthuizen, S. (1994) 'Saxon commons in South Cambridgeshire', *Proceedings of the Cambridge Antiquarian Society* 82, 93–100.

Oosthuizen, S. (2005) 'New light on the origins of open-field farming?', *Medieval Archaeology* 49, 165–94

Oosthuizen S. and Taylor C. (2000) 'John O'Gaunt's house: Bassingbourne, Cambridgeshire: a fifteenth-century landscape', *Landscape History* 22, 61–71.

Oppl, F. ed. (1982) *Austrian Historic Towns Atlas I*, F.Denticke, Wien.

Ormerod, G.revised and enlarged by T.Helsby (1882; 2nd edn) *The History of the County Palatine and City of Chester*, George Routledge, London.

Orwin, C.S. and Orwin, C.S. (1938) *The Open Fields*, Clarendon Press, Oxford.

OS (1869–70) *The First Edition of the Ordnance Survey Six-Inch Map of Aberdeenshire*, Ordnance Survey, Southampton.

Ottaway, P. (1992) *Archaeology in British Towns from the Emperor Claudius to the Black Death*, Routledge, London.

Owen, D. M. (1971) *Church and Society in Medieval Lincolnshire*, History of Lincolnshire 5, History of Lincolnshire Committee, Lincoln.

Owen, D. M. (1975) 'Medieval chapels in Lincolnshire', *Lincolnshire History and Archaeology* 10, 15–22.

Oxley, J (1982) 'Nantwich: an eleventh-century salt town and its origins', *Transactions of the Historic Society of Lancashire and Cheshire* 131, 1–20.

Øye, I. (1994) *Bergen and the German Hanse*, Bryggens Museum, Bergen.

Padel, O. (1985) *Cornish Place-Name Elements*, English Place-Name Society 56–7, English Place-Name Society, Nottingham.

Padel, O. (1999) 'Place-names' in eds R. Kain and W. Ravenhill, *Historical Atlas of South-West England*, Exeter University Press, Exeter, 88–94.

Page, M. and Jones, R. (2003) 'Medieval settlements and landscapes in the Whittlewood area: interim report 2002–3', *Medieval Settlement Research Group Annual Report* 18, 27–36.

Page, P., Atherton, K. and Hardy, A. (2005) *Barentin's Manor: Excavations on the Moated Manor at Harding's Field, Chalgrove, Oxfordshire 1976–9*, Thames Valley Landscapes monograph 24, Oxford Archaeological Unit, Oxford.

Page, W. ed. (1908) *The Victoria History of the Counties of England: Hampshire and the Isle of Wight, Volume 3*, Archibald Constable, London.

Palliser, D. M. (1995) 'Town defences in medieval England and Wales' in eds A. Ayton and J. L. Price, *The Medieval Military Revolution*, Tauris, London, 105–20.

Palliser, D. M., Slater, T. R. and Dennison, E. P. (2000) 'The topography of towns 600–1300' in ed. D. M. Palliser, *The Cambridge Urban History of Britain, I, 600–1540*, Cambridge University Press, Cambridge, 153–86.

Palmer, J. J. N. (1987) 'The Domesday manor' in ed. J. C. Holt, *Domesday Studies*, Boydell, Woodbridge, 139–59.

Parker, J. H. (1846) *An Architectural Description of Saint Leonard's Church, Kirkstead, Published under the Superintendence of the Lincolnshire Architectural Society*, Oxford.

Parker, R. (2000) 'Measuring Suffolk's hedgerows', *Suffolk Natural History* 36, 105–7.

Parsons, D. and Styles, T. (2000) *Vocabulary of English Place-Names: Brace-Cæster*, Centre for English Name-Studies, Nottingham.

Paul, J. B. ed. (1984) *Registrum Magni Sigilli Regum Scotorum, 1424–1513*, Edinburgh.

Pearce, S. (1978) *The Kingdom of Dumnonia*, Lodenek Press, Padstow.

Pearce, S. (2004) *South-Western Britain in the Early Middle Ages*, Leicester University Press, London.

Penhallurick, R. D. (1986) *Tin in Antiquity*, Institute of Metals, London.

Penoyre, J. and Penoyre, J. (1999) 'Somerset Dendrochronology Project', *Somerset Archaeology and Natural History* 142, 311–15.

Perring, D. ed. (2002) *Town and Country in England: Frameworks for Archaeological Research*, Council for British Archaeology, London.

Pevsner, N. (1962) *The Buildings of England: North-West and South Norfolk*, Penguin, Harmondsworth.

Pevsner, N. and Harris, J. (1964) *The Buildings of England: Lincolnshire*, Penguin, Harmondsworth.

Pevsner, N. and Harris, J. (1989; 2nd edn) *The Buildings of England: Lincolnshire*, Penguin, Harmondsworth.

Phillips, A. D. M. and Phillips, C. B. (2002) *A New Historical Atlas of Cheshire*, Cheshire County Council, Chester.

Phillips, C. B. and Smith, J. H. (1994) *Lancashire and Cheshire from AD 1540*, Longman, Harlow.

Phillips, E. N. M. (1966) 'Excavation of a Romano-British site at Lower Well Farm, Soke Gabriel, Devon', *Proceedings of the Devon Archaeological Society* 23, 2–62.

Phythian-Adams, C. (1987) *Rethinking English Local History*, Department of English Local History occasional papers fourth series 1, Leicester University Press, Leicester.

Phythian-Adams, C. (2000) 'Environments and identities: landscape as cultural projection in the English provincial past', ed. P. Slack, *Environments and Historical Change: The Linacre Lectures 1998*, Oxford University Press, Oxford, 118–46.

Platt, C. (1973) *Medieval Southampton: The Port and Trading Community, AD 1000–1600*, Kegan Paul, London.

Platt, C. (1984a) *The Abbeys and Priories of Medieval England*, Secker and Warburg, London.

Platt, C. (1984b) *Medieval Britain from the Air*, George Philip, London.

Platt, C. and Coleman-Smith, R. eds (1975) *Excavations in Medieval Southampton 1953–1969*, Leicester University Press, Leicester.

Pollack, M. (1992) 'Military architecture and cartography in the design of the early modern city' in ed. D. Buisseret, *Envisioning the City. Six Studies in Urban Cartography*, University of Chicago Press, Chicago, 109–24.

Pollard, J. and Reynolds, A. (2002) *Avebury: The Biography of a Landscape*, Tempus, Stroud.

Pollard, S. M. H. (1966) 'Neolithic and Dark Age settlements on High Peak, Sidmouth, Devon', *Proceedings of the Devon Archaeological Society* 23, 35–59.

Porsmose, E. (1987) *De Fynske Landsbyers Historie*, Odense University Studies in History and Social Sciences **109**, Odense.

Postan, M. M. (1975) *The Medieval Economy and Society: An Economic History of Britain in the Middle Ages*, Penguin, Harmondsworth.

Poulsen, B. (1997) 'Agricultural technology in medieval Denmark' in eds G. G. Astill and J. Langdon, *Medieval Farming and Technology. The Impact of Agricultural Change in Northwest Europe*, Brill, Leiden, 115–45.

Pounds, N. J. G. (1991) 'The chapel in the castle', *Fortress* **9**, 12–20.

Pratt, D. (1965) 'The medieval borough of Holt', *Denbighshire Historical Society Transactions* **14**, 9–74.

Preston-Jones, A. and Rose, P. (1986) 'Medieval Cornwall', *Cornish Archaeology* **25**, 135–85.

Pryde, G. S. (1965) *The Burghs of Scotland: A Critical List*, London.

Pudełko, J. (1959) 'Rynki w planach miast Śląska', *Kwartalnik Architectury I Urbanistyki* **4**, 235–49.

Pudełko, J. (1960) 'Zagadnienie wielości i proporcji rynków w badaniach nad rozplanowaniem niektórych miast średniowiecznych Zeszyty', *Naukowe Politechniki Wrocławskiej* **36**, 25–45.

Pugh, R. B. ed. (1969) *The Victoria History of the Counties of England: A History of Warwickshire, Volume 8*, University of London Institute of Historical Research, London.

Quinn, G. F. (1995) 'A new survey of the prehistoric field system on Kerswell Down and Whilborough Common', *Proceedings of the Devon Archaeological Society* **53**, 131–4.

Quinnell, H. (1986) 'Cornwall during the Iron Age and the Roman period', *Cornish Archaeology* **25**, 111–34.

Quinnell, H. (2004) *Trethurgy. Excavations at Trethurgy Round, St Austell: Community and Status in Roman and Post-Roman Cornwall*, Cornwall County Council, Truro.

Quinnell, H., Blockley, M. R. and Berridge, P. (1994) *Excavations at Rhuddlan, Clwyd 1969–73, Mesolithic to Medieval*, Council for British Archaeology research report **95**, Council for British Archaeology, York.

Rackham, O. (1976) *Trees and Woodlands in the British Landscape*, Dent, London.

Rackham, O. (1986) *The History of the Countryside*, Dent, London.

Ragg, J. M., Beard, G. R., George, H., Heaven, F. W., Hollis, J. M., Jones, R. J. A., Palmer, R. C., Reeve, M. J., Robson, J. D. and Whitfield, W. A. D. (1984) *Soils and their Uses in Midland and Western England*, Soil Survey of England and Wales, Harpenden.

Rahtz, S. and Rowley, R. T. (1984) *Middleton Stoney: Excavation and Survey in a North Oxfordshire Parish 1970–1982*, Oxford University Department for External Studies, Oxford.

Rahtz, P. A. and Watts, L. eds (2004a) *Wharram: A Study of Settlement on the Yorkshire Wolds, IX. The North Manor Area and North-West Enclosure*, York University Archaeological Publications **11**, University of York, York.

Rahtz, P. A. and Watts, L. (2004b) 'The North Manor Area Excavations' in eds P. A. Rahtz and L. Watts, *Wharram: A Study of Settlement on the Yorkshire Wolds, IX. The North Manor Area and North-West Enclosure*, York University Archaeological Publications **11**, University of York, 1–138.

Raine, J. ed. (1884) *Testamenta Eboracensia, or, Wills registered at York, Volume 5*, Surtees Society **79**, J. B. Nichols, London.

Ramey, R. L. (2004) 'An archaeology of hospitality. The Stoneleigh Abbey gatehouse' in ed. R. Bearman, *Stoneleigh Abbey: The House, its Owners, its Lands*, Stoneleigh Abbey, Stratford-upon-Avon, 62–81.

Rawcliffe, C. (2005) 'The earthly and spiritual topography of suburban houses' in eds K. Giles and C. Dyer, *Town and Country in the Middle Ages: Contrasts, Contacts and Interconnections, 1100–1500*, Society for Medieval Archaeology monograph **22**, Maney Publishing, Leeds, 251–74.

RCAHMS (1995) *Mar Lodge Estate, Grampian: An Archaeological Survey*, Edinburgh.

RCAHMS and HS (2002) *But the Walls Remained: A Survey of Unroofed Rural Settlement Depicted on the First Edition of the Ordnance Survey Six-Inch Map of Scotland*, Historic Scotland and RCAHMS, Edinburgh.

RCHME (1981) *City of York: Volume V The Central Area*, HMSO, London.

RCHME (1982) *An Inventory of the Historical Monuments in the County of Northamptonshire, Vol. 4: Archaeological Sites in South-West Northamptonshire*, RCHME, London.

Reaney, P. H. (1935) *The Place-Names of Essex*, English Place-Name Society 7, Cambridge University Press, Cambridge.

Reed, S. J. and Manning, P. T. (2000) 'Archaeological recording of a hillslope enclosure at North Hill Cleave, Bittadon, North Devon', *Proceedings of the Devon Archaeological Society* **58**, 201–14.

Renes, J. (1988) 'Some aspects of open fields in the southern part of the Province of Limburg (the Netherlands)', *Geografiska Annaler* **70B**, 161–7.

Renn, D. (2003) 'Burhgeat and gonfanon: two sidelights from the Bayeux tapestry' in ed. R. Liddiard, *Anglo-Norman Castles*, Boydell, Woodbridge, 69–90.

Reynolds, A. (2003) 'Boundaries and settlements in later sixth to eleventh-century England', *Anglo-Saxon Studies in Archaeology and History* **12**, 98–136.

Reynolds, S. (1977) *An Introduction to the History of English Medieval Towns*, Clarendon Press, Oxford.

Richards, J.D. (1992) 'Anglo-Saxon settlement at Wharram Percy: a general introduction' in eds G. Milne and J.D. Richards, *Wharram: A Study of Settlement on the Yorkshire Wolds, VII. Two Anglo-Saxon Buildings and Associated Finds*, York University Archaeological Publications 9, University of York, York, 89–94.

Richards, J.D. (1997) 'Anglian and Viking settlement in the Yorkshire Wolds', in ed. G. de Boe, *Rural Settlements in Medieval Europe*, Papers of the Medieval Europe Brugge 1997 conference 6, Instituut voor het Archeologisch Patrimonium, Zellik (Belgium), 233–42.

Richardson, A. (2005) *The Forest, Park and Palace of Clarendon, c.1200–c.1650*, British Archaeological Reports British Series 387, Archaeopress, Oxford.

Riden, P. (2002) *The Victoria County History of Northamptonshire, Vol.5: Cleley Hundred*, Boydell Press for the Institute of Historical Research, Woodbridge.

Rigold, S.E. (1972) 'Eynsford Castle and its excavation', *Archaeologia Cantiana* 86, 109–72.

Riley, H. and Wilson-North, R. (2001) *The Field Archaeology of Exmoor*, English Heritage, London.

Rippon, S. (1997) *The Severn Estuary: Landscape Evolution and Wetland Reclamation*, Leicester University Press, London.

Rippon, S. (2000) *The Transformation of Coastal Wetlands*, British Academy, Oxford.

Rippon, S. (2004) *Historic Landscape Analysis*, Council for British Archaeology, York.

Rippon, S. (2006) 'Landscapes of pre-medieval occupation' in ed. R.J.P. Kain, *Landscapes of South-West England*, English Heritage/Harper Collins, London.

Rippon, S. (forthcoming) *Landscape and Community on the North Somerset Levels: The Creation of an Historic Landscape*, Council for British Archaeology research report, Council for British Archaeology, York.

Rippon, S., Fyfe, R. and Brown, A.G. (2006) 'Beyond villages and open fields: the origins and development of a historic landscape characterised by dispersed settlement in South West England', *Medieval Archaeology* 50, 31–70.

Roberts, B.K. (1973) 'Field systems of the West Midlands' in eds A.R.H. Baker and R.A. Butlin, *Studies of Field Systems in the British Isles*, Cambridge University Press, Cambridge, 188–231.

Roberts, B.K. (1977) *Rural Settlement in Britain*, Hutchinson, London.

Roberts, B.K. (1987) *The Making of the English Village: A Study in Historical Geography*, Longman, Harlow.

Roberts, B.K. (1996) *Landscapes of Settlement: Prehistory to the Present*, Routledge, London.

Roberts, B.K. and Glasscock, R.E. eds (1983) *Villages, Fields and Frontiers: Studies in European Rural Settlement in the Medieval and Early Modern Periods*, British Archaeological Reports international series 185, British Archaeological Reports, Oxford.

Roberts, B.K. and Wrathmell, S. (2000) *An Atlas of Rural Settlement in England*, English Heritage, London.

Roberts, B.K. and Wrathmell, S. (2002) *Region and Place: A Study of English Rural Settlement*, English Heritage, London.

Roberts, E. (1988) 'The Bishop of Winchester's deer parks in Hampshire, 1200–1400' *Hampshire Field Club and Archaeological Society* 44, 67–86.

Roberts, E. (2003) *Hampshire Houses 1250–1700: Their Dating and Development*, Hampshire County Council, Winchester.

Robertson, J. ed. (1857) *Illustrations of the Topography and Antiquities of the Shires of Aberdeen and Banff*, vol.3, Spalding Club, Aberdeen.

Robey, T. (1993) 'The archaeology of Cressing Temple' in ed. D.D. Andrews, *Cressing Temple. A Templar and Hospitaller Manor in Essex*, Essex County Council, Chelmsford, 37–50.

Robinson, D. (1998) *The Cistercian Abbeys of Britain. Far from the Concerns of Men*, Batsford, London.

Robinson, D.H. (1949; 13th edn) *Fream's Elements of Agriculture*, John Murray, London.

Robinson, M. (1973) 'Excavations at Copt Hay, Tetsworth, Oxon', *Oxoniensia* 38, 41–115.

Robinson, M. (1992) 'Environment, archaeology and alluvium on the river gravels of the south Midlands' in eds S. Needham and M.G. Macklin, *Alluvial Archaeology in Britain*, Oxbow monograph 27, Oxbow, Oxford, 197–208.

Roden, D. (1973) 'Field systems of the Chiltern Hills and their environs' in eds A.R.H. Baker and R.A. Butlin, *Studies of Field Systems in the British Isles*, Cambridge University Press, Cambridge, 325–74.

Rodwell, K. and Bell, R. (2004) *Acton Court: The Evolution of an Early Tudor Courtier's House*, English Heritage, London.

Rodwell, W. (1978) 'Relict landscapes in Essex' in eds H.C. Bowen and P.J. Fowler, *Early Land Allotment*, BAR British series 48, British Archaeological Reports, Oxford, 89–98.

Rodwell, W.J. and Rodwell, K. (1977) *Historic Churches – A Wasting Asset*, CBA research report 19, Council for British Archaeology, London.

Rodwell, W.J. and Rodwell, K. (1982) 'St Peter's Church, Barton-upon-Humber: excavation and structural study, 1978–81', *Antiquaries Journal* 62, 283–315.

Roffe, D. (2000) 'The early history of Wharram Percy' in eds P. A. Stamper and R. A. Croft, *Wharram: A Study of Settlement on the Yorkshire Wolds, VIII. The South Manor Area*, York University Archaeological Publications 10, University of York York, 1–15.

Rogerson, A. (1995) *Fransham: An Archaeological and Historical Study of a Parish on the Norfolk Boulder Clay*, unpublished PhD thesis, University of East Anglia.

Rogerson, A. (1997) 'An archaeological and historical survey of the parish of Barton Bendish' in eds A. Rogerson, A. Davison, D. Pritchard and R. Silvester, *Barton Bendish and Caldecote: Fieldwork in south-west Norfolk*, East Anglian Archaeology 80, Norfolk Museums Service, Dereham, 1–42.

Rose, P. (2004) 'Shadows in the imagination: encounters with caves in Cornwall', *Cornish Archaeology* **39–40**, 95–128.

Rose, P. and Preston-Jones, A. (1995) 'Changes in the Cornish countryside AD 400–1100' in eds D. Hooke and S. Burnell, *Landscape and Settlement in Britain AD 400–1066*, Exeter University Press, Exeter, 51–68.

Rosser, G. (1996) 'Myth, image and social process in the English medieval town', *Urban History* **23**, 5–25.

Rosser, G. (2000) 'Urban culture and the church 1300–1540' in ed. D. M. Palliser, *The Cambridge Urban History of Britain, I, 600–1540*, Cambridge University Press, Cambridge, Cambridge University Press, Cambridge, 335–69.

Rotuli Hundredorum, ed. W. Illingworth and J. Caley (1812–18) 2 vols, Record Commission.

Round, J. H. ed. (1913) *The Great Roll of the Pipe for the Thirty-first Year of the Reign of Henry II, AD 1184–1185*, Publications of the Pipe Roll Society **34**, The St Catherine Press, London.

Rowley, T. ed. (1981) *The Origins of Open Field Agriculture*, Croom Helm, London.

Roy, W. (1747–55) *Military Survey of Scotland*, photocopy held at RCAHMS, Edinburgh from original sheets in the British Library.

Rudkin, E. H. and Owen, D. M. (1960) 'The medieval salt industry in the Lindsey marshland', *Reports and Papers of the Lincolnshire Architectural and Archaeological Society* new ser. 8, 76–84.

Ryan, P. M. (1993) 'Cressing Temple: its history from documentary sources' in ed. D. D. Andrews, *Cressing Temple. A Templar and Hospitaller Manor in Essex*, Essex County Council, Chelmsford, 11–24.

Sanders, I. J. (1960) *English Baronies: A Study of their Origins and Descent, 1086–1327*, Clarendon Press, Oxford.

Saunders, C. (1972) 'The excavations at Grambla, Wedron, 1972: interim report', *Cornish Archaeology* **11**, 50–2.

Saunders, T. (1990) 'The feudal construction of space: power and domination in the nucleated village' in ed.

R. Samson, *The Social Archaeology of Houses*, Edinburgh University Press, Edinburgh, 181–96.

Sawyer, P. H. (1968) *Anglo-Saxon Charters: An Annotated List and Bibliography*, Royal Historical Society, London.

Sawyer, P. H. (1985) 'Domesday Book: a tenurial revolution?' in ed. P. H. Sawyer, *Domesday Book: A Reassessment*, Edward Arnold, London, 71–85.

Sayers, J. (1994) *Innocent III*, Longman, London.

Schein, R. H. (1997) 'The place of landscape: a conceptual framework for interpreting an American scene', *Annals of the Association of American Geographers* **87**, 660–80.

Schofield, J. (1994) *Medieval London Houses*, Yale University Press, New Haven.

Schofield, J. (2000) 'London: buildings and defences 1200–1600' in eds I. Haynes, H. Sheldon and L. Hannigan, *London Underground: The Archaeology of a City*, Oxbow, Oxford, 223–38.

Schofield, J. and Vince, A. (1994) *Medieval Towns*, Leicester University Press, London.

Scott, S. (2000) *Art and Society in Fourth-Century Roman Britain*, Oxford University School of Archaeology monograph **53**, Oxford University School of Archaeology, Oxford.

Scrase, A. (1999) 'Geometry and medieval town planning: a comment', *Urban Morphology* **3**, 115–6.

Scrase, A. (2002) *Medieval Town Planning, A Modern Invention*, Faculty of the Built Environment occasional paper **12**, University of the West of England, Bristol.

Seebohm, F. (1890) *The English Village Community*, Longmans, London.

Semple, S. (1998) 'A fear of the past: the place of the prehistoric burial mound in the ideology of middle and later Anglo-Saxon England', *World Archaeology* **30**, 109–26.

Seymour, J. (1996) *The Complete Book of Self-Sufficiency*, Faber, London.

Shaw, M. (1993) 'The discovery of Saxon sites below field-walking scatters: settlement evidence at Brixworth and Upton', *Northamptonshire Archaeology* **25**, 77–92.

Sheppard, F. (1998) *London: A History*, Oxford University Press, Oxford.

Sheppard, J. A. (1966) 'Pre-enclosure field and settlement patterns in an English township', *Geografiska Annaler* **48**, 59–77.

Sheppard, J. A. (1974) 'Metrological analysis of regular village plans in Yorkshire', *Agricultural History Review* **22**, 118–35.

Sheppard, J. A. (1976) 'Medieval village planning in northern England: some evidence from Yorkshire', *Journal of Historical Geography* **2**, 3–20.

Silvester, R. J. (1978a) 'A hillslope enclosure at Collomoor, Bittadon', *Proceedings of the Devon Archaeological Society* **36**, 245–9.

Silvester, R.J. (1978b) 'Cropmark sites at North Tawton and Alverdiscott', *Proceedings of the Devon Archaeological Society* **36**, 249–54.

Silvester, R.J. (1980) 'An enclosure in Staverton Ford Plantation', *Proceedings of the Devon Archaeological Society* **38**, 119–21.

Silvester, R.J. (1981) 'An excavation on the post Roman site at Bantham, South Devon', *Proceedings of the Devon Archaeological Society* **39**, 88–118.

Silvester, R.J. (1988) *The Fenland Survey, Number 3: Norfolk Survey, Marshland and Nar Valley*, East Anglian Archaeology **45**, Norfolk Archaeological Unit, Dereham.

Silvester, R.J. (1993) '"The addition of more-or-less undifferentiated dots to a distribution map"?: The Fenland Project in Retrospect' in ed. J.Gardiner, *Flatlands and Wetland: Current Themes in East Anglian Archaeology*, East Anglian Archaeology **50**, Scole Archaeological Committee, Norwich.

Silvester, R.J. and Balkwill, C.J. (1977) 'Three hillslope enclosures in the Lyd Valley, West Devon', *Proceedings of the Devon Archaeological Society* **35**, 81–4.

Simpson, S.J., Griffith, F.M. and Holbrook, N. (1989) 'The prehistoric, Roman and early post-Roman site at Hayes Farm, Clyst Honiton', *Proceedings of the Devon Archaeological Society* **47**, 1–28.

Sims, R.E. (1978) 'Man and vegetation in Norfolk' in eds S.Limbrey and J.G.Evans, *The Effect of Man on the Landscape: the Lowland Zone*, Council for British Archaeology research report **21**, Council for British Archaeology, London, 57–62.

Slater, T.R. (1981) 'The analysis of burgage patterns in medieval towns', *Area* **13**, 211–16.

Slater, T.R. (1985) 'Medieval new town and port: a plan-analysis of Hedon, East Yorkshire', *Yorkshire Archaeological Journal* **57**, 23–41.

Slater, T.R. (1987) 'Ideal and reality in English episcopal medieval town planning', *Transactions of the Institute of British Geographers* new series **12**, 191–203.

Slater, T.R. (1990a) 'Starting again: recollections of an urban morphologist' in ed. T.R.Slater, *The Built Form of Western Cities*, Leicester University Press, Leicester, 23–37.

Slater, T.R. (1990b) 'English medieval new towns with composite plans: evidence from the Midlands' in ed. T.R.Slater, *The Built Form of Western Cities*, Leicester University Press, Leicester, 60–82.

Slater, T.R. (1997) 'Domesday village to medieval town: the topography of medieval Stratford-upon-Avon' in ed. R.Bearman, *The History of an English Borough: Stratford-upon-Avon 1196–1966*, Sutton Publishing, Stroud, 30–42.

Slater, T.R. (1998) 'The Benedictine order and medieval town planning: the case of St Albans' in eds T.R.Slater and G.Rosser, *The Church in the Medieval Town*, Ashgate Press, Aldershot, 155–76.

Slater, T.R. (1999a) 'Whose urban heritage? Character, managerialism and representation in conserving Europe's historic towns' in ed. E.P.Dennison, *Conservation and Change in Historic Towns*, Council for British Archaeology research report **122**, Council for British Archaeology, York, 13–23.

Slater, T.R. (1999b) 'Geometry and medieval town planning', *Urban Morphology* **3**, 107–11.

Slater, T.R. (2001) 'Planning plots in Grenade-sur-Garonne', *Urban Morphology* **5**, 48–50.

Slater, T.R. (2004) 'Planning English medieval 'street towns': the Hertfordshire evidence', *Landscape History* **26**, 19–35.

Slater, T.R. (2005a) 'Plan characteristics of small boroughs and market settlements: evidence from the Midlands', in eds K.Giles and C.Dyer, *Town and Country in the Middle Ages: Contrasts, Contacts and Interconnections, 1100–1500*, Society for Medieval Archaeology monograph **22**, Maney Publishing, Leeds, 23–42.

Slater, T.R. (2005b) 'The landscape of medieval towns, some European comparisons', unpublished paper presented to ISUF/INTBAU symposium on 'Tradition and Modernity in Urban Form', London.

Smith, G. (1996) 'Archaeology and environment of a Bronze Age cairn and prehistoric and Romano-British field system at Chysauster, Gulval, near Penzance, Cornwall', *Proceedings of the Prehistoric Society* **62**, 167–219.

Smith, J.T. (1992) *English Houses 1200–1800. The Hertfordshire Evidence*, HMSO, London.

Smith, K., Coppen, J., Wainwright, G.J. and Beckett, S. (1981) 'The Shaugh Moor project: third report – settlement and environmental investigations', *Proceedings of the Prehistoric Society* **47**, 205–74.

Snooks, G.D. (1996) *The Dynamic Society: Exploring the Sources of Global Change*, Routledge, London.

Somerset County Council (1992) *A Palaeoenvironmental Investigation of a Field off White's Drove, Godney Moor, Near Wells, Somerset: Interim Report*, unpublished report, Somerset County Council Environment Section, Taunton.

Soulsby, I. (1983) *The Towns of Medieval Wales*, Phillimore, Chichester.

Spearman R.M. (1988) 'The medieval townscape of Perth' in eds M.Lynch and G.P.Stell, *The Scottish Medieval Town*, Edinburgh University Press, Edinburgh, 42–59.

Speight, S. (1993) *Family, Faith and Fortifications: Yorkshire 1066–1250*, unpublished PhD thesis, University of Nottingham.

Spring Gardens (1878) *The Spring Gardens Sketch Book, volume VII*, Spring Gardens Sketching Club, London.

260

Spring Gardens (1890) *The Spring Gardens Sketch Book, volume VIII*, Spring Gardens Sketching Club, London.

Stacy, N.E. (2004) 'The state of the demesne manors of Glastonbury Abbey in the twelfth century' in ed. R.Evans, *Lordship and Learning: Studies in Memory of Trevor Aston*, Boydell, Woodbridge, 109–23.

Stadt Braunschweig (1985) *Braunschweig – Führer zum Stadthistorischen Rundgang*, Braunschweig.

Stamper, P.A. and Croft, R.A. (2000) *Wharram: A Study of Settlement on the Yorkshire Wolds, VIII. The South Manor Area*, York University Archaeological Publications 10, University Of York, York.

Stat. Acct. (1791–9) *The Statistical Account of Scotland*, Edinburgh.

Steane, J.M. (2001) *The Archaeology of Power: England and Northern Europe AD 800–1600*, Tempus, Stroud.

Steedman, K. (1994) 'Excavation of a Saxon site at Rigby Cross Roads, Lincolnshire', *Archaeological Journal* 151, 212–306.

Stell, C. (2002) *An Inventory of Nonconformist Chapels and Meeting Houses in Eastern England*, English Heritage, Swindon.

Stocker, D. ed. (2003) *The City by the Pool: Assessing the Archaeology of the City of Lincoln*, Lincoln Archaeological Studies 10, Oxbow, Oxford.

Stocker, D. (2005) 'How serious were Lincoln's medieval defences?', unpublished paper given at 'City Walls and City Identities AD 900–1650' conference, Rewley House, Oxford.

Stocker, D. and Everson, P. (2003) 'The straight and narrow way: Fenland causeways and the conversion of the landscape in the Witham Valley, Lincolnshire' in ed. M.Carver, *The Cross Goes North: Processes of Conversion in Northern Europe, AD 300–1300*, Boydell and Brewer, Woodbridge, 271–88.

Stoob, H. ed. (1973–93) *Deutscher Städteatlas* I–V, GSV Städteatlas Verlag, Dortmund, Grösschen.

Strahm, H. (1948) 'Der Zähringische Gründungsplan der Stadt Bern', *Archiv des historischen Vereins des Kantons Bern* 39, 361–90.

Strappa, G., Ieva, M., and Dimatteo, M.A. (2003) *La Cittàcome Organismo. Lettura di Trani alle Diverse Scale*, Mario Adda Editore, Bari.

Stringer, K.J. (1985) *Earl David of Huntingdon 1152–1219: A Study in Anglo-Scottish History*, Edinburgh.

Stuart, J. (1844) *List of Pollable Persons within the Shire of Aberdeen, 1696*, Spalding Club, Aberdeen.

Surtees, F.R. (1883) ['Boxley Abbey'], *Archaeologia Cantiana* 15, xli.

Sykes, N. (2004) 'The dynamics of status symbols: wildfowl exploitation in England AD 410–1550', *Archaeological Journal* 161, 82–105.

Sympson, E.M. (1889–90) 'On Lincolnshire rood-screens and rood-lofts', *Associated Architectural Societies Reports and Papers* 20, 185–213.

Taylor, A.J. (1963) 'Some notes on the Savoyards in North Wales, 1277–1300, with special reference to the Savoyard element in the construction of Harlech castle', *Genava* new series 11, 289–315.

Taylor, A.J. (1986) *The Welsh Castles of Edward I*, Hambledon Press, London.

Taylor, C.C. (1983) *Village and Farmstead: A History of Rural Settlement in England*, George Philip, London.

Taylor, C.C. (1988) 'Introduction and commentary' in W.G.Hoskins, *The Making of the English Landscape*, Hodder and Stoughton, London, 7–9.

Taylor, C.C. (1989a) 'Whittlesford: the study of a river-edge village' in eds M.Aston, D.Austin and C.Dyer, *The Rural Settlements of Medieval England*, Blackwell, Oxford, 207–27.

Taylor, C.C. (1989b) 'Somersham Palace, Cambridgeshire: a medieval landscape for pleasure?' in eds M.Bowden, D.Mackay and P.Topping, *From Cornwall to Caithness*, British Archaeological Reports British series 209, British Archaeological Reports, Oxford, 211–24.

Taylor, C.C. (1997) 'Dorset and beyond' in eds K.Barker and T.Darvill, *Making English Landscapes: Changing Perspectives*, Oxbow, Oxford, 9–25.

Taylor, C.C. (2000) 'Medieval ornamental landscapes', *Landscapes* 1, 38–55.

Taylor, C.C. (2002) 'Nucleated settlement: a view from the frontier', *Landscape History* 24, 53–71.

Taylor, C.C. and Fowler, P.J. (1978) 'Roman fields into medieval furlongs?' in eds H.C.Bowen and P.J.Fowler, *Early Land Allotment*, BAR British series 48, British Archaeological Reports, Oxford, 159–62.

Taylor, C.C., Everson, P. and Wilson-North, R. (1990) 'Bodiam Castle, Sussex', *Medieval Archaeology* 34, 155–7.

Tebbutt, C.F., Rudd, G.T. and Moorhouse, S. (1971) 'Excavation of a moated site at Ellington, Huntingdonshire', *Proceedings of the Cambridge Antiquarian Society* 63, 31–73.

Terrett, I.B. (1962) 'Cheshire' in eds H.C.Darby and I.S.Maxwell, *The Domesday Geography of Northern England*, Cambridge University Press, Cambridge, 330–91.

Tesch, S. (1993) *Houses, Farmsteads, and Long-term Change. A Regional Study of Prehistoric Settlements in the Köpinge Area, in Scania, Southern Sweden*, Department of Archaeology, Uppsala University, Uppsala.

Thacker, A.T. (1987) 'Anglo-Saxon Cheshire' in ed. B.E.Harris, *Victoria County History of Cheshire I*, Oxford University Press for the Institute of Historical Research, Oxford, 237–92.

Thacker, A.T. (2000) 'The early medieval city and its buildings' in ed. A.Thacker, *Medieval Archaeology, Art and Architecture at Chester*, Maney, Leeds, 16–30.

Thew, N. (1994) 'Geology and geoarchaeology in the Yeo Valley at Ilchester' in ed. P. Leach, *Ilchester Volume 2: Archaeology, Excavations and Fieldwork to 1984*, Department of Archaeology and Prehistory, University of Sheffield, Sheffield, 157–71.

Thirsk, J. (1964) 'The common fields', *Past and Present* **29**, 3–29.

Thomas, C. (1958) *Gwithian: Ten Years' Work*, West Cornwall Field Club, Cornwall.

Thomas, C. (1981) *A Provisional List of Imported Pottery in Post-Roman Western Britain and Ireland*, Institute for Cornish Studies, Redruth.

Thomas, C. (1990) ''Gallici Nautae de Galliarum Provinciis' – a sixth/seventh century trade with Gaul, reconsidered', *Medieval Archaeology* **34**, 1–26.

Thomas, C. (1993) *Tintagel: Arthur and Archaeology*, English Heritage, London.

Thomas, C. (1994) *'And Shall These Mute Stones Speak?' Post-Roman Inscriptions in Western Britain*, University of Wales Press, Cardiff.

Thomas, G. (2005) *Excavations at Bishopstone, 2004: Third Interim Report*, unpublished report, Sussex Archaeological Society.

Thompson, M. (1998) *Medieval Bishops' Houses in England and Wales*, Ashgate, Aldershot.

Thorpe, H. (1949) 'The green villages of County Durham', *Transactions and Papers of the Institute of British Geographers* **15**, 155–80.

Tibbles, J. (2003) *An Archaeological Evaluation at Kitchen Lane, Beverley, East Yorkshire*, Humber Field Archaeology Report **146**, Humber Field Archaeology, Hull.

Tilley, C. (1994) *A Phenomenology of Landscape: Places, Paths and Monuments*, Berg, Oxford.

Tilley, C. (2004) *The Materiality of Stone: Explorations in Landscape Phenomenology 1*, Berg, Oxford.

Todd, M. (1987) *The South West to AD 1000*, Routledge, London.

Todd, M. (1998) 'A hillslope enclosure at Rudge, Morchard Bishop', *Proceedings of the Devon Archaeological Society* **56**, 133–52.

Toulmin Smith, L. ed. (1907) *The Itinerary of John Leland in or about the Years 1535–1543, Parts I to III*, George Bell and Sons, London.

Tout, T.F. (1934) *Mediaeval Town Planning, A Lecture*, Manchester University Press, Manchester.

Tracy, J.D. (2000) 'To wall or not to wall: evidence from medieval Germany' in ed. J.D. Tracy, *City Walls: The Urban Enceinte in Global Perspective*, Cambridge University Press, Cambridge, 71–87.

Trist, P.J.O. (1971) *A Survey of the Agriculture of Suffolk*, County Agricultural Surveys 7, Royal Agricultural Society of England, London.

Trollope, E. (1875–6) 'The churches of Horncastle and other parishes, visited by the Society on the 14th and 15th of June 1876', *Associated Architectural Societies Reports and Papers* **13**, 153–76.

Turner, H.L. (1970) *Town Defences in England and Wales*, John Baker, London.

Turner, S. (2003) 'Making a Christian landscape: early medieval Cornwall' in ed. M. Carver, *The Cross Goes North: Processes of Conversion in Northern Europe, AD 300–1300*, Boydell Press, Woodbridge, 171–94.

Unwin, R. (1909) *Town Planning in Practice – An Introduction to the Art of Designing Cities and Suburbs*, Fisher Unwin, London.

Unwin, T. (1983) 'Townships and early fields in north Nottinghamshire', *Journal of Historical Geography* **9**, 341–6.

Upex, S. (2003) 'Landscape continuity and the fossilization of Roman fields', *Archaeological Journal* **159**, 77–108.

Van Emden, W. (1984) 'The castle in some works of medieval French literature' in eds K. Reyerson and F. Powe, *The Medieval Castle: Romance and Reality*, Kendall/Hunt, Dubuque, Iowa, 1–36.

Verhulst, A. (2002) *The Carolingian Economy*, Cambridge University Press, Cambridge.

Vico, G. (1744) *New Science: Principles of the New Science Concerning the Common Nature of Nations* (3rd edn 2001, Penguin Books, London).

Waddell, H. (1982) *Songs of the Wandering Scholars*, edited with preface by Dame Felicitas Corrigan, Folio Society, London.

Wade-Martins, P. (1980a) *Excavations in North Elmham Park 1967–1972*, East Anglian Archaeology **9**, Norfolk Museums Service, Gressenhall.

Wade-Martins, P. (1980b) *Village Sites in the Launditch Hundred*, East Anglian Archaeology **10**, Norfolk Museums Service, Gressenhall.

Walker, J. (1998) 'Essex medieval houses: type and method of construction' in eds D.F. Stenning and D.D. Andrews, *Regional Variation in Timber-Framed Building in England and Wales Down to 1550*, Essex County Council, Chelmsford, 5–15.

Wallace, C., Lawson, J.A. and Reed, D. (2004) ''Ye toun salbe wallit and and stankeit about, with ane substantious wall'. Mural ideology in 16th century Edinburgh and southern Scotland?', *History Scotland* **4**, 35–42.

Walter, J.C. (1899) *Records of Woodhall Spa and Neighbourhood; Historical, Anecdotal, Physiographical and Archaeological with other matter*, Morton, Horncastle.

Ward, S. (1994) *Excavations at Chester, Saxon Occupation within the Roman Fortress*, Cheshire County Council, Chester.

Ward, S. (2001) 'Edward the Elder and the re-establishment of Chester' in eds N.J. Higham and D.H. Hill, *Edward the Elder, 899–924*, Routledge, London, 160–6.

Warner, P. (1987) *Greens, Commons and Clayland Colonisation*, Department of English Local History occasional paper, fourth series **2**, Leicester University Press, Leicester.

Warnock, S. (2002) *The Living Landscapes Project: Landscape Characterisation – Handbook: Level 2 (version 4.1)*, Department of Geography, University of Reading, Reading.

Warren, J.C. (1919) 'From Puritanism to Unitarianism in Lincoln', *Transactions of the Unitarian Historical Society* **2, 1**, 1–31.

Waton, P.V. (1982) 'Man's impact on the chalklands: some new pollen evidence' in eds M. Bell and S. Limbrey, *Archaeological Aspects of Woodland Ecology*, British Archaeological Reports international series **146**, British Archaeological Reports, Oxford, 75–91.

Watts, V. (2002) *A Dictionary of County Durham Place-Names*, English Place-Name Society popular series **3**, English Place-Names Society, Nottingham.

Weddell, P.J. and Reed, S.J. (1997) 'Excavation at Sourton Down, Okehampton 1986–1991: Roman road, deserted medieval hamlet and other landscape features', *Proceedings of the Devon Archaeological Society* **55**, 39–147.

Westman, A. (1999) *Project Area 430: Parsonage Farm ARC PFM 98. Archaeological Excavation Interim Report*, unpublished report, Museum of London.

Whitaker, T.D. (1878; 3rd edn) *The History and Antiquities of the Deanery of Craven*, Dodgson, Leeds.

White, G. (1995) 'Open fields and rural settlements in medieval west Cheshire' in eds T. Scott and P. Starkey, *The Middle Ages in the North West*, Leopard Head Press, Liverpool, 15–36.

Whitehand, J.W.R. and Larkham, P.J (1992) 'The urban landscape: issues and perspectives' in eds J.W.R. Whitehand and P.J. Larkham, *Urban Landscapes – International Perspectives*, Routledge, London, 1–19.

Whitehead, D. (2001) *Historic Parks and Gardens in Herefordshire*, Herefordshire and Worcester Gardens Trust, Hereford.

Whitelock, D. ed. (1930) *Anglo-Saxon Wills*, Cambridge University Press, Cambridge.

Whitelock, D. ed. (1961) *The Anglo-Saxon Chronicle*, Eyre and Spottiswoode, London.

Widgren, M. (1997) 'Fields and field systems in Scandinavia during the Middle Ages' in eds G. Astill and J. Langdon, *Medieval Farming and Technology. The Impact of Agricultural Change in Northwest Europe*, Brill, Leiden, 173–92.

Wiedenau, A. (1983) *Katalog der Romanischen Wohnbauten in Westdeutschen Städten und Siedlungen*, Das Deutsche Bürgerhaus **34**, Ernst Wasmuth, Tübingen.

Willan, T.S. (1980) *Elizabethan Manchester*, Chetham Society 3rd series **27**, Manchester University Press, Manchester.

Williams, A. (1992) 'A bell-house and a burh-geat: lordly residences in England before the Norman Conquest' in eds C. Harper-Bill and R. Harvey, *Medieval Knighthood IV: Papers from the Fifth Strawberry Hill Conference 1990*, Boydell, Woodbridge, 221–40.

Williams, B. (1987) 'Excavations of a medieval earthwork complex at Hillesley, Hawkesbury, Avon', *Transactions of the Bristol and Gloucestershire Archaeological Society* **105**, 147–63.

Williams, H. (1998) 'Monuments and the past in Early Anglo-Saxon England, *World Archaeology* **30**, 98–108

Williams, R.J. (1993) *Pennyland and Hartigans: two Iron Age and Saxon sites in Milton Keynes*, Buckinghamshire Archaeological Society monograph series **4**, Buckinghamshire Archaeological Society, Aylesbury.

Williamson, T. (1987) 'Early co-axial field systems on the East Anglian Boulder Clays', *Proceedings of the Prehistoric Society* **53**, 419–32.

Williamson, T. (1988) 'The working landscape' in ed. B. Ford, *The Cambridge Guide to the Arts in Britain, 2. The Middle Ages*, Cambridge University Press, Cambridge, 252–61.

Williamson, T. (1993) *The Origins of Norfolk*, Manchester University Press, Manchester.

Williamson, T. (2003) *Shaping Medieval Landscapes: Settlement, Society, Environment*, Windgather Press, Macclesfield.

Williamson, T. and Bellamy, L. (1987) *Property and Landscape: A Social History of Landownership and the English Countryside*, George Philip, London.

Wilson, D.R. (1982) *Air Photo Interpretation for Archaeologists*, Batsford, London.

Wiltshire, P.E.J. (forthcoming) 'Palynological assessment and analysis' in eds T. Ashwin and A. Tester, *Excavations at Scole, 1993–4*, East Anglian Archaeology.

Wiltshire, P.E.J. and Murphy, P. (1999) 'Current knowledge of the Iron Age environment and agrarian economy of Norfolk and adjacent areas' in eds J. Davies and T. Williamson, *Land of the Iceni. The Iron Age in Northern East Anglia*, University of East Anglia, Norwich, 141–8.

Wiltshire, P.E.J. and Murphy, P. (2004) 'Palynological and macrofossil analyses of palaeochannel sediments at BRS' in eds R. Havis and H. Brooks, *Excavations at Stansted Airport 1986–91. Volume 1: Prehistoric and Romano-British*, East Anglian Archaeology **107**, Essex County Council, Chelmsford, 68–78.

Windell, D., Chapman, A. and Woodiwiss, J. (1990) *From Barrows to Bypass: Excavations at West Cotton, Raunds, Northamptonshire, 1985–89*, Northamptonshire County Council, Northampton.

Wood, M. (1981) *Burton Agnes Old Manor House*, for the Department of the Environment, HMSO, Edinburgh.

Wood, S. ed. (1975) *Domesday Book 3: Surrey*, Chichester, Phillimore.

Woodfield, P., Conlon, R. and de Broise, A. (2005) *Whittlewood Project: Historic Buildings Surveys*, 12 vols, unpublished report deposited with the Archaeology Data Service.

Wrathmall, S. (2002) 'Some general hypotheses on English medieval peasant house construction from the seventh to the seventeenth century' in ed. J. Klápště, *The Rural House From the Migration Period to the Oldest Still Standing Buildings* (Ruralia IV), Institute of Archaeology, Academy of Sciences of the Czech Republic, Prague, 175–86.

Wymer, J. J. and Brown, N. R. (1995) *Excavations at North Shoebury: Settlement and Economy in South-East Essex 1500 BC–AD 1500*, East Anglian Archaeology 75, Essex County Council, Chelmsford.

Young, A. (1786) 'Minutes relating to the dairy farms etc of High Suffolk' *Annals of Agriculture* 27, 193–224.

Young, A. C. (1995) 'Excavations at Harry Stoke, Stoke Gifford, Northavon', *Bristol and Avon Archaeology* 12, 24–55.

Youngs, S., Clark, J. and Barry, T. (1986) 'Medieval Britain in 1985', *Medieval Archaeology* 30, 114–98.

Index